Depressive Disorder in Childhood and Adolescence

Richard Harrington
University of Manchester, UK

JOHN WILEY & SONS
Chichester · New York · Brisbane · Toronto · Singapore

Copyright © 1993 by John Wiley & Sons Ltd,
Baffins Lane, Chichester
West Sussex PO19 1UD, England

Published in paperback July 1995

Other Wiley Editorial Offices

John Wiley & Sons, Inc., 605 Third Avenue,
New York, NY 10158-0012, USA

Jacaranda Wiley Ltd, 33 Park Road, Milton,
Queensland 4064, Australia

John Wiley & Sons (Canada) Ltd, 22 Worcester Road,
Rexdale, Ontario M9W 1L1, Canada

John Wiley & Sons (SEA) Pte Ltd, 37 Jalan Pemimpin #05-04,
Block B, Union Industrial Building, Singapore 2057

British Library Cataloguing in Publication Data

A catalogue record for this book is available from the British Library

ISBN 0-471-92917-4
ISBN 0-471-96141-8 (paper)

Typeset in 10/12pt Times by Inforum, Rowlands Castle, Hants
Printed and bound in Great Britain by Bookcraft (Bath) Ltd

Stepping Hill Hospital

Poplar Grove

Depressive Disorder in Childhood and Adolescence

Stockport 7JE

WILEY SERIES ON
STUDIES IN CHILD PSYCHIATRY

Series Editor
Michael Rutter
Institute of Psychiatry
London

Contents

Series Preface

During recent years there has been a tremendous growth of research in both child development and child psychiatry. Research findings are beginning to modify clinical practice but to a considerable extent the fields of child development and child psychiatry have remained surprisingly separate, with regrettably little cross-fertilization. Much developmental research has not concerned itself with clinical issues and studies of clinical syndromes have all too often been made within the narrow confines of a pathological condition approach with scant regard to developmental matters. This situation is rapidly changing, but the results of clinical-developmental studies are often reported only by means of scattered papers and scientific journals. This series aims to bridge the gap between child development and clinical psychiatry by presenting reports of new findings, new ideas, and new approaches in a book form that may be available to a wider readership.

The series includes reviews of specific topics, multi-authored volumes on a common theme, and accounts of specific pieces of research. However, in all cases, the aim is to provide a clear, readable, and interesting account of scientific findings in a style that makes explicit their relevance to clinical practice or social policy. It is hoped that the series will be of interest to both clinicians and researchers in the fields of child psychiatry, child psychology, psychiatric social work, social paediatric, and education—in short, all concerned with growing children and their problems.

This latest volume in the series provides an up-to-date appraisal of what is known about depression arising in childhood and adolescence. Until relatively recently, there was a widespread belief that depressive disorders as they occur in adult life were quite rare in childhood. It is now appreciated that they are in fact much commoner than hitherto realized, although their prevalence is substantially lower than in adulthood. The issues surrounding depression involve many key questions of crucial importance to both developmentalists and clinicians. What is the connection between ordinary feelings of misery and major depressive disorders requiring hospital treatment? Why do children and their parents so often disagree on their reporting of depression? What is the place of standardized interviews and questionnaire assessments? What is the role of cognitive processes (such as those concerned with feelings of guilt, helplessness, and attributions of blame) in the initiation and perpetuation of depressed mood? How do these psychological features interconnect with the neuroendocrine, and other biological, changes associated with serious depressive conditions? Why does depression seem to become more frequent during adolescence, and why are depressive disorders in young people apparently more frequent now than they were half a century ago? Why, if depressive disorders in childhood are so likely to recur in adult life, are they not as responsive to antidepressant medication as they are in adulthood? These and other issues are clearly and authoritively discussed by Richard Harrington, indicating what is, and what is not, known, as well as suggesting possible ways ahead by which further progress may come about. The approach taken is broad-ranging and integrative and the book should be of interest to clinicians of all disciplines who are concerned with emotional disturbances in young people.

MICHAEL RUTTER

Preface

Until quite recently the conventional wisdom was that major depressive disorders were exceedingly rare in children and adolescents. Most recent evidence indicates, however, that rates of these disorders are much higher at younger ages than previously recognized. Indeed, they are now seen as a major public health problem. Depression in young people tends to be associated with much impairment of psychosocial functioning, and the available data suggest that the recurrence risk is high with strong continuity into adulthood. The public health importance of depressive conditions among the young is further underlined by recent changes in the prevalence of suicide. In most Western countries rates of adolescent suicide have been increasing, and several recent studies have reported a strong association between depressive disorder and suicide in this age group.

The result of this growing concern about depressive disorders among the young has been a major research effort directed towards investigation of the characteristics of depressed children and adolescents. There is now much information on the clinical features of young people who become depressed, and on the problems they face. Knowledge has also gradually accumulated about how best to help them. It is to these issues that this book, which is primarily a review of recent research findings, is particularly addressed. The book is intended to be of use to all professionals dealing with depressed children and their families, but especially to psychiatrists and psychologists.

The book begins with discussion of concepts of depression across the age span. There then follows an overview of concepts of depression in young people. The next two chapters are concerned with the assessment of depression. Chapter 2 is primarily a clinical account. The importance of structured interviews, rating scales, and observational ratings is discussed in Chapter 3. The fourth chapter provides a description of the epidemiology of affective conditions in young people. Epidemiological studies have all found that depressive disorders among the young frequently occur in conjunction with other psychiatric conditions. Chapter 5 therefore discusses the extent and meaning of this overlap, so-called comorbidity. In the next two chapters the principal findings concerning the factors that appear to cause depressive disorders, and the psychological and biological mechanisms that may link these factors to the clinical state of depression, are reviewed. Chapter 8 describes psychological approaches to management. Pharmacological treatments are discussed in Chapter 9. Chapter 10 deals with the outcomes of early-onset depressive disorders. The final chapter summarizes some of the important issues and needs in the field.

Acknowledgements

During five years at the Institute of Psychiatry in London I was fortunate to have stimulating colleagues in the Department of Child and Adolescent Psychiatry. The sharing of ideas about research issues and concepts was a feature of our work over several years, and I hope this is reflected in the contents of this book. Anyone familiar with the field will appreciate how much this book owes to Michael Rutter. He encouraged me to write it, and has since then given continuous advice and support. I am particularly grateful for his comments on an earlier draft. I am also indebted to the Depression Research Team in the Department of Child Psychiatry at the Institute, which has at various times included the following: Hazel Fudge, Christine Groothues, Diana Bredenkamp, Jacqueline Pridham, and Jonathan Hill. Special thanks are due to Hazel, Chris and Diana. Their ideas, endurance and efforts contributed a great deal to our various projects. Financial support for these projects was received from the MacArthur Foundation, and from the Medical Research Council. The Mental Health Foundation is supporting our current research on treatment. Finally, there is the incalculable debt I owe my wife, Lesley, and my son James, who have borne the inordinate demands on their leisure with remarkable good will and tolerance. Without their constant enthusiasm and support I have little doubt that this book would not have been completed.

The author and publishers are grateful to the American Psychiatric Association who gave permission for the DSM-III-R criteria for major depression (American Psychiatric Association, 1987) to be reproduced.

Chapter 1

Definition and Classification

INTRODUCTION: CONCEPTS OF DEPRESSION

The concept of childhood depression is still a matter of considerable controversy. Until relatively recently the prevailing view was that depressive disorders rarely occurred in children or that if they did occur they took a "masked" form. In the last fifteen years, however, there has been an increasing recognition that depressive conditions resembling adult depression can and do appear in childhood (see reviews by, for example: Rutter, 1988a; Angold 1988a; Harrington, 1990). Indeed, it has been suggested that they are quite common in clinical samples. Nevertheless, there are continuing uncertainties about the comparability of depressive disorders in children with the major depressive disorders of adults and many writers remain doubtful about the true frequency of depressive syndromes in prepubertal children (Lefkowitz & Burton, 1978; Graham, 1981; Shaffer, 1985).

It is necessary to appreciate that the concept of depressive disorder in adults has also involved some controversial issues. Although great progress has been made in recent years in the diagnosis and classification of affective disorders occurring in adulthood, it is obvious that there are a large number of unresolved problems (Farmer & McGuffin, 1989). Indeed the problems that arise in the study of childhood depressive disorders are in many respects closely comparable to those that occur in the study of adult depression. Accordingly, this first chapter begins with a brief review of issues in the classification of depressive conditions in adults. These may be summarized as:

1. Where should the line be drawn between the concept of affective disorder and, on the one hand, normality, and on the other hand non-depressive psychiatric disorders?
2. How should affective disorders be subtyped?

Depressive disorder versus normality

Feelings of sadness are part of normal experience. The concept of depression, however, is not synonymous with sadness or unhappiness. Although unhappiness is a common component of the depressive mood associated with depression, the negative mood of depression may be represented more by features such as emotional emptiness or a feeling of flatness. For example, some depressed patients describe their mood as being like "a black cloud" (Hamilton, 1982). These feelings may vary in severity and may show *diurnal variation*, worse at one time of the day or another. Also related to depressed mood is the symptom of *anhedonia*, an inability to obtain pleasure from pursuits that the subject had previously enjoyed.

In recent years many writers have emphasized the importance of the so-called *cognitive features* of depression, and some believe that these features are essential to the concept. Beck (1976), for example, considered that depressed people were characterized by a negative "cognitive set"; they have a negative view of themselves, the world, and the future. Thus some depressed patients have intense feelings of personal inadequacy and a tendency to engage in *self-depreciation*. The patient may have a low opinion of himself, and often believes that others take a depreciatory view of him. These cognitive features have been described by many other investigators, although their role in aetiology has been the subject of much contention (Wilner, 1984).

The next step in the clarification of the concept of depression is the distinction between depression as a symptom and as a syndrome. Depressed affect and depressive cognitions are experienced by many people at some time during their lives, and can be regarded as part of the normal range of human emotional reaction. By contrast, the term syndrome implies more than just an isolated symptom, but the combination with other symptoms to form a symptom complex. In most classification systems, the syndrome of depression is defined by the combination of depressed mood with certain associated symptoms. The third revised version of the American *Diagnostic and Statistical Manual* (DSM-III-R) (American Psychiatric Association, 1987) definition of major depression, for example, requires the presence of at least five out of nine symptoms (see Table 1.1). At least one of the symptoms is either depressed mood or loss of interest or pleasure. Other operationally defined diagnostic systems provide similar lists (Feighner et al, 1972; Spitzer, Endicott & Robins, 1978).

It will be apparent that to define these syndromes of depression in terms of numbers of symptoms only may give rise to error. For example, one person with many minor symptoms causing no impairment may be regarded as suffering from the depressive syndrome, while another whose few symptoms cause much impairment may not be so regarded. Accordingly, most diagnostic systems include additional criteria that are intended to sharpen the differentiation between depressive symptoms and the syndrome of depression. For instance, the Research Diagnostic Criteria (RDC) (Spitzer et al, 1978) definition of major depression requires that symptoms persist for two weeks and that there is evidence of social impairment or help-seeking behaviour. A rather different approach was taken by Wing et al (1978) in the construction

Table 1.1   DSM-III-R criteria for a major depressive episode

---

A At least five of the following symptoms have been present during the same two-week period and represent a change from previous functioning. At least one of the symptoms is either (1) depressed mood, or (2) loss of interest or pleasure.

   (1) Depressed mood most of the day, nearly every day
   (2) Markedly diminished interest or pleasure in all, or almost all, activities most of the day, nearly every day
   (3) Significant weight loss or weight gain when not dieting, or decrease or increase in appetite nearly every day
   (4) Insomnia or hypersomnia nearly every day
   (5) Psychomotor agitation or retardation nearly every day
   (6) Fatigue or loss of energy nearly every day
   (7) Feelings of worthlessness or excessive or inappropriate guilt nearly every day
   (8) Diminished ability to think or concentrate, or indecisiveness, nearly every day
   (9) Recurrent thoughts of death, recurrent suicidal ideation without a specific plan, or a suicide attempt or a specific plan for committing suicide

B (1) It cannot be established that an organic factor initiated and maintained the disturbance
   (2) The disturbance is not a normal reaction to the death of a loved one

C At no time during the disturbance have there been delusions or hallucinations

D Not superimposed on schizophrenia, schizophreniform disorder, delusional disorder, or psychotic disorder NOS

Source: *Diagnostic and Statistical Manual of Mental Disorders*, 3rd revised edn, Washington D.C., American Psychiatric Association, 1987. Reproduced with permission.

of the Index of Definition. This system is based on the number, type and severity of Present State Examination symptoms (Wing, Cooper & Sartorius, 1974). In DSM-III-R, the only additional requirement for the diagnosis of major depression is that symptoms have been present during the same two-week period, but DSM-III-R also recognizes that dysthymic disorders characterized by chronic mild depressive symptoms can occur.

Despite these methodological developments the differentiation of depressive "states" from "normal reactions" remains a challenging problem. This is especially so in community surveys, where many subjects have symptomatology near the threshold for diagnosis. Brown and Harris (1978), for example, found that 17% of women in their London studies were definite "cases" and a further 19% were "borderline". It has been argued (Tennant & Bebbington, 1978) that these common depressive syndromes have few similarities with those seen by psychiatrists. Finlay-Jones et al (1980), however, reviewed the diagnoses of the women interviewed by the Bedford College team and found that the great majority of their cases met the appropriate standards for depression and anxiety set by the Research Diagnostic Criteria.

Nevertheless, there is still reluctance to accept that the cases of depression identified in community samples are comparable to those treated by psychiatrists, and this reluctance has often been expressed by importing the distinction between "distress" and "disease". A key issue here has been the differentiation between "depression" and "normal" reactions to stress and adversity such as "demoralization". Sadly, the evidence on this issue is inconclusive and often contradictory. It is now well established that in adults there is a relationship between the onset of depressive episodes and adversity, usually in the form of life events (Paykel et al, 1969; Brown & Harris, 1978). Brown et al (1973), for instance, examined a mixed group of depressed female patients, 50 "neurotic" depressives and 64 "endogenous" depressives. Their life-event histories were compared with those of a community sample free of psychiatric disorder. In the nine months before onset the depressed women experienced a four-fold excess of threatening events. Paykel et al (1969) matched 185 depressed patients on socio-demographic variables with subjects from the community. In the six months prior to onset the depressed subjects reported three times as many events as did the control subjects. Paykel (1974) attempted to evaluate the importance of recent loss in the genesis of depression, and calculated that about 8% of depression could be attributed to "exit" events such as separations.

However, some depressions are encountered that appear unrelated to any adversity. Accordingly, many researchers have attempted to differentiate subgroups of affective disorders by the presence of environmental stressors. The evidence so far indicates that unprecipitated depressions only weakly show the expected "endogenous" symptom pattern (Paykel, 1982; Brugha & Conroy, 1985). Bebbington et al (1988), for instance, found that whatever the definition of preceding adverse experience there were no significant differences between "endogenous" and "neurotic" categories of depression. Moreover, it seems that the relationship between depressive subtype and adversity is influenced by methodological biases of one kind or another. For instance, there is evidence that clinical psychiatrists make the distinction between endogenous and reactive depression on grounds both of symptoms and the presence or absence of adversity. Since clinicians' judgements are often used as the basis for validating the distinction between endogenous and reactive depression, it is not surprising that the relationship with preceding adversity appears highly significant (Bebbington et al, 1988). Finally, it seems that environmental stress can precede the onset of severe psychotic depressions (Leff, Roatch & Bunney, 1970) and mania (Ambelas, 1979).

Another approach to this question is provided by the prospective study, in which all subjects undergoing a specific event are followed up to observe the effects. Clayton (1982), for example, has carried out a number of follow-up studies in which men and women were interviewed in the first month after the deaths of their spouses and were seen again one year later. It seemed that the full range of depressive symptoms was common in the first year of bereavement. Indeed, many subjects fulfilled standardized diagnostic criteria for depression. However, certain symptoms were rare. Thus psychomotor retardation and morbid guilt were uncommon at any time, as were suicidal thoughts after the first month. These data indicate both similarities and differences between grief reactions and major depression.

All these studies raise the basic question of whether the most appropriate classification scheme should be categorical or dimensional. The categorical approaches to "caseness' described above are based on diagnostic systems that attempt to determine whether the subject does or does not meet criteria for depression as a categorical disorder. By contrast, dimensional approaches are based on the assumption that depression should be defined along a continuum of, say, increasingly severe symptoms of depression. Thus, they sidestep the problem of deciding in an often arbitrary fashion whether or not a depression should be counted as a "case" or as "normal". Moreover, such approaches avoid the loss of information that inevitably occurs through the imposition of cut-offs. They are inherently more flexible than categorical approaches.

On the other hand, that a subject has an extreme score on a depression scale does not necessarily mean that he or she would be diagnosed as having a mood "disorder". In addition, dimensional approaches to affective disturbances assume that these disturbances have the same meaning throughout the continuum. This assumption may be true for some forms of depression but, as we shall see later, conditions such as bipolar disorder probably involve qualitative as well as quantitative deviations from normal. Another important problem is that dimensions do not provide the same ease of description and conceptualization as a typology. Finally, as Kendell (1976) pointed out, it is somewhat illogical to decide that depression is best described by a dimensional model but then to study it as a category in isolation from other psychiatric conditions.

It would seem that we need to make use of both approaches in studying depression. Indeed, there are many examples of conditions that can be conceptualized in both categorical and dimensional terms. Intelligence, for example, works well as a continuous dimension, even within the low range. Yet, we know that there are many discrete syndromes associated with moderate or severe mental handicap. It could be that the same model can be applied to depression.

In summary, the present evidence suggests that it is better to characterize depressions by their correlates, course and response to treatment rather than by terms such as "normal" or "pathological". Indeed, delineation of a system that will consistently differentiate "normal" depression from depressive "disease" has so far proved impossible.

Depressive disorders and other psychiatric disorders

The boundary between affective disorders and other psychiatric conditions is equally unclear. Depressive symptoms can occur in many types of psychiatric disorders, such as schizophrenia, anorexia nervosa, obsessive–compulsive disorders, and anxiety states. In addition, it is quite common for the depressive *syndrome*, as defined above, to occur in conjunction with these conditions. For example, many patients with anorexia nervosa will at some time meet diagnostic criteria for major depression (Hendren, 1983; Swift, Andrews & Barklage, 1986; Rothenberg, 1988) and a substantial proportion of patients meeting DSM-III criteria for anxiety disorders also meet the criteria for additional depressive diagnoses (Barlow et al, 1986).

The two main psychiatric classification systems, DSM (American Psychiatric Association, 1987, 1991) and the International Classification of Diseases (World Health Organization, 1992: ICD-10) differ in their approach to these multiple overlapping diagnoses. For the most part DSM allows for the generation of multiple diagnoses, with the consequence that with mixed clinical pictures it is common for subjects to have several different diagnoses. ICD-10, by contrast, assumes that in most cases one diagnosis will take precedence. Psychiatrists are expected to use the overall pattern of clinical findings to diagnose the "main" disorder, although it is possible to make multiple diagnoses.

It is not at all clear which is the best approach. Diagnostic hierarchies can have a substantial effect on estimates of the prevalence of "excluded" psychiatric disorders, which cannot always be corrected for (Kendler, 1988). Moreover, in most cases we lack the evidence to decide which syndrome should have priority. On the other hand, common sense suggests that a mixed clinical picture is more likely to be the result of one disorder with variable manifestations, rather than the result of several different disorders that happen to occur in the same individual at the same time. Furthermore, the consequence of making multiple diagnoses is that the *same* subjects will appear in several supposedly *different* diagnostic groupings. This makes it difficult to identify specific aetiological factors for each of the supposedly separate disorders.

SUBCLASSIFICATION OF AFFECTIVE DISORDERS

Similar nosological problems occur in the subclassification of adult affective disorders. The result has been the proliferation of a large number of competing methods of classifying depression, both in research settings and in clinical practice (see reviews by, for example: Kendell, 1976; Andreasen, 1982). In this chapter, just two of the major current clinical classifications will be considered: DSM-III-R/DSM-IV and the International Classification of Diseases.

Table 1.2   DSM-III-R classification of affective disorders

Mood disorders
  Bipolar disorders
    Manic
    Depressed
    Mixed
    Cyclothymia
    Bipolar disorder NOS
  Depressive disorders
    Major depression
      Single episode or recurrent
    Dysthymia (or depressive neurosis)
      Primary or secondary
      Early- or late-onset
    Depressive disorder NOS

Psychotic disorders not elsewhere classified
  Schizoaffective disorder
    Bipolar type or depressive type

Adjustment disorder
  With depressed mood

Source: As Table 1.1

DSM-III-R/DSM-IV

Table 1.2 shows a summary of the DSM-III-R classification of affective disorders. DSM-III-R differentiates between mood disorders in which there may or may not have been episodes of mania (bipolar disorders and depressive disorders respectively). Mania is not used as a separate category—it is classified under bipolar disorders whether or not there have been depressive disorders.

The current state of major depression and bipolar disorder is characterized further according to severity, the presence of psychotic features, or whether there is partial or full remission. Major depressive episodes can additionally be specified as chronic and/or melancholic in type. "Psychotic" is used to mean "delusions or hallucinations". The term "chronic" is used when "the current episode has lasted two consecutive years without a period of two months during which there were no significant depressive symptoms".

The term "melancholic type" is used to mean a major depression in which symptoms such as loss of interest, lack of reactivity to pleasurable stimuli and significant anorexia occur. The diagnostic criteria for "major depression: melancholic type" also include nonsymptomatic features such as "no significant personality disturbance before first major depressive episode", "one or more previous major depressive episodes followed by complete, or nearly complete, recovery", and "previous good response to specific and adequate somatic antidepressant therapy". The diagnosis requires the presence of at least five out of the nine symptomatic and nonsymptomatic criteria.

It is also possible to specify whether or not there has been a seasonal pattern. Here, there has to be a temporal relationship between episodes and remissions of bipolar disorder or major depression and a particular period of the year. This must have occurred at least three times, and seasonal episodes of mood disturbance must have outnumbered nonseasonal episodes by three to one.

The other main mood disorders in DSM-III-R are cyclothymia and dysthymia (or depressive neurosis). Both these categories refer to long-standing mood disorders that last at least two years. Cyclothymia is characterized by mild depression and hypomania, while dysthymia refers to a chronic mild depressive syndrome. Other mild depressive syndromes, which do not meet criteria for major depression or dysthymia, are placed under "adjustment disorder with depressed mood". When a depressive syndrome is thought to be a reaction to the death of a loved one the DSM-III-R category of "uncomplicated bereavement" can be used.

DSM-III-R will soon be replaced by DSM-IV. A number of options for dealing with the subclassification of affective disorders have been considered, but these options have not yet been finalized (American Psychiatric Association, 1991). The criteria for major depressive disorder are likely to remain essentially unchanged except for one important possible addition: a criterion requiring impairment or distress. Another important option concerns the criteria for dysthymic disorder, which would be changed to apply only in cases in which the criteria have never been met for a major depressive episode. Parallel options have been prepared for cyclothymic disorder. DSM-IV may also include a new category, "minor depressive disorder", which will be defined by criteria similar to those used in the RDC for minor depressive disorder. The approach taken to depressive disorders in young people is likely to be the same as in DSM-III-R (Shaffer et al, 1989).

ICD-10

Table 1.3 summarizes the ICD-10 classification of affective disorders (World Health Organization, 1992). As the table indicates, the classification is in some respects similar to that of DSM. For instance, in common with DSM the distinction between bipolar and unipolar affective disorders is explicit. ICD-10 also contains diagnostic guidelines, which attempt to provide an explicit specification of the concepts that underlie each disorder. These indicate the number and balance of symptoms usually required before a diagnosis can be made and are much more detailed than the glossary of ICD-9. They also give an indication of the level of knowledge represented in each category.

In line with DSM-III-R, depressive disorders that can occur at any age are not separately categorized when they happen to occur in children. Bipolar

Table 1.3   ICD-10 classification of affective disorders

F3   Mood (affective) disorders
  F30   Manic episode
  F31   Bipolar affective disorder
  F32   Depressive episode
  F33   Recurrent depressive disorder
  F34   Persistent affective disorders
  F38   Other mood (affective) disorders
  F39   Affective disorder, unspecified

F4   Neurotic, stress-related and somatoform disorders
  F41   Other anxiety disorders
      .2   Mixed anxiety and depressive disorder
  F43   Reaction to severe stress, and adjustment disorders
      .2   Adjustment disorder
        .20   Brief depressive reaction
        .21   Prolonged depressive reaction
        .22   Mixed anxiety and depressive reactions

F2   Schizophrenia, schizotypal and delusional disorders
  F20   Schizophrenia
      .4   Post-schizophrenic depression
  F25   Schizoaffective disorders

F9   Behavioural and emotional disorders with onset usually occurring in childhood or adolescence
  F92   Mixed disorders of conduct and emotions
      .0   Depressive conduct disorder

Source: World Health Organization, 1992

disorder, for example, is classified in the same ICD-10 category regardless of age of onset. There is, however, a separate childhood category for mixed disorders characterized by the combination of conduct disorder and depression ("depressive conduct disorder"). ICD continues to be different from DSM in its use of such combination categories.

VALIDITY OF DIAGNOSTIC SUBGROUPS

There is no biological test that can be used reliably to distinguish one functional psychiatric disorder from another. Accordingly, a variety of different research strategies have been employed in order to validate these nosological distinctions within the affective disorders. The aims have been both to establish the predictive validity of the various categories and to identify a specific correlate that distinguishes one category from another.

One of the most consistent findings from research into the adult-onset affective disorders has been that these disorders tend to aggregate in families (e.g. Tsuang, Winokur & Crowe, 1980; Gershon et al, 1975; Weissman et al, 1984a). As a result, there have been many attempts to validate subcategories of depression by the type of affective disorder found in relatives of the depressed proband. Indeed, many family studies have supported the distinction between unipolar and bipolar disorder. Bipolar probands have often been found to have high rates of both bipolar and unipolar disorders in their relatives, whereas unipolar probands generally show a high rate of unipolar but not bipolar disorder in relatives (Gershon et al, 1982; Weissman et al, 1984a; Andreasen et al, 1987). There have, however, been some negative findings and the interpretation of these results has been the subject of some disagreement (McGuffin & Sargeant, 1991). In particular, it is not known whether the pattern of results is better interpreted in terms of there being two separate but overlapping conditions, or in terms of a common predisposition.

Family studies have also been used to investigate the validity of the diagnosis of "melancholic" depression, but the results have been contradictory. Andreasen et al (1986) found no excess of depressive disorders in the relatives of probands with melancholia, whereas Leckman et al (1984) reported significant increases in familial prevalence. On the other hand, studies of response to treatment have tended to show that melancholic features predict a better response to electroconvulsive therapy (Scott, 1989) and possibly to tricyclic antidepressants (Paykel, 1989).

A number of follow-up studies have investigated differences between the outcomes of "neurotic" and "psychotic" or "endogenous" depressions. (Terminology has been very confusing here, since the term "psychotic" does not necessarily imply the presence of delusions or hallucinations, and has often been used to describe depressions characterized by "melancholic" or "endogenous" features.) Both short- and long-term follow-ups have indicated that patients with "endogenous" depression are more likely to require readmission during the follow-up period (Copeland, 1983; Kiloh, Andrews & Neilson, 1988; Lee & Murray, 1988). However, it is unclear whether the overall outcome differs significantly between the groups (*Lancet*, 1989). Lee and Murray (1988) reported that, in the long term, psychotic depressed subjects became more severely and chronically disabled than neurotic depressed subjects. On the other hand, Kiloh et al (1988) found that the prognosis for the two types of depression was the same.

A variety of mathematical techniques, such as cluster analysis, have been employed to subclassify affective disorders. However, these techniques will almost invariably yield a classificatory system if the sample is large enough (Everitt & Dunn, 1983). So, it is always necessary to validate the mathematical classification by other means. Nonetheless, on the whole the results have separated a group with severe psychotic or melancholic features (Andreasen, 1982).

Biological measures have also been used in the attempt to subdivide depressive disorders. A large number of possible psychobiological measures have been studied, of which perhaps the best known is the Dexamethasone Suppression Test (DST). In the early 1980s, nonsuppression on this test was proposed both as a biological marker of melancholic depression (Carroll, 1982) and as a guide to treatment (*British Medical Journal*, 1981). However, the findings of subsequent studies have been inconsistent and have often failed to support these suggestions (Berger et al, 1984). Nonsuppression may be strongly influenced by weight loss and stress (Cowen & Wood, 1991; Mellsop, Hutton & Delahunt, 1985) and it has become clear that the test provides little differentiation within the depressive disorders.

In summary, it is evident that all is not well with the classification of depression arising in adulthood. There is little agreement on where the line should be drawn between major affective disorders and conditions in which either mood disturbances are mild or in which they are part of another psychiatric syndrome. Even greater uncertainty exists concerning the subtyping of depressive disorders, although there is evidence to support a separation of bipolar and unipolar forms (Perris, 1982).

Nevertheless, most clinicians would agree that the concept of depression arising in adulthood has proved useful, and few would eschew it altogether. The same cannot be said for the notion of depression as a disorder that affects children. The remainder of this chapter considers the development of the concept of depressive disorder in childhood and some of the uncertainties surrounding it.

CONCEPTS AND CLASSIFICATION OF DEPRESSIVE DISORDER IN CHILDHOOD

Current concepts of depressive disorders in childhood use criteria that are closely comparable to those in adults. However, we shall see later that there have been problems in using adult criteria with children. Accordingly, it is helpful to consider first earlier views in order to highlight some of the key dilemmas and issues.

Anaclitic depression

One of the first studies to suggest links between depression in children and the major depressive conditions of adult life was conducted by Spitz (1946), who described the syndrome of "anaclitic depression". The Spitz study involved nursery infants separated from their mothers. In addition to weepiness and withdrawal, the infants showed retardation of development, slow reactions, retardation of movement, sometimes stupor, and loss of appetite. Spitz and Wolf (1946) postulated that the most important aetiological factor was "loss of the love object". Other authors have observed similar behavioural changes in institutionalized children. Goldfarb (1943), for instance, found that such children were often passive or apathetic.

Spitz's paper (1946) has been the subject of a number of methodological criticisms, particularly with respect to the suggestion that "anaclitic depression" can lead to severe developmental retardation. Pinneau (1955) pointed out that Spitz's measures were unstandardized and that his design did not take sufficient account of other factors that might have led to the outcomes. Nevertheless, the notion of a syndrome of anaclitic depression has persisted. Harmon, Wagonfeld and Emde (1982), for instance, described the case of an infant who was placed in a residential nursery at eight days of age. At eight months the child displayed symptomatology of "anaclitic depression", including weeping, withdrawal, apathy, weight loss and sleep disturbance. This episode lasted until the child was 17 months of age. Sadly, he experienced three further episodes during which he was depressed. Each began with agitation and was followed by apathy. All these episodes were associated with separation from a primary attachment figure.

Several authors regard Spitz's notion of anaclitic depression as an example of depressive disorder. It has even been suggested that deprivation is a key variable in the aetiology of depressive conditions among the young. For instance, Trad (1986) emphasized the similarities between the "portrait of the maternally deprived child and the clinically depressed child". Indeed, it is clear that the phenomena observed in institutionalized infants, together with the protest–despair–detachment sequence seen in some toddlers admitted to hospital (Bowlby, 1969), constitute a kind of affective reaction. However, whether or not these inhibitory reactions of infancy are isomorphic with the major depressive disorders of adulthood remains uncertain. Thus, the responses of toddlers admitted to hospital usually disappear rapidly when the parent returns, whereas major depression in adulthood is often a recurrent problem. Moreover, these responses occur most frequently between about six months and four years of age, and appear to decline thereafter. The implication is that the affective states of infancy do not represent the same kind of condition as depressive disorders in adults.

Masked depression

During the 1960s the predominant view in the psychoanalytic literature was that depressive conditions resembling adult depression could not occur in children because the personality structure of the child was too immature (Rie, 1966). Rochlin (1959), for example, considered that depression was impossible in middle childhood because the child does not have a sufficiently formulated superego to direct aggression against his own ego. However, middle childhood has also been seen as a time when depression does occur, but in a "masked" form. In this formulation children between roughly the ages of six and ten years of age are in a transition period. They are able to experience adult-like depressive conditions but they express these feelings in a different way. Glaser (1967), for instance, hypothesized that masked depression included symptoms such as phobias, delinquency, and somatic symptoms. Other symptoms that have been viewed at one time or another as "depressive equivalents" include social withdrawal, aggression, fears about death, and enuresis.

In an early attempt to study the notion of masked depression, Frommer (1968) hypothesized that there were three types of depression in childhood: uncomplicated or pure depression, enuretic depression, and phobic depression. Children with uncomplicated depression were the only group in which spontaneous complaints of depression were common. This group was characterized by symptoms such as irritability, weepiness, difficulty sleeping and suicidal ideation and/or attempts. Monoamine oxidase inhibitors were considered the drugs of choice. The group with enuretic depression often had serious difficulties at school and learning problems. Antisocial behaviour was common and these children frequently came from families where there was discord and rejection by parents. Frommer (1968) hypothesized that these children were suffering from maturational delays, of which enuresis was just one feature. The group of children with phobic depression had marked anxiety and somatic complaints as well as some depressive symptomatology. This group was also said to do well with monoamine oxidase inhibitors.

Cytryn and McKnew (1972) proposed that the most common type of depression in childhood was masked depression, which could be diagnosed on the basis of features such as facial expression, and fantasy content. However, these authors also described a "typical" depressive syndrome occurring in children. This consisted of symptoms such as hopelessness, psychomotor retardation, sleep problems, appetite disturbance, social withdrawal and other symptoms seen in adult depressive disorders. They divided these typical depressive syndromes into acute and chronic forms. The acute form was said to occur in children without previous psychiatric disorder and without marked family psychopathology. Children with the chronic type of typical depression were often poorly adjusted prior to the onset of the disorder and tended to come from a more disturbed background. The fact that children with the acute form of depression recovered quickly when removed from adversity has led some authors to suggest that these children would not meet present-day criteria for major depressive disorder (Puig-Antich & Gittelman, 1982). However, in a more recent assessment of these children, Cytryn et al (1980) rediagnosed the original sample using DSM-III criteria. Eleven out of the 12 children with acute depression met DSM-III criteria for major depressive disorder. By contrast, only four of the 13 children originally diagnosed as masked depression met criteria for a DSM-III depressive diagnosis. Most of the remainder were found to have conduct disorder.

We shall see later that there is some evidence to support the idea that the presence or absence of nondepressive symptoms such as antisocial behaviours may be a useful way of subclassifying children with overt depression. In addition, there is no doubt that the notion of masked depression has proved useful in some clinical settings in drawing attention to modes of presentation of depression that are easily missed. Moreover, it is not unreasonable to think that if depressive disorders do occur in prepubertal children then they may assume a different form. After all, young children differ from adults in their ability to experience many of the so-called cognitive features of depression, such as hopelessness (Rutter, 1986a).

However, the idea that depression in young children is mostly expressed through nondepressive symptoms, with few obvious signs of a primary mood state, has proved very difficult to put into practice. The problem is that no one has been able to devise a set of criteria that can reliably distinguish between symptoms that are due to depression and identical symptoms that occur as part of a different underlying disorder. When, for example, is enuresis "true enuresis" and when is it a "depressive equivalent"? Furthermore, the symptoms that were thought to be due to masked depression included practically all the possible psychiatric symptoms of childhood (Gittelman-Klein, 1977; Puig-Antich & Gittelman, 1982). Since our current classification systems are mostly specified in descriptive rather than aetiological terms, it is somewhat confusing to classify an individual as depressed when he or she shows few overt signs of depression. Finally, as Kovacs and Beck (1977) pointed out, the term "masked depression" is not only misleading but also probably unnecessary. They noted that many of the behaviours listed as masking depression in children were often a prominant part of the clinical picture in adults. Moreover, Carlson and Cantwell (1980a) found that other psychiatric symptoms did not usually mask depressive symptoms. Careful clinical examination would usually reveal the underlying depression. Similar observations have been made in more recent studies (Kolvin et al, 1991).

Operational criteria for syndromes resembling adult depression

The next major development in this field was the attempt by several authors to specify operational diagnostic criteria for depression in children that resembled the criteria used to diagnose depression in adults (Ling, Oftedal & Weinberg, 1970; Weinberg et al, 1973; McConville, Boag & Purohit, 1973; Pearce, 1974, 1978). These early operationalized systems stemmed from the idea that depression in children had many similarities with depressions arising in adults as well as a number of features seen only in childhood. Weinberg et al (1973), for instance, used criteria that were broadly similar to the adult criteria of Feighner and his colleagues (1972). They proposed that the diagnosis of depression in children required all four of the following:

1. The presence of both dysphoric mood and self-deprecatory ideation.
2. Two or more of the following eight symptoms—aggressive behaviour (agitation), sleep disturbance, a change in school performance, diminished socialization, change in attitude towards school, somatic complaints, loss of usual energy, and an unusual change in appetite or weight.
3. These symptoms represent a change in the child's usual behaviour.
4. Symptoms present for at least one month.

Weinberg and colleagues found that 45 out of 72 prepubertal children presenting to a clinic with school performance difficulties or behavioural problems, or both, met these criteria for depressive illness. Interestingly there was a family history of depressive illness among the first-degree relatives of 40 of the depressed cases, compared with only 8 of 26 nondepressed controls.

At about the same time, Pearce (1974, 1978) devised a similar set of criteria for depression in children. His elegant study was based on child psychiatric patients attending the Maudsley Hospital during the years 1968 to 1969, after the exclusion of those with infantile or schizophrenic psychoses, organic states or an IQ below 50. Pearce (1974) used a variety of statistical techniques to identify symptoms that discriminated between depressed and nondepressed children and that were positively associated with the symptom of depression. On the basis of these statistical analyses he proposed that childhood depressive disorder should be defined by the symptom of depressed mood plus at least two of the following symptoms: suicidal and morbid thoughts, disturbance of sleep, disturbance of appetite, obsessions, irritability, hypochondriasis, alimentary symptoms, school refusal, and altered perception, such as delusions or overvalued ideas of guilt and worthlessness. The symptoms must represent a change in the child's usual functioning and be persistent and severe enough to be a handicap (Pearce, 1978). Using these criteria, Pearce (1974) identified 80 out of 673 child psychiatric patients (12%) as having depressive disorder.

These operationalized diagnostic criteria represented an important advance in the evolution of the current concept of depressive disorder in children. However, both sets of criteria were rather nonspecific to the extent that a depressive disorder could still be diagnosed in the absence of a majority of symptoms of depression. For example, in the Pearce system it was possible to diagnose a depressive condition on the basis of just depressed mood, school refusal and hypochondriasis (though in practice the majority of cases met RDC criteria for a depressive disorder—see Harrington et al (1990)). Moreover, in order to make assessments more applicable for children, certain assumptions had to be made about the equivalence of child and adult symptoms. For example, in the Weinberg criteria "desire to run away from home" was taken as evidence of self-depreciatory ideation. Furthermore, the existence of several different sets of criteria for childhood depressive disorder meant that there was little uniformity within the field.

Full adult criteria

As a result, several authors suggested that depressive disorders among children should be diagnosed using the standardized criteria that were used with adults, particularly DSM-III (American Psychiatric Association, 1980). According to this viewpoint the essential features for major depression were identical for prepubertal children, adolescents and adults. Puig-Antich et al (1978), for example, identified 13 prepubertal children who met RDC criteria for major depressive disorder for at least one month. All were able to describe depressed mood and 11 had suicidal thoughts. These children appeared to have a severe form of depression as judged by the fact that three of them had an endogenous symptom pattern and three had depressive hallucinations. Since then, there have been reports that such syndromes may be relatively common in children referred to psychiatrists (Carlson & Cantwell, 1980b; Kolvin et al, 1991) and it has been suggested that major depressive disorders occur in preschoolers (Kashani, Holcomb & Orvaschel, 1986).

Indeed, the main current classification systems make no distinction in the diagnostic criteria for prepubertal, adolescent or adult depression. DSM-III-R does state in the text that there may be age-specific associated features that differ across these age periods. For instance, irritable mood may substitute for depressed mood in both children and adolescents. In prepubertal children with major depression, somatic complaints, agitation and mood-congruent hallucinations are said to be particularly frequent. In adolescence, wanting to leave home, restlessness, grouchiness and aggression are common and school difficulties are likely. In addition, withdrawal from social activities and a reluctance to cooperate in family ventures are said to be frequent. However, none of these features are actually part of the diagnostic criteria in DSM-III-R. Major depressive disorders are seen as occurring at any age, including infancy. In ICD-10 no mention is made of the features of major depression as they occur in children. Presumably, therefore, the criteria are identical across the age span.

Thus, in the space of a few years the field has advanced from the position that depressive disorders cannot occur in children, or that they occur in a "masked" form, to the point where childhood disorders with features similar or identical to adult depression are part of our classification systems. Indeed, as Shaffer (1985) pointed out, for a time the idea of depression as a psychiatric disease affecting children became so popular that papers on it dominated scientific journals and meetings. Moreover, since there seems to be little doubt that disorders meeting the full criteria for adult major depression can and do occur in children, it might be thought that the issue of the validity of childhood depressive disorder has been resolved. However, this is very far from being the case and many uncertainties still exist about the concept.

Some of these uncertainties apply equally to depressive disorders arising in adulthood, and have been dealt with briefly above. Thus, for example, Graham (1981) considered that depression as a biologically determined disorder occurs only rarely in children. In line with many critics of the biological model of adult depression, he proposed that depressive disorder in children was usually a social response to stress. He suggested that childhood depressive disorders should be viewed as reactions until proved otherwise.

In addition, the strategy of applying unmodified adult criteria to children has been criticized because it fails to take into account developmental research on *age changes* in the frequency and expression of affective phenomena. Three developmental issues are especially relevant here. First, we shall see in Chapter 4 that there are substantial age differences in the occurrence of depressive phenomena (Rutter, 1986a; Angold, 1988a,b). Depressive symptoms in the community are considerably more prevalent in adolescence than in childhood and these changes seem to show an association with puberty (Rutter, Tizard & Whitmore, 1970; Rutter et al, 1976; Rutter, 1980). Data on depressive disorders in clinical samples (Pearce, 1978) and in the general population (Fleming, Offord & Boyle, 1989) show the same trend. Moreover, suicide rates rise dramatically after puberty (Shaffer, 1986; McClure, 1988; Shaffer, 1988) and it seems that the same is true of mania (Strober, Hanna & McCracken, 1989). Furthermore, there is some evidence of a change in sex ratio at around the time of puberty: among prepubertal children it seems that depressive symptoms and depressive disorders are more common in boys, whereas after puberty they are more common in girls (Rutter, 1986a, 1988a; Fleming, Offord & Boyle, 1989). Clearly, all these findings suggest that there may be important *dissimilarities* between child and adult depressive conditions.

Secondly, children differ from adults in their ability to *experience* some of the *cognitive features* said to characterize adult depressive disorders (Rutter, 1986b). For example, if children are to experience guilt and a sense of failure it is necessary that they can understand the concept of failure. It seems that children as young as four or five years old are aware that other people may feel ashamed of them, but it is not until around the age of eight years that most children talk of being ashamed of themselves (Harter, 1983).

Thirdly, the valid application of adult criteria to children requires not only that they are capable of experiencing the features said to be characteristic of adult depression, but also that they can *report* them accurately. It seems that children have limitations in this last respect. Kovacs (1986), for example, reported that young children had difficulties differentiating basic emotions, and often mislabelled emotions such as sadness and anger. Moreover, the young child's capacity to give an account of duration of problems and past events is limited. This may pose problems for the diagnosis of some categories of depressive disorder, such as "recurrent depression", in which historical data are required to make the diagnosis.

Validity of adult-based depressive syndromes in children

Despite these problems, there is considerable evidence to support the validity of an adult-like depressive syndrome occurring in children and adolescents. The two most important pieces of evidence are the longitudinal and family-genetic findings. The results of these studies will be considered in more detail later in this book. However, it is worth noting here that several longitudinal studies have found that children with depressive disorders are at increased risk of subsequent depression when compared with nondepressed cases. It appears that this increased risk is specific to depressive disorder; no disorder other than depression is increased at follow-up (Harrington et al, 1990). Similarly, several family studies have found that there are increased rates of depressive disorder in the relatives of depressed child probands. Moreover, once again this risk seems to be relatively specific for depression (Harrington et al, 1992). A third validating feature, which is not as strong as the first two, concerns the age and sex trends for depressive disorders that were described in the previous section. No other disorder shows these trends in quite the same way.

Developmental perspectives on classification

Nevertheless, the problems of using adult criteria for depressive disorders in young people have led several investigators to propose alternative approaches to diagnosis (Harrington, 1991). Indeed, it has been argued that since the nature of the symptoms expressed at different ages may differ greatly, perhaps it is futile to try to define criteria that can be applied across the age span. According to this viewpoint it might be better to identify age-appropriate signs and symptoms that take into account the child's level of functioning in the various cognitive and affective domains (Garber, 1984; Carlson & Garber, 1986).

To some extent it is probably already the case that many clinicians who apply adult criteria for depression to young children draw upon their knowledge of child development to adapt these criteria to the developmental levels of their patients (Cicchetti & Schneider-Rosen, 1986). Indeed, early attempts to define adult-like operational criteria for childhood depression often made assumptions about the equivalence of child and adult symptoms. For instance, the criteria devised by Weinberg and his colleagues (1973) treated the symptom of being "negative and difficult to please" as a sign of "dysphoric mood". Moreover, DSM-III-R in effect advocates the notion of using age-specific criteria for depression when it lists the ways in which the manifestations of depression vary with age.

However, the problem with both the intuitive approach of the clinician and the more formal approach of DSM-III-R is that neither specifies exactly how the "developmental perspective" should be put into practice. It is all very well to suggest that the manifestations of depression may vary with age but it is quite another thing to operationalize this idea in the form of criteria that can be used reliably and that will be widely accepted. Thus, one of the first attempts to classify childhood depression (Malmquist, 1971) was based on both aetiology and developmental level. There were five major groups. Two were classed according to aetiology (depressions associated with organic disease and deprivation syndromes) and three according to developmental stage (individuation, latency and adolescent types). However, no systematic studies were done on the validity of these distinctions, and as a result the criteria were never widely used. Similarly, McConville, Boag and Purohit (1973) proposed that there were three types of depression in childhood. "Affectual" type occurred in children aged six to eight years and was thought to be characterized by expressions of sadness, hopelessness and helplessness. The second form was said to be more common after the age of eight and was characterized by low self-esteem. In the third type, which occurred in children of eleven years or older, feelings of guilt were common. Once again, however, there has been little published research on the relationship between the various proposed subtypes.

More recently Carlson and Garber (1986) have suggested that current diagnostic systems such as DSM could be revised to take into account developmental differences. They proposed a set of diagnostic rules involving a two-tiered process that takes into account different base rates at different ages. The first tier would consist of a set of core indicators that occur at roughly the same rate across the age span. A certain number would be required for the diagnosis of depression. A second set of indicators would consist of those symptoms found rarely in children, such as suicidal ideation. These symptoms would contribute to the diagnosis if present, but would not alter the diagnosis if absent. The third set would consist of symptoms highly associated with depression in children, such as social withdrawal, which would also contribute to the diagnosis if present. In essence, then, this classification scheme proposes that depression in children could be conceptualized as having a basic similarity with adult-onset depression, but with some age-specific features. The system has merit but it remains to be seen whether or not it will become widely used.

It is important to appreciate that the developmental perspective is concerned not only with the definition and diagnosis of depression in children but also with the much wider issues of the mechanisms and processes involved in the developmental changes that take place. These processes will be discussed in greater detail later in this book. In the meantime it should be noted that it is not sufficient to know that adult concepts can be extended down to childhood, nor is it enough to consider disorders arising in childhood *sui generis* (Rutter, 1986a). Rather, we need also to ask questions concerning the reasons for the age trends, and to establish the degree of continuity across age periods. Knowledge of these developmental processes is fundamental to any understanding of the aetiology of depression at all ages.

CONCLUSIONS

The validity of the diagnostic concept of depressive disorder in adulthood is now well established, though continuing uncertainties remain concerning its boundaries. The application of the same concept to the study of affective phenomena in children has generated much research and has led to great progress in recent years. In particular, there is now evidence from longitudinal, family-genetic and epidemiological sources that supports the validity of an adult-like depressive syndrome occurring in young people. Nevertheless, the classification and diagnosis of depressive disorder in children using unmodified adult criteria remains a matter of controversy. A number of alternative classifications have been proposed, some of which take a "developmental" approach. However, these alternative approaches have yet to be fully evaluated with respect to symptomatology, aetiology and course.

Chapter 2

Assessment of Depression in Children

INTRODUCTION

For many years information from parents and teachers was the main source of data in the diagnosis of child psychiatric disorders. Rutter, Tizard and Whitmore (1970), for instance, found that the interview with the parents was the single best method for detecting children with psychiatric problems. It was uncommon for children thought to be normal by their parents to be diagnosed as suffering from a psychiatric disorder on the basis only of the interview with the child.

In the past fifteen years or so, however, interest in depressive disorders among the young has been spurred by the recognition that children can give accurate information regarding their own mental state. As a result, the same symptoms assessed in adult depression are now routinely assessed during the interview with a depressed child. Indeed, we shall see later in this chapter that information that is obtained directly from the child may be essential in order adequately to assess symptoms that reflect subjective phenomena, such as feelings and worries.

In spite of this development, information from other sources continues to play an important role in the diagnosis of childhood depressive disorder. Such sources are important not only because young children find it difficult to report accurately on certain aspects of psychopathology, but also because parents or teachers are usually the best informants on observable behaviour. So, the assessment of depressed children often requires that information be obtained from both parents and teachers, as well as from the child. It is also important to emphasize that the assessment of depressed children only starts with the diagnosis, and does not end with it. Depressed children usually have multiple problems that impinge on most aspects of their lives, particularly on their social functioning and scholastic attainments. Assessment needs therefore to include knowledge about many other aspects of the child's life and the circumstances in which the child and the family are living.

This chapter is concerned with the clinical assessment of depressive symptoms in young people. The chapter begins with a review of the symptomatology of depressive disorder. Next, interviews with parents and children are considered, with a particular focus on developmental aspects. Finally, the important issue of the level of agreement between parent and child reports is reviewed. Structured interviews, rating scales and observational ratings will be covered in the next chapter.

SYMPTOMATOLOGY OF DEPRESSIVE DISORDER IN ADULTS

Before going on to discuss affective symptoms in children, it is appropriate to consider briefly the clinical picture of depressive conditions as they present in adults. The main symptom of adult depressive disorder, though not necessarily the presenting complaint, is *depression of mood*. The mood does not improve substantially in circumstances where ordinary feelings of sadness would be alleviated and is often described as qualitatively different from normal unhappiness. Patients may speak of a "black cloud" or sometimes of a complete inability to experience any kind of emotion. Such feelings are commonly accompanied by a *loss of enjoyment* of usual activities and *loss of energy*. Frequently there is *loss of concentration*, which may impair the patient's ability to carry out even simple tasks.

The so-called *"biological"* symptoms of depression are often present. They include diurnal variation of mood (usually worse in the morning), loss of appetite, loss of weight, constipation, and problems sleeping. Sleep disturbance is of several different kinds but characteristic is early morning waking. In some patients there is increased appetite and weight gain.

Depressive cognitions may be prominent. Typically, the depressed patient expects the worst, and sees no hope for the future. Such thoughts are commonly linked to *suicidal ideation*. Depressed people also experience feelings of guilt, which may become extremely intense and occasionally of delusional proportions. They readily become preoccupied with past trivial misdemeanours for which they blame themselves. The patient may also think that he is a failure and discount his previous achievements.

Finally, in severe depressive disorder a number of other symptoms may be present. There may be agitation or retardation of movements. The patient may feel that his thoughts have slowed down. Delusions of worthlessness or ill-health are not uncommon. For example, the patient may become convinced that he suffers from cancer. Auditory and visual hallucinations are less common but are usually depressive in content. For instance, the patient may hear voices saying that he is worthless or evil and deserves to be punished.

SYMPTOMATOLOGY OF DEPRESSION IN CHILDREN

Comparisons across ages

Several investigators have systematically compared the symptoms of depressed children with those of depressed adolescents or adults (Kovacs &

Paulauskas, 1984; Ryan et al, 1987; Carlson & Kashani, 1988; Mitchell et al, 1988). In the largest such study (Ryan et al, 1987) symptom frequency and severity were compared in two clinically referred samples of 95 children and 92 adolescents with major depression. There was no difference between children and adolescents with major depressive disorders in the overall severity of depressive symptoms, or in the severity of the majority of individual depressive symptoms, including depressed mood, insomnia, irritability and suicidal ideation. However, prepubertal children had more somatic complaints, psychomotor agitation, separation anxiety, phobias and hallucinations. Adolescents had greater hopelessness/helplessness, anhedonia, hypersomnia, and use of alcohol and drugs.

Although prepubertal children seemed to have just as much suicidal ideation as depressed adolescents, the potential lethality of their suicidal attempts was lower. Ryan et al (1987) suggested that younger children have equal suicidal intent but lack the cognitive ability to formulate successful suicidal plans. By contrast, adolescents choose a more effective method, such as gunshot. In adolescents there was a strong association between all measures of suicidality and duration of episode over two years.

Carlson and Kashani (1988) compared the symptom profiles of the children and adolescents in the Ryan et al study (1987) with the symptomatology of nine preschool children with DSM-III major depression and with 100 adults who had been hospitalized with unipolar depression. Anhedonia, diurnal variation, hopelessness, psychomotor retardation, and delusions increased with age. Depressed appearance, low self-esteem, and somatic complaints decreased with age. However, in a similar study, Mitchell et al (1988) found there were very few differences between the symptomatology of depressed children and adolescents. Moreover, their combined group of children and adolescents differed little in symptom presentation from adults with major depression. Similarly, Kovacs and Paulauskas (1984) found that there were few differences in depressive symptomatology across developmental stages.

It will be appreciated that because all these studies were based on children who had previously been diagnosed as having DSM-III major depression, and because this diagnosis was based on the number and type of depressive symptoms, the amount of variation in depressive symptomatology was necessarily very limited. Nevertheless, even with this constraint the findings of the study of Ryan et al (1987) point not only to substantial similarities between child and adult depressive disorders, but also to important dissimilarities. Indeed, as these authors commented, some symptoms that are not part of the adult criteria for major depression, such as somatic complaints and social withdrawal, were so common among depressed children and adolescents that consideration should be given to including them in the criteria for depressive disorder in this age group. Perhaps development may alter some of the features of depressive conditions. As we shall see in the next section, mathematical studies produce a similar pattern of phenotypic continuities and discontinuities between child and adult depressive disorders.

Mathematical studies

Several types of mathematical approach have been used to study the symptomatology of depressed children and to examine the degree of similarity with depressive disorders arising in adulthood. *Principal components analysis*, which forms groups of *symptoms* based on the co-occurrence of those symptoms in individuals, was used by Ryan et al (1987) with the Pittsburgh sample described earlier. These authors found five clinically interpretable factors: an endogenous factor (anhedonia, fatigue, psychomotor retardation, social withdrawal, depressed mood, anorexia, decreased weight, diurnal variation, and hypersomnia); a negative cognitions factor (negative self-image, hopelessness/helplessness, suicidal ideation, and brooding/worrying); an anxiety factor (separation anxiety, somatic complaints, insomnia, brooding/worrying, psychomotor agitation); an appetite and weight factor (increased appetite, increased weight, anorexia, and decreased weight); and a disturbed conduct factor (suicidal ideation, psychomotor agitation, conduct disorder and irritability). The group was then divided into prepubertal children and adolescents. The adolescent group gave essentially the same factor structure. However, in the child group the endogenous factor combined with the negative cognition factor, while the other three factors remained basically unchanged.

Similar component structures were identified by Kolvin et al (1991) who applied the same statistical techniques in a study of successive referrals to a university child psychiatry unit in Newcastle, England. In their principal components analyses of a sample containing less than 50 cases of depressive disorder, four clinically interpretable components were identified: (1) depressed, anhedonia, increased fatigue, and psychomotor retardation; (2) negative cognitions and thoughts of suicide; (3) an anxiety component (including separation anxiety and fear); and (4) an anger, agitation, and irritability component. In contrast to Ryan et al (1987), neither conduct nor appetite–weight components were identified. The smaller size of the Newcastle sample did not allow separate analysis of pre- and postpubertal groups.

It should be borne in mind that while principal components analysis permits the exploration of relationships between *attributes* (such as symptoms), it does not permit conclusions about the classification of *individuals*. Another mathematical technique, *cluster analysis*, is better suited for this task since it works by grouping like patients together. In the Pittsburgh research the results of a cluster analysis were rather inconclusive. However, Kolvin et al (1991) were able to identify distinct clusters. Thus, when using combined child–parent data three clusters were obtained: depressive cognitions, endogenous depression, and a mixture of conduct disturbance and neurotic disorder.

All in all, these two studies provide some support for the concept of an endogenous form of depression occurring in older children and adolescents that is phenomenologically distinct from other forms of the disorder in this age group. This finding parallels the results from a large number of factor and cluster analysis studies conducted with samples of depressed adults. Indeed, probably the most consistent finding from these studies has been the identification of a group of patients with an "endogenous" depression characterized by symptoms such as nonreactivity of mood in the face of pleasurable events, terminal sleep disturbance, diurnal variation and distinct quality of mood (Kendell, 1976; Nelson & Charney, 1981). Similarly, there is also support for the validity of an "anxious" factor, which again has been identified in several of the adult mathematical studies. Paykel (1971), for instance, produced four groups from a cluster analysis of the ratings of 165 adult patients with depression: psychotic depressives, anxious depressives, hostile depressives and young depressives with personality disorder. Similar factors were produced in Overall et al's study (1966) of adult depression.

On the other hand, the syndrome of depressive cognitions, which was found in both the Pittsburgh and the Newcastle studies, is less easy to relate to adult typologies. Perhaps, as some cognitive theories of depression postulate, these cognitions are the precursors of later depression. Or, could it be that they are simply the result of a previous episode? This is certainly a group that warrants further study and probably follow-up into late adolescence. In either event, the implication is that depression in young people may not have the same underlying factor structure as depression in adults. It may be that depression in childhood shows developmental heterogeneity, with some varieties being more or less specific to children, while others are isomorphic with depressions arising in later age periods.

The studies of Ryan et al (1987) and Kolvin et al (1991) were primarily concerned with defining the mathematical structure of symptoms within a group of children who had, for the most part, already been diagnosed as depressed. That is, they were concerned mainly with the *subclassification* of depressive disorders. The same statistical methods can also be used to tackle the issue of whether or not major depression in young people is a diagnostic entity distinct from other syndromes—that is, with the validity of the concept of depressive disorder within the overall *classification* of child and adolescent disorders.

There have been many factor analytic studies of disturbed children, and in a review of 37 of them, Quay (1979) found none in which a clear depressive factor emerged. However, many of these studies used measures of depression that would be considered rather crude by current standards and so they constitute a rather weak test of present-day approaches to classification. More recently, Achenbach et al (1989) presented data on a very large sample of outpatients (8194 individuals aged from 6 to 16 years) who had been assessed using a well standardized and widely used questionnaire, the Child Behaviour Checklist (CBCL). They extracted a syndrome that they designated as "anxious/depressed", which included the features of DSM-III-R overanxious disorder for children, as well as dysthymia. No clear depressive factor could be identified. On the other hand, Williams et al (1989) studied the factor structure of self-reports of DSM-III symptomatology obtained from over 700 eleven-year-olds using a standardized psychiatric interview. For boys, anxiety and depression were inseparable, but in girls separate factors representing anxiety and depression emerged. Similarly, in a multivariate study of a clinical sample, Thorley (1987) reported a depression factor that included symptoms such as depressed mood, suicidal ideas and disturbance of sleeping. Highly significant age effects were found: the depression factor was found only in the age range 12–18 years, and not among younger subjects.

It may be relevant that Thorley's study (1987) was based on psychiatric referrals that included inpatients, and that the depression ratings were based on clinical assessments (including face-to-face interviews) rather than questionnaire measures. Perhaps, then, a clear factor for depression will emerge only when the overall severity and prevalence of depression are high, and when the measures are sufficiently sensitive. Support for the idea that a depression factor may appear only in samples where depressive disorder is relatively severe comes from the study of Nurcombe et al (1989), which was based on a small sample of inpatients (216 adolescents aged between 12 and 16 years). These authors found three behavioural syndromes by principal components analysis of CBCL ratings. Of the three groups of patients identified by a subsequent cluster analysis, one was consistent with the concept of a categorically defined nuclear depression. Interestingly, a continuously distributed depressive syndrome appeared in a larger number of individuals. Nurcombe et al therefore proposed that adolescent depression might represent a heterogeneous group of conditions, one of which could be a categorical syndrome (major depression) and the other a dimension (dysthymia).

In concluding it is important to note that all these studies illustrate the truism that what comes out of mathematical attempts to derive syndromes depends very largely on what goes in. It may be that the failure to demonstrate a distinct syndrome of depression in many community studies is simply the result of the possibility that they were based on samples containing very few cases of depression. It seems that it is easier to identify a depression factor in samples of patients, especially in the older age groups. It should also be borne in mind that even if a sample contains a sufficient number of cases with a depressive syndrome, no mathematical technique can derive this syndrome if the measures lack sensitivity. For example, two of the recent studies cited above (Achenbach et al, 1989; Nurcombe et al, 1989) were based on parent ratings, and we shall see in later sections of this chapter that parents are often unaware of depressive feelings in their offspring.

SYMPTOMATOLOGY OF MANIA IN CHILDREN

Carlson (1983, 1990) has systematically reviewed the literature on the phenomenology of mania in children and adolescents. In older children (9 to 12 years) aberrations in thought content such as grandiosity and paranoia are common whereas irritability and emotional lability are common in younger children. Hyperactivity, pressure of speech and distractibility are common in both age groups. Strober, Hanna and McCracken (1989) suggested that pre-pubertal bipoplar children have an illness characterized by frequent cycles of brief duration in which dysphoria and hypomania are intermixed; with the onset of puberty the cyclical extremes of depression and mania occur.

The differential diagnosis of bipolar disorder in young people can be very difficult (Bowring & Kovacs, 1992). Clearly, there are some superficial similarities between hypomania and hyperactivity. However, follow-ups of hyperactive children have not found an excess of affective disorders (Gittelman et al, 1985). Strober et al (1989) considered that the child with bipolar illness has a more pronounced shift in mood than the hyperactive child, activity tends to be more goal directed, and there may be delusions or hallucinations. The distinction between bipolar illness and schizophrenia can also be a problem. Werry, McClellan and Chard (1991) reported that over half of bipolar adolescents were misdiagnosed as schizophrenic when first seen. Patients with schizophrenia manifested more abnormal personalities and had a lower level of adaptive functioning before the illness. However, symptomatology during the index episode was quite similar. Zeitlin (1986) found few differences in presenting symptomatology between children subsequently diagnosed as schizophrenic or manic–depressive in adulthood.

INTERVIEWS WITH PARENTS

The clinical assessment usually begins with a parental interview. It is best to start this interview with a detailed discussion of the reasons why the child has been referred to the clinic. In common with many other child psychiatric disorders, it appears that the presence of depressive disorder is rarely a *sufficient* reason for referral. Only a small minority of depressed children ever see a mental health professional and many get no help at all (Keller et al, 1991). In some cases this is because parents are unaware of the child's problems. In others the parents may recognize that there is a problem but may attribute it to "adolescent turmoil" that the child will grow out of. It is therefore well worthwhile spending time with the parents establishing the manner of the referral since this will often provide important information on the parents' attitudes to the child's difficulties. Sometimes the reason for referral may lie as much in the parents or in the family as in the child. For example, Shepherd,

Oppenheim & Mitchell (1971) found that mothers of children with psychiatric disorders attending clinics had higher rates of nervous disorders than mothers of children with similar disorders who were not attending clinics.

Once the reasons for referral have been clarified the parents should be allowed to give a spontaneous account of the presenting problems. Open questions are particularly important at this part of the interview where a chronological account of what has happened should be obtained. A detailed description of each item of behaviour that is mentioned spontaneously should be recorded. It is not enough to know that the child was "depressed". The term "depression" has many different meanings, even among professionals (Angold, 1988a), so the interviewer needs to establish exactly what the parents mean by their use of this word. Similarly, when going on to systematic questioning additional probing will frequently be required to clarify the meaning of initial answers (Cox, Hopkinson & Rutter, 1981). It is important to obtain an account of the onset, frequency and severity of each symptom.

THE INTERVIEW WITH THE CHILD: DEVELOPMENTAL ISSUES

The importance of the direct interview with the child has been emphasized by many researchers and clinicians who have been interested in prepubertal and/ or adolescent depression (Carlson & Cantwell, 1980a; Puig-Antich et al, 1983a; Kovacs, 1986). As described earlier, in some centres this represents a major shift from the past, when the traditional interview with the child was based largely on observation in free-play situations. Advocates of direct verbal examination of children emphasize the fact that many crucial symptoms of depression are "subjective" symptoms that may completely escape observation by others. Much emphasis is therefore placed on the direct questioning of children about symptoms and complaints.

It cannot of course be assumed that young children can comply with the demands of a symptom-orientated interview in the same way as depressed adults. For example, techniques such as open-ended questions can be confusing to the child. Moreover, it may be that children differ from adults in the basic competencies that are required to meet the operational criteria for major depression. Clearly, then, it is essential to know about the developmental changes in these competencies. Kovacs (1986) described three developmental dimensions that are relevant to the clinical diagnosis of depressive disorders in children:

1. Knowledge of emotion and mood.
2. Understanding of the self.
3. Time concepts and memory.

Knowledge of emotion and mood

By the age of two years many children have a vocabulary describing basic emotions, and between the ages of two and five years children learn to recognize and label situations denoting different feelings. By age five most children can differentiate basic emotions in others. However, developmental changes still occur in the understanding of several aspects of emotion after this age. For example, as they grow older children increasingly understand that real feelings may be different from those that are observed. Studies in which children hear stories and are asked to describe the feelings of the person in that story suggest that four-year-olds have limited understanding of the idea that a person can look one way and feel another, whereas six-year-olds seem to understand the distinction clearly (Harris et al, 1986). In addition, there is increased understanding that the source of emotions can be internal as well as situational. Younger children are more likely to rely on situational cues, or cues arising from recent somatic experiences, than older ones.

Accordingly, Kovacs (1986) suggested that although younger children could differentiate basic emotions, enquiries about sadness or irritability should be posed in the context of specific environmental events. In the absence of external cues, children younger than ten may confuse basic emotions, such as anger and sadness. Kovacs (1986) also noted that the findings concerning developmental competencies in normal children may not generalize to children with psychiatric problems. She pointed out that such children seem often to have a poor command of psychological constructs and may be particularly likely to mislabel emotions. It is important therefore to check children's responses to questions in this area.

Understanding of self

Feelings of self-depreciation and self-devaluation are commonly found in people with depressive disorders, and as we shall see later such feelings have often been considered a defining characteristic of depression, especially by psychoanalysts and cognitive therapists. As with emotions, there are regular developmental changes in the ability to evaluate oneself and to communicate self-knowledge to others.

The beginnings of self-awareness appear during the second year of life. Between 18 months and 24 months of age children recognize their own face and point to pictures of themselves when someone says their name (Damon & Hart, 1982). Self concepts in older children are usually measured by asking children to describe themselves and there are developmental changes in the ways children do this. Until about the age of seven years "self" is conceived in terms of favourite activities and physical characteristics. Children describe themselves in terms of observable features such as hair colour and play activities ("I like to play football", "I have red hair"). However, by around age eight years childrens' descriptions of self become less concrete and focus more on psychological aspects. Children of this age become concerned with their own competencies and frequently make comparisons with others.

It may therefore be the case that young children cannot experience certain cognitive symptoms of major depression in the same way as adolescents or adults. For instance, since the symptom of worthlessness implies the denigration of self in relation to others, it could be that young children cannot develop this symptom.

Time concepts and memory

Most current operational definitions of major depressive disorder require that symptoms must be present for a specified length of time before the diagnosis can be made. In addition, symptoms must occur together during the same time period. To provide this information children must therefore have an adequate sense of time.

Kovacs (1986) identified a number of developmental changes in time concepts and memory that are likely to influence the young child's ability to give an accurate account of an episode of major depression. First, although even preschoolers can give an accurate account of specific activities, constructs of *calendar time* appear only around age eight years. Second, children have difficulties conceiving *temporal order* until concrete operational thinking is established, also at around the age of eight. Third, it is not until children are about twelve years old that they can correctly estimate *duration* from an event (such as the end of term).

On the basis of these observations, Kovacs (1986) suggested that patients aged six to nine years are unlikely to be able to estimate correctly the overall duration of their complaints or to give accurate data on the duration of one symptom in relation to another. They are unlikely therefore to be good informants about previous episodes of depression. They may, however, be able to give accurate information about current depressive symptoms.

THE INTERVIEW WITH THE CHILD: ELICITING DEPRESSIVE SYMPTOMS

The interview with the child should at an early point include a brief assessment of time concepts and language abilities, so that questions to the child can be presented appropriately. First, however, it is necessary to establish rapport with the child. It is particularly important to bear in mind that symptoms of depression such as social withdrawal and loss of concentration can make depressed children very difficult to assess. For example, depressed children may have great difficulties with open questions that invite descriptive answers. Such children sometimes require assistance in formulating their answers and it may on occasion be necessary to provide some kind of commentary to enable younger children to recognize symptoms that they might otherwise have difficulty describing. For instance "some of the children I see feel sad about x, do you feel like that?".

Once the initial conversational part of the interview has been concluded, and an informal assessment of the child's verbal abilities has been made, it is appropriate to continue with a detailed enquiry into the child's mental state. Puig-Antich, Chambers and Tabrizi (1983a) described some of the techniques that may be necessary to elicit key symptoms of depressive disorder, including depression of mood, excessive guilt, suicidal ideation/behaviour and psychotic symptoms such as delusions and hallucinations.

Children may have no name for the *persistent dysphoric mood* that they experience, or their name for it may be unfamiliar to the interviewer. Accordingly, several different labels for depression should be used, such as "sad, blue, empty, or down in the dumps". Depressed prepubertal children can usually identify one of these labels.

As noted earlier, the young child may not be able to estimate the duration of this dysphoric mood as well as older children or adults. They frequently do not clearly understand units of time such as hours. However, other types of time unit may work rather better, especially if they mean something to the child and can be placed in the context of his average day. Thus, for example, duration can be estimated in units such as "from dinner to the time you go to sleep", or "from breakfast to lunch".

The assessment of the symptoms of *guilt* can also be difficult, but for rather different reasons. The problem here is that the child may not understand the concept. Puig-Antich et al (1983a) advocate the use of very concrete questions: 'How do you feel after you have done something wrong?"; "Do you sometimes feel bad for things other people did wrong, but you felt it was your fault?"; "Do you ever feel (guilty) and don't know why?". It may in addition be necessary to give examples.

Parents are often unaware of *suicidal ideation* in their child, and sometimes they do not know of significant suicidal attempts (Walker, Moreau & Weissman, 1990). Indeed, there is often reluctance among clinicians to question children regarding suicidal feelings. However, there is no evidence that such questions are harmful to the child, and depressed children can gain relief from being able to talk openly about their suicidal thoughts and plans. The kinds of techniques employed to question depressed children about suicidality are very similar to those used with adults. It is important to obtain a full account of the strength of suicidal ideation and of any plans that the child may have had.

Another feature of the child's mental state that requires careful examination is the presence of hallucinations. At first sight, it might be thought that hallucinations would be very uncommon among depressed prepubertal children. After all, psychotic disorders are rare among young children, increasing in frequency during adolescence (Rutter, 1988b). However, in clinical samples of prepubertal depressed children hallucinations have been reported to occur in about one-third of cases (Ryan et al, 1987; Mitchell et al, 1988). For example, Mitchell et al (1988) found that 31% of depressed children and 22% of depressed adolescents "endorsed" the symptom of hallucinations during the child version of the Schedule for Affective Disorders and Schizophrenia (KSADS). Ryan et al (1987) reported that one-third of depressed prepubertal children scored "mild", "moderate" or "severe" on the KSADS ratings of hallucinations.

Unfortunately, the psychopathological significance of these phenomena remains unclear. For instance, in only half of the cases described as having hallucinations by Mitchell et al (1988) were both the patient and the interviewer convinced that the hallucinations were real. So, prepubertal children need to be questioned very carefully in this area. In particular, it is important to distinguish hallucinations from the various other types of perceptual phenomena that can occur in children. Visual illusions, in which there is a false perception of a real stimulus, are quite common in young children under conditions of semi-darkness. They will usually disappear when the light conditions improve. Similarly, the vivid images that young children can sometimes create are usually under voluntary control and often experienced as pleasurable. Depressive hallucinations also need to be distinguished from hypnogogic and hypnopompic hallucinations that can occur as the child goes off to sleep or wakes up. Finally, depressive hallucinations should be distinguished from the hallucinations of other functional psychiatric disorders. Typical depressive hallucinations in children usually occur only during episodes of depression and the content is congruent with depressive mood.

CORRESPONDENCE OF PARENT AND CHILD REPORTS OF DEPRESSIVE SYMPTOMS

Level of agreement

As the previous section showed, it is clearly possible to obtain information on certain depressive symptoms by interviewing children directly. However, young children have difficulties understanding some specific concepts, such as *slowed down thoughts*, and are generally less reliable reporters of dates and durations than adults. In addition, parents are usually knowledgeable about their children across situations and over time and may be better able to give an account of certain symptoms. So, as a general rule it is always necessary to corroborate the child's account of depression with an account from a parent or other adult who knows the child well.

A great number of studies have published data on the agreement between parent and child reports of depressive symptomatology (see, for example; Leon, Kendall & Garber, 1980; Weissman, Orvaschel & Padium, 1980; Orvaschel et al, 1981; Herjanic & Reich, 1982; Kazdin et al, 1983a; Lobovits & Handal, 1985; Moretti et al, 1985; Edelbrock et al, 1986; Angold et al, 1987a; Mokros et al, 1987; Breslau, Davis & Prabizki, 1988; Kazdin, 1989a; Barrett et al, 1991). The findings regarding the level of agreement on any single depressive symptom have varied greatly across these studies. In general, however, agreement between parent and child has been found to be only moderate. For instance, in the Newcastle study, Barrett et al (1991) reported that the range of overall agreement on depressive symptoms (i.e. agreement on absence combined with agreement on occurrence) extended from 40% to 86%, with the majority falling between 60% and 70%. Since one could achieve 50% overall agreement simply by tossing a coin, these results are not especially encouraging. Symptoms with high levels of overall agreement included psychomotor retardation, loss of appetite, suicide attempts, loss of interest and weeping.

Angold et al (1987a) used the kappa statistic to measure the level of agreement between parent and child in a sample containing proband parents who had previously been depressed or parents with no psychiatric diagnosis. The kappa statistic takes into account chance agreement and ranges from 0 (agreement no better than chance) to 1 (perfect agreement). Agreement between parent and child on interview-based measures of depressive symptoms was low, with kappas ranging from $- 0.07$ to $+ 0.52$. In only 6 out of 21 symptoms did the level of agreement reach statistical significance: diurnal variation, weight loss, hypersomnia, feelings of worthlessness, thoughts of death, and suicidal ideas.

Factors influencing agreement between parent and child

There are a variety of different types of explanations for this low level of agreement. Doubtless, it is in part simply the result of the fact that ratings of certain items of behaviour or types of emotion are inherently unreliable. Unfortunately, since few papers on parent–child agreement have simultaneously presented data on the reliability of the instrument during the study, it is difficult to estimate the magnitude of this effect. Interestingly, however, Wierzbicki (1987) found that although the parent form of the Children's Depression Inventory (see later) had good inter-rater and test–retest reliability, mother's ratings were consistently lower than their children's own ratings of depression.

This suggests that disagreement in the study of Wierzbicki (1987) was not completely random, since random disagreement would lead to similar overall levels of symptomatology. Many other studies have found that children report more depressive symptomatology than their parents do about them (e.g. Weissman, Orvaschel & Padium, 1980; Orvaschel et al, 1981; Moretti et al, 1985; Angold et al, 1987a; Barrett et al, 1991). For example, in the study of Barrett et al (1991) 39 out of the 52 depressive symptoms studied were reported more often by the child than by the parents and only four symptoms were reported more often by the parents. In the study of Angold and his colleagues (1987a) all 21 symptoms were reported more often by the child.

Some of these studies have found that the symptoms reported more often by the child are "internalizing" or "emotional" kinds of symptoms, whereas symptoms reported more often by parents tend to be "externalizing" or conduct symptoms. Thus, for instance, in the Newcastle study the six symptoms reported three times more often by children were *deja vu*, self-dislike, general anxiety, obsessions, suicidal ideation, and suicidal attempts (Barrett et al, 1991). The four symptoms reported more often by parents were hypersomnia, increased appetite, anhedonia and exaggerated illness behaviour. Edelbrock et al (1986) found that children reported significantly more affective/neurotic problems and alcohol/drug abuse than their parents, whereas parents reported significantly more behaviour/conduct problems than their children. Herjanic and Reich (1982) found that parents reported significantly more relationship problems, school difficulties, aggression and disobedience than their children. Children reported more fears, obsessions and depression.

It seems, then, that certain types of symptom can occur in the child without the parent knowing. It should be noted, however, that some studies have reported a trend in the other direction: that is, for parents to report more depressive symptomatology in their children than the children themselves report (e.g. Kazdin et al, 1983a; Mokros et al, 1987; Treiber & Mabe, 1987). Mokros et al (1987), in a study of 34 children attending a university-based affective disorders clinic, found that parent summary scores on a depression rating scale were significantly higher than child scores. However, this excess was largely due to scores on "behavioural" items such as schoolwork and social withdrawal. The mean ratings on "ideational" items such as depressed feelings, guilt and suicidal ideation did not differ between the children and their parents. Moreover, the same researchers showed that children from a *nonclinical population* had a tendency to rate themselves more severely than their parents. The implication is that the relationship between parent–child ratings of depression may vary according to the type of population that is studied. Perhaps, for example, the parents of children attending a special clinic for depression are especially keen to highlight the depressive aspects of their child's problem. Or, it could be that children with severe types of depression tend to minimize their symptoms or lack the ability to communicate them clearly.

It may therefore be relevant that one of the other studies that found parents reporting more symptoms in their offspring was based on severely disturbed children who had been admitted as inpatients (Kazdin et al, 1983a). Similarly, Tisher and Lang (1983) found that the parents of severe outpatient cases of school refusal scored a little higher than their children on a depression scale, although the reverse occurred in their normal control group.

Thus, it appears that although agreement between parent and child is influenced by the *type of symptomatology* that is being rated, the findings may also differ according to the *setting* in which these children are studied. Several other factors have been found to be related to child–parent agreement on depressive symptomatology, though there has been little consistency across studies.

Edelbrock et al (1986) examined the relationship between the *age of the child* and the level of agreement with the parent and found that agreement was substantially higher among children aged 14–18 years than those aged 10–13 and 6–9 years. On the other hand, Barrett et al (1991) found that prepubertal children had significantly higher child–parent agreement than pubescent/postpubertal children on two-thirds of items. The average difference between child–parent kappas in the two groups was large (0.44), and the authors concluded that in general teenagers reveal less of their feelings to their parents than do younger children. By contrast, Mokros et al (1987) found that age had no influence on depression ratings either in a normal population or in a referred group. Angold et al (1987a) found no consistent differences in parent–child agreement between older and younger children, though the comparability of their sample with others is limited by the fact that the average age of the young people in their study was 17 years.

The findings regarding the *sex of the child* have also been rather inconsistent. Angold et al (1987a) found that both boys and girls reported more symptoms than their parents did about them, but the difference was statistically significant only in the case of girls. Parent–child agreement on the symptom of dysphoria was however much higher for the boys ($\kappa = 0.55$) than for the girls ($\kappa = 0.28$), leading Angold et al (1987a) to suggest that depression was less readily recognized or admitted by boys than girls. Barrett et al (1991) found that agreement between girls and their mothers was higher only on those symptoms that they might be expected to share with their mothers, such as suicidal behaviour. Neither Herjanic et al (1975) nor Mokros et al (1987) found consistent sex differences in child–parent ratings.

The child's *intelligence* had also been found to be relevant in some studies. Barrett et al (1991), for instance, divided their sample into two groups by intelligence quotient. There was much greater agreement in the case of brighter children in respect of the number of hospital admissions, some somatic symptoms and symptoms associated with depression. These authors suggested that the key factor leading to increased agreement was not so much intelligence as increased communication between parent and child. The same authors found that agreement tended to be higher in the higher occupational strata. However, Mokros et al (1987) found that socioeconomic status, as measured on the Duncan Scale, had no influence on either the parents' or the child's ratings of depression.

Another factor that might be expected to influence agreement between parent and child is the *parent's mental state*. Moretti et al (1985) found that parents' ratings of their own depression correlated with their ratings of their children's depression. McGee et al (1983) reported a strong association between a mother's current depression and her reports of behavioural problems in her child. The mother's reports were not confirmed by those of the child or the teacher, suggesting that the association could be the result of response bias on the part of the mother.

Of course, these results are in the opposite direction to those described above (where parents seemed to be relatively insensitive to their child's symptoms), so we cannot exclude the possibility that depressed mothers may be correctly picking up more symptoms in their children. Perhaps depressed mothers are more "tuned in" to depression in their offspring. Or, could it be that depressed children are more likely to "show" their depression to their parents when the parents are themselves depressed?

There is no infallible "gold standard" against which the validity of these hypotheses can be tested. However, if more accurate reporting was the explanation, then one would expect not only that depressed parents would report higher levels of depression in their offspring, but also that parent–child agreement was higher when the parent was depressed. There was some suggestion in the data of Angold et al (1987a) that agreement between parent and child was higher in the group where the parent was depressed than in the group where the parent was "normal". The implication is that the higher levels of depression in offspring that are reported by depressed parents may not entirely be the result of bias caused by the parent's mental state. However, there was no significant difference in the rates of child reports of dysphoria between the children of depressed and normal proband parents, whereas there was a significant excess of parent reports of dysphoria in the depressed proband parent group.

Clearly, then, this is an issue that requires further study. Parents play a major part in the decision to refer the child and are closely involved in treatment. Clinicians need therefore to be aware of the discrepancies that can occur between parent and child reports and how these may be related to the parent's mental state. It is also important to note that these discrepancies may influence our understanding of aetiology, and in particular of how depressive disorders are transmitted in families. For instance, Breslau et al (1988) found that the data from child reports supported a depression-specific transmission in families where the mother was depressed. That is, the children reported high rates of depression but not high rates of other psychiatric symptoms such as anxiety. By contrast, mothers reported that the children had high rates of all psychiatric symptoms (including depression, anxiety and oppositional behaviours), suggesting that the familial links were rather nonspecific.

It follows that if parental mental state has such a marked effect on reports of psychopathology in the child, then the weight given to such reports may need to be changed. However, at this stage it would be unwise to assume that parental reports are less valid when the parent is depressed. Indeed, it would seem that parents rarely report the presence of affective disorders that are not present according to the children themselves (Angold et al, 1987a). So, their reports need to be taken seriously.

COMBINING PARENT AND CHILD REPORTS

The lack of correspondence between parent and child reports clearly raises the question of how these two disparate accounts are to be combined. This is an important issue because the manner in which parent and child accounts are reconciled will probably have a great influence both on the rates of depressive disorder that we find in our studies and on the aetiological factors that are found to be correlated with the disorder. For instance, it would seem that studies relying on child accounts will, in general, find higher rates of problems than studies relying on parental accounts. Presumably, therefore, some individuals will be counted as "cases" with one method and as "normal" with another. So, the factors that are found to be associated with childhood depressive disorder may vary simply because the criterion is defined in a different way across different studies. This could be a particular problem in community surveys, where many individuals will be near the threshold for diagnosis.

A variety of different methods have been proposed for dealing with this issue. Puig-Antich and Gittelman (1982) suggested that the parent should be interviewed first and that while interviewing the child the clinician should monitor agreement between parent and child. If the reason for disagreement is not obvious, then Puig-Antich and Gittelman suggested that it is useful to "confront" the child with the parental report and ask why the parent had said that. Unfortunately this approach may lead to one informant being pressured into agreeing with the other, which may not necessarily lead to a more valid response.

Another way of combining data from the parent and child is to use some kind of "best estimate" procedure. This kind of approach has been extensively used in adult psychiatry to combine information from several sources (e.g. Leckman et al, 1982) and is becoming widely used in child psychiatry (Bird, Gould & Staghezza, 1992). Basically, all available data on the subject are given to a rater who combines the data to make a single consensus diagnosis using a predetermined set of decision rules. For example, it is quite common clinical practice to accept any symptom as positive if any informant reports it as definitely present. Reich and Earls (1987) used two working rules when reviewing diagnostic discrepancies between parent and child reports: (1) that the child's age should be taken into account, and (2) that information from the teacher should be used to resolve discrepancies. They concluded that in most cases the diagnosis can be made on the basis of the child's account alone, though teachers' reports are particularly important for behavioural diagnoses.

The attraction of these approaches is that they produce a unitary diagnosis without the need to confront the patient with the question of which account is "true". However, at the moment we do not know the best way of combining parent and child data, so any decision rules will have to be somewhat arbitrary. Moreover, it would be desirable to be able to take into account possible sources of bias such as may occur when the parent is depressed.

Recently, statistical techniques such as confirmatory factor analysis have been used in order to model the way in which such biases may act (see, for example: Fergusson & Horwood, 1987; Fergusson, Horwood & Lloyd, 1991). The models proposed assume that measures of behaviour or emotions reflect underlying continuous dimensions that measure the extent to which the child manifests these behaviours or emotions. It is assumed that each source of information (say the child's report or the parent's report) will be measuring the hypothesized underlying latent variable, but there will be error in this measurement. One component of this error will be specific to the source of information that is used. The models attempt to distinguish the variance in reports which reflects generalized differences in child behaviour or emotions (e.g. depression) from the component of variance that is method-specific.

These statistical methods, like the two clinical methods described above, usually assume that there is a single underlying disorder and attempt to combine data from different sources in order to measure it. However, it is not of course always necessary to combine parent and child reports. It may be, for instance, that each source of data has validity. Indeed, Kazdin (1990) pointed out that child ratings of depression may correlate better with some associated features, such as hopelessness and suicidal ideation, whereas parental reports may be better predictors of other phenomena, such as diminished social interaction. According to this point of view the two sources of data should be kept separate since each has its own particular set of strengths, as well as weaknesses. Disagreements between sources do not necessarily mean that one source is "right" and another "wrong". Children may be relatively untroubled by symptoms that their parents find extremely irksome. Conversely, children may be very distressed by feelings that for one reason or another they are unable to share with their parents.

So, until we know more about the validity of each source of information it may be premature to combine all of them together. Certainly, it is important in clinical work to be aware of discrepancies between parent and child reports.

They can often reveal much about relationships within the family. Moreover, lack of parental awareness about certain problems, such as suicidality, may become a focus for intervention.

SUMMARY

Depressive disorders in children are now diagnosed using clinical interview methods that are very similar to those used in adults. In particular, there is a focus on direct, symptom-orientated interviews with children. This strategy has been successful to the extent that it seems that adult-like depressive disorders can be identified using these techniques. Moreover, the symptomatic features of these disorders are similar to those found in adults. Statistical studies of the distribution of symptoms also support the idea of phenotypic similarities with adult disorders, to the extent that several studies have identified in children a form of depression resembling the "endogenous" depressions of adults.

Some difficulties remain in the assessment of depressive disorders among the young. For instance, it seems that children under the age of ten years or so may have difficulties in understanding and/or reporting certain key symptoms of depressive disorder. Interviews with parents offer only a partial solution to these difficulties since the correlations between parent and child reports are usually low and it is not clear which account is more valid. In the next chapter we shall examine the contribution that standardized schedules and rating scales have made towards solving these difficulties.

Chapter 3

Standardized Interviews and Rating Scales

INTERVIEWS: SOME GENERAL ISSUES

One of the major advances in the measurement of psychopathological phenomena has been the development of standardized psychiatric interviews. The first interview schedules were developed for use with adults (Wing, Cooper & Sartorius, 1974; Endicott & Spitzer, 1978; Robins et al, 1981) and, to a large extent, paralleled the trend towards the use of defined diagnostic criteria in research settings. They were soon followed by equivalent schedules that could be used with children. Indeed, there is now a range of standardized child interview measures that are designed to give replicable diagnoses for most of the diagnostic categories.

While such diagnostic interviews are most frequently used by researchers, they provide advantages for the clinician as well. For example, they enable the clinician to evaluate a wide range of symptoms in a standardized fashion. Standardized psychiatric interviews have a number of advantages over traditional free-style undirected interviews. In particular, they give much more extensive information and the available data suggest that they are more reliable (Cox & Rutter, 1985). They have, in addition, certain advantages over other methods of assessment such as rating scales and direct observation. For instance, they allow the investigator to check ambiguous responses and to obtain data on chronology and onset.

Two different types of interview approach have been included under the broad umbrella of the "standardized interview". *Highly structured,* questionnaire-style interviews place much reliance on the use of pre-determined standardized questions that usually require only a "yes/no" response. The exact order, wording and coding of each item is specified. Such interviews can be regarded as *respondent-based* to the extent that the decision as to whether or not the criterion is met is essentially left to the interviewee. Highly structured interviews are designed to minimize the role of clinical inference in the assessment process. This has two advantages:

1. One potential source of unreliability is reduced.

2. The interview can be administered by so-called "lay interviewers" who have had only interview-specific training.

However, there is the corresponding disadvantage of relying on the assumption that all respondents will interpret the questions in the same way and that their concepts of, say, "sadness" will match those of the investigator. In addition, there is evidence that highly structured interviews will miss possible behaviours of interest that are outside the range of standard enquiry (Harrington et al, 1988).

By contrast, *investigator-based* interviews provide only general and flexible guidelines for conducting the interview and recording information. Such interviews seek to obtain detailed descriptions of behaviour, which are then coded by the interviewer using pre-specified diagnostic criteria. Thus, the structure of the interview resides in the concepts and codings rather than in the questions. Because they permit greater latitude in phrasing questions and interpreting responses, investigator-based interviews are usually designed for experienced interviewers. These interviewers must usually undergo a lengthy period of training and/or have clinical experience of the concepts in question. By contrast, respondent-based interviews can be administered by interviewers who have little or no prior experience and who are trained specifically for that interview. As we shall see later, this makes highly structured interviews an attractive proposition in large-scale epidemiological studies where it may be necessary to interview many subjects.

There are as yet little systematic data on the relative merits and demerits of these two different approaches in child populations. Much of the research conducted up to now has been limited by issues such as small sample sizes (Carlson et al, 1987) and order effects (Cohen et al, 1987). Nevertheless, the available data suggest that there are both similarities as well as differences between the approaches (Carlson et al, 1987; Hodges et al, 1987; Cohen et al, 1987). It seems that respondent-based interviews tend to overestimate psychopathology in the case of unusual behaviours. Breslau (1987) studied examples of replies to questions from the Diagnostic Interview Schedule for Children (DISC), a respondent-based interview. Replies were recoded as negative when the examples indicated that the respondents had misunderstood the question. The editing reduced the rate of obsessions and compulsions by one-third, and the rate of delusions by a factor of five to ten. It may be that highly structured, respondent-based approaches also tend to overestimate the frequency of more common psychiatric symptoms, such as depression. Cohen et al (1987) found that rates of separation anxiety as assessed by the DISC were "implausibly high" when compared with those obtained with a semi-structured interview.

Interviews also differ in many other ways, such as their age range, item content and coverage, length and organization. The choice between them should be guided by the purpose of the study. Research involving large populations may require a different instrument from that concerned with the evaluation of treatment response in a small clinical population. The interviews described below should not therefore be viewed as competing with one another: they were originally designed for different purposes and each has strengths and weaknesses. In the descriptions that follow, the focus is on interview schedules that have been used in studies of depression or that show promise in this field. Four features of each interview will be discussed in relation to the assessment of depressive phenomena:

1. A general description.
2. Administration.
3. Information obtained.
4. Psychometric properties.

The Kiddie-SADS

The Kiddie-SADS (Puig-Antich & Chambers, 1978) is a semi-structured interview for children aged 6 to 17 years. It was originally developed as a children's version of its adult counterpart, the Schedule for Affective Disorders and Schizophrenia (SADS) (Endicott & Spitzer, 1978). The child schedule was initially used for the assessment of psychiatric disorders in studies of childhood depression and it continues to be widely used in studies of affective disorders occurring in young people. However, it has been revised on several occasions and now covers a wide spectrum of DSM disorders (Ambrosini et al, 1989). It is currently available in two forms, the Present Episode form (K-SADS-P) and the Epidemiological Version (K-SADS-E).

The K-SADS is designed to be administered by clinically sophisticated interviewers who are familiar with the diagnostic criteria and who are experienced in the assessment of children with psychiatric disorders. The usual procedure is to interview the parent first and then to resolve any discrepancies between parent and child during the interview with the child. The interview takes approximately one hour to administer to each informant. The first part of the interview is relatively unstructured, during which a chronological history of the present illness is obtained and details of current symptoms are determined. Next, there are detailed questions on specific symptoms or behaviours. Interviewers have considerable flexibility in choosing the wording of questions and are encouraged to probe in order to substantiate answers. The K-SADS embodies a skip structure whereby, if an initial screening question is negative, subsequent questions in the section can be missed. Finally, ratings are made of observational items and of the overall level of functioning.

Information is obtained on many DSM diagnoses, including most of the affective disorders. Most symptoms on the K-SADS are rated twice, for the worst period during the present episode and during the previous week. The K-SADS also yields scores on summary scales, such as depressed mood and ideation, endogenous features and suicidal ideation and behaviour. The K-SADS-E is designed to assess past as well as current episodes of psycho-pathology (Orvaschel et al, 1982).

Short-term test–retest reliability was first evaluated in a sample of 52 psychi-atrically referred children. Correlations for depressive symptoms ranged from 0.28 to 0.88, with the majority of ratings over 0.50 (Chambers et al, 1985). The reliability of the diagnosis of major depression was 0.54, which was higher than that for anxiety disorder ($\kappa = 0.24$) but a little lower than for conduct disorder ($\kappa = 0.63$). Apter et al (1989) also found that the scale had satisfactory test–retest reliability. The most recent revision of the KSADS (the KSADS-III-R) can also rate depressive disorders reliably (Ambrosini et al, 1989).

Since the primary use of the K-SADS has been to select children with affec-tive disorders it has strong face validity. The validity of K-SADS ratings of depression is further supported by the results of family studies (Puig-Antich et al, 1989) and psychobiological research (Puig-Antich et al, 1981). The K-SADS has also been used as a quantitative measure of change in pharmacological studies and seems to work well in this setting (Puig-Antich et al, 1987).

The Interview Schedule for Children (ISC)

Like the K-SADS, the Interview Schedule for Children (Kovacs, 1982a) was initially constructed for a research project on childhood depression. Two forms are available, one for initial assessment and one for follow-up. The ISC is a semi-structured interview suitable for use with children 8 to 17 years old. Interviewers must have clinical experience and be trained in the use of the interview. Mothers are interviewed about their children and then the children are seen alone. Each interview takes about 40 to 60 minutes.

The ISC begins with an unstructured interview and then covers a number of core symptoms which are rated on a 0–8 scale. The order of the questions may vary. The interview also makes observational ratings. The ISC is symptom-orientated with a focus on depressive symptoms. Information on most DSM-III disorders is obtained. Inter-rater reliability on symptoms is good, with an aver-age intra-class correlation of 0.89 (range 0.64–1.00) (Kovacs, 1983). The sched-ule seems to generate diagnoses with predictive validity (Kovacs et al, 1984a,b).

The Child Assessment Schedule (CAS)

The Child Assessment Schedule (Hodges et al, 1982) is a semi-structured interview designed for clinical or research assessments. It is appropriate for use with children aged between 7 and 16 years and a parallel version exists for use with the parents. Interviewers need to have some clinical experience since some clinical judgement is necessary in the administration and rating of CAS items. The first part of the interview is composed of about 80 items, which are grouped so that the interview can appear like a conversation. The interviewer also rates observational items. The CAS covers many depressive diagnoses, including major depression, dysthymia and cyclothymia, but only screens for bipolar disorder. The focus is on current episodes of illness.

The CAS has been reported to have good test–retest reliability for depressive disorder (Hodges et al, 1989). Hodges et al (1987) reported good concordance between the CAS and the K-SADS for affective disorder either when diagnoses were based on the parent interviews alone or when diagnoses were based on combinations of parent and child interviews. Hodges et al (1990) demonstrated that the child version of the CAS had high internal consistency for depressive symptoms in psychiatric patients, medically ill patients and in a community-based sample.

The Diagnostic Interview Schedule for Children (DISC)

The Diagnostic Interview Schedule for Children (Costello et al, 1984) is a highly structured interview that is appropriate for use with children aged 6 to 17 years. A parallel version, the DISC-P, is available for administration to the parents about the child. The child version has 264 items and takes about 40–60 minutes to complete with clinically referred children (Edelbrock & Costello, 1988a). The time frame is the past year.

The order, wording and coding of all items in the DISC are pre-specified. In many cases the criterion can be met with a positive response to just one question. It can therefore be administered by clinicians or lay interviewers having 2–3 days training and requires no clinical judgement. The interview begins with some general questions and then proceeds to cover items necessary to make virtually all DSM-III diagnoses. The DISC questions were designed to reflect the DSM-III criteria. The interview incorporates a skip structure that reduces interviewing time with children who have few symptoms. Diagnoses are generated by the application of computer algorithms to DISC data. However, lay interviewers record descriptions of many symptoms, which can be reviewed by a clinician after the interview.

Inter-rater reliability has been examined by comparing symptom scores for ten videotaped child interviews. Correlations ranged from 0.94 to 1.00, with an average of 0.98 (Costello et al, 1984). Test–retest reliability for parent reports on 242 child patients ranged from 0.44 to 0.86, with an average intraclass correlation of 0.76 for symptom clusters (Edelbrock et al, 1985). The reliability of the child interview was strongly related to age and averaged 0.43, 0.60 and 0.71 respectively for children aged 6–9, 10–13 and 14–18 years. The reliability of behavioural problems was higher than for affective–neurotic problems (Edelbrock et al, 1985). The stability of self-report from children under 10 years over a mean test–retest interval of 11 days was very poor, particularly for affective symptoms (Edelbrock et al, 1985). Findings on parent–child agreement are mostly in line with other studies (see above). Costello et al (1985) showed that the DISC discriminated well between paediatric referrals and psychiatric referrals.

The DISC has been used in a number epidemiological studies (e.g. Costello, 1989; Velez, Johnson & Cohen, 1989; McGee et al, 1990), but there are some uncertainties about its efficacy in clinical samples. For instance, Weinstein et al (1989) reported that agreement between DISC diagnoses made by clinicians and the clinical diagnosis recorded on the admission summary was very poor. Agreement on the diagnosis of major depression was little better than chance ($\kappa = 0.17$).

The Diagnostic Interview for Children and Adolescents (DICA)

Like the DISC, the DICA is a highly structured interview in which the order, wording and coding of items are specified in detail. It can be administered by clinicians or trained lay interviewers and the interviewer does not need clinical judgement to complete the ratings. It is appropriate for use with children aged 6 to 17 years and there is a parallel version that can be administered to the parent about the child (DICA-P). Symptoms are designed to be coded "yes" or "no". Questions are phrased in the present tense for all children, but children over the age of 12 years can be asked about past symptoms. The DICA gives information on 185 symptoms, as well as their onset, duration and severity. The DICA-P also includes information about medical and developmental history.

An early study indicated that the DICA had satisfactory inter-rater reliability (Herjanic & Reich, 1982), and in a later study Welner et al (1987) found good test–retest reliability over an interval of 1–7 days. The kappa for affective disorder was 0.90. Agreement with discharge summary diagnoses was less good (kappa for affective disorder 0.52) but clinical discharge diagnoses are probably a less than entirely reliable gold standard against which to compare research interviews. Interestingly parent–child agreement in the study of Welner et al (1987) was much improved over that found in an earlier study with the DICA (Reich et al, 1982). However, there are no data available on the reliability of the symptom scales, and the validity data from the DICA are weaker than for the other interviews (Hodges, 1992).

The Child and Adolescent Psychiatric Assessment (CAPA)

The most recent schedule that has been constructed, the Child and Adolescent Psychiatric Assessment, was developed by Angold and his colleagues at the MRC Child Psychiatry Unit in London. It is based on interviews used in the Isle of Wight study and the K-SADS, but it differs from both instruments in several crucial respects:

1. There is a wider coverage of psychiatric symptoms than in either of its predecessors.
2. There is separate measurement of symptom intensity and accompanying social incapacity.
3. While it can be used to derive ICD-10 and DSM-III-R diagnoses, the approach is not hierarchical so that it can be adapted for use with any classification system.

The schedule is designed to be administered by experienced interviewers who must undergo a period of training. They need not, however, be clinicians. The CAPA is a semi-structured, symptom-orientated interview, that is designed to be used flexibly. Interviewers are expected to probe the subject's responses until they are satisfied that the criterion is met. The interview is accompanied by a manual that specifies in detail the rating for each symptom. There is a parallel version for use with parents about the child. Each version takes about 60–90 minutes to administer, though the skip structure means that the interview can be completed more quickly in subjects with little psychopathology.

The interview starts with an open section during which the subject is asked about leisure activities, the family and schooling. A history of the presenting problem is taken, and there follow direct questions on symptoms. At the end of the interview ratings of incapacity due to psychiatric symptoms are made.

A small pilot study has shown that the interview has good inter-rater reliability (Angold, 1988c). Further data are being gathered on test–retest reliability and parent–child agreement.

Selecting a structured interview to assess depressive disorders in young people

At the moment, no single interview has emerged as better for all purposes than another. All the schedules described above can be recommended for certain specialized purposes. In choosing between them, it is helpful to bear the following considerations in mind.

The *intended age range* of the sample is of some importance in the study of affective disorders since, as we saw earlier, there are a number of potential problems in obtaining reliable accounts of affective phenomena from young children. Although all of the above interviews are used with children aged between 8 and 10 years, there have been very few studies in which the effects of the child's age on the reliability of the interview have been systematically assessed. However, the available data suggest that the reliability of affective symptoms may be particularly low in children under the age of 10 years

(Edelbrock et al, 1985). The difficulties that young children have in reporting affective symptoms may mean that semi-structured interviews are particularly appropriate in this age group. In such cases the less structured format of interviews such as the K-SADS, CAPA and ISC may make it easier to establish rapport, and the ability to reword questions and alter the format of the interview could be especially important. There are, however, no empirical data to support these suggestions.

The *personnel* available to interview the children will be an important determinant of the choice of diagnostic interview. Both the DICA and the DISC can be administered by trained lay interviewers and involve a minimum of clinical inference. These factors may make them especially useful for screening large numbers of subjects in population surveys.

The *time frame* covered by the interviews varies greatly. All of them cover the "present", though the definition of present varies greatly. For instance the ISC focuses on the past two weeks for depressive symptomatology, the K-SADS targets the past week, the CAPA the past three months and the DISC the past six months. The short time frame of the ISC and the K-SADS may make them especially useful for measuring *change* in treatment studies. Their ability to do this is enhanced by the design of their scales; both schedules rate symptoms on quantitative scales.

The K-SADS and the DICA can make *"lifetime" psychiatric diagnoses*. This may make them especially suitable for longitudinal studies where it is expected that many subjects will be well currently but will have suffered from episodes of illness in the interval between the index episode and follow-up. The ISC is of proven value in longitudinal research on childhood depression (Kovacs et al, 1984a,b) and a version is available specifically for follow-up assessments.

Some schedules, such as the K-SADS, are *organized* according to diagnostic categories. This makes it easier to rate lifetime diagnoses, where it is crucial to establish not only that symptoms have occurred but that they occurred during the same period of time. In general, this structure also makes it easier to make diagnoses quickly, which is of course an advantage in clinical practice. However, there is the disadvantage that the schedule becomes tied to the prevailing diagnostic system (e.g. DSM-III) and must be revised every time this is changed. Schedules can therefore evolve to the point where much of the earlier work on reliability and validity becomes obsolete.

Symptom-orientated interviews are not immune from this problem, and indeed all schedules must be revised in line with ongoing research on their reliability and validity. However, it is likely that schedules such as the CAPA and the DISC will prove to be more flexible in adapting to new diagnostic systems than schedules that are organized around the official nomenclature. They may also be better able to describe phenomenology and to explore new ways of classifying disorders.

All the schedules described here can generate most of the major affective diagnoses. The main differences between them in respect of *diagnostic content* concern their coverage of nonaffective syndromes. These differences are too numerous to be considered in detail here, but it is important to note that comorbidity with nonaffective disorders is becoming an increasingly important issue for research in juvenile depression. Indeed, as we shall see in subsequent chapters, it is now hard to envisage a research project on depressed young people that does not include systematic coverage of nondepressive symptoms.

The *psychometric properties* of the interviews have been discussed earlier. Preliminary studies have established that all of them can be rated reliably, although it has to be said that most of the psychometric research carried out so far has been based on relatively small sample sizes. Also, the samples chosen for reliability studies have differed greatly in respect of sex ratio, age range, in/outpatient status, and so on. For these, and other reasons, data from these studies may not necessarily generalize to other research settings.

Finally, the balance between the *sensitivity and specificity* of an interview can be an important determinant of the choice of diagnostic schedule. Sensitivity is the rate of positive diagnoses among subjects with the index disorder. Specificity is the rate of negative diagnoses among those who do not have the index condition. Ideally, an interview would have both high sensitivity and high specificity for depressive disorder. In practice, however, no such interview exists and so in choosing between interviews it is necessary to consider carefully the tradeoff between sensitivity and specificity. The clinical, investigator-based interviews appear to have been designed to maximize specificity. Thus, for instance, there is detailed cross-questioning to establish whether or not criteria are met. Such interviews seem better suited for clinical studies where it is often very important that samples are homogeneous and relatively uncontaminated by false positives. By contrast, the respondent-based, questionnaire-style interviews seem to have been designed to maximize sensitivity. They would seem to be better suited to those epidemilogical studies where a large number of cases must be screened for the disorder of interest.

SCREENING FOR DEPRESSIVE DISORDER IN COMMUNITY SAMPLES

So, one approach to ascertaining cases of depressive disorder in community samples would be to interview large numbers of subjects using a highly structured interview. However, although such an approach may work well when dealing with relatively common disorders and risk factors, it is likely to be inefficient when dealing with relatively rare disorders such as childhood depression. Very many normal subjects would have to be assessed in order to identify a small number with depressive disorder.

Another approach to case ascertainment in psychiatric research is the two-stage design, which is probably a more cost-effective method than a one-stage procedure (Shrout, Skodel & Dohrenwend, 1986). A screening process, usually in the form of a pencil and paper checklist, is used at stage 1 to pick out individuals likely to have disorders. During stage 2, these individuals are interviewed using a more definitive diagnostic procedure. These interviews can be investigator- or respondent-based.

Two-stage screening procedures are becoming increasingly popular in child psychiatric epidemiology. Nevertheless, if such a design is to be employed successfully to screen for depressive disorders, several methodological issues require careful attention. First, because of the low level of agreement between parent and child responses to a clinical interview (see above) it will be necessary to give careful consideration to the choice of criterion at the second stage of the study. For instance, as Costello and Angold (1988) pointed out, if the criterion is to select children from a community sample who will report depressive symptoms when they are interviewed then it will be necessary to include a *child* depression questionnaire. On the other hand, if the criterion is to identify children in whom both children *and* parents agree on the presence of depressive symptomatology then one need only screen with a *parental* questionnaire, since in community studies most depression identified by parents will be endorsed by children.

Second, it is important to bear in mind that the type of questionnaire that is used at the first stage may have a great effect on the pattern of associations that is found at the second stage. For example, broad-band questionnaires that assess a wide range of child psychiatric symptoms will tend to miss monosymptomatic disorders such as depression and oversample children whose psychopathology includes symptoms of many different types. This is because children who have symptoms of several different disorders will score higher on a broad-band questionnaire and will therefore have a greater chance of being selected for the second stage. This kind of detection bias may lead to the appearance of spurious associations between depression and other psychiatric problems. The best way of avoiding this problem is to use narrow-band depression questionnaires at the first stage and to assess the other phenomena at the second stage.

Third, it will be necessary to interview a random sample of individuals who were screen negative in order to test the efficiency of the screening method and to calculate a corrected prevalence figure.

A fourth methodological consideration in the design of two-stage epidemiological studies of depressive disorder stems from the fact that the efficiency of this design will depend greatly on the sensitivity and specificity of the initial screening instrument. Indeed, it should be borne in mind that a screening instrument may have high reliability and internal consistency and yet have low sensitivity and specificity. As we shall see later, there is a paucity of data on the sensitivity and specificity of most narrow-band depression questionnaires in community samples of children and adolescents. However, the available data suggest that, while depression questionnaires are likely to be relatively good at identifying true positives, they are much less efficient at detecting true negatives (Carlson & Cantwell, 1980b; Costello, 1986). Moreover, even if a scale has a specificity of 90%, it is a mathematical certainty that when a disorder is rare many false positives will be generated for each true positive. This means that in screening for juvenile depression, many young people who are interviewed at the second stage of the study will be found not to be depressed.

The potential size of this problem is well illustrated by the screening data from the Oregon Adolescent Depression Project (Lewinsohn and colleagues). The population for this study was taken from high-school adolescents, who were interviewed using the K-SADS and who also completed two depression questionnaires on two separate occasions. Roberts, Lewinsohn and Seeley (1991) calculated that even after using the optimal cut-off point on the questionnaires (i.e. the point that maximized sensitivity and specificity) the false positive rate was still about 20%. Or, to put it another way, if these questionnaires had been used as first-stage screens in a two-stage survey, then second-stage interviews would have been conducted with about seven false positives for every true positive who was eventually identified at interview. Very similar findings were reported by Garrison et al (1991) in a two-stage epidemiological study of adolescents. These authors reported that about 80% of probable cases on the screen did not have the disorder at interview.

So, even two-stage surveys can be very inefficient. Indeed, it would seem inevitable that when screening for rare disorders with devices that are less than completely accurate, some false positives will be generated. Nevertheless, since the interview assessments that are employed in the second stage of these studies are expensive and time-consuming, it is important to consider the various ways in which these false positives can be reduced. One approach to this problem is to use a questionnaire that covers symptoms that overlap closely with those of the criterion diagnosis. For example, if the criterion is "DSM major depression" then a questionnaire that includes many symptoms of this diagnosis is likely to have a higher screening efficiency than a questionnaire that covers only a few symptoms.

Another approach is to use a multiple screening procedure in which screening questionnaires are administered twice. Roberts et al (1991) examined the efficiency of multiple screens using both parallel and serial strategies in their community sample of adolescents. Parallel administration means that the subject is counted as a case if the results are positive on either screen; in serial administration a subject must have positive results on both screens to be a case. For current major depression (assessed independently by the K-SADS interview), serial screening increased the accuracy of the prediction of caseness, whereas the effects of parallel screening were negligible.

Perhaps, as Roberts et al (1991) suggest, a combination of these two approaches offers the best alternative. That is, subjects would be screened first with a brief questionnaire (Roberts and colleagues calculated that one of the depression questionnaires could be shortened from 21 to just four items with little loss of screening efficiency!), and then a detailed questionnaire would be administered that covered all of the symptoms included in the criterion diagnosis. The purpose of the second screen would be to distinguish between true and false positives.

Alternatively, to screen efficiently for depressive disorders in two-stage surveys, it may be necessary to use criteria other than symptomatology. For example, it may be that greater attention needs to be paid to associated features such as impairment of peer relationships or decline in academic performance.

It will be appreciated, however, that the cutpoints for distinguishing cases from noncases can be altered to suit the needs of a particular study. Let us suppose, for example, that a researcher is not especially interested in establishing the "true" rate of depression, but rather is using an epidemiological design in order to obtain a homogenous group of nonreferred cases. Such a researcher may decide to select a cutpoint that would include only true cases, since the risk of missing some cases would be of little consequence to that researcher's primary aims. Incidentally, it is worth noting that this strategy will have the effect of producing a sample whose average degree of disturbance is greater.

On the other hand, some investigators may want to find as many cases of depression as possible in order to arrive at an accurate estimate of prevalence. Obviously, if one needs to be certain that absolutely no cases of depression have been missed, then it will be necessary to interview everyone. However, another way of approaching this is to lower the threshold of the screening questionnaire to the point where sensitivity is maximized.

Of course the strategy of altering the threshold on a screening questionnaire presupposes that data are available on the true positive rate and false positive rate at various cutpoints. Fortunately, these data can now be presented graphically in the form of Receiver Operating Characteristic (ROC) curves. These curves plot the true positive rate (sensitivity) against the false positive rate (1 − specificity) for a variety of cutpoints and can be used to compare two or more questionnaires directly. The researcher can select the threshold score that is most suitable for the purpose in hand, which will depend on the relative costs and benefits associated with classifying a patient with an illness as normal and classifying a normal person as ill. Examples of the use of these curves in studying childhood depression can be found in the papers by Garrison et al (1991) and Costello and Angold (1988).

Clearly, then, there is unlikely to be a single optimal cutpoint on a depression scale that will apply to all samples. For instance, it is possible that different caseness criteria should be used for females and males and cutpoints for adolescents may be higher than for adults (Garrison et al, 1991; Roberts, Lewinsohn & Seeley, 1991). Certainly, there can be no guarantee that the cutpoints established in clinical samples that are enriched with cases will work satisfactorily in community samples.

Finally, it should be emphasized that the methodological problems encountered in screening programmes for juvenile depressive disorders are not so great that such programmes are infeasible in routine practice. Reynolds (1991), for example, describes the successful application of multiple-stage screening procedures for depressed and suicidal youngsters in school settings. These were linked to a treatment programme.

SELF-REPORT SCALES AND CHECKLISTS

General issues

As the preceding discussion indicated, one of the main purposes of pencil and paper tests is to provide a relatively cheap method of detecting cases of depression in a population. Such tests are relatively quick and easy to complete and may be suitable for group administration, which means that very large numbers of subjects can be assessed. Rating scales have, however, a number of other uses. Indeed, some scales have attempted to embrace a wide range of depressive symptoms and so they can be used to study the nature of depressive psychopathology further. For instance, techniques such as factor analysis can be used to examine the underlying factor structure of the symptoms. Depression rating scales are also frequently used to measure change during the course of treatment.

It is important to remember, however, that questionnaires are not a substitute for the standard method of making categorical diagnoses, which is the interview. As we saw earlier, agreement between questionnaires and interviews is very far from perfect. Self-report questionnaires rely on the child understanding the concept being considered, and do not permit the clarification of the subject's responses. There is therefore no way of establishing that the child and the investigator have a common perception of the emotions or behaviours in question. Moreover, self-report questionnaires require a basic level of literacy, though they can be read to the child.

Despite these problems questionnaires still have many advantages over other forms of assessment and so a large number exist for research on psychopathology in children. The self-report depression scales selected for more detailed discussion in this section are those on which a reasonable amount of experience has accumulated in the measurement of juvenile depressive phenomena and on which some psychometric data exist. Almost all of them have a parallel parent version (the use of other sources of information in assessment will be described later in this chapter). For each measure a brief general description is given, psychometric properties are described and the main applications are outlined.

The Children's Depression Inventory (CDI)

Probably the best known of the self-report measures for children is the Children's Depression Inventory (Kovacs, 1982b). This is a questionnaire for individuals aged 7 to 17 years that was derived from the Beck Depression Inventory (Kovacs & Beck, 1977). The measure includes 27 items regarding a broad range of depressive symptoms. Each item consists of three statements describing symptoms at three different levels of intensity from "not a problem" to "severe". The children read the items or have the items read to them. The CDI takes between 10 and 20 minutes to complete. A parallel parent version is available, and there are published data on the correspondence of parent and child reports (e.g. Wierzbicki, 1987) and on the level of agreement with broadband questionnaires such as the CBCL (Jensen et al, 1988). A short 13-item version of the CDI has been developed (Carlson & Cantwell, 1980b).

The CDI has been shown to have good test–retest reliability and high internal consistency (Costello & Angold, 1988). Factor analyses of CDI ratings made by teachers have revealed four subdomains: affective behaviour, image ideation, interpersonal relations and guilt irritability (Helsel & Matson, 1984). Some studies have found that the CDI can distinguish between children with and without depressive disorder (Moretti et al, 1985), but others have found that the discrimination was relatively poor (e.g. Fundudis et al, 1991). Data on age and sex norms are available (Finch, Saylor & Edwards, 1985; Smucker et al, 1986; Nelson et al, 1987). Finch and colleagues, for instance, used group administration of the CDI to test nearly 1500 school children aged between 7 and 16 years. Small but significant age and sex differences were found: very young children reported less depression than very old children, and girls tended to report less depression, especially in the younger age groups.

Concerns have been expressed about the CDI's ability to select children with depression from community samples (Costello & Angold, 1988). Nevertheless, it has been used in a variety of studies, including several treatment studies (see, for example: Stark, 1990; Fine et al, 1991) and remains one of the most widely used of the self-report measures for children.

The Beck Depression Inventory (BDI)

The Beck Depression Inventory was first introduced in 1961 (Beck et al, 1961) and has since been revised. The BDI contains 21 items that assess cognitive, behavioural, affective and somatic aspects of depression. Each question provides for a response of 0 (not present) to 3 (severe) so that overall scores can range from 0 to 63.

The Beck inventory has been shown to have good psychometric properties in adult samples (Beck, 1967) and data have been accumulating on its use in community samples of adolescents (e.g. Teri, 1982; Kaplan, Hong & Weinhold, 1984; Barrera & Garrison-Jones, 1988; Larsson & Melin, 1990; Whitaker et al, 1990). In one of the more recent community studies, the BDI was found to have high internal consistency (0.89) but only moderate test–retest stability (0.67) and low specificity. There was low concordance between the BDI and the Centre for Epidemiological Studies Depression Scale (see below), though the BDI was slightly superior as a screen for depressive disorder (Roberts, Lewinsohn & Seeley, 1991). Ambrosini et al (1991) found that the BDI had good test–retest stability ($r = 0.87$ for adolescents with major depression), and high internal consistency (0.91) in outpatient adolescents referred to a clinic for depression. In their study the BDI discriminated well between depressed and nondepressed adolescents, with "major depression" on the K-SADS as the criterion variable. Kashani et al (1990) also found that the BDI differentiated depressed from nondepressed adolescent outpatients.

The BDI is becoming a popular measure for the assessment of depression in adolescence. One of its advantages is that it has been extensively used with adults, which should facilitate comparisons across ages.

The Centre for Epidemiological Studies Depression Scale (CES-D)

Another measure that was first developed for use with adults is the Centre for Epidemiological Studies Depression Scale. This is a 20-item self-report rating scale developed at the National Institute of Mental Health to measure current (past week) depressive symptoms in adult community studies (Radloff, 1977). The CES-D presents statements to which the subject responds on a three-point scale. The adult version has been used with adolescents (Schoenbach et al, 1982) and a version specifically designed for children and adolescents has been developed (Weissman, Orvaschel & Padium, 1980). A form for completion by the parent is available.

Several groups have used the CES-D as a screening questionnaire for depressive disorders in community samples of adolescents (e.g. Garrison et al, 1991; Roberts, Lewinsohn & Seeley, 1991). Garrison et al (1991) found that in younger adolescents (aged 12–14 years) the CES-D had high internal consistency ($\alpha = 0.87$) and distinguished individuals diagnosed as depressed from those without affective disorder. However, it was not a good predictor of cases of depression, and the authors concluded that in a two-stage screening procedure a very large proportion of probable cases (about 80%) who would be screened as "positive" would at interview have no disorder. Similar conclusions were reached by Roberts et al (1991) in a sample of older adolescents (aged 15–18 years), where predictive power was lower than with the BDI. The CES-D does not appear to be an effective discriminator between depressed and nondepressed cases in clinical samples of young people (Weissman et al, 1980).

The Depression Self-Rating Scale (DSRS)

The Depression Self-Rating Scale was developed to measure moderate to severe depression in childhood (Birleson, 1981; Birleson et al, 1987). The child is asked to make a judgement of whether or not a particular statement applies to him or her over the previous week, and then to estimate whether this is true for most of the time or only sometimes. There are 18 items on the questionnaire and a 21-item version exists (Asarnow & Carlson, 1985). No parent version is available.

Birleson et al (1987) found that the scale distinguished between child psychiatric outpatients given a clinical ICD-9 diagnosis of depressive disorder and outpatients who had other disorders. Asarnow and Carlson (1985) found that the scale significantly discriminated depressed from nondepressed children in a sample of 82 child psychiatric inpatients. There was a high correlation (0.81) with scores on the CDI but no significant correlation with ward ratings of depression. Asarnow and Carlson considered that the format of the DSRS made it easier to use than the CDI. Firth and Chaplin (1987) developed a modified version for use in nonclinical samples, but as yet little data are available on the use of this instrument in community settings.

Since the scale is short and covers the previous week, the DSRS may prove to be useful in treatment studies or in other studies where frequent measurement of depression is required. The lack of a parent version is however a disadvantage, and the DSRS cannot yet be recommended for use in nonclinical settings.

The Children's Depression Scale (CDS)

The Children's Depression Scale (Lang & Tisher, 1978) is a 66-item self-report scale that contains five depression subscales (affective response, social problems, self-esteem, preoccupation with own sickness and death, guilt) and a nondepressive subscale (pleasure) (Tisher & Lang, 1983). It is designed for use with children aged between 9 and 16 years. The scale employs a card-sort format that requires that children post a card into one of five boxes. This was designed to reduce stereotyped responses. A pencil and paper version is available (Rotundo & Hensley, 1985), and a parallel version has been developed so that adults can rate the child's depression (Tisher & Lang, 1983). The scale has been translated into several languages (Tisher & Lang, 1983).

The CDS seems to discriminate well between depressed and nondepressed children in referred samples (Tisher & Lang, 1983; Rotundo & Hensley, 1985; Kazdin, 1987). Kazdin (1987) reported that the CDS had high internal consistency ($\alpha = 0.94$) and that depression scores for both children and parents correlated significantly with other depression measures and measures of associated symptoms (e.g. self-esteem). Parents' scores were significantly higher than child scores, but this may be related to the fact that the subjects were all psychiatric inpatients.

Tisher and Lang (1983) surveyed some of the research projects that were using the CDS. These included studies of school populations, sex differences in depressive symptoms, and the relationship with Eysenck Personality Inventory scores.

The Mood and Feelings Questionnaire (MFQ)

The Mood and Feelings Questionnaire (Angold et al, 1987b) is a relatively new 32-item questionnaire that covers all the items of depression mentioned in ICD-10 and DSM-III-R. It was developed to select children for an epidemiological study of depression. Items are scored on a three-point ("true"; "sometimes"; "not true") response scale. It exists in both parent and child forms and is designed for the age range 8–18 years. A short form, which consists of the 11 items with the highest internal consistency and discriminating power, has also been developed.

In a study of 20 adolescent inpatients, the child version has been found to have good test–retest stability (0.81) although there is a fall-off in scores between the first and second administration (Angold, 1989). The mean MFQ score of 17 patients whose discharge diagnosis included depression was 23.1 compared with 12.1 for nine nondepressed patients. Using a cutpoint of 12 or over, this gave a sensitivity of 88%, and a specificity of 70% (Benjamin et al, cited by Costello & Angold, 1988). In a separate study, the MFQ was found significantly to distinguish children attending a primary-care paediatric clinic and children being evaluated in an assessment clinic of a psychiatric unit (Costello & Angold, 1988).

The MFQ has yet to be fully evaluated, but it does have the advantage of being specifically designed to screen for DSM-III-R diagnoses. Several ongoing epidemiological studies are using the MFQ.

Other self-report scales

Many other narrow-band self-report measures of depression have been developed for use with children or adolescents. Reynolds (1987) developed a 30-item scale (the *Reynolds Adolescent Depression Scales*—RADS) that was based on DSM-III. The scale was found to distinguish depressed from nondepressed children and to correlate well with the CDI (Reynolds, 1989). Sokoloff and Lubin (1983) adapted the *Children's Depression Adjective Checklist* (C-DACL) from the adult Adjective Checklist. It is designed for use with adolescents and children and has been shown to have satisfactory internal reliability (Eddy & Lubin, 1988).

In addition to these narrow-band scales, a variety of broad-band scales have been used to assess depression in young people. These scales assess a wide range of emotional and behavioural symptoms, as well as depression. Probably the best known is the *Child Behaviour Checklist* (CBCL). The CBCL (Achenbach & Edelbrock, 1983) includes more than 100 items and is available in both parent and child versions (the child version is suitable for children aged over 11 years). It is probably the most widely used instrument of its kind. Although its coverage of depressive symptoms is somewhat limited, Nurcombe and colleagues (1989) have reported that principal components analyses and cluster analysis of CBCL ratings revealed a depressive factor. Rey and Morris-Yates (1991) found that CBCL ratings of the depressive symptoms included in this factor were able to discriminate between child and adolescent patients with and without major depression. Edelbrock and Costello (1988b) found a significant relationship between the CBCL depression scales and the diagnosis of depression or dysthymia.

Measures of variability of mood

Most of the scales described above attempt to measure depression over defined periods of time. However, scales have also been devised to measure the degree of *variability* of depression from day to day. Costello et al (1991) used the Adolescent Mood Scale, a set of visual analogue scales, to examine the variability of mood in child psychiatric inpatients. The scales were completed three times daily for seven consecutive days. Larson et al (1990) used radio-pagers to signal children and adolescents at regular intervals, who then rated their mood on semantic differential or adjective checklist scales. Interestingly, using the same technique, Larson and Lampman-Petraitis (1989) found that, contrary to popular belief, the mood states of adolescents were not significantly more variable than those of children.

ASSESSMENT OF DEPRESSION IN PRESCHOOL CHILDREN

Although this book is primarily concerned with depressive disorders in children and adolescents, it is worth considering briefly the assessment of depression in preschoolers. A variety of broad-band measures are available for the assessment of emotional and behavioural problems in preschool children. Probably the best known is the *Behavioural Screening Questionnaire* (BSQ) (Richman & Graham, 1971), which was developed as a means of identifying psychiatric disturbance in preschool children. The BSQ is a parent interview that covers about 60 questions on the behaviour, health and development of the child. Its validity has been demonstrated in several studies (e.g. Richman, Stevenson & Graham, 1975; Earls et al, 1982).

A number of studies have attempted to diagnose mood disorders in pre-school children, but until recently most had relied on reports obtained from parents or teachers. For instance, Kashani, Holcomb and Orvaschel (1986) developed the *General Rating of Affective Symptoms for Preschoolers* (GRASP) as an observer rating to be completed by parents and/or teachers who had watched the preschooler interact with other children or adults for at least 20 minutes. Recently, however, several investigators have described measures that attempt to obtain reports of affective symptomatology directly from children. Martini, Strayhorn and Puig-Antich (1990) developed a pic-torial self-report instrument (*Preschool Symptom Self-Report*—PRESS) that was adminstered directly to the child. It consists of 25 items, each comprising two illustrations on a page. One drawing shows a problem or behaviour, and the other illustrates its absence. The instrument was found to have high inter-nal consistency and good retest reliability. Children's responses did not corre-late well with parents' or teachers' responses, but of course the same has been found in studies of older children.

Kranzler et al (1990) developed a standardized *Affect Interview* for the assessment of preschoolers who had experienced a bereavement. Although the sample size was small, it was clear that children as young as three years could express some of the emotions of grief. The authors concluded that bereavement may be a useful model for affective disorder in young children.

OTHER SOURCES OF INFORMATION ABOUT CHILDHOOD DEPRESSION

As described earlier, ratings by children are important because children are probably the best source of information about "internal" symptoms of de-pression. Ratings by parents are also important both because they can identify symptoms different from those reported by the child and because their per-ception of the problem may be very important in clinical work.

In addition, there are a variety of other sources that may be used to provide information about depression in children. Thus, rating scales exist for clini-cians' "best estimate" assessments, teachers' assessments, peer nominations and direct observations.

Clinicians' ratings

Kolvin et al (1984, 1992) developed the *Kolvin–Berney–Bhate Scale* (KBB) that was geared to screen populations for depressive syndromes. Information on symptoms was derived from interviews with the parent and child.

Symptoms were rated on a four-point scale (1–2–3–4), and were then recoded to give a dichotomous score indicating the presence or absence of a symptom (0–0–1–1). Kolvin, Berney and Bhate (1984) showed that there were 11 key symptoms that distinguished between depressed and nondepressed children with school phobia and that using a cutpoint of six or more symptoms gave the best discrimination between the groups (sensitivity 100%, specificity 80%).

The *Johns Hopkins Depression Scale—Child Version* (HDCL—C) was specifically designed to be based on the diagnostic criteria of DSM-III (Joshi, Capozzoli & Coyle, 1990). The HDCL-C is a 38-item instrument in which the diagnostic criteria of DSM-III were transformed into descriptions of depressive symptoms. The questions fall into five main categories: mood, energy, behaviour, somatic complaints and vegetative symptoms. The time period covered by the checklist is two weeks. Items are scored on a severity scale of 0 to 4. The scale can be completed by clinicians or other adults who know the child well. In a study of psychiatric inpatients, Joshi et al (1990) showed that HDCL-C ratings made by nursing staff distinguished between depressed and nondepressed patients. In addition, normative data based on parental ratings are available on more than 1000 children (Joshi et al, 1990).

The *Hamilton Depression Rating Scale* (HDRS) is one of the most widely used rating scales for depression in adults. In its original form the 17-item scale was intended to be completed by a skilled psychiatrist (Hamilton, 1960). Information about the patient is collected from a variety of sources. It should only be used with depressive disorders that have already been diagnosed and is intended primarily as a measure of the severity of depression. The HDRS has been very popular in clinical trials with depressed adults and has been used in drug trials of depressed adolescents (e.g. Strober et al, 1990a). The *Children's Depression Rating Scale* (CDRS) (Poznanski, Cook & Carroll, 1979) is an adaptation of the Hamilton Rating Scale for Depression. As with the adult version, evaluation of the 17 symptoms depends on the judgement of the clinician, who may use multiple sources of data (e.g. child interview, parent interview and observations) to make a rating. The scale has been found to have high inter-rater reliability, and high test–retest reliability (Poznanski et al, 1979, 1984). Cniles, Miller and Cox (1980) described a 27-item rating scale that also included items derived from the Hamilton scale and was designed to be administered in the same way.

The *Bellvue Index of Depression* (BID) (Petti, 1978) was devised on the basis of the Weinberg criteria. It comprises 40 items, each rated on a four-point scale. Kazdin et al (1983a) modified the BID to a scale with just 26 items.

Teacher ratings

Teachers are rarely used as primary sources of information about depression in children and many of the studies of teacher ratings have been based on straightforward adaptations of self-report scales (Hoier & Kerr, 1988), which is not ideal. Lefkowitz and Tesiny (1980) reported that ratings on the *Teacher Nomination Inventory of Depression* correlated positively both with parent ratings and self-report. Kazdin et al (1983a) found moderate to low concordance between teacher ratings and other sources of information. They suggested that this might be due in part to teachers having different opportunities to observe behaviours. Stark (1990) discussed some of the reasons why depression may be unrecognized by teachers and concluded that the biggest reason was that depressed children rarely "act out" and are easily forgotten. It seems unlikely that teachers will prove to be accurate informants on the internal symptoms of depression, though of course they can provide very useful accounts of other kinds of symptoms.

Peer ratings

Peers generally see a child in a wider variety of settings and for longer periods of time than a teacher does. It might therefore be expected that peer-based ratings would provide a suitable source of data on depressed children. The best known of these measures is the *Peer Nomination Inventory for Depression* (PNID) (Lefkowitz & Tesiny, 1980). The measure includes 20 items in which children are asked specific questions. The items are divided into three subscales: depression, happiness and popularity. The child identifies the peer to whom each characteristic applies. A child's own score is the sum of the nominations he receives from his classmates. Scores range from 0 (no one has nominated the child as depressed) to 13 (everyone has nominated the child on every item) (Lefkowitz & Tesiny, 1985).

The PNID has been found to have reasonable internal consistency (Ezpeleta et al, 1990) and to correlate with school performance, self-concept, peer ratings of popularity and self-ratings of depression (Lefkowitz, Tesiny & Gordon, 1980; Lefkowitz & Tesiny, 1985; Worchel et al, 1990). Data on a large sample from the general population are available (Lefkowitz & Tesiny, 1985) and a self-report version of the PNID has recently been developed (Lefkowitz, Tesiny & Solodow, 1989). It should be borne in mind, however, that peer nominations are time-consuming and have not so far been shown to add very much to data obtained from other sources.

Direct observations

Some of the features of depression, such as retardation of speech and movement, and facial expression, are overt and observable. Research with depressed adults has shown that ratings of observable behaviour can be of value. For instance, Williams, Barlow and Agras (1972) observed the talking, smiling and motor behaviours of depressed adults. These behaviours were found to be correlated with clinician and self-report ratings of depression.

As yet, few observational measures of depressed children have been developed and most studies have used different measures so it is difficult to compare them. Kazdin et al (1985a) made direct observations on 62 inpatient children aged 8 to 13 years, who were observed during free time periods. During the free period, children could play in an activity area where games and play materials were available. Behaviours for observation were (1) social activity (e.g. talking, playing in a game), (2) solitary behaviour (e.g. playing alone, straightening one's room), and (3) affect-related expression (e.g. smiling, arguing). Children who scored highly on a parent measure of depression engaged in less social behaviour and affect-related expression than did children low in depression.

Observational ratings of depressive behaviours can also be made during interviews. Kazdin et al (1985b), for instance, assessed nonverbal behaviours during a 15-minute interview with child psychiatric inpatients. These behaviours were assessed as the child answered questions on everyday activities. The nonverbal behaviours included facial expression, eye contact and bodily movements. Inter-rater reliability on most of these scales was high, with a mean correlation of 0.79. However, most of the behaviours did not correlate with measures of depression obtained from parents and children, and the DSM-III diagnosis of depression was unrelated to nonverbal behaviours.

In spite of the fact that parental observational ratings can be made relatively cheaply (Reid et al, 1988) they have not become widely used in research into juvenile depressive disorders. This is probably because there is no good evidence that they add anything to the information that can already be collected from parents by simple questionnaires. Ratings during interviews may prove to be more useful, and indeed many of the diagnostic interviews include codings for direct observations. For example, the K-SADS contains codings for depressed appearance and blunting of affect. However, these do not generally have a great influence on the diagnosis.

Probably the most important area for observational ratings is in inpatient settings. Here, they can add important information about the persistence and severity of depressive symptoms, and can sometimes play an important role in diagnosis.

And, of course, direct observations of depressed children need not be restricted to measurement of their depression. It is possible to gain much useful information about other constructs through observational studies. For example, Altmann and Gotlib (1988) observed the social behaviour of depressed 10-year-old children who were selected through schools using the CDI. Depressed children spent more time alone and less time interacting with peers than nondepressed children. Interestingly, when depressed children did interact with their peers they were more aggressive and negative than were the nondepressed children. The implication is that the social isolation of depressed children may arise from peer rejection as well as from social withdrawal.

MEASURES OF CONSTRUCTS RELATED TO DEPRESSION

There are a number of other constructs that are commonly associated with depression and which it may be necessary to measure. We shall see later that *hopelessness* is a key symptom in many formulations of depression (e.g. Brown, Harris & Bifulco, 1986) and correlates with suicidal behaviour in adults. A scale to measure hopelessness in children has been developed (Kazdin et al, 1983b), which is correlated with suicidal attempts and has good test–retest reliability in clinical samples (Kazdin et al, 1986). Loss of enjoyment can also be measured (Kazdin, 1989b). Low *self-esteem* also plays an important role in some models of depression and can be assessed using standardized inventories (e.g. Coopersmith, 1967). Several scales exist for the assessment of suicidal ideation in children and adolescents, such as the *Suicidal Intent Questionnaire* (Reynolds, 1989) and the *Suicidal Behaviours Interview* (Reynolds, 1990).

It is important to assess *impairment of social functioning* both because depressed children frequently have problems in this area and because severity of social impairment is often a good indicator of the clinical significance of a disorder. The *Children's Global Assessment Schedule* was developed by Shaffer and his colleagues (1983) to assess the DSM-III-R axis-5 Global Assessment of Functioning scale in individuals aged 4 to 16 years. This single scale ranges from 100–91 (superior functioning) to 10–1 (persistent danger of harming self, failure to maintain personal hygiene). A more detailed assessment of social functioning is provided by the *Social Adjustment Inventory for Children and Adolescents* (John et al, 1987). The *Child Behaviour Checklist* also provides information on social functioning.

Social skills are often impaired in depressed children and social skills training is an important component of some treatments for depression in young people. Helsel and Matson (1984) found a strong association between scores on the *Matson Evaluation of Social Skills with Youngsters* (MESSY) and depression on the CDI. A large number of other measures of social behaviour are available, but few have been systematically assessed in depressed children.

Finally, it is important to measure other child psychiatric symptoms. All the interview measures described in this chapter assess nondepressive psychiatric problems, though as noted earlier they differ somewhat in the extent to which they do so. Many broad-band questionnaire measures of child psychopathology also exist, such as the CBCL and the Rutter scales (reviewed by Barkley, 1988).

CONCLUSIONS: CHOOSING AN INSTRUMENT

It is clear from this review that a large number of interviews, questionnaires and rating scales now exist for the purpose of assessing depression in children. Indeed, it could well be argued that there is little need for new measures of depression in young people. Rather, we need much more data on existing measures, especially those that have already been well developed and standardized. At the moment, no single measure has been shown to assess all aspects of childhood depression and all measures have weaknesses, as well as strengths. Researchers wishing to choose between these measures can therefore expect some difficult decisions.

The primary consideration in selecting measures of depression is, of course, the question that the investigator wants to answer. Nevertheless, it is possible to delineate certain basic principles regarding the choice of an instrument to assess depression in young people. First, it is necessary to decide whether or not to make the *diagnosis of depression*. None of the questionnaire measures described above can generate a categorical diagnosis, and indeed many of them are based on a dimensional view of psychopathology rather than a categorical one. The correlation between scores on depression questionnaires and the diagnosis of depression at interview is low. So, although direct interviews are time-consuming and relatively expensive, at the moment they are the only way of generating a categorical diagnosis.

Second, there is the issue of what *sources of information* to use. Many investigators now appear to regard the child as the primary source of information on depressive symptomatology so any assessment of depression in young people must include information obtained from the child. In general, the correlation of child ratings and parental ratings of the child's depression has been low, but the two sources of information may predict different correlates so parental data will also continue to be important.

The role of information from other sources is less clear. Teacher ratings do not correlate well with child ratings of depression, but some researchers have found reports from teachers are of help in resolving diagnostic discrepancies (Reich & Earls, 1987). Teacher ratings are probably going to be of more use in the assessment of externalizing problems. Observer ratings of depression in children have been subjected to little research, and warrant more extensive study. At the moment, relatively little data exist on these measures and they cannot be recommended for routine use.

A third decision concerns the *content* of the assessment. Most of the interview-based measures cover the symptoms of depression included in DSM, but there is great variability in the symptoms covered by the various questionnaires and rating scales. In some studies it may be necessary to cover many areas of depressive symptomatology, whereas in others all that may be required is coverage of a few specific symptoms. As Costello and Angold

(1988) pointed out in their helpful review, questionnaire measures are often expected to perform two different kinds of tasks. On the one hand, they may be required to give an indication of the number and types of depressive symptoms that are present. On the other hand, their main use may be as a means of distinguishing cases of depression from the rest of the population. Scales that are good at one of these tasks may not necessarily be good at the other.

A fourth consideration is the degree of coverage required of *other areas of functioning and psychopathology*. This is likely to depend greatly on the particular needs of the researcher or clinician, but it should be borne in mind that juvenile depressive disorders seldom occur without other psychopathology.

Finally, there is the need for comparability with other studies. The number of measures for use in assessing depressed children is increasing so rapidly that it is becoming difficult to generalize the results from one study to another. So, it will often be important to use instruments that have been used by other investigators.

Chapter 4

Epidemiology

Epidemiological studies of general population samples are expensive and difficult to undertake. Nevertheless such studies are important not only because they provide data on prevalence but also because variations in the rates of disorder with correlates will generate hypotheses about aetiology. Of course, investigations of clinical samples can contribute much to our understanding of the mechanisms leading to depression in children. Indeed, since epidemiology is concerned with the distribution of disorders in defined populations, epidemiological methods can and are being used to study depression in referred groups. However, clinic populations may be unrepresentative in ways that may distort findings on correlates and aetiology. For example, whenever less than 100% of subjects are referred, clinical studies will tend to overestimate the proportion of subjects with multiple diagnoses because the probability of referral with two conditions is greater than the probability of referral with one (Berkson, 1946). Biases may be particularly prominent in referrals of children to mental health settings because the referral may be partly related to parental characteristics (Shepherd, Oppenheim & Mitchell, 1971). Also, since clinical studies are concerned with children who have for the most part been identified as having a problem, it is not possible to study *escape* from risk.

For these reasons, and others, over the past decade or so there have been a number of published studies of depressive conditions in community samples of children and/or adolescents. This chapter will review these studies with an emphasis not only on the prevalence of disorder but also on other aspects such as correlates and age trends. Data from clinical studies will also be reviewed. First, however, findings from early studies of depressive phenomena in the community will be considered briefly since they raise important methodological issues that later epidemiological work has attempted to tackle.

HISTORICAL BACKGROUND AND METHODOLOGICAL ISSUES

Early studies of the prevalence of psychiatric disorders in childhood often did not describe the frequency of discrete disorders but instead reported the occurrence of overall mental or behavioural impairment (Brandenberg, Friedman & Silver, 1990). Those studies that did report rates for individual depressive symptoms tended to find that these symptoms were quite common. Shepherd, Oppenheim and Mitchell (1971), for example, found the symptom of crying to occur in 25% of 5-year-olds and low appetite in 15%. Irritability is also reported quite commonly, occurring in 11% in the study of Shepherd et al.

Many of these studies used questionnaires completed by teachers or parents as sources of information (Lapouse & Monk, 1964; Shepherd et al, 1971). Children were rarely used as sources of information about depressive symptomatology. Moreover, in some studies it was not at all clear how much of the reported symptomatology represented psychopathology. As Angold (1988a) pointed out, the term "depression" has come to be used in many different ways, from "depression" as a description of the low end of the ordinary fluctuation of normal mood to "depression" as a disease accompanied by a distinctive aetiology. In addition, few of the earlier studies provided sufficient information on the reliability and validity of the assessment procedures.

Recent research has attempted to address many of these methodological issues. Most of the epidemiological studies conducted recently have used standardized methods of data collection and operationalized diagnostic criteria for depressive disorder (usually DSM-III). Information has generally been collected from both parent and child and some studies have also collected information from teachers. Greater attention has been paid to sampling procedures.

In spite of these developments there are still problems in the interpretation of the available epidemiological data on depressive conditions in young people. First, although it might be thought that the wisdespread use of DSM-III in interview-based studies would solve the problem of diagnostic certainty, or "caseness", this is far from being the case. In fact, it is still very difficult to arrive at comparable estimates of the prevalence of depressive disorder in young people. Thus, although comparable criteria have been used in many of the recent interview-based studies, the threshold for defining a "case" in these studies has varied widely. For instance, in community studies of depressive disorder in adolescents, caseness has been defined on the basis of symptoms only (McGee et al, 1990), need for treatment (Kashani et al, 1987), social impairment (Bird et al, 1990) or a combination of various definitions of caseness (Fleming, Offord & Boyle, 1989).

A further problem of comparison is the certainty with which a case is decided upon. Fleming et al (1989) showed that the prevalence of depression depended hugely on the level of diagnostic certainty, which was defined on the basis of severity of symptoms. Among children aged between 12 and 16 years the rate of "high diagnostic certainty" depression was 1.8%, the level of "medium diagnostic certainty" depression was 7.8%, and the level of "low diagnostic certainty" depression was 43.9%! Moreover, it would appear that the certainty of diagnosis differs greatly between studies. In the J. Anderson et al (1987) survey of 11-year-olds only about two-fifths of depressive disorders were diagnosed with "weak" certainty, whereas in the study of Fleming et al (1989) cases of depression (aged between 6 and 11 years) at low diagnostic certainty far outnumbered cases at high or medium certainty. Compounding this problem is the fact that the kinds of instruments used in these studies have varied a great deal. As we saw in the previous chapter, different kinds of interview might give different results, especially when defining "caseness" in community surveys.

A second important area that has been inconsistent across studies concerns the way in which information from different sources has been combined. Some studies have used different measures with parents and children. For instance, in the assessment of 15-year-olds in the Dunedin Multidisciplinary Health and Development Study (DMHDS) (McGee et al, 1990), scores on the Revised Behaviour Problem Checklist (Quay & Peterson, 1987) were used to confirm the adolescent self-report. In line with other studies, less than one-third of anxiety–depressive disorders were confirmed by the parent. Other studies have used basically the same kind of measure with parents and children (e.g. Kashani et al, 1987) but have placed greater reliance on the child's report. Often, only the final "best-estimate" diagnosis is presented and very few studies have provided data on how associations with risk factors varied according to the source of information that was used.

A third area of inconsistency is the type of prevalence rate reported. Prevalence rates will vary according to the length of the survey period. Period prevalence (the prevalence of disorder during a given period of time) is a function of point prevalence (the prevalence at a particular point in time) and incidence (the number of new cases). One-month period prevalence will therefore be less than six months, which will in turn be less than one year. The time frames that have been covered by recent population surveys of children and adolescents have varied between "current" and six months.

A fourth source of variation across studies arises because of differences in the sampling frame. In their excellent review of recent epidemiological studies of juvenile depressive disorders, Fleming and Offord (1990) suggested that sampling from schools may underestimate the rate of these disorders since school dropouts and nonattenders will be omitted. On the other hand, studies that use only one randomly selected child per household (e.g. Bird et al, 1988) could underestimate the prevalence of conditions that run in sibships. Fleming and Offord calculated that response rates were less than 75% in over half of the studies. It was difficult to assess the biases caused by differential response rates because information about non-participants was often inadequate.

Bearing in mind all these differences between studies, it is not surprising to find that the rates of depressive disorders have varied somewhat. The following sections will therefore concentrate on studies appearing since 1980 and using DSM-III, so that at least the diagnostic criteria are similar. As a background to these studies, however, the series of epidemiological studies carried out by Rutter and his colleagues will be outlined because they set the standard for many of the studies that have followed. Brief consideration will also be given to studies using self-report checklists since they give information on the prevalence of depressive phenomena below the cutpoints usually employed by studies using diagnostic criteria for depressive disorder.

THE ISLE OF WIGHT STUDIES

The study carried out on the Isle of Wight during the 1960s (Rutter, Tizard & Whitmore, 1970) was one of the first large-scale epidemiological studies that focused on psychiatric disorders in children. The authors used a two-stage design in which the entire population at risk was surveyed using parent and teacher questionnaires; school, clinic and hospital records; and paediatric records. Children at risk were then interviewed, as were some low-scoring children. Interviews were conducted by psychiatrists who were carefully trained in the use of the semi-structured interviews designed for the study. Parent and child were interviewed separately and the results combined to produce the diagnosis. Diagnoses were based on behavioural features. A similar study design was used to follow up the original sample in order to examine risk factors prospectively and to examine the course of the disorders.

The study found that depressive disorder was very rare in children aged 10–11 years (0.14% at the time of the interview) and still relatively rare in those aged 14–15 years (1.5%). However, individual depressive symptoms were common at both ages (sad/miserable 12% and 45% respectively). Adolescents reported much higher rates of affective symptomatology than was evident from parental reports. The Isle of Wight study also found that depressive symptoms were common in all types of psychiatric disorders, including conduct disorder. This distinguished them from anxiety/phobic symptoms, which did not show an association with conduct problems.

The Isle of Wight study used measures of depression that were relatively crude by present standards (Rutter, 1989) and it is likely that the threshold for making a diagnosis was high. Thus, for example, the study employed broad-band screening questionnaires that probably have a lower sensitivity for depressive disorders than the scales available nowadays (see the previous chapter). Nevertheless, as we shall see later, many of the findings from the Isle of Wight study, such as that adolescents report higher levels of depressive symptomatology than children, have been replicated in subsequent research.

STUDIES USING DSM-III

In one of the first published studies to use DSM-III to diagnose depressive conditions in children, Kashani and Simonds (1979) found that 1.9% of those aged 7 to 12 years had a depressive disorder, a rate that was far in excess of that found among children aged 10–11 years in the Isle of Wight study. Seventeen per cent had the symptom of depressed mood. However, these findings were limited by methodological issues: the study used a clinical interview of unknown reliability and the numbers were very small (total sample size was 103 subjects). Another study by the same author had access to a much larger cohort ($n = 641$) and reported an even higher rate of depressive disorder (Kashani et al, 1983). This study was based on an ongoing longitudinal study of a consecutive series of births in Dunedin, New Zealand, and used a standardized psychiatric interview (K-SADS-E). The point prevalence of either major or minor depression among 9-year-olds was 4.3%, and about one out of ten subjects were reported to have had a previous episode at some time in their lives. The response rate in the Kashani et al (1983) study was less than 60%, but in a re-examination of this sample at age 11 years, J. Anderson et al (1987) achieved a 70% response. The one-year prevalence of depressive disorder based on DISC interviews was 1.8%. The prevalence of DSM-III disorders in the Dunedin sample was re-examined when the subjects were 15 years old (McGee et al, 1990). On this occasion 94% of subjects were re-assessed, using an abbreviated version of the DISC. The prevalence of current major depression was 1.2% and of dysthymia 1.1%.

Several other recent studies have used the DISC. Cohen et al (1987) assessed a randomly selected subsample of a sample originally drawn in 1975 and followed up in 1983–84. The DISC and DISC-P were administered by trained "lay" interviewers and the K-SADS was then administered about three months afterwards by clinicians. Parent and child data were combined to make a diagnosis. The prevalence of "definite" major depression was 3% among 100 individuals aged 9–12 years. The combined rate of "possible" and "probable" major depression on the DISC was 11%, compared with 6% on the SADS. There was, however, virtually no agreement on who actually had a depressive disorder! In most instances the different interviews nominated different individuals as depressed.

Bird et al (1988) used a two-stage design to survey children aged between 4 and 16 years. In the first stage, CBCLs were obtained from parents and in the second stage DISC interviews were conducted by psychiatrists with children who scored above the published cutpoint on the screen, and with a random sample of the screened children. Parents were also interviewed and the two sources of information were combined by the clinician. "Caseness" was defined both by the DSM-III criteria and a low score on the Children's Global Assessment Scale (see back and also Bird et al, 1990). The period prevalence (past 6 months) for major depression among those aged 11 to 14 years was 2.5%. Costello (1989) also used a two-stage design involving the CBCL and the DISC to estimate rates of psychiatric disorders in a primary-care paediatric sample. Interviews were conducted with 300 parents and children drawn from a first-stage screening sample of 789 children aged 7 to 11 years. The one year prevalence estimate for major depressive disorder was 0.4%.

A different kind of two-stage design was used by Whitaker et al (1990) to study DSM-III disorders in secondary school children aged between 14 and 17 years. Whitaker and colleagues used a battery of narrow-band self-report questionnaires, including the BDI, to screen for disorders, rather than a single broad-band scale. The second-stage interview was conducted by a clinician using an unstandardized interview that included sections obtained from several other interviews. The lifetime prevalence of major depression was 4.0% and of dysthymic disorder 4.9%.

One of the largest of the DSM-III-based studies to use a one-stage design was conducted in Ontario. It was based on a sampling frame that consisted of all household dwellings listed in the 1981 census of Canada (Boyle et al, 1987). Diagnostic rates were based on responses to the CBCL (Achenbach & Edelbrock, 1983), to which some items were added. Psychiatric interviews were carried out to validate the checklist but estimates of the prevalence of depressive "disorder" were based on questionnaire responses. Fleming, Offord and Boyle (1989) estimated that among children aged between 6 and 11 years the rate of a "DSM-III-like" depressive syndrome (high diagnostic certainty) was 0.6% and among adolescents aged between 12 and 16 years the rate was 1.8%. Adolescents identified themselves as more often depressed than their parents. Clearly, the lack of interview-based measures of depression is a disadvantage, and the validity of the DSM-III-like disorder was not studied in the original validation study (Boyle et al, 1987). Nevertheless, some support for the validity of the "DSM-III-like" depressive disorder came from the finding that depressed subjects were more likely than nondepressed subjects to use mental health or social services, to have poor school performance and to have problems getting along with others.

Another study that used a one-stage strategy sampled from high-schools in urban and rural areas of Oregon (Lewinsohn and colleagues). Adolescents were interviewed with an epidemiological version of the K-SADS that could generate past and present episodes of depression. The response rate was 61%, with nonresponders more likely to be women and of lower socioeconomic status. Preliminary findings indicated that the prevalence of DSM-III-R major depression was 2.5% for current episode and 18.5% for past episodes. For dysthymia the rates were 0.5% and 3.3% respectively (Roberts, Lewinsohn & Seeley, 1991).

STUDIES USING SELF-REPORT CHECKLISTS

The Beck Depression Inventory (BDI) has been used in numerous community surveys of adolescents (e.g. Albert & Beck, 1975; Teri, 1982; Kaplan, Hong & Weinhold, 1984; Gibbs, 1985; Larsson & Melin, 1990; Roberts, Lewinsohn & Seeley, 1991). In one of the first, Albert and Beck (1975) surveyed 63 adolescents using a short version of the Beck questionnaire. Around one-third were found to have "moderate" or "severe" depression according to the cutpoints established in studies of adults. Teri (1982) surveyed 568 adolescents and also found a high rate of moderate or severe depression (32%). By contrast, Kaplan et al (1984) found that only 8% of 385 high-school adolescents who completed the BDI had moderate or severe depression. The older children and those of lower socioeconomic status had the higher scores. Roberts et al (1991) estimated that the prevalence rate on the BDI for severe depression was 4%, similar to that reported by Teri (1982) but higher than the rate for severe depression reported by Kaplan et al (1.3%). The prevalence of severe BDI depression at 4% was much closer to the point prevalence of major depression and dysthymia obtained at interview (3%) than the 12.1% obtained with the CES-D, though in most instances it was not the same individuals who were identified as depressed.

Garrison et al (1991) pointed out that the distribution of CES-D scores is different in adults and adolescents and that different "case" criteria may need to be used. Indeed if the CES-D cutpoint used in adults to correspond to the presence of major depression (>16) is used in studies of adolescents, then the rates of depression are very high. Schoenbach et al (1982) found that one-half of their sample of 384 adolescents were depressed, and in the study of Wells, Klerman and Deykin (1987), the rate of depression was 33%. Much lower rates of depression were found when attempts were made to make ratings more closely comparable with current diagnostic systems. For instance, in the study of Schoenbach et al (1982) when CES-D items were used to make RDC diagnoses the rate of depression dropped to 2.9%. Similarly, in the study of Wells et al (1987) the depression rate dropped to 16% when only symptoms that lasted three or more days of the week were counted.

Garrison et al (1989) replicated the study of Schoenbach et al (1982) in a sample of 677 students from the same junior high-school. In general the findings were strikingly similar to those reported by Schoenbach et al. Thus, for example, 56% of students in the Garrison et al study scored 1 or more on the CES-D symptom of "felt depressed" compared with 54% in the study of

Schoenbach et al. Garrison et al (1989) also constructed a "DSM-III-like" depressive syndrome using the CES-D responses and found that 30 (4.4%) of subjects had symptom profiles that conformed to this syndrome.

A variety of other scales have been used to estimate rates of depression in community samples, such as the CDI (Kaslow, Rehm & Siegel, 1984) and the six-item scale used in the study of Kandel and Davies (1982). Little will be gained by detailing every study that has used self-report scales to determine rates of depression in community surveys. Suffice to say that although these rates have varied widely, as a general rule they have been far in excess of those found in interview-based studies. Clearly, the problem of defining "caseness" in studies based entirely on self-report measures is just as acute as in interview-based studies. Indeed, the exceedingly high rates of depression found in a few of these studies suggest that some of this symptomatology may be part of "normal" misery or sadness.

CORRELATES OF DEPRESSIVE DISORDERS IN COMMUNITY SURVEYS

Many of the risk factors for depression in young people, together with the possible risk mechanisms that these factors represent, will be discussed in greater detail in later chapters. This section will therefore consider only briefly some of the correlates that community-based epidemiological studies have suggested may be associated with juvenile depressive disorders.

Social class

In general, interview-based studies have reported that low social class was not significantly associated with depressive disorder in young people (Costello, 1989; Bird et al, 1989). For instance, in a longitudinal analysis of risk factors that predicted the subsequent development of psychiatric disorders in middle childhood and adolescence, Velez, Johnson and Cohen (1989) found that major depression was the only disorder *not* predicted by low social class. However, several self-report surveys of depressive symptoms have found an association of these symptoms with income or class. Kaplan et al (1984) found that lower social class adolescents were more depressed than higher social class adolescents. Kandel and Davies (1982) found that low family income was associated with depressive symptoms.

Race

The findings in respect of race have also varied. Some studies have detected no effect of race (Kandel & Davies, 1982; Costello, 1989). Schoenbach et al

(1982) found that depressive symptoms were more common in black than in white males.

Family functioning

Several community-based studies have shown that depressive disorder is associated with some aspect of family dysfunction (Bird et al, 1989; Kashani, Burbach & Rosenberg, 1988; Velez, Johnson & Cohen, 1989). For instance, one of the few factors that predicted major depression in the study of Velez et al (1989) was the presence of emotional problems in parents. Similar findings have been reported in studies of depressive symptoms. For instance, Kandel and Davies (1986) found that family dysfunction was one of the factors that predicted continuity of depressive symptoms to early adulthood, though this effect disappeared when the effects of intervening events were controlled for.

Sex

In prepubertal children it seems that depressive disorder is just as common in boys as in girls (Kashani et al, 1983; Fleming, Offord & Boyle, 1989; Costello, 1989; Velez, Johnson & Cohen, 1989), and some studies have reported that there is a male preponderance (J. Anderson et al, 1987). There is also good evidence that by adulthood women have higher rates of depression than men (Weissman & Klerman, 1977). So, at some point between the two age periods there must be a shift in the sex ratio for depressive disorder. It is not clear when this shift occurs, but several studies have found a female preponderance for depressive disorder in adolescents (Rutter, Tizard & Whitmore, 1970; Kashani et al, 1987; Fleming, Offord & Boyle, 1989; McGee et al, 1990). The Dunedin studies suggest that the switch occurs somewhere between the ages of 13 and 15 years. J. Anderson et al (1987) reported a 5:1 excess of males at age 11, whereas by age 15 there was a 1.8:1 excess of girls (McGee et al, 1990).

It is not clear whether the rates of depressive disorder in boys change during adolescence. From the data provided by Fleming et al (1989) it would seem that there may be an increase in rates of depression in both boys and girls, but the increase is particularly marked in girls. However, sex of child was only significant in the low diagnostic confidence group (see page 66 above). In the Dunedin studies the rate of depressive disorder in boys seemed to be about the same across ages: J. Anderson et al (1987) reported that the rate of major depression or dysthymia was 2% in 7-year-old boys, and in the study of McGee et al (1990) the rate of major depression plus dysthymia was around 1.6% in 15-year-old boys. In the Puerto Rico and New York State studies the rates of depressive disorder remained fairly stable for boys, but for girls more than doubled in New York, and in Puerto Rico increased from 4.9% to 13.1% (Costello, 1989).

Age

Perhaps the most consistent finding from epidemiological studies of depressive phenomena in young people has been the association with increasing age. For example, in the Isle of Wight study about 13% of individuals aged 10 or 11 years showed depressed mood at interview. When the same children were assessed at age 14–15 years depressive feelings had become considerably more prevalent. At interview, over 40% of adolescents reported feelings of misery or depression and 7–8% reported that they had suicidal feelings (Rutter et al, 1976). Depressive disorders also showed an increase with age: there were only three cases among 2000 children aged 10 or 11 years, but at age 14–15 years there were nine cases of "pure" depressive disorder and 26 cases where depressive disorder occurred in conjunction with other psychiatric problems.

Several other studies of depressive disorders that have included both children and adolescents have found that rates of the disorder increase with age (Bird et al, 1988; Fleming et al, 1989). Fleming and colleagues, for instance, found that there was a three-fold increase in the prevalence of a DSM-like depressive condition (high diagnostic certainty) between the age periods 6–11 years and 12–16 years. By contrast, Kashani et al (1989) found that although symptoms of depression increased with age there was no significant increase in the prevalence of depressive disorder. However, this study was based on very small numbers of cases.

It should also be noted that the age trends that seem to occur in affective *disorders* may not occur in other manifestations of negative mood. Indeed, some symptoms, such as crying, are more common among children than among adolescents, whereas other symptoms, such as irritability, show no particular age trends (Shepherd, Oppenheim & Mitchell, 1971). It is also notable that although depressive disorder and anxiety disorder commonly occur in conjunction with each other, the available data suggest that anxiety disorders probably do not show marked age trends (Rutter, 1988b). Similarly, it seems that specific fears actually decrease with increasing age, though "adult-like" phobic disorders such as social phobia and agoraphobia increase during adolescence (Marks, 1987). It seems, therefore, that the age trends that are found in depressive disorders distinguish them from some of the other emotional problems of childhood.

PREVALENCE OF DEPRESSIVE DISORDER IN REFERRED SAMPLES

Reported rates of depressive disorder in children and adolescents seen at mental health clinics have varied enormously. Angold (1988b) reviewed studies reporting rates of depression in referred populations and found that the rates ranged from 0% to 61%. However, since the introduction of operational diagnostic criteria such as DSM-III there has been less variation in these rates, with most studies reporting that about 10% to 30% of child psychiatric outpatients have a depressive disorder (Angold, 1988b). For instance, Carlson and Cantwell (1980b) screened 210 referrals for the symptom of depression. Sixty per cent of the children has depressive symptoms, 49% had a depressive syndrome and 28% met criteria for the presence of an affective disorder. Kolvin and his colleagues (1991) screened successive referrals to a university child psychiatry outpatient department using the CDI. Ninety-five children were examined further by a structured clinical interview. About one-third were felt to have "significant" depression and marked or severe depression was present in about a quarter of subjects. The rate of depressive disorder was very similar irrespective of whether the diagnosis was based on DSM-III criteria applied to the case notes (25%), a symptom algorithm (25%) or the Weinberg criteria (23%).

It will be appreciated that all kinds of biases may influence the prevalence of disorders found in referred samples. Nevertheless, studies of clinical groups have the advantage that they can often generate much larger numbers of depressed cases than community surveys. Indeed, much more is known about the correlates of depressive disorders in referred samples than in the community. For instance, virtually all studies of psychobiological markers have been conducted in referred samples, as have most of the systematic family-genetic studies. These studies will be described in greater detail in subsequent chapters. For the time being, it is worth noting that the findings from general population studies regarding sex ratio and age trends in depressive phenomena have also been reported in clinical samples. Thus, several studies of child psychiatric patients have shown that among prepubertal children the sex ratio is about equal, whereas among postpubertal children there tends to be a female preponderance (Ryan et al, 1987; Harrington et al, 1990; Kolvin et al, 1991). Carlson and Strober (1983) found that admissions to psychiatric hospitals with depressive diagnoses increased steadily with age.

There is some suggestion from clinical studies that the prevalence of depressive phenomena may follow a U-shaped distribution. Zeitlin (1986) studied Maudsley child psychiatric patients who had also attended the Maudsley as adults. About 22% of those aged 4–5 years had the symptom of depression, under 10% of those aged 8–9 years had the symptom, and nearly 50% of those aged 14–15 years had depression. Similar findings were obtained when the syndrome of depression, defined by operational criteria devised by Pearce (1978), was considered. Zeitlin's data also suggested that the "switch" between a male and a female preponderance for depression occurs much earlier than has been reported in the epidemiological studies described above. By the age of 10 years there was a clear female preponderance among children with the depressive syndrome, which became progressively greater during adolescence. In both sexes, rates of the depressive syndrome increased with age, until the endpoint of the study at 16 years.

Further evidence for the switch in sex ratio occurring at around the age of 10 years comes from two other studies. Weissman et al (1987) studied rates of major depression in the children of depressed parents. After the age of 10 years the incidence rates for girls increased much more quickly than those for boys. In both sexes, rates of depressive disorder increased steadily with age. This research estimated age of onset of depressive disorder retrospectively, which raises the question of whether or not these differences could be due to biased recall. However, similar findings were obtained by Angold and Rutter (1992) using Maudsley clinical data on around 2400 consecutive attenders at the Maudsley during the calendar years 1973 to 1982. The clinical data sheets were completed at the time of the initial presentation by a psychiatrist and contained data that allowed the investigators to define depression in several different ways: as a symptom, as a depressive syndrome, and as an ICD-9 diagnosis. The results were substantially the same for all these different definitions of depression. Until the age of 10 the rates in boys and girls were very similar, but after this age girls were between one-and-a-half to twice as likely to be depressed as boys. In this study, as in the studies of Weissman et al (1987) and Zeitlin (1986), the rates of depression in boys increased steadily with age.

POSSIBLE EXPLANATIONS FOR AGE TRENDS IN DEPRESSIVE DISORDER

At this point, it is appropriate to consider briefly the range of possible explanations for these age and sex trends in depressive disorder. One possibility is that the age changes could represent some kind of measurement artifact. For instance, it could be that there is no real increase in rates of depressive disorder, it is just easier to measure it in older subjects. Indeed, it does seem that it is more difficult to measure DSM-III-like depressive syndromes in children under the age of 10 than it is in 16-year-olds (Chapter 3). However, it is not obvious why measurement artifacts should lead to a steady increase in rates of depression after the age of 10 years or why they cause a shift in sex ratio.

Another possibility is that the age trends are linked in some way to puberty. Of course, in order to study the effects of puberty it is necessary to control for age, since age and puberty are strongly correlated. Rutter (1980) was able to do just this in the second phase of the Isle of Wight study. Boys at age 14–15 years include those who are prepubertal as well as those who have passed puberty, so it was possible to study the relationship between puberty and depression within a group of similar age. Hardly any of the prepubescent boys showed depressive feelings, whereas about one-third of the postpubertal boys did do (the pubescent boys were intermediate on these measures). The implication is that the increase in rates of depression was linked to puberty and not to age. Unfortunately, it was not possible to conduct similar comparisons for girls since almost all of them had reached puberty by the age of 15 years.

The larger sample of children with depressive disorder available to Angold and Rutter (1992) in their study of Maudsley child patients meant that they were able to examine the effects of age and puberty in both males and females (though even in this study the cell sizes for some of the analyses were rather small!). To their surprise, there was no evidence of an effect of puberty in either sex once age was controlled for. The measures of puberty available in this study were, however, very crude, and of course there are problems in interpreting data that are based entirely on referrals to a psychiatric clinic.

We shall see later that research with depressed adults has implicated hormonal changes in the aetiology of depressions occurring in the puerpurium and in association with the menstrual cycle. Moreover, abnormalities of sex hormone secretion have been found in depressive adult patients. So, it is possible that the hormonal changes experienced by girls at puberty are partly responsible for the sex difference in rates of depression. Perhaps, for instance, these changes have a direct effect on mood, or act in combination with some other factor, such as a genetic predisposition. However, Brookes-Gunn and Warren (1989) found that, although negative affect was associated with the rapid oestrogen rise that occurs during early puberty in girls, social factors were also important. Puberty is, after all, a time when there are important social changes, such as in the social network, and coincides with several other transitions, such as school transfer. It may be, for example, that the kinds of social stressors that are thought to be important in the aetiology of some adult depressions become more frequent during early adolescence.

Alternatively, the increase in rates of depression during adolescence may be due to a decrease in protective factors rather than an increase in risk factors. For instance, it seems that during early adolescence there is a marked decline in the amount of time that the young person spends with the family (Larson & Richards, 1991). Perhaps the reduction of family support associated with becoming independent makes adolescents more susceptible to stress. Or, maybe young children are protected from depression by their limited ability to experience the cognitions that some theorists consider are so important in aetiology.

Probably, there are several different factors involved. If it is the case that rates of depression rise steadily in both sexes but that the increase is more rapid in girls, then it would be necessary to postulate at least two different mechanisms. Perhaps, for instance, there is a general factor that operates in both sexes, plus an additional factor that is responsible for the sex difference in adolescence. Whatever the reasons for the age trends, on current evidence it would seem that the sex difference is well established by mid-adolescence.

AGE TRENDS IN DEPRESSION-RELATED PHENOMENA

In adults, there seems to be a strong relationship between depression and suicide. Barraclough et al (1974) found that 93 of 100 suicides were mentally ill and 64 of these had a depressive disorder uncomplicated by other serious physical or mental disorder. Similar findings were reported in St Louis by Robins et al (1959). In young people, there is also a strong association with depression. Shaffer's (1974) study of completed suicide in children under the age of 15 indicated that a substantial proportion of the victims had some features of mood disturbance. In a separate study, Shaffer (1988) reported that 21% of teenagers who committed suicide had major depression. Brent et al (1988) estimated that 63% of adolescents who committed suicide had some form of affective disorder. Similar findings were reported by Marttunen et al (1991).

So, could age differences in suicidal phenomena help us to understand age trends in depressive disorders? Suicide is very uncommon before the age of 10 but then increases steadily through puberty and adolescence. Shaffer (1986) thought that this was not simply because young children do not know how to kill themselves. He suggested that there were two possible reasons. First, many suicides take place in the context of social isolation and childhood is a time when there is usually a large network of social supports. Perhaps the adolescent's drive for individuation weakens these supportive systems and increases the vulnerability to suicide. Second, changes in the ability to experience certain cognitions may also be relevant. Hopelessness and guilt are often seen as important in the genesis of suicidal behaviour, and as described earlier there are developmental changes in the ability to experience these constructs.

However, too close an analogy between depression and suicide in young people may be misleading. Suicide occurs more often in males than in females at all ages, and does not show the switch in sex ratio during early adolescence that seems to occur in depression. In addition, suicide in adolescents is associated not only with depression but also with several other symptoms, especially behavioural problems and drug use (Brent et al, 1988; Shaffer, 1988). Moreover, any explanations of the age trends in suicide must also explain why these rates carry on increasing until they reach a peak in middle age.

Perhaps attempted suicide provides a better parallel with depression. Attempted suicide is also relatively infrequent during childhood and shows a great increase during adolescence (Hawton & Goldacre, 1982). In addition, there is a female preponderance. However, although adolescents who attempt suicide frequently have the symptom of depression, many do not meet criteria for affective disorder (Pfeffer, 1992). Clearly, then, factors other than depressive disorder are likely to be important in the aetiology of adolescent suicidal attempts.

Mania and hypomania would seem to offer a better analogy since they are strongly associated with depression in adults. However, the problems of diagnosing mania and hypomania in children are at least as difficult as those occurring in the diagnosis of depression. Probably, "classical" mania is very rare before puberty. However, whether or not *forme frustes* occur in prepubertal children is unclear. The boundaries with conditions such as attention deficit disorder and schizophrenia are not well understood (Carlson, 1990). At the moment, then, it is difficult to say much about developmental trends in mania.

SECULAR TRENDS IN DEPRESSIVE DISORDERS

Up to now we have been concerned with *age effects* on depressive disorders and depression-related phenomena; that is, with the possibility of a change in age-specific rates during the lifespan of an individual. Two other kinds of variations in rates over time exist. First, there is the *period effect*. Period effects occur when there is a change in the rate of an illness during a particular historical period. Such effects are well recognized in psychiatry, one example being the fall in rates of suicide during each of the world wars (Registrar General, 1961). Second, *cohort effects* occur when variations in rates of illness are related to some shared temporal experience, usually the year or decade of birth.

In the 1970s a number of investigators became concerned that rates of depression might be increasing, especially in the younger cohorts. Klerman (1988) summarized the observations that led to this concern. First, treatment settings were experiencing an increase in patients diagnosed as depressed. Second, patients diagnosed as depressed were younger than the textbook descriptions of depressed patients. Indeed, childhood depression was becoming a focus for attention. Third, although overall rates of suicide were falling, there seemed to be an increase in the younger groups.

There are, however, formidable technical problems in the investigation of cohort effects for depression. For instance, to separate period effects from cohort effects with an infrequent disorder like major depression requires large numbers of subjects. The ideal design would involve multiple samples from successive cohorts who would be followed up and assessed periodically using standardized assessments. Such studies would be expensive and time-consuming, but there are several strategies that can approximate to it. One of these is to use lifetime prevalence data and age of onset of depression from community samples or from family studies.

Lifetime prevalence studies

Analyses of data from these sources have suggested that there may indeed be an increase in the lifetime risk for major depressive disorder among recently born cohorts. In the Epidemiological Catchment Area Study, estimates of the lifetime prevalence of specific mental disorders were made by means of the Diagnostic Interview Schedule, which is a highly structured respondent-based interview that can be used by lay interviewers (L.N. Robins et al, 1981). Data were collected from several different sites, and in all of them it seemed that individuals born after 1936 had an earlier age of onset and higher rates of depression than those born earlier in the century (reviewed by Klerman, 1988). Similar findings have been reported in family studies of depressed adults (e.g. Klerman et al, 1985) and in studies of the relatives of depressed child probands (Ryan et al, 1992).

Several explanations have been put forward to account for these findings. For example, perhaps some kind of biological mechanism linked to puberty is operating. After all, there has been a steady decline over the past century of the mean age of menarche (Rubin, 1990). Or, it could be that the apparent increase in rates of depression among the young is linked in one way or another to social factors, such as unemployment or divorce.

Some of these possibilities will be discussed in later chapters. In the meantime it should be noted that there are also a number of measurement artifacts that could simulate these supposed cohort effects for depression. For example, selective mortality or migration of depressed young people could deflate the rates of depression in the elderly. It may also be that there has been a change in attitudes towards mental illness rather than a change in rates. Perhaps younger people are more likely to report depression than older people.

Probably the most serious methodological issue concerns the biases that may arise from relying on retrospective accounts of age of onset of depression. As described earlier, much of the evidence for an increase in major depression among the young comes from studies that have relied on retrospective accounts of previous episodes of depression. Cohorts born earlier in the century report not only lower rates of depression but also that the first episodes occur later in life than those occurring in cohorts born later in the century. It could be, however, that older subjects have more difficulty recalling events earlier in life than younger subjects, and/or when they do recall these events they tend to bring them forward in time. So, their lower rates and later ages of onset of depression arise from limitations of recall and memory.

Giuffra and Risch (1991) simulated the effects of forgetting in cohorts of up to 2000 individuals born in 1900, 1930 or 1960, and interviewed in 1990. It was assumed that subjects would "forget" previous episodes of depression at a rate proportional to the length of time since the past episode. The forgetting rate was based on data from real depressed patients who in another study had been asked to recall their index episode. Using the same methods of analysis that were used in studies finding a cohort effect, they showed that large differences between their simulated cohorts could be caused by relatively small forgetting rates.

On the other hand, Warshaw, Klerman and Lavori (1991) analysed data from a follow-up of a very large sample of relatives (about 1700 subjects) who were interviewed on two occasions about six years apart. There was good agreement on the presence of an episode of major depression before the first interview. Large secular trends were found but there was no evidence that the changes in age of onset were related to age at interview. Older relatives did not change their ages of onset more than younger relatives. Nor were they more likely than younger people to "lose" a diagnosis between the two occasions.

A further challenge to the hypothesis of cohort effects for depression arises from the finding that similar trends have been found for many other disorders when their prevalence has been assessed by retrospective "lifetime" interviews. For instance, in the ECA studies the lifetime prevalence of many disorders was higher in the youngest age groups despite the fact that they had passed through less of the age of risk than older groups. Thus, in all three of the sites of the ECA study that were reported by Robins et al (1984), the lifetime prevalence of drug abuse, antisocial personality, major depression and mania was greater in the age group 25-44 years than in the next older group. Schizophrenia and alcohol abuse had significantly higher prevalence in the younger age group in two of the three sites (Robins et al, 1984). The finding that drug abuse and dependence is high in the younger age groups is understandable given that the drug epidemic which occurred in the United States during the late 1960s affected predominantly younger age groups. However, all other things being equal the lifetime rate in the younger age groups should not exceed the rate in older cohorts. Clearly, then, there is a real possibility that these trends represent some kind of measurement artifact.

Other evidence supporting a secular trend

On the other hand, some support for the findings in respect of major depression comes from data on secular trends for suicide. Over the past 25 years suicide has become less common among middle-aged and elderly Americans but more common among the young. For instance, Shaffer (1988) estimated that among white males aged between 15 and 19 years the rate had increased from 8 per 100 000 in 1968 to nearly 16 per 100 000 in 1984. Similar trends have been found in the United Kingdom (McClure, 1984, 1986). Suicide is now the second most common cause of death among young people aged 15–24 years (OPCS, 1990). There seems to have been no change in suicide rates among young children.

Since these trends are based on coroner's records they cannot be due to recall bias. They could be the result of under-reporting of suicide in older age groups, but if anything under-reporting (as judged by the proportion of un-determined verdicts) is greater in younger age groups (Shaffer, 1986).

Shaffer (1986) reviewed some of the other possible explanations for the change in rates of suicide among the young. He considered it unlikely that a period effect was operating because the effect was so specific to the 15–29 age group. Rather, it seemed that there was a cohort effect. One possible source of this effect would be some form of environmental stress. However, one of the groups that has not shown an increase in suicide rates, young blacks from the south of the United States, will be experiencing more stress and greater employment and educational pressures than whites.

A more probable explanation, according to Shaffer (1986), would be that blacks are protected by some cultural factor. In extending this idea, he suggested that the cohort effect operates through the "release" of a propensity to commit suicide rather than through a factor that generates it. After all, suicide was until recently regarded as a profane and illegal act but is now often seen as a manifestation of mental illness. So, he concluded, we must look for factors within the individual to explain the origins of the condition.

Support for the idea that this factor is depressive illness comes from Carlson et al's study (1991) of secular trends in suicide. Psychiatric diagnoses of two cohorts of suicide victims, one from the 1950s in St Louis and the other from the early 1980s in San Diego, were compared. Depression appeared to have increased in the younger age groups, especially depression that was comorbid with substance/alcohol abuse. Unfortunately, confidence in these findings is limited by the fact that there is no way of knowing whether these differences reflect secular trends, or whether they are simply an indication of geographical differences in the causes of suicide.

The final piece of evidence for a secular trend in depression comes from the long-term prospective Lundby study in Sweden, from 1947 to 1972 (Hagnell et al, 1982). Rates increased in the most recent period for depression associated with mild or medium impairment, but *not* for the most severe psychotic type of depression. An elevated incidence was noticed among subjects in the age range 20–39 years, with a sharper rise for men than women.

CONCLUSIONS

Epidemiological studies of depression among the young are still difficult to interpret because of differing definitions of "caseness" and variations in sampling procedures between studies. Nevertheless, when analysis is restricted to recent studies using DSM-III criteria, then the point prevalence of major depression among *children* has generally been found to fall in the range 0.5–

2.5%. Epidemiological studies of *adolescents* have generally reported higher rates of depressive disorder than among preadolescents, with most investigators finding current rates in the range 2.0–8.0%. Studies that have examined *both* preadolescents and adolescents have generally confirmed that there is an increase in rates of depression with age. Interestingly, it seems that among depressed children the sex ratio is about equal, but by adolescence the female preponderance found in adult depression becomes evident. The numbers of depressed cases in community samples have been too small to allow accurate estimates of the age at which the switch of sex ratio occurs. Data from several other sources suggest that the switch occurs at around the age of 10 years. There are also strong age trends for depression-related phenomena, such as suicide and parasuicide. Possible reasons for these age trends and sex differences include measurement artifacts, an increase in risk factors and a decline in protective factors. However, apart from age trends and sex differences, the correlates of depressive disorder have been found to vary from study to study.

There is some evidence that depressive disorder is becoming more common among the young. Most of the evidence comes from retrospective accounts of age of onset, and may therefore be unreliable. However, some support for a real increase in the incidence of depression in this age group comes from changes in the rates of suicide. Certainly, both depression and suicide are becoming an increasing cause for concern among professionals dealing with young people.

Chapter 5

Overlap with other Disorders

Many people will find it surprising that the prevalence estimates for major depression that were described in the previous chapter were so high. However, it should be borne in mind that in most of these studies the diagnosis of depressive disorder was made without a diagnostic hierarchy. In other words, although these children met the criteria for major depression (see Chapter 1) it was perfectly possible for them to have many other psychiatric diagnoses as well. Indeed, as we shall see in the present chapter, it seems the *majority* of children who are diagnosed as having a depressive disorder also meet the criteria for one or more nondepressive diagnoses.

The co-occurrence or comorbidity of depression with other disorders raises fundamental questions about the validity of the concept of depressive disorder among the young. For example, is it better to regard children suffering from major depression and conduct disorder as primarily depressed, and therefore perhaps needing antidepressants, or as conduct disordered, and therefore perhaps in need of behaviour therapy? Or, should such children be treated as having both depression and conduct disorder?

This chapter will describe the overlap of depression and other conditions. It is divided into two parts:

1. A description of the level and types of comorbidity of juvenile depression in both clinical and epidemiological samples.
2. A discussion of the possible reasons for comorbidity.

OVERLAP OF DEPRESSION AND OTHER DIAGNOSES IN REFERRED SAMPLES

The overlap of depression and other psychiatric diagnoses has been one of the most consistent findings from research in clinical populations, where an association has been found with conditions as diverse as conduct disorder (Puig-Antich, 1982; Marriage et al, 1986), anxiety states (Bernstein & Garfinkel, 1986, 1988; Puig-Antich & Rabinovich, 1986; Mitchell et al, 1988), and learning problems (Weinberg & Rehmet, 1983). Indeed, the majority of children who meet criteria for depressive disorder are given some other diagnosis by the clinicians involved in their care (Harrington et al, 1990).

Anxiety disorders

The most prevalent comorbid diagnoses are the anxiety disorders, especially separation anxiety. Ryan et al (1987) found that moderate to severe separation anxiety disorder occurred in 58% of children and 37% of adolescents with depressive disorders, a significant difference. Moderate to severe phobias with avoidance were found in 45% of children and 27% of adolescents. Mitchell et al (1988) reported similarly high rates of separation anxiety disorder in children (42%) and adolescents with depression, though there was no significant difference between the two age periods.

Strauss et al (1988) found that nearly 30% of their anxiety disorder patients had major depression. In a large sample of school refusers, Bernstein (1991) found that around 50% of adolescent school refusers were depressed. Kolvin, Berney and Bhate (1984) reported that 45% of school refusers had significant depression.

Conduct disorders

The other group of disorders that commonly occur in conjunction with depressive conditions are the conduct disorders. Numerous studies have suggested that conduct problems are prominent in the clinical presentation of depression in young people. Indeed, antisocial behaviour was seen as one of the most frequent "masks" of depression (Cytryn & McKnew, 1972) in the days when "masked" depression was a popular concept. More recently, it has become clear that it is not necessary to evoke the idea of "masks"; careful clinical examination will usually provide a clear answer as to whether or not a child presenting with conduct symptoms also has a depressive syndrome (Puig-Antich, 1982; Kolvin et al, 1991). As might be expected, reports of the frequency of conduct symptoms in depressed children seen in clinical settings have varied. However, most studies of referrals to psychiatric clinics have suggested that between 15% and 35% of depressed children have conduct disorder.

Thus, for example, one of the first systematic studies of the relationship between depression and conduct disorder in children found that more than a third (37%) of 43 prepubertal boys with major depression referred to a child depression clinic had conduct disorder (Puig-Antich, 1982). Marriage et al (1986) reported that of 60 children and adolescents referred for possible depression, 33 received DSM-III diagnoses of affective disorder and 11 of these also had conduct disorder. Mitchell et al (1988) found 26% of depressed preadolescent boys had conduct disorder, although the rate of conduct disorder was lower among adolescent boys (10%). In one of the largest clinical studies of the phenomenology of child and adolescent depressive disorders, Ryan et al (1987) also found that the overlap of depression and conduct disorder was a little less in the older age groups. Mild conduct problems were present in 38% of children and 25% of adolescents. Conduct disorder of sufficient severity to have substantial disruptive effects on social functioning was present in 16% of children and 11% of adolescents.

Overlap with other disorders

Depressive disorders also occur in conjunction with a variety of other disorders. Thus, several studies have documented an association with substance abuse, though as might be expected such problems are more common among older depressed children. Ryan et al (1987) found that 18% of adolescents with depression used soft drugs at least occasionally, whereas none of the prepubertal children had. Similarly, 7% of adolescents and 2% of children reported drinking alcohol about once a week. Greenbaum et al (1991) studied the prevalence of substance abuse (alcohol or marijuana) among 547 adolescents, aged 12–18 years, who had been identified through either mental health or school systems as having severe emotional disturbances. The findings were striking in showing that, even after controlling for other factors, depression was one of the disorders that was most strongly associated with substance abuse. Nearly one-half of children with severe depression also had substance abuse. Milin et al (1991) studied the prevalence of psychopathology among juvenile offenders: 18% of those adolescents who abused either drugs or alcohol met DSM-III criteria for some form of depressive disorder, compared with 5% in those who did not abuse substances.

Although only a small proportion of depressed subjects meet criteria for anorexia nervosa, the overlap of these two disorders is noteworthy because of the high rates of affective disorders among subjects with eating disorders. Reports of the frequency of depressive disorder among subjects with eating disorder vary, but the studies have been consistent in suggesting that the rates are high (between 25% and 80%: Strober & Katz, 1987).

Findings regarding the degree of overlap of depressive disorder and attention deficit disorder have been less consistent (Biederman, Newcorn & Sprich, 1991). Carlson and Cantwell (1980b) found that 7 out of 28 children with affective disorder had had hyperactivity before the onset of the depression. McClellan et al (1990) pointed out that several investigators have found an increase in attention deficit disorder in the children of depressed mothers. Weissman et al (1987), for instance, reported that attention deficit disorder was the second most common disorder in the children of depressed mothers. On the other hand, neither Ryan et al (1987) nor Mitchell et al (1988) make any mention of the occurrence of attention deficit disorder among children and adolescents with major depression.

OVERLAP WITH PSYCHIATRIC DISORDERS IN COMMUNITY SAMPLES

It will be appreciated that apparent comorbidity between child psychiatric disorders in referred samples may be artifactual, as a result of referral biases. For instance, a clinician who has a particular interest in cases showing co-morbidity is more likely to be referred such cases. Moreover, as discussed earlier, for statistical reasons rates of comorbidity in clinical samples will be greater than those in community samples (Berkson's bias).

In view of this it is perhaps surprising that only about a half of recent general population studies measured nonaffective diagnoses (Fleming & Offord, 1990). Nonetheless, the available epidemiological data suggest that the co-occurrence of depression and other child psychiatric disorders far exceeds that expected by chance. J. Anderson et al (1987), for example, found that of 14 children (aged 11 years) with depressive disorders, 11 had at least one other psychiatric condition as well. Indeed 8 of the 14 children had depression and an anxiety disorder and an attention deficit disorder and a conduct disorder! McGee et al (1990) reported on this sample at age 15 years; the greatest degree of comorbidity was present in the case of affective disorders. Almost two-thirds of the 40 adolescents with a depressive disorder had a coexisting psychiatric condition. A high comorbidity rate was also found in the study of Kashani et al (1987), who reported that none of the 12 cases of depression was "pure". Similarly, Fleming, Offord and Boyle (1989) reported that 96% of subjects with depression (at a high level of diagnostic certainty) had either conduct disorder, hyperactivity, emotional disorder or somatization.

A slightly lower rate of comorbidity was reported by Rohde, Lewinsohn and Seeley (1991) who found that 42% of adolescents currently had at least one comorbid diagnosis. This report from the Oregon epidemiological project also included data about depressed adults. Confidence in the adolescent–adult comparison is somewhat reduced by high rates of nonparticipation in both groups and the use of different diagnostic criteria (RDC with adults and DSM-III-R with adolescents; see Lewinsohn et al, 1991). Nevertheless, the results were striking in showing that the likelihood that an adult currently had an additional psychiatric disorder (8%) was considerably lower than for an adolescent (42%).

In general, the pattern of comorbidity in epidemiological studies has been similar to that found in referred samples. That is, the greatest degree of overlap occurs with the anxiety disorders and conduct or oppositional disorder. Several community studies have found the rate of conduct disorder among depressed young people was similar to that found for anxiety disorders. Thus, McGee et al (1990) reported that one-third of depressed adolescents had conduct disorder and one-third an anxiety disorder. Kashani et al (1987) reported that 10/12 cases of depression had conduct/oppositional disorder and 9/12 had an anxiety disorder. These findings are slightly different from those found in most clinical studies, where among depressed children the rate of anxiety disorders has generally exceeded the rate of conduct disorders (e.g. Ryan et al, 1987; Kolvin et al, 1991).

Less is known about the degree of overlap with other child psychiatric problems in community surveys. The finding that substance abuse occurs in around one-quarter of depressed adolescents (Kashani et al, 1987) supports the results of studies of clinical samples. J. Anderson et al (1987) found much overlap of depression and attention deficit disorder among children (see above). However, McGee et al (1990) were unable to replicate these findings when the same sample was seen again in adolescence, in spite of the fact that attention deficit disorder was still very prevalent. Only one out of 20 cases of attention deficit disorder had an additional depressive diagnosis.

POSSIBLE EXPLANATIONS FOR COMORBIDITY

The extent of the overlap between depression and other child psychiatric problems raises fundamental questions about the validity of the diagnosis in this age group. Indeed, it could be argued that since depression usually occurs in conjunction with some other psychiatric condition it might be better to dispense with the concept altogether and instead to diagnose the comorbid disorder. Alternatively, perhaps mixed states of depression and some other psychiatric disorder should be assigned to a separate diagnostic category. This is an important issue because until we know how to deal with these mixed clinical pictures in classification schemes it will be difficult to identify homogeneous groups with respect to aetiology, treatment responsiveness, or prognosis.

Clearly, then, it is important to consider the range of possible explanations for comorbidity. These may be divided into three principal groups (Caron & Rutter, 1991): (1) artifacts of detection, (2) artifacts arising from nosological considerations, and (3) explanations of true comorbidity.

Detection artifacts

These have already been touched on at various parts of this book. *Referral factors* are likely to be very important in child psychiatric samples, since relatively few cases of disorder in the community actually come to see a psychiatrist. However, it is very unlikely that such factors could explain the overlap of depression and other psychiatric problems since this overlap has repeatedly been found in community samples. Indeed, if anything the degree of overlap of depression with other disorders is actually a little greater in community surveys.

As described in Chapter 3, *detection biases* may occur when broad-band questionnaires are used to select subjects for subsequent interview during two-stage epidemiological surveys. This procedure will tend to miss cases with monosymptomatic disorders since such cases will have a relatively low score on the broad-band questionnaire. However, this is unlikely to be a major problem in the interpretation of community surveys of juvenile depression, since up to now most studies that have assessed comorbidity have used one-stage strategies.

A related problem concerns the extent to which the diagnoses made at interview in these surveys have been made independently. Perhaps some kind of *'halo' effect* was operating such that having one diagnosis increased the chances of having another. For instance, since the comorbid diagnoses were made by the same interviewer it may be that in some cases comorbidity was simply the result of the interviewer imposing his or her preconceptions on the ratings.

It is difficult to be certain about the degree to which the kinds of detection biases described above could have inflated the observed rates of comorbidity in studies of depression. However, it was very unlikcly that they constitute the complete explanation because high rates of comorbidity have been such a consistent finding across studies using very diverse methodologies.

Nosological considerations

As Caron and Rutter pointed out, the concept of comorbidity implies the co-occurrence of two independent disorders. So, another source of difficulty in the study of comorbidity arises from the possibility that the nosological concepts may themselves be mistaken. One type of nosological confusion arises from the fact that the same symptom appears in the list of diagnostic criteria for several supposedly separate diagnostic categories. The problem of *overlapping diagnostic criteria* is most immediately obvious in the comorbidity of major depression and anorexia nervosa. Many of the symptoms of starvation, such as loss of energy, decreased concentration and reduced libido, closely resemble the accessory symptoms of major depressive disorder. There is also some overlap of the DSM-III-R criteria for major depressive disorder and generalized anxiety disorder. The same or similar symptoms (restlessness, easy fatigability, difficulty concentrating and irritability) appear in both disorders. And, of course, the two main DSM-III-R depressive diagnoses, major depression and dysthymia, have very many symptoms in common.

It is not surprising that many disorders should share symptoms, especially those items of behaviour that are rather nonspecific indicators of psychopathology. Indeed, in general medicine there are many examples of symptoms that occur across a range of different and otherwise well validated disorders. Nevertheless, the overlap of symptoms will undoubtedly lead to some degree of artifactual comorbidity. It is unlikely, however, that overlapping diagnostic criteria can adequately explain the overlap of juvenile depression and its main comorbid diagnoses, separation anxiety disorder and conduct disorder. Neither of these disorders is defined by criteria that closely resemble those for major depression.

An altogether more substantial challenge to the notion of comorbidity arises from the possibility that the basic conceptual nature of our nosological schemes is misconceived. Most studies conducted up to now have conceived comorbidity between depression and other child psychiatric disorders as the co-occurrence of two independent *categories*. However, it could be that the concept of disorder categories is itself misconceived. Indeed, it may be that psychopathology is best thought of as the extreme of a *continuous dimension*, rather than as a discrete category. According to this viewpoint, there is no qualitative cut-off point but rather quantitative variations along the range of behavioural dimensions. Apparent comorbidity is simply the result of the fact that some individuals will inevitably have high scores on two dimensions (Caron & Rutter, 1991).

One strategy to compare the validity of categorical and dimensional approaches would be to determine if a behavioural dimension related to one diagnostic category functioned as a risk factor for another condition at levels below the diagnostic threshold. Robins and McEvoy (1990), for example, found that conduct problems predicted substance abuse at all levels of severity. The implication was that conduct problems should be thought of as a continuous dimension. To date, few studies have taken this approach to the study of comorbidity in childhood depression. However, data from our study of the overlap of childhood depression and conduct disorder support a categorical view of comorbidity. Thus, children with one or two conduct symptoms had a prognosis that was very similar to that of children without conduct problems, and significantly different on most measures from that of children with three or more conduct problems (Harrington et al, 1991). A categorical approach that assumed comorbidity between two separate disorders seemed to account for the findings better than a dimensional one.

A related issue concerns the extent to which the findings could be the result of a nonspecific increase in severity along a single dimension or entity rather than the true overlap of two disorders or dimensions. This could occur because severe conditions with many symptoms will necessarily have a greater chance of meeting criteria for more than one disorder than mild conditions with few symptoms. One test of this possibility would be to see whether or not correlates of the disorders, such as social impairment or adverse outcomes, increased linearly with severity. In our study of depression and conduct disorder (Harrington et al, 1991) there were some cross-sectional data to support this view. Thus, it seemed that children with depression and conduct disorder had greater problems with social relationships than children with depression alone (though the differences just failed to reach significance). Moreover, children with depression and conduct disorder were significantly more hand-icapped at the time of discharge than children with "pure" depression.

On the other hand, if the results were simply a reflection of a single underlying dimension of increasingly severe psychiatric problems, then an increase in all forms of adult psychiatric disorder would be expected. The finding in our research that adult depressive disorders tended to be *less common* among children with depression and conduct disorder than among children with "pure" depression suggests that the results cannot entirely be explained by the confounding of severity and comorbidity (Harrington et al, 1991). So, the longitudinal data suggest that depression and conduct disorder are better conceptualized as independent entities or disorders rather than as being on the same continuum.

A dimensional approach that assumes there is a continuum of increasing severity may, however, provide a better model when the relationship between depression and anxiety is considered. Several studies have found that children with depressive disorder and anxiety disorder tend to have more severe forms of the disorders than those with a single disorder alone. For example, Mitchell et al (1988) reported that depressed young people with comorbid separation anxiety rated many of their depressive symptoms higher in severity than young people with depressive disorder alone. They were also more likely to show an endogenous symptom pattern. Similarly, Strauss and colleagues (1988) demonstrated a significantly increased severity of anxiety symptomatology in anxiety disorder patients with major depression compared with patients with anxiety disorder only. Bernstein (1991) found that children and adolescents with school refusal who met criteria for both anxiety and depressive disorders scored higher than patients with anxiety alone or depression alone on all anxiety and depression scales. These findings are in line with clinical studies of adults with major depression and anxiety disorder (e.g. Bronisch & Hecht, 1990).

This idea of a continuum of increasing severity assumes that depression and anxiety are more or less equally placed on the continuum. However, another "unidimensional" way of looking at these two conditions is as *different underlying phases of the same disorder* (Brady & Kendall, 1992). Thus, for example, Kovacs et al (1989) found that among cases of childhood depression with a comorbid anxiety disorder the anxiety disorder preceded the depression about two-thirds of the time and often persisted after the depression had remitted. Psychopathology in the mother increased the risk of anxiety disorder in the child. On the basis of these findings Kovacs et al (1989) proposed that, during the time a child is more dependent on maternal care, a pattern of maternal unavailability and inconsistency may "threaten the child's sense of stable attachment", which in turn leads to anxiety and depression. They felt that the finding of anxiety preceding depression in many cases supported

Bowlby's ideas on the chronology of the two conditions (Bowlby, 1980). Puig-Antich and Rabinovitch (1986) also observed that in many cases it seemed as if the depression was superimposed on the anxiety rather than the anxiety on the depression. On the other hand, Geller et al (1985) found that separation anxiety disorder began after the onset of the depression in about four-fifths of cases.

Possible explanations of true comorbidity

If it is assumed that apparent comorbidity of depression and other problems is not due to the kinds of artifacts described above, then a number of possible explanations of "true" comorbidity need to be considered. The first is that the overlapping disorders *share risk factors*, such as a family history of psychiatric disorder or environmental adversity. Thus, family history studies comparing child probands with anxiety disorders with child probands with depressive disorders indicate no differences between these groups in respect of rates of psychiatric disorders among relatives. For example, Livingston et al (1985) found very high rates of psychiatric disorders among the relatives of anxious and the relatives of depressed children, mostly depression and alcoholism. The family histories of the two groups were similar, suggesting that childhood depressive and anxiety disorders may be familially related. Similarly, Goodyer, Wright and Altham (1988) found that depressed children and anxious children were equally likely to have experienced environmental adversity of one kind or another.

Another possibility is that *the disorders have different risk factors but these factors are correlated*. For instance, Caron et al (1992) suggested that the association of depression and conduct disorder might be due to the association of depression and marital discord, which is much more common when a parent is depressed (Rutter & Quinton, 1984). Comorbidity of depression and conduct disorder arises because parental depression is associated both with a genetic risk for depression in offspring and with marital discord, which in turn leads to conduct disorder.

A third possibility is that *one disorder increases the risk of the other*. For example, perhaps conduct disorder increases the likelihood of later adverse experiences, which in turn lead to depression. Robins (1966), for example, showed that conduct disorder in childhood was often followed by marital breakdown and unemployment in adulthood. Alternatively, perhaps prolonged depression eventually leads to anxiety or to conduct problems.

A fourth possibility is that the *comorbid pattern constitutes a meaningful syndrome*. The two main diagnostic systems, DSM-III-R and ICD-10, take different approaches to this issue. In the DSM, there are no separate categories for conditions characterized by two problems. Rather, it is assumed that comorbidity between, say, depression and conduct disorder represents the co-occurrence of separate conditions. The implication is that the presence of comorbidity does not alter the meaning of either of the two disorders.

By contrast, in ICD-10, comorbid states showing a mixture of depression and conduct problems are separately coded as "depressive conduct disorder". Here, the assumption is that a mixed clinical picture is more likely to mean a single disorder with varied manifestations, rather than two different disorders that happen to occur in the same individual at the same time. The implication is that one or other of the problems will have a different meaning when the problems occur together.

In our follow-up study of depressed children (Harrington et al, 1991) the findings in respect of adult antisocial outcomes seemed to support the position that is implicit in DSM-III-R. The presence of depression during the index episode appeared to have little effect on the long-term course of the conduct disorder. The antisocial outcomes of depressed children with conduct disorder were very similar to those of nondepressed children with conduct disorder. These data are consistent with the findings of Kovacs and her colleagues (1988) who reported that depressed children who had ever had a conduct disorder were more likely to have had antisocial problems during the follow-up interval than depressed children without CD.

When depressive outcomes were considered, however, a different picture emerged. There was a strong trend for children with depression and conduct disorder to have *lower* rates of major depression in adulthood than depressed children without conduct problems. This trend just failed to reach significance at the 5% level, but it was notable that there was a four-fold difference between these groups in the cumulative probabilities of major adult depression. By contrast, the difference between the comorbid group and the "pure" conduct disorder group was not only a nonsignificant one but also trivial in absolute terms. Moreover, further support for the distinction between "pure" depression and "depressive conduct disorder" comes from the family-history study of Puig-Antich et al (1989). These authors found that children with conduct disorder and major depression had significantly lower rates of depression and alcoholism among relatives than depressed children without conduct disorder.

It is important to note that our longitudinal study and the family study of Puig-Antich et al (1989) were both based on relatively small numbers. A strong case exists, therefore, for replicating these studies with larger samples. Nonetheless, it was striking that these different forms of inquiry, in different places, and using different research methods, gave similar results. Children with depression and conduct disorder seemed to differ from children with "pure" depression in respect of both longitudinal and familial correlates. If future research should confirm the reality of these differences then the implication would be that mixed states of depression and conduct disorder should either be assigned to a separate diagnostic category or classified together with the conduct disorders. They are incompatible with the hypothesis that the conduct disturbance is part of the depression.

The picture looks rather different when the overlap of depression and anxiety is considered. Thus, for example, preliminary analyses of our child to adult follow-up data have indicated that children with depression and anxiety cannot be distinguished from children with depression and no anxiety either in terms of rates of depression in adulthood or in terms of rates of anxiety disorders. Similar findings were reported by Kovacs et al (1989) who found that comorbid anxiety disorder did not seem to affect the risk of subsequent depression in children with major depression.

Once again the longitudinal data are consistent with the family history findings of Puig-Antich et al (1989). These authors reported that comorbid separation anxiety in children with major depression was not associated with any significant differences in familial rates of any diagnosis except for "other" psychiatric disorders in second-degree relatives.

The implication is that comorbid anxiety disorder has a different meaning from comorbid conduct disorder. Comorbid conduct disorder seems to indicate a nonfamilial form of childhood depression that is relatively transient, and is seldom followed by major depression in adulthood. Comorbid anxiety disorder appears to have little impact on either familial aggregation or long-term prognosis, though it does seem to indicate a more severe form of child psychiatric problem. We can tentatively conclude that, although children with "depressive conduct disorder" still need to be identified as a separate group, the data do not yet justify the separation of a group with "depressive anxiety disorder".

Finally, however, it is worth noting that these research strategies for investigating comorbidity rely on the presence of correlates that are fairly strongly associated with the "pure" disorders. Since both depression and conduct disorder have been shown to have predictive validity in terms of course and familial correlates (see later), it is possible to use these features to examine the meaning of the mixed state. The findings regarding anxiety disorders are, however, more difficult to interpret. For example, preliminary analyses of our adult follow-up data show that childhood anxiety disorders have less powerful longitudinal associations than either depressive disorder or conduct disorder. So, the failure to establish differences between the mixed group and the "pure" groups could simply be the result of a lack of validity of the measures in respect of anxiety disorders. This is not a new problem. For many years, one of the great difficulties in the study of childhood anxiety disorders has been the lack of a specific correlate that can be used to study links with other conditions. For example, studies of the families of school-phobic children have produced inconsistent findings regarding the familial rates of anxiety diagnoses (Bernstein & Borchardt, 1991). Similarly, though childhood emotional disorders do show some persistence into adulthood, most children with emotional disturbance become psychiatrically normal adults (Rutter, 1988b). By contrast, conduct disorders show a consistent pattern of links with sociopathy in adulthood (Robins, 1991). Moreover, they have repeatedly been found to be associated with problems in the home environment, such as marital discord and a broken home, and with a family history of criminality and alcoholism (Robins, 1991). It remains to be seen whether research into the anxiety disorders will identify a correlate that will be as robust as course and family factors have been in conduct disorder. Such a correlate would greatly assist the investigation of comorbid cases.

OVERLAP WITH MEDICAL CONDITIONS

Depressive disorders overlap not only with other psychiatric diagnoses but also with physical disorders. For instance, Ling, Oftedal and Weinberg (1970) studied 25 children referred for diagnostic evaluation of headache: 40% met criteria for depression, and many of these showed an improvement in both mood and headache when treated with antidepressants. Garber, Zeman and Walker (1990) studied children with recurrent abdominal pain with no identifiable organic cause, children with an organic diagnosis for their abdominal pain, children with psychiatric disorders and healthy normal controls. Both groups of children with abdominal pain had significantly more psychiatric disorders (mostly depression and anxiety) than did the physically healthy group.

It may be that the factors leading to depression in physically ill children are similar to those occurring in healthy children. Burke et al (1990) suggested that depression in children with organic bowel disorders was likely to be the result of an interaction with social factors and familial predisposition to depression. Children with inflammatory bowel disease (IBD) who became depressed had more life events and experienced more family conflict than did nondepressed children with IBD.

Clearly, then, symptoms of depression are not uncommon in children presenting with physical illness. It should be borne in mind, however, that somatic complaints may also be a symptom of depression. For example, Ryan et al (1987) reported that somatic complaints were very common among both children and adolescents with major depressive disorder. Larsson (1991) found a high correlation between scores on a somatic symptom checklist and the BDI. Tiredness, headache and sleep problems were most strongly associated with depression. Children with unexplained physical symptoms therefore require careful assessment in order to determine whether or not they are depressed.

Since depression and anxiety commonly co-occur the question arises as to whether the somatic symptoms are linked more to the depression or more to the anxiety. McCauley, Carlson and Calderon (1991) found that 70% of children who met criteria for depression had somatic complaints and that the frequency of the somatic complaints increased with the severity of the depression, regardless of coexisting anxiety. These data suggest that somatic complaints are more strongly associated with depression than with anxiety.

COMORBIDITY: CONCLUDING REMARKS

The co-occurrence of depressive disorders and other psychiatric conditions is now established in both clinical and community samples. This overlap has important implications both for our classification systems and for our understanding of aetiology. In recent years some progress has been made in differentiating between the various explanations for comorbidity, with perhaps the most important finding being that the meaning of comorbidity seems to depend greatly on the type of comorbid diagnosis. In particular, mixed states of depression and anxiety seem to have a different meaning from mixed states of depression and conduct disorder. At the moment, the available data suggest that children with depression and conduct disorder need to be distinguished from children with "pure" depression. One of the challenges for the future will be to see whether or not children with depression and anxiety have more in common with children with "pure" depression or children with "pure" anxiety.

Chapter 6

Predisposing and Precipitating Factors

The aetiology of depressive disorders is usually regarded as being multifactorial, implying genetic, sociological and psychological antecedents. In adult psychiatry, a distinction has traditionally been made between those factors that increase the individual's *vulnerability* to depression, such as early adverse experiences or personality, and factors that *precipitate* an episode of depression at a particular time. We shall see later that when the aetiology of depressive conditions among the young is considered, a straightforward downward extension of these models developed with adult cases is not always adequate. For example, many acute events in childhood occur in the context of long-standing adversity. Indeed, in depressed children acute "precipitating" events are so commonly interwoven with long-standing adversities, family problems and personality features (Hammen, 1991) that at times the distinction between them becomes very blurred. Nevertheless, this distinction between predisposing and precipitating factors does provide a useful way of thinking about the mechanisms that are involved in the aetiology of childhood depression, and so it will be retained here.

This chapter, then, is divided into two parts:

1. Consideration of the factors that seem to make the individual vulnerable to depressive disorder.
2. A look at the events that can precipitate an episode.

PARENTAL DEPRESSIVE DISORDER

There are three main reasons for thinking that depressive illness in parents may be an important risk factor for depressive disorder in children. First, studies of depressed adults have suggested that adult depressive disorders are often familial, and some varieties have an important genetic component. Second, family studies of depressed children indicate that there are high rates of psychiatric disorders among relatives. Third, the children of depressed parents are at risk for a variety of psychiatric disorders, including depressive conditions.

Family-genetic factors in adult affective disorders

Although methods and samples have varied a great deal, one of the most consistent findings from studies of adults has been that affective disorders tend to be familial (Gershon et al, 1982; Andreasen et al, 1987). Familial aggregation does not of course necessarily imply genetic mechanisms. Both environmental and genetic factors may be important in the familial loading of depression, since psychosocial adversities as well as depression tend to aggre- gate in families (McGuffin et al, 1988). Moreover, depressive conditions in adults are probably a heterogeneous group of disorders. For example, it seems that unipolar and bipolar disorders have different patterns of familial transmission (Perris, 1982).

Nevertheless there is now well replicated evidence from twin and adoption studies of a major genetic component in the bipolar disorders. For instance, McGuffin and Katz (1986) estimated an 86% heritability for manic– depressive illness based on data from several twin studies. Mild "neurotic" types of unipolar depression appear to have weaker, though still significant, heritability (McGuffin, 1991; Kendler et al, 1992). Thus, for example, McGuffin and Katz (1986) estimated a heritability of just 8% for milder depressions seen in outpatients.

Advances in molecular biology have been used to determine whether the severe forms of bipolar affective disorder are linked to genetic markers. The assumption is that there is a single major gene for affective disorder. Early findings from an examination of a large Amish family suggested that severe affective disorders might be linked with a marker on chromosome 11 (Ege- land et al, 1987). However, a study of a more extended pedigree did not confirm the linkage nor has it been confirmed in other samples (reviewed by Baron, Endicott and Ott, 1990). The validity and generalizability of the Amish findings therefore remains uncertain.

Age at onset and familial loading

It will be appreciated that since all these studies have been concerned with adult probands, their relevance to child and adolescent depressions may be limited. In fact, however, several family studies of depressed adults have suggested that early onset of depression is associated with an *increased* famil- ial loading (Mendlewicz & Baron, 1981; Weissman et al, 1984b; Strober, 1992a). For instance, Weissman et al (1984b) found that an onset before the age of 20 years was associated with a markedly increased familial loading of depression, whereas there was no increased familial loading when the onset was after the age of 40 years. The same research group also found that the onset of major depression in the offspring of depressed probands was several years earlier than in the offspring of controls. The children of probands with an onset of major depression under the age of 20 years had a risk of developing major depression under the age of 15 years that was 14 times that of controls (Weissman et al, 1988)!

Family studies of child and adolescent depressive disorders

Two kinds of family studies have been used to investigate rates of illness among the relatives of depressed child and adolescent probands: family history studies (which rely on information provided by a key informant) and family interview studies (which involve direct interview of the proband's relatives). Several family history studies have reported high rates of affective disorder in the first-degree relatives (FDRs) of depressed child probands. In an uncontrolled family study of 20 children with major affective disorders, Dwyer and Delong (1987) found that two-thirds of the parents had similar disorders. Livingston et al (1985) compared 127 relatives of 12 anxious and 11 depressed probands: 72% of the sample received family history RDC diagnoses, most commonly depression and alcoholism, but the family histories of the two groups were similar. More recently, Kutcher and Marton (1991) obtained family history data on the first-degree relatives (parents and siblings) of adolescent patients with bipolar disorders or unipolar disorders, and normal controls. The rate of bipolar illness in the FDRs of bipolar patients was 15%, significantly higher than in the FDRs of the unipolar probands or the controls. The rate of unipolar depression in the FDRs of both bipolar and unipolar adolescent probands was significantly higher than in the FDRs of the controls.

Family history studies will tend to underestimate rates of psychiatric disorders among relatives. However, family interview studies have broadly confirmed the finding that there are high rates of affective disorders among the relatives of depressed children. Puig-Antich et al (1989) compared 48 probands aged 6–12 years with a major depressive disorder, 20 probands with anxiety disorders and 27 normal controls. Systematic interview data were obtained on about half of the FDRs. Major depression and alcoholism were about twice as common in the first-degree relatives of children with depression as in the other two groups. Mitchell et al (1989) also found that alcoholism was more common among the relatives of depressed child probands than among the relatives of nondepressed child psychiatric patients, but did not find a significantly increased rate of depression among these relatives.

The finding in these two studies that an early onset of depression was associated with an increased rate of alcoholism among relatives is consistent with the results of several studies of depression in adults. For instance, Winokur (1979) found an excess of alcoholism among the relatives of probands with an early onset of depression. He therefore proposed that there was a subtype of depressive disorder, called "depressive spectrum disease", which was characterized by early onset and a family history of affective disorder, alcoholism and antisocial personality. Puig-Antich et al (1989) suggested that a similar constellation ran in the families of depressed child probands. However, other family studies have produced findings that conflict with these suggestions. For instance, Merikangas et al (1985) reported that depressed subjects without alcoholism did not transmit alcoholism.

One of the problems with many of the family history and family interview studies of childhood depression conducted up to now has been that none of them have achieved close matching between the depressed and control groups. This issue is important because, as we saw in the previous chapter, depression in young people tends to occur in conjunction with many other child psychiatric problems such as anxiety states and conduct disorders. The question therefore arises as to whether or not the familial aggregation of disorders in the relatives is a function of the depression in the proband, or whether it might be better explained by these other nondepressive diagnoses. An additional methodological issue relates to the fact that all these studies have, understandably, investigated relatives when the probands were still young. The problem is that many of the first-degree relatives (i.e. the siblings) will not have entered the peak period of risk for the disorders in question or will have been at risk for a few years only.

In an attempt to overcome these methodological issues, Harrington et al (1992) conducted a family interview study that was based on an 18-year follow-up of depressed children into adulthood. The clinical data summaries of Maudsley child patients attending during the years 1968 to 1972 were used to identify a group of 80 children meeting operational criteria for depression, together with 80 closely matched controls. At follow-up, on average 18 years after the initial contact, information was obtained on the adult outcomes of 62 depressed subjects and 69 controls. The first-degree relatives of these pro-bands were deemed "in scope" for a family interview study of rates of lifetime psychiatric disorders. The lifetime prevalence of RDC depression was significantly higher (nearly double) in the 128 interviewed relatives of the childhood depressed subjects than in the 151 relatives of the child psychiatric controls. Higher rates of depression were found among the female relatives of both the depressed and control probands. These findings suggest that there *is* some specificity in the familial aggregation of affective disorder in the relatives of depressed young people. Moreover, the finding of a female preponderance among affectively ill relatives is consistent with the results of family studies of depressed adults (e.g. McGuffin et al, 1988).

Studies of early-onset bipolar disorder

In line with family studies of unipolar adult patients, family studies of bipolar adults have suggested that early onset is associated with an increased familial loading. Strober (1992a) reviewed eight studies that had reported rates of major affective disorder among relatives of probands with bipolar disorders and which had provided separate estimates for early and late onset of illness. In six of these studies the relatives of early-onset bipolar probands were at increased risk for the development of affective disorder compared with late-onset probands.

It might therefore be expected that adolescence-onset cases would have particularly high rates of affective disorders among relatives. Some evidence in support of this proposition comes from the systematic family interview study conducted by Strober et al (1988) on cases of bipolar disorder and schizophrenia admitted to an adolescent unit. Major affective disorder was found in 30% of the first-degree relatives of bipolar probands compared with 4% of those of schizophrenic probands. The corresponding figures for bipolar disorder were 15% and 0%. These rates are somewhat higher than those reported in studies of adult probands with bipolar disorders. The familial loading for major affective disorder was greater when the bipolar disorder in the proband was preceded by symptoms before the age of 12 years.

Children of parents with depressive disorders

So, the findings from "bottom-up" studies of juvenile probands with affective conditions suggest that, like their adult counterparts, these cases have increased familial rates of affective disorders. However, it is also necessary to know whether this association applies "top-down". That is, do depressed parents have children who have increased rates of depression?

It has been recognized for many years that parental mental disorder is a risk factor for psychopathology in children, but it was not until relatively recently that much attention was paid to the offspring of depressed parents. Early studies suggested that these children were at high risk for psychiatric disorders and impairment, but they were limited by methodological issues such as small numbers, inadequate control groups and lack of direct interviews with children (Beardslee, 1983).

The results of more recent studies have for the most part confirmed the earlier findings. In a benchmark study, Weissman et al (1987) interviewed 125 children (aged 6 to 23 years) of depressed parents and 95 children of control probands from the general population. Compared with the children of normal subjects, the children of depressed parents had significantly higher lifetime prevalence rates of major depression, substance abuse and a number of DSM-III diagnoses. Similar findings were reported in a longitudinal design (Weissman et al, 1992). High lifetime rates of psychopathology have been found in several other recent studies of the children of depressed parents (e.g. Keller et al, 1986; Hammen et al, 1987; Grigoroiu-Serbanescu et al, 1991; Radke-Yarrow et al, 1992).

Mechanisms underlying the problems in the offspring of depressed parents

Since major affective disorders in parents seem to have a genetic component, it is often assumed that the psychiatric risk to children stems to some extent from genetic mechanisms. Indeed, some support for a genetic hypothesis comes from the finding that the children of depressed parents tend to show the same psychiatric disorders as their parents. Thus, Weissman et al (1987) found that 38% of children had had a major depressive disorder, and Keller et al (1986) reported that major depression was the most common diagnosis among 47 children of depressed probands (rate = 24%).

On the other hand, it should be borne in mind that depressive disorders are common in the general population, occurring for instance in 24% of the children of normal parents in the study of Weissman and her colleagues (1987). Moreover, as the latter study demonstrated, the risk to children is not specifically for depression but includes several other psychiatric disorders, such as substance abuse. Clearly, then, even if the parental condition is genetically determined it does not necessarily follow that the risk to children is similarly mediated. Parental mental disorder is frequently accompanied by important environmental disturbances such as impaired parenting (Weissman & Paykel, 1974), lowered parental responsiveness (Cox et al, 1987) and marital discord (Rutter & Quinton, 1984). The importance of environmental factors is further underlined by the study of Keller et al (1986). They found that almost every measure of severity and chronicity of depression in the parent had a significant association with impaired adaptation in the child. Genetic factors would be expected to increase the risk to the child regardless of the amount of exposure to the parent's illness.

What, then, are the environmental mechanisms that might account for this association between parental depression and problems in the child? Several different mechanisms could be involved. It may be, for instance, that parental depressive symptoms *directly* impinge in one way or another on the child, perhaps in the ways that Rutter (1966) described. For example, depression and withdrawal in the parent could lead to restrictions in the child's social activities. However, in a subsequent study of a more representative sample, Rutter and Quinton (1984) found that direct involvement in parental symptoms was uncommon. Exposure to parental depressive symptoms was not associated with psychiatric problems in the children once other factors had been controlled for. By contrast, parental behaviour was strongly associated with psychiatric disorder in the child, regardless of the parental diagnosis. Marital discord was an important source of such behaviour. Several other studies of depressed parents have found an association between marital discord and psychiatric disorders in children (e.g. Keller et al, 1986; Cox et al, 1987). The risk seems to be greatest when parental criticism or hostility is directly focused on the child.

Some support for the idea that *hostility and criticism* directed at the child may be important in the aetiology of depression in young people came from a study of parents with affective disorders, nonaffective psychiatric disorders, and no psychiatric illness (Schwartz et al, 1990). Higher levels of criticism were found in mothers from families where at least one parent had affective illness. Such families had a higher risk of having children with major depression, substance abuse, or conduct disorder than families where there was only nonaffective psychiatric illness or no psychiatric illness at all. Interestingly, this increased risk remained even after controlling for the presence of affective illness in the families. Similarly, Asarnow et al (1992) found that child inpatients with depressive disorders who returned to families in which there were high levels of expressed emotion were much less likely to recover than depressed children returning to families where there were low levels of expressed emotion.

Observational studies have shown that depressed women often have *other problems in parenting*. Radke-Yarrow et al (1985) have found that insecure attachment in the strange situation was more frequent in the young children of severely depressed mothers than controls. A pattern of ambivalence and avoidance was particularly prominent. Cox et al (1987) showed that depressed women were less likely to be involved in extended patterns of interaction with their 2-year-old children than nondepressed mothers. It seemed as if they were less able to "pick-up" cues from their children. Of course, these studies were concerned with young children, and may not therefore generalize to older children and adolescents with affective disorders. Nevertheless, they underline the point that depressed women may not only express more negative affect towards their children but also may have impaired problem-solving and coping skills. Interestingly, parenting problems may persist after women have recovered from depression (Stein et al, 1991), suggesting that in some instances these problems are just one manifestation of a more generalized personality disturbance.

Finally, it may be that depressive disorder in the parent increases the likelihood that children will be exposed to adversity, which in turn leads to depressive disorder in the child. Thus, for example, Hammen (1991) reported that some depressed women contributed to the causation of stressful events, especially interpersonal difficulties, which then impacted on the child. She speculated that these events might impair important mothering activities, such as attachment. Hammen (1991) emphasized the point that events could also be a "marker" of certain maternal characteristics that reflect parental impairment, such as personality difficulties.

Depressive disorders in parents and children: conclusions

To summarize, recent research suggests that there are strong familial links between depressive disorders in young people and their parents. Youngsters with major depression have high rates of depression among relatives, and the offspring of depressed parents are at increased risk of depression. Moreover, it seems that within samples of adult probands, earlier age of onset is associated with an increased familial loading of major depression.

Although these findings are suggestive of a genetic component, it will be appreciated that just because a disorder runs in families does not necessarily mean that it is genetic. To demonstrate the importance of genetic factors in childhood depression would require designs that can more effectively separate the effects of genes and environment, such as twin or adoption studies (Rutter et al, 1990a,b). Such genetic studies will need to consider not only the possibility of *direct* genetic effects on mood regulatory systems, but also the ways in which there may be *indirect* genetic effects, as when individuals create their own adverse environments (Scarr, 1992). To date no such studies on juvenile affective disorders have been published, though there is no reason to think that the severe bipolar disorders of adolescence are any less genetic than their adult counterparts.

In the meantime, the available data suggest that environmental factors are also likely to be important. Indeed, two recent longitudinal studies reported that the children of mothers with unipolar depression actually had a higher risk of depression than the children of mothers with bipolar disorder (Hammen et al, 1990a; Radke-Yarrow et al, 1992). These findings run counter to the prediction from genetic theories, which would suggest that the risk should be greater in the children from bipolar families, as bipolar disorder has the stronger genetic component. The implication is that depressive disorders in parents are likely to vary in the extent to which their impact on children is environmentally or genetically determined. Parental depression should not therefore be treated as a single homogeneous variable with uniform effects. In some varieties the continuities may be mediated genetically and in others environmentally, but in most it is likely that both genes and environment will play a part.

Similarly, it is important to note that children differ in their responses to parental depression. Indeed, as with many other kinds of psychological disorder in childhood, only a minority of those who experience the risk factor succumb to it. So, it will also be necessary to look at factors within the individual that may either increase resilience or make the child vulnerable, such as temperament. In this regard, it is important to note that *bidirectional effects* are also likely (Dodge, 1990). For example, depressed mothers may have offspring who are more difficult to manage, which in turn leads to further depression in the mother. Or, their offspring may act in ways that increase the likelihood of them experiencing adversity. Several recent studies have documented the importance of such effects (Field et al, 1990; Hammen, Burge & Stansbury, 1990b; Hammen, 1991). Moreover, it must also be considered that the factors leading to depression in the mother also cause depression in the child. Indeed, the finding in one study of a close *temporal* relationship between maternal and child depression (Hammen, Burge & Adrian, 1991) supports the idea of a common risk factor.

We can conclude that depression in parents is associated with depression in offspring through several different mechanisms, though data on their relative importance are lacking. First, there may be direct genetic effects on mood regulatory systems, as seems to be the case in adult-onset bipolar disorder. Second, there may be other genetic effects, mediated through factors such as the child's temperament, that increase the risk of depression indirectly. Third, there may be direct environmental effects of parental symptoms on children. Fourth, there may be effects on parenting. Finally, we should remember that depression in children and parents may be linked by some third factor, such as parental personality or social circumstances.

SOCIAL RELATIONSHIPS

Studies of depressed adults

In adults, there is much evidence of an association between poor social bonds or difficulties in interpersonal relationships and depression (e.g. Weissman & Paykel, 1974; Brown & Harris, 1978). Brown and Harris (1978) identified the absence of a close, intimate, confiding relationship with someone as a vulnerability factor for depression in women. They argued that a close confiding relationship provided a woman with a sense of being valued and that in the absence of another source of value (such as social activities or a job outside the home) this would act as a vulnerability factor for depression.

However, alternative models exist for the association of lack of social support and depression. Perhaps, for example, depression leads to a lack of social support rather than the other way round. Some support for this suggestion comes from longitudinal studies of depressed adolescents. Garber et al (1988) found that adolescent patients with a depressive disorder were significantly more impaired in social and intimate relationships than a psychiatric control group when they were followed up about 8 years after discharge. Similarly, Kandel and Davies (1986) reported that self-ratings of depressive symptoms in adolescents were associated with selective effects on interpersonal relationships in early adulthood. Earlier depression seemed to affect the individual's ability to form close interpersonal relationships with a member of the opposite sex. As Kandel and Davies (1986) pointed out, the implication is that the association of depression and absence of a supporting social network could reflect social selection as much as social causation.

Alternatively, it could be that some third factor leads to both the depression and lack of social support. Henderson (Henderson et al, 1980; Henderson, Byrne & Duncan-Jones, 1981; Henderson, 1982) found an association of deficiencies in social relationships and neurosis in a cross-sectional study, and undertook a longitudinal study in order to tackle the issue of causality. Contrary to expectation, it was not the lack of relationships which had the strongest predictive power, but the perception of these as inadequate under adversity. In other words, it was the personality of the individual that was crucial for the development of symptoms rather than the immediate social environment. Henderson excluded those with psychiatric symptoms at time 1 because the reporting of social relationships would have been open to contamination. Indeed, it would seem logical to control for previous psychiatric symptoms since they were likely to be risk factors for future symptoms and could affect personality. However, this strategy may have obscured the effects of social support. Clearly, then, there are considerable conceptual difficulties in researching the relationship between social support and depression.

Supportive relationships and depression in young people

It will be appreciated that the young child's social world is in many respects different from that of an adult. For instance, young children usually develop a specific set of attachment relationships with caregivers. These parent–child attachment relationships are probably not isomorphic with the kinds of intimate relationships that develop between adults. For example, intimate relationships in adults do not seem to be so reliant on physical proximity. So, theories regarding the role of social support in depressed adults may not generalize to studies of depressed children.

On the other hand, both attachment relationships between parent and child and intimate relationships between adults have as one component the provision of emotional security. Moreover, as children develop, the balance between relationships within the family and relationships outside changes (Hartup, 1983; Goodyer, 1990). During the pre-school years brief immature social exchanges are abandoned for more complex social relationships that contain some of the elements of adult relationships. During middle childhood school attendance results in increased social contact, and there is a decline in egocentricity with an increasing recognition that individuals have their own point of view. Children increasingly confide in other children. Nevertheless, at times of crisis even adolescents are more likely to turn to their parents for support and advice than to their peers (Rutter, 1980).

Many studies have reported that depression in young people is associated with impairments in various types of interpersonal relationship (e.g. Altmann

& Gotlib, 1988; Kazdin et al, 1985a; Puig-Antich et al, 1985a; Goodyer, Wright & Altham, 1989). Probably the most thorough study of these problems in children with depressive disorders was conducted by Puig-Antich et al (1985a,b). They assessed a variety of different aspects of psychosocial functioning during episodes of major depression in prepubertal children. Compared with normal controls, most aspects of psychosocial relationships were found to be impaired. Thus, depressed children showed significantly worse mother–child relationships, sibling relationships and relationships with peers than normal controls. Few of these deficits were specific to depression, occurring also in nondepressed child psychiatric controls. However, poor communication and lack of warmth were specific to children with major depression. Puig-Antich and colleagues suggested that the relationship difficulties of depressed children could therefore have two components: a depression-specific component and a nonspecific component found in many other child psychiatric disorders. The sample was followed up after the depressed children had recovered from the episode of major depression. Deficits in the child's intra- and extra-familial relationships had only partly recovered.

The meaning of the association of depression in young people and impaired interpersonal relationships remains, however, poorly understood. Goodyer, Wright and Altham (1989) found that friendship difficulties before the onset of depression did not predict the type of diagnosis (anxiety or depression), but that after the onset of disorder depressed but not anxious children were at risk for poor friendships (Goodyer et al, 1991a). The implication is that depression was associated with the maintenance or worsening of friendship problems. Goodyer et al (1991a) suggested that there were two possible explanations: either the social behaviour of depressed children had a negative impact on the social behaviour of their friends; or the negative thinking state of depression reduces the prosocial behaviour necessary for friendship development or maintenance.

A different point of view was put forward by Cole (1990, 1991) who hypothesized that social competence had a direct effect on depressive symptoms. He studied the relationship between self-report questionnaire measures of depressive symptomatology and peer/teacher ratings of social competence and academic competence in a sample of school children aged around 10 years. This study had the disadvantage of using questionnaire measures of symptoms but the advantage of using measures of peer relationships that were independent of measures of depression. Low social competence and depression scores were correlated.

Kupersmidt and Patterson (1991) also used peer reports of social preference, but their study had an additional longitudinal component. At time 1, assessments were made of social competence and aggression (peer ratings) together with self-reports of behavioural difficulties and self-esteem. At follow-up, two years later, students completed a modified version of the CBCL. Among boys, depression (as measured on the CBCL) was best predicted by feelings of low self-worth. In girls, peer status was a broad indicator of subsequent behaviour problems, and lack of same-aged school friendships was most important in predicting subsequent depression. The implication is that in girls peer relationship difficulties may have a role in the development of depressive *symptomatology*. It remains to be seen whether prospective studies will demonstrate the same for depressive disorders.

Because there seems to be an association between impaired interpersonal relationships and depression in young people, and because there also seem to be age changes in the characteristics of children's friendships (see above), it is also necessary to consider whether these age changes may account for the age trends in depressive phenomena that were described in Chapter 4. For example, could it be that the increase in depression during adolescence occurs because adolescents are less able to use their parents as a source of support but have not yet developed the love relationships that seem to protect adults from depression? Probably not. In fact, it seems that as children grow older their friendships become more intense and involve more emotional sharing (Goodyer, 1990). Moreover, it is necessary to take into account sex differences. The greatest rise in depression is seen among adolescent females yet it is just this group who tend to maintain close, more intimate friendships (Berndt, 1983). Of course, this could make girls more vulnerable to depression since they might find friendship failures more distressing. However, overall it seems unlikely that developmental changes in sources of social support can adequately explain the developmental changes in depression.

It must also be remembered that positive peer relationships may protect young people from depressive disorders. Beardslee, Schultz and Selman (1987) reported that among the adolescent offspring of parents with affective disorders high levels of interpersonal skills appeared protective. Social charm—having qualities that elicit positive social responses from others—was one of three protective factors reported by Radke-Yarrow and Sherman (1990) in a study of children in whom both parents had affective disorders.

In conclusion, there is no doubting the very strong association between difficulties in peer relationships and depression in young people. However, it has to be said that the meaning of this relationship is poorly understood. Some studies suggest that the deficits are secondary to depression, others that they are part of a wider problem that predisposes to the disorder. The available data do not yet allow us to choose between these different viewpoints, and more longitudinal research on this issue is certainly required. It is possible that problems in peer relationships are both a consequence and a cause of depression.

TEMPERAMENT

We also need to consider whether these risk variables can be taken back to earlier childhood in relation to temperamental features. In other words, are there simple, nonmotivational stylistic characteristics that represent stable differences between individuals and which predispose to depression in childhood?

Longitudinal studies from both normal samples and samples at risk for psychiatric problems have shown that temperamental features predict the subsequent development of psychopathology (Prior, 1992). In the New York study children who later developed behavioural difficulties showed different temperamental characteristics from those without behavioural problems (Thomas & Chess, 1982). Graham, Rutter and George (1973) studied children who had a parent under psychiatric care. Temperamental characteristics were associated with a high risk of the children developing a psychiatric disorder in middle childhood.

There are many possible mechanisms that could link temperamental attributes to psychopathology. First, it could be that some extreme forms of temperament constitute in themselves a form of psychiatric disorder. However, there are a number of reasons for thinking that this is not the case, the main one being that the symptoms of psychiatric disorders are, for the most part, quite different from the features of temperament. Second, it may be that temperamental characteristics of children have a direct impact on the response to a stressful event. Dunn and Kendrick (1982) found that temperamental characteristics were strongly associated with an increase in emotional disturbance after the birth of a sibling. Adaptable children may find it easier to cope with adversity. Third, certain temperamental features may make it more likely that children will experience adverse events, such as accidents. Fourth, children's temperamental characteristics, such as aggression, may lead to the child becoming the target of criticism by others (Quinton & Rutter, 1985). Prior (1992) underlined the importance of both temperamental characteristics *and* the mother–child relationship in the genesis of behavioural problems in children.

Clearly, then, there are a number of ways in which temperamental features could either predispose a child to depressive disorder, or protect him/her from it. Indeed, it has been suggested that temperamental characteristics are closely linked to depression in young people. For instance, Trad (1986) has hypothesized that the biological elements of temperament may be linked to the neuroendocrine systems that are thought to be involved in depression. Kagan, Reznick and Snidman (1987) suggested that the temperamental characteristic behavioural inhibition is a function of a low threshold of responsivity in limbic and hypothalamic structures. We shall see later that activity in these systems has also been seen as important in the aetiology of depression.

To date, however, very little has been written about the temperamental characteristics of children with depressive disorder (Benfield et al, 1988). Chess, Thomas and Hassibi (1983) identified six cases of depression in the 133 subjects of the New York Longitudinal Study. A review of the longitudinal data did not show a significant earlier life tendency to negative mood temperamentally. Indeed, they found little evidence that any of the child's temperamental characteristics played a role in the aetiology of the two cases of major depression. On the other hand, all four cases of depressive neurosis showed an extreme score on one or other temperamental trait. Examination of these cases suggested that there might be indirect mechanisms linking "difficult" temperamental features, through secondary psychosocial reactions, to depression. Temperamental features seemed to make it more likely that children would behave in ways that increased the likelihood of adversity, which in turn predisposed them to depression.

Clearly, more needs to be known about the ways in which temperamental features may predispose either directly, or indirectly, to depressive disorders.

EARLY ADVERSE EXPERIENCES AND LATER DEPRESSIVE DISORDER

For many years it was widely believed that early separation was linked to depressive disorder in adults. This idea grew out of psychoanalytic ideas about the importance of early loss and was developed further by Bowlby in the notion of attachment theory. So far as the aetiology of depression is concerned, perhaps the most important concept that has come from attachment theory is the idea of the *attachment behaviour system* (Hinde, 1982). This is a behaviour system that is seen as existing in the individual and that has coherence over time. It is different from other uses of the term attachment (such as when it is used to describe attachment behaviours seen in infancy) in that it is an explanatory rather than a descriptive concept. The postulated system incorporates sensitivity to and expectations of other people. The child's expectations about and behaviour in subsequent relationships are in part determined by those he has already experienced. There is what Bowlby (1973) called a "working model", which constantly changes as the child experiences new relationships. In other words, as we accumulate relationships our models of these relationships are changed.

Bowlby hypothesized that the experience of secure attachments in infancy fosters self-efficacy and makes it more likely that later social functioning will be adaptive. Insecure attachments in infancy are likely to predispose infants to react adversely to later stressful experiences (Bowlby, 1980) and so to become depressed. The key point in the model is not that there should be stability of traits over time but that there are meaningful links between early selective attachments and other kinds of social relationship.

A large number of studies have examined the association between early loss and depression in adulthood, but despite the large volume of research on this topic the relationship remains in doubt. Granville-Grossman (1968) reviewed 17 studies and concluded that the relationship of depression and loss is probably absent. Paykel (1982) identified 14 studies in which the rate of early parental death in patients with affective disorders was compared with that in one or more control groups. Seven studies showed an excess of early parental death, seven did not. Crook and Elliot (1980) conducted a similar review and concluded that social class is a confounding variable that has led to a spurious association in some studies of loss and depression.

It may be, however, that the focus of these studies on loss and parental death was misplaced, and that the key issue is whether or not there was *early lack of care* (Parker, 1992). In other words, it is not so much the early loss that is crucial, but the circumstances surrounding it that lead to later depression. Indeed, Brown, Harris and Bifulco (1986) found that the relationship between early loss and depression was mediated to a large extent by indices of lack of care, such as indifference on the part of the parent/s who had continued to look after the child following the loss and a stay in an institution. Further support for this idea came from another study by the same research team, which was conducted in Islington, North London (Bifulco, Brown & Harris, 1987). They found that one-third of those with childhood lack of care were depressed, compared with one-sixth of those without lack of care. The effect of loss of mother on later depression seemed to be dependent on lack of care.

Rodgers (1990) reported on the childhood precursors of symptoms of depression and anxiety in a national population sample of over 3000 men and women aged 36 years. Early factors had a relatively small effect on the risk of adult depression, but once again it seemed that separation from parents *per se* did not appear to be an important factor, whereas family disruption and parental attitudes were associated with subsequent depression.

Brown et al's (1986) study also underlined the importance of events occurring later in life, such as early pregnancy, as intervening factors between early adversity and later depression. Quinton et al's study (1984) of institution-reared women gave rise to a closely comparable finding. When followed up into their mid-20s, the institution-reared women showed parenting as good as that of the control group provided that they had a supportive spouse and lived in good social conditions. However, they fared much worse than the controls if they lacked adequate housing or marital support. Their adverse early experiences seemed to have left them without resilience.

Different views have been put forward regarding the mechanisms by which these adversities lead to later depression. The notion of *vulnerability* has received particular attention. The key feature of a vulnerability factor, as it is usually conceptualized, is that in isolation it does not increase the risk of depression. It only does so in association with precipitating events. That is, there is an *interaction* between the vulnerability factor and the precipitant. Brown and Harris (1978), for example, suggested that women were made vulnerable to the development of depression by vulnerability factors such as early adversity, but that depression would occur only if the woman also experienced *provoking agents* such as life events or chronic difficulties. However, Tennant and Bebbington (1978) have argued that vulnerability factors do not appear to be conceptually distinct from provoking agents. They reanalysed the data of Brown and Harris and found that the so-called vulnerability factors acted in an additive way: that is, they contributed independently to the risk of depression. Moreover, Rodgers (1990) has suggested that whether a factor acts as a vulnerability agent seems to depend on what the criterion is. In his study, variables that acted as vulnerability agents for acute depressive disorders appeared to act independently for chronic conditions.

In conclusion, it seems that childhood "loss" as such has only a weak association with depression in adulthood, and this association is mediated largely through the psychosocial adversities that follow the loss. Other forms of adversity are likely to be more important in predisposing to depression, with the key factor being early lack of care. Probably, early adversity predisposes to later psychopathology both through increasing vulnerability to later stresses, and directly.

Early experiences and vulnerability to later depression in young people

Some of the psychological mechanisms that might be involved in these child to adult links will be described in later sections. First, however, it is necessary to consider the question of whether earlier experiences increases vulnerability to childhood depression in the same way as it has been hypothesized that they do in adult-onset disorders. Developmentalists have argued that they can, but not in a simple linear fashion (Cicchetti & Schneider-Rosen, 1986). Thus, for example, children who are insecurely attached are thought to have less *competence* across a range of social domains and might therefore behave in a way that may make it more likely that they will experience later adversities. Also, the experience of an insecure attachment may leave cognitive biases, such as pessimism regarding self-abilities. Such feelings of hopelessness and lack of self-worth may lead directly to major depression, or indirectly predispose to the disorder by creating a vulnerability through impairments of social relationships.

So, although adaptational failures early in childhood are probably not sufficiently specific for the prediction of later depression they may operate together with other factors to produce the disorder. Thus, for example, Lewis et al (1984) reported that in addition to the attachment relationship, several other factors, including life stress and family demographic variables, seemed to influence the risk of psychopathology. They concluded that "although the child's attachment relationships play an important role in the development of psychopathology, the child is neither made invulnerable by an early secure attachment nor doomed to psychopathology by an insecure attachment".

We saw earlier that parents of depressed children often suffer from mental illness, and that sometimes their relationship with the child is characterized by rejection and hostility. In addition, there is some evidence that depressed children have problems communicating with their families and that these deficits in social relations persist after the depression has remitted (Puig-Antich et al, 1985a,b). Is it possible, then, that these problems are a reflection of early insecure attachments (caused by, say, depression in the mother) which in turn lead to depression in the child?

Unfortunately, there have been no large-scale longitudinal studies of the relationship between early attachment status and major depressive disorder in young people (though data from one cross-sectional study support the idea of a link between the two — see Armsden et al (1990)). However, several studies have "looked backwards" and examined the links between early loss or separation and depression among young people. Thus, Goodyer and Altham (1991a,b) explored this issue in a cross-sectional study of school-aged children attending a university department of psychiatry. All cases were classified as "anxiety dominant" or "depressive dominant". Lifetime "exit" events were assessed during an interview with the mother, and included events like deaths, divorce, and separations. Events occurring in the previous 12 months were regarded as "recent exits" and excluded from the analyses. Two or more lifetime exit events were reported significantly more often in depressed and anxious children than in community controls. There were no differences in the number of lifetime exits between depressed and anxious cases.

Goodyer and Altham (1991b) hypothesized that a likely causal chain would involve earlier adverse alterations to family relationships connecting to recent family adversities. They tested this hypothesis by examining the relative contributions to emotional disorder in the presence and absence of other family and social adversities. They found no evidence of an interaction between previous exit events and recent family or social adversities, such as maternal distress and lack of friendships. Thus lifetime exits appeared to exert their effects independently of recent adversities.

Goodyer and Altham (1991b) suggested a number of other possible mechanisms whereby previous exit events could be linked to emotional disorders, such as through the reactions of family members, or through continuity of psychopathology (i.e. that the exit event had previously been associated with psychopathology, and that the link was simply due to continuity of the first disorder). Some support for this last suggestion comes from the longitudinal study of Kandel and Davies (1986). These authors studied continuity of self-reported depressive symptomatology from adolescence into early adulthood. Depressive symptoms in young adulthood were predicted most strongly by depressive symptoms in adolescence, and neither closeness to parents nor separation before 11 years had a significant influence on subsequent levels of depression. Berney et al (1991) found that bereavement in the pre-school years was actually less common among depressed children than among non-depressed psychiatric cases, whereas loss occurring in the school years was significantly more common among children with the endogenous subtype of depression. The number of depressed cases was too small to determine whether or not there was an interaction with recent adversities.

On the other hand, in a longitudinal study of children in a lower-middle-class community, Reinherz et al (1989) found that in girls death of a parent was a predictor of depressive symptoms in adolescence. Girls who had experienced a parental death were more than nine times more likely to score above 12 on the CDI than girls who had not. Early physical illness was also a risk factor. The impact of these earlier risk factors was independent of current adversities. Unfortunately, this longitudinal study did not include measures of depression at the early time points (e.g. age 9 years) and we cannot be certain as to how far the results would generalize to children with depressive disorders. Nevertheless, the results do support the view that early experiences may predispose to depression later in childhood.

In conclusion, the results regarding the effects of early loss in childhood depression parallel those found in adults. Some studies have reported a significant association and others have failed to find one. We need to know much more about this issue. In particular we need a firmer understanding of the mechanisms that may be involved in linking early adversity to later depression.

PREDISPOSITION TO DEPRESSION AMONG THE YOUNG: CONCLUSIONS

There is ample evidence of an association between depression in young people and mental illness of one kind or another in relatives. The finding of some specificity in these links clearly raises the possibility of a genetic component, though the presence of such a component remains to be conclusively demonstrated. Juvenile affective disorders represent a heterogeneous group of conditions, and it is quite likely that some varieties (e.g. the bipolar disorders) are more heritable than others (e.g. mild nonpsychotic unipolar depressions). Certainly, there are many plausible environmental mechanisms that could link mental illness in family members to depression in their offspring, and the evidence, such as it is, suggests that these mechanisms are likely to be significant.

In common with investigators of adult depression, researchers into the aetiology of childhood depression have looked for links with early adversity. The findings so far have been quite similar: there do seem to be links, but these are indirect and are not for the most part specifically tied to loss. By contrast, there is much evidence of an association between juvenile depression and disturbances of social relationships. The meaning of this association is, however, unclear, and it may well be that disturbed relationships are in many cases secondary to depression. The association is important because it raises the possibility that some individuals have a personal disposition either to depression or to factors that may precipitate it. We shall see in the next section that, although depression in young people is commonly associated with acute adversities of one kind or another, most young people who experience adversity do not become depressed. So, the factors that make children and adolescents either resilient or vulnerable to depression are likely to be of great importance in our attempts to understand aetiology.

RECENT LIFE EVENTS: STUDIES OF DEPRESSED ADULTS

For many years acute adverse life events have been seen as important in the aetiology of adult depressive disorders. For example, Paykel et al (1969) found depressed patients to report three times as many events as control subjects. When events were dichotomized, depressed subjects reported five times as many exits from their social fields and more undesirable events, yet experienced the same number of entrance or desirable events as the controls. Using female subjects, Brown et al (1973) found that the rate of all events was elevated only in the three weeks before onset of depression, but for events rated as markedly threatening it was increased over the whole of the 48-week period that was studied. The magnitude of the link between life events and depression has been calculated in various ways. Paykel (1978) applied a modified form of the epidemiological measure, relative risk, and found that the risk of depression increased six-fold in the six months following a markedly threatening life event.

One of the problems encountered in this kind of research is deciding whether the life events precede the depression, or whether the insidious onset of the disorder brings about certain events. This problem can be tackled by distinguishing between dependent and independent events. Independent events are those that are most unlikely to have been brought about by the behaviour of the subject, such as losing a job because a factory closes. Dependent events are those that could have been due to the behaviour of the respondent, such as losing a job when no one else has. Finlay-Jones and Brown (1981) reported that the association between life events and depression remained even when dependent and possibly dependent events were removed from the analysis.

A more fundamental issue relates to the fact that, although there is a methodological need to distinguish between dependent and independent events, it does not follow that dependent events are unimportant in the aetiology of depression. It could be that the adverse life experiences that stem in one way or another from the individual are just as potent a cause of depression as the so-called independent events. Indeed, many of the "life events" that have been found in association with adult depression (such as bad marriages, social isolation, housing problems and so on) are predicted by earlier behaviour such as conduct problems (Robins, 1966). In other words, we need to know where life events come from.

LIFE EVENTS AND DEPRESSION IN CHILDREN

Research on the psychosocial correlates of childhood depression is at a very early stage and, as was noted at the beginning of this chapter, there are a number of reasons for thinking that models developed with adult cases will not always be adequate. Thus, many acute life stresses in childhood arise in the context of chronic adversities (e.g. parent–child separations), so acute life events may need to be conceptualized as one class of social adversity, rather than as something different. Also, Brown et al's (1986) studies of parental loss suggest that the risk for psychiatric disorder stems from the deficient parental care that follows the loss rather than from the loss *per se*. So, it will be important to study the circumstances surrounding life events as well as the events themselves.

Some of these complexities are well illustrated by Goodyer's systematic studies on life events and psychiatric disorders in children (see Goodyer, 1990). Goodyer, Wright and Altham (1988) found that the onset of emotional disorders in children was strongly associated not only with undesirable life events (relative risk of about 5) but also with maternal distress and poor maternal confiding relationships. They suggested that some children could become "life event prone" as a result of a decrease of maternal protective effects on the child. For example, mothers who are very preoccupied with their own concerns may be less able to protect the child from adverse events.

It is important to note that there appeared to be no specificity between these stressful factors and the types of emotional symptoms in the children. Thus, in the presence of adversity the children were equally likely to become anxious as they were to become depressed (Goodyer, Kolvin & Gatzanis, 1985; Goodyer, Wright & Altham, 1988). Comparable findings were reported by Berney et al (1991) who found that, although a variety of environmental adversities were associated with childhood disturbance, few were specifically linked with depression. Clearly, these findings suggest that the links between life events and depression in young people may be rather nonspecific. Similarly, it would appear that as a general rule there are no life events that are particularly associated with depression in young people (Wilde et al, 1992).

As is the case in adult depression, the question also arises as to whether or not life events in young people precede the depression or whether the depression precedes the life events. In other words, to what extent are negative events a consequence of depression? Hammen, Adrian and Hiroto (1988) studied this question in a sample that included offspring of women with affective disorders. The children were assessed using the K-SADS and then followed up six months later when information was collected on depressive diagnoses and life events. The strongest predictor of depression at follow-up was depression at the time of the initial evaluation, but life events were also a significant additional predictor of later depression. Similar findings have been reported in a longitudinal study of depressive symptoms (Nolen-Hoeksema, Girgus & Seligman, 1992).

It seems, then, that adverse life events are not simply a consequence of depression: they can and do precede it. However, as noted earlier, much more needs to be known about the ways in which these events come about. In particular, we need to know the degree to which depressed children and/or their families act in ways that put them at increased risk of negative events. Many of the events that are associated with depression in young people, such as illness in a family member or changes in living situation, are clearly not independent. Indeed, Hammen (1991) found that the children of depressed parents were exposed to higher levels of adversity than a control group. In part this seemed to be a by-product of living in a home with a depressed mother. In part, however, these adversities were dependent on the child's behaviour.

SPECIFIC LIFE EXPERIENCES AND DEPRESSION IN YOUNG PEOPLE

Another way of approaching the issue of the relationship between adversity and depression in young people is to study children who have experienced a particular form of negative event. Of course even apparently simple indices of risk may turn out to be more complicated than seemed at first sight. For instance, we shall see later that divorce involves a complex series of events and stressors. Nevertheless, since this approach takes as its starting point children who have experienced an event, rather than children who are already depressed, it has proved a useful (if under-used) way of studying not only vulnerability to depression but also resilience to it.

Bereavement

Despite the stress placed on children by the death of a parent, and the attention paid to childhood bereavement in the literature on adult depression, there have been surprisingly few prospective studies of bereaved children (Garmezy, 1986; Goodyer, 1990). Retrospective studies have indicated that children aged between 5 and 10 years may be the most vulnerable, perhaps because children in this age group have the most difficulties with institutionalization (Tennant, Hurry & Bebbington, 1982). Younger children seem to grieve with less intensity than older children, probably because older children have a greater understanding of death as universal, inevitable and irreversible (Garmezy, 1986).

In one of the first systematic prospective studies of bereaved children, Van Eerdewegh et al (1982) studied 105 individuals aged from 2 to 17 years (mean age 11) who were children of a consecutive sample of young widows and widowers in the community. Community controls were also studied. The childrens' reactions to parental death were recorded at one month and 13 months after the event by interview with the surviving parent. There was a significant increase in dysphoria among bereaved children, and compared with the controls the bereaved group contained significantly more children with a "depressive syndrome" (14% versus 4%). The six children with the depressive syndrome comprised four boys and two girls, all except one were aged over 13 years, and all had lost their fathers.

This study did not conduct face-to-face interviews with the child, and since many of the informants would have been depressed at the time of the interview, the question arises as to the accuracy of these assessments. To overcome this problem, Kranzler et al (1990) developed a standardized affect interview in order to assess bereavement reactions in 26 children aged between 3 and 6 years who had lost a parent. The bereaved children showed significantly more psychiatric problems than nonbereaved controls, particularly symptoms of depression and anxiety. They expressed a full range of affect, not just simple sadness. Bereaved boys were more vulnerable than girls. Interestingly, it seemed that depression in the surviving parent was the most powerful predictor of child disturbance. Similarly, Weller et al (1991) conducted direct interviews with 38 prepubertal children who had recently experienced the death of a parent. A considerable number developed the clinical symptoms of a major depression and nearly one-third met criteria for a major depressive episode.

All in all, the findings of these prospective studies indicate that grieving is possible even in young children. Depressive symptoms are prominent at all ages but only a minority of children develop a depressive syndrome. It is uncommon for bereaved children to show guilt, impaired self-esteem (Kranzler et al, 1990) or pessimism about the future (Van Eerdewegh et al, 1982). The presence of these symptoms should therefore alert the clinician to the possibility of a major depressive disorder. And, finally, the study of Kranzler and colleagues reminds us once again of the importance of associated adversity in the genesis of psychopathology in children who have experienced loss or separation.

Divorce

Studies of children whose parents have divorced provide another excellent example of how several different factors can contribute to the psychopathology that is associated with adverse experiences.

The first point to note is that divorce is usually an outcome of chronic difficulties between two parents. Children may have been exposed to marital discord for many years and there is much evidence of an association between marital discord and emotional disorders in children (Quinton, Rutter & Gulliver, 1990). Similarly, Block, Block and Gjerde (1988) reported that marital environment prior to divorce was an important determinant of child adjustment.

Secondly, divorce has lasting consequences (Hetherington, Cox & Cox, 1982; Wolkind & Rutter, 1985). There is often a marked decrease in the standard of living. Sometimes, parents experience emotional symptoms over a prolonged period. They may become depressed, anxious, angry and feel rejected. Many divorced parents experience disruption of their social lives. Family disorganization can also be prolonged with features like erratic bedtimes and irregular meals. There may be difficulties in parenting, with divorced mothers being harassed by their children, especially their sons.

Third, the effects on children seem to differ according to the child's *developmental stage* (Wallerstein & Kelly, 1980). Preschool children tend to regress behaviourally, with acting out, anxieties and greater attention-seeking. By middle childhood, the child's responses are likely to be dominated by depression; children may begin to fear replacement of the father through maternal remarriage. In adolescents, the short-term impact can be quite marked, and some may show severe depression. Anger also occurs, with blame placed on the parent who left the family home.

Disasters

The importance of developmental stage in determining the individual's affective response to life experiences is also underlined by some of the research on the psychological consequences of disaster. Amongst the most thorough of these studies was that based on the Buffalo Creek flood (Gleser, Green & Winget, 1981), which was the consequence of a dam bursting above the mining town of Buffalo Creek in America. The flood killed 125 people and left hundreds injured or homeless. Children showed fewer symptoms than adults. About 20% were thought to have moderate or severe anxiety, 30% some degree of depression, and about the same proportion had some form of psychiatric disorder. There was an overall increase in the rate of psychiatric disturbance with age; children tended to respond with anxiety symptoms and adults with depressive symptoms. In children, the presence of anxiety following the disaster was the strongest predictor of subsequent difficulties, whereas depression was the strongest predictor in adults.

In the Buffalo Creek study, disturbances in children tended to parallel those in the parents. Disturbance in fathers was associated with disturbance in sons; mothers and daughters showed an analogous association. Children in supportive households showed less psychopathology. Similar findings were reported by McFarlane (1987, 1988) who studied children between the ages of 5 and 12 years who attended schools within a region of Australia that had been affected by severe bushfires. Questionnaire measures of psychopathology were administered at 2, 8 and 26 months after the disaster. The continuing effects of the disaster on parental mental state, as shown by such features as the father continuing to have recurring thoughts, were the strongest predictor of children's psychopathology.

The findings of these two studies suggest that parental reactions to disaster are very important in mediating the psychological impact on children. What kind of impact does a disaster have when the parents are not physically involved during the incident itself? Yule, Udwin and Murdoch (1990) studied the psychopathology of 25 girls aged between 14 and 16 years who were on board the Jupiter cruise liner for an educational cruise when it was hit by an oil tanker. The Jupiter sank 45 minutes later and many of the children had to jump into the sea. Ratings of depression on the Birleson self-report scale were significantly higher among the girls who had been on the Jupiter when compared with girls from the same year in school. Clearly, then, symptoms of depression can in some instances be directly linked to a disaster and do not always depend on the reactions of others.

Academic problems

An association between depressive disorder in young people and impaired academic performance has been documented in several studies. Puig-Antich et al (1985a) found that depressed children were more impaired than normal controls for the items measuring school behaviour and school achievement that were included in a parental interview. The school performance of depressed children did not differ significantly from that of nondepressed child psychiatric patients, suggesting a rather nonspecific link between academic performance and depressive disorder. These authors found that recovered depressed children were functioning better in school than they had while depressed. They had better relationships with their teachers and showed better academic achievement than during their depressive episode (Puig-Antich et al, 1985b). The implication is that the school problems were secondary to the depression.

Berney et al (1991) reported that children with depressive disorder were much more likely to absent themselves from school than nondepressed psychiatric controls. As part of a larger study of school placement of psychiatric patients, Forness (1988) found that nearly one-third of pupils with "pure" depression (that is, accompanied by no other behavioural or learning difficulties) continued to require various special educational placements.

There may be sex differences in the association between academic problems and depression. Cole (1990) found in a sample of 10-year-olds that, although teachers rated girls as more academically competent than boys, girls' self-ratings were no higher than boys'. Indeed, compared with teacher ratings, girls tended to underestimate their academic competence whereas boys tended to overestimate theirs. The tendency to underestimate academic competence was significantly related to self-report depression questionnaire ratings (the CDI), suggesting that children who underestimated academic competence were more likely to report depressive symptoms. Cole linked these findings to the results of Dweck et al (1978) who found that boys tended to attribute academic failure to lack of effort whereas girls attributed failure to lack of ability. The implication is that preadolescent girls have a cluster of cognitive biases that predispose them to depression: they tend to underestimate their own abilities and when they do fail blame their failure on this lack of ability. Of course, we cannot be certain about the direction of causality. It could be that depression leads to an underestimation of academic abilities. Nevertheless, this is an interesting notion that warrants further study, preferably in a longitudinal design.

Physical and sexual abuse

Much of the research on the psychological consequences of physical abuse has been understandably concerned with the risks of antisocial behaviour and violence. Indeed, the data do certainly suggest that physically abused children show more physical aggression (George & Main, 1979; Kinard, 1982), and are at risk of a variety of developmental and cognitive difficulties (Friedrich & Einbender, 1983). Nevertheless, there are two main reasons for thinking that physically abused children will be at increased risk of depressive symptomatology (Kinard, 1982; Kazdin et al, 1985c; Allen & Tarnowski, 1989). First, although abused children vary in their characteristics, many of them show anhedonia, poor self-esteem, withdrawal and poor social interaction. Oates, Forrest and Peacock (1985), for example, reported that abused children had lower self-esteem than nonabused children, though it seems that such problems may improve with therapeutic day treatment (Culp et al, 1991). Second, the parenting that physically abused children suffer might be expected on theoretical grounds to induce learned helplessness (Kazdin et al, 1985c). We shall see in the next chapter that such feelings have been linked to depression.

In one of the first systematic studies of this issue, Kazdin et al (1985c) examined the level of depressive symptomatology among 33 consecutive admissions to an inpatient unit who had been physically abused. Comparisons were made with child psychiatric inpatients who had not been abused. The proportion of cases with primary or secondary depressive diagnoses did not differ between abused and nonabused children. However, children who had been abused showed significantly higher levels of self-reported depression on the CDI and had lower self-esteem than nonabused controls. Children with both past and current abuse were the most severely depressed. Interestingly, the abused and nonabused groups did not differ on levels of nondepressive symptoms as measured by the Child Behaviour Checklist. The implication is that there may be a specific link between physical abuse and depressive symptoms in children.

Since the study of Kazdin et al (1985c) was based on a sample referred to a psychiatric inpatient facility, the question arises as to the generalizability of the results. However, similar findings were reported by Allen and Tarnowski (1989) in a study of 18 physically abused children attending either an abuse clinic or social services. Compared with nonabused controls from the community, the abused group scored significantly higher than controls on self-report measures of depression and hopelessness, and had lower self-esteem.

It will be appreciated that the results of these questionnaire studies of depressive symptoms may not apply to depressive disorders. Moreover, the design of the study of Allen and Tarnowski does not allow conclusions regarding the specificity of the links between physical abuse and depression, though there is some suggestion from the study of Kazdin et al (1985c) that there is a specific link. Nevertheless, taken together the results of these studies do suggest that physically abused children are at risk for depressive symptoms.

Retrospective community studies have suggested that there may also be a link between sexual abuse in childhood and depression in adult life (Mullen et al, 1988). Bifulco, Brown and Adler (1991), for example, found that 9% of working class mothers living in North London reported sexual abuse involving physical contact before the age of 17 years. Sixty-four per cent of those with childhood sexual abuse were depressed at "caseness" level compared with 26% of the rest of the women. While sexual abuse was associated with other earlier stressful experiences, such as parental indifference, it was associated with an increased risk of depression *above* these other factors.

The results of psychiatric studies conducted with children and adolescents who have been sexually abused have suggested that a variety of psychiatric symptoms can occur. These include anxiety, guilt, shame, aggression as well as depression (Krener, 1985; Adams-Tucker, 1982; Livingston, 1987). In one of the largest studies to date, Sirles, Smith and Kusama (1989) investigated the initial psychiatric profiles of abused children presenting at an outpatient child psychiatry unit. All 207 cases had been victims of intrafamilial sexual abuse. The majority of victims did not have a psychiatric diagnosis. Of the 38% that did, most suffered from an adjustment reaction, with the most common adjustment disorder being with depressed mood. A variety of other psychiatric disorders were diagnosed, including conduct disorder and attention deficit disorder, but no subject was diagnosed as major depression or dysthymia. Risk factors for having a psychiatric diagnosis were age of the victim (adolescents were at greater risk), relationship to the perpetrator (abuse by a parent was associated with a greater risk than abuse by an extended family member), and frequency and duration of abuse (the more frequent and longer the abuse occurred the greater the risk of disorder). It is necessary to be cautious in interpreting the results of this study since the diagnoses were not made using a standardized interview and it is unclear how sexual abuse was defined. Moreover, it is possible that the victims suffered from symptoms and/or disorders that were not classifiable in DSM-III. Nevertheless, the results suggest that many victims of sexual abuse do not have a formal psychiatric diagnosis in childhood, and that there does not appear to be a specific link with depressive disorder.

Goldston, Turnquist and Knutson (1989) compared 128 girls who had been sexually abused, and who had attended one of the three clinical services, with nonabused controls attending the same services. Among abused girls aged between 2 and 11 years, 36% had the symptom of depression of mood, a significantly higher rate than in the controls. The rate of depressed mood among adolescent girls aged between 12 and 18 years who had been sexually abused was very high (72%) but this was no higher than in the nonabused controls. Nearly one-half of abused adolescents had suicidal ideation and a fifth had made a suicidal attempt, but again this did not distinguish them from the controls.

All in all, these findings suggest that, although abusive experiences can certainly be associated with depressive symptomatology, the link is rather nonspecific.

ACUTE ADVERSITY AND DEPRESSION IN CHILDREN: CONCLUSIONS

The responses of children to many other specific adverse experiences have been studied. Recent reports have included children with burns (Stoddard et al, 1989), adolescents who had been in concentration camps (Kinzie et al, 1989), and homeless children (Fox et al, 1990). Little will be gained by considering all of these studies here. Suffice to say that there are obviously marked individual variations in childrens' affective responses to specific adverse experiences. Although levels of depressive symptomatology have for the most part been quite high, on current evidence it seems that the majority of children who experience an adverse event will not develop a depressive disorder. It is important to emphasize that this is not to say that adverse experiences are not important in the aetiology of depressive disorders of young people. Most people who smoke do not develop lung cancer yet most people with lung cancer have been smokers. Similarly, many children with depressive disorder (perhaps a half) have experienced a life event (Goodyer, Kolvin & Gatzanis, 1985; Berney et al, 1991; Wilde et al, 1992). Nevertheless, these findings remind us that for one reason or another some children seem to be remarkably resilient in the face of adversity.

At the moment, the available data suggest that there is little specificity in the association of adverse experiences and depression in young people. Such experiences can be followed by a number of psychiatric symptoms, including symptoms of post-traumatic stress disorder, anxiety, behavioural problems, as well as depression. Moreover, in general, depressed children seem to have had the same number and types of adverse experiences as children with other psychiatric problems. Furthermore, as is the case in adults, there is no evidence that depressed children with an "endogenous" symptom pattern differ from children with other types of depression in respect of the proportion suffering a life event (Berney et al, 1991). So, it seems that adverse life experiences constitute a rather nonspecific risk factor for depression in young people.

We shall see in the next chapter that a number of psychological theories exist that attempt to explain the mechanisms linking environmental adversity to the mental state of depression. At this point, it should be noted that whatever the nature of the intrapsychic mechanisms, there is evidence that factors external to the child also play a part in linking adverse experiences to depression in children. Thus, studies of bereavement, divorce and disasters have all found evidence suggesting that the psychopathological reactions of other family members may be important in the links with psychopathology in the child. Unfortunately, the mechanisms that might be responsible for these links are not yet fully understood. Perhaps, for example, parents who suffer psychiatric symptoms after an experience such as a divorce or bereavement are less able to provide emotional support for their children. Or, it could be that the association is spurious and induced by the fact that parents who have a tendency to react to stress with depression pass the same tendency on to their child. Whatever the reason, it is clear that in some instances there are important links between psychopathology in the child, adverse experiences and psychopathology in the parents.

Finally, it should be borne in mind that much of the research on the consequences of specific events has been primarily concerned with depressive symptomatology. It may therefore be of only limited application to the study of depressive disorders. Further prospective studies of children who have experienced specific events using interview-based measures of depressive disorders would be most informative. In addition, we need to continue to ask "where do life events come from?" (Rutter & Sandberg, 1992). As was described earlier in this chapter, children with depression often come from families where there are high rates of adversity. Moreover, they commonly have difficulties forming social relationships. Both these features could act to increase the rates of so-called acute life events. A better understanding of the mechanisms involved in these processes would have important implications for prevention.

Chapter 7

Psychological and Biological Mechanisms

Several kinds of mechanism have been put forward to explain how the risk factors described in the previous chapter could lead to the symptoms of depression. These may broadly be divided into psychological and biological, although it will be appreciated that the two are not mutually exclusive.

PSYCHOLOGICAL MODELS

Cognitive–behavioural models

Among investigators of childhood depression probably the most influential of the psychological approaches have been the so-called cognitive–behavioural models. There is much overlap between the ideas behind these models, but three stand out:

1. Seligman's theory of depression, in which one particular cognitive style, helplessness, is crucial.
2. Beck's cognitive theory of depression.
3. Lewinsohn's behavioural viewpoint.

Learned helplessness
Seligman's (1975) theories of depression are rooted in animal experiments. Seligman and his coworkers observed that dogs exposed to uncontrollable electric shocks failed subsequently either to learn the response to terminate the shock or to initiate as many escape attempts. In human terms, there was an expectation of helplessness that was generalized to the new situation.

These findings were thought to have direct implications for the development of depression. Seligman suggested that reactive depression in humans is a state of learned helplessness. The individual has learned expectations that external events are largely beyond his control and that unpleasant outcomes are probable. It is the *expectation* of loss of control rather than the event that is crucial. This state can produce many of the features of depression, such as some of the cognitive deficits and motivational difficulties (e.g. psychomotor retardation). However, a particular problem for learned helplessness theory was to explain why depressed people so often had guilt. If depressed subjects thought they were unable to control events then why did they so often experience guilt?

These, and other, discrepancies between the theory and clinical observations led to a reformulation of the theory within an *attributional framework* (Abramson, Seligman & Teasdale, 1978). Attribution theory states that the causes of events cannot be observed, but rather are interpreted by the individual to make the environment meaningful. Abramson and colleagues suggested that when a person fails at something he attributes it to a cause. The cause may be stable or unstable, internal or external, and global or specific. It was asserted that the expectation of uncontrollable adverse events leads to depression, but only if the person attributes them to *internal*, *stable* and *global* causes. For example, "I failed the exam because I am useless". In its reformulated form the theory was better able to explain some of the features of depression that were unexplained by the original model. However, since the reformulated theory did not explicitly present a clearly articulated model of depression (it was mainly concerned with the general issue of human helplessness) there were still many discrepancies between the theory and clinical observations on depressed patients (see Wilner, 1984). Accordingly, there have been several attempts to revise the reformulated theory, most notably by Abramson, Metalsky and Alloy (1989) who de-emphasized the role of attribution theory and highlighted the role of negative cognitions, especially hopelessness.

Depressive cognitions

The central feature of Beck's (1976) theory of depression is a *negative "cognitive set"*. Depressed people are seen as having a negative view of themselves, of the world and of the future. It is these depressive cognitions that lead to depressed mood. Beck proposed that we have an automatic style of thinking that largely determines the conclusions we derive from experiences. People who are prone to depression have a tendency to interpret events negatively. Early traumatic experiences, especially loss, are seen as important in the origins of these negative views. The recurrence of situations similar to these early experiences may bring the negative schemata into existence. It is not the events themselves which produce depression, but rather their meaning to the individual. For instance, a rebuff in a social situation would be more likely to cause depression in a person who feels that he needs to be liked and who takes such a rebuff to mean that he is disliked.

Low rate of social reinforcement

Early behavioural formulations of depression tended to analyse depressive behaviour in operant conditioning terms. The depressed person was seen as on an "extinction" schedule: active responses decrease because of the lack of positive reinforcement, while depressive behaviour is reinforced. Lewinsohn

(1974) also proposed that depression is the result of a low rate of response-contingent positive reinforcement. However, this low rate occurs not only because few positively reinforcing events are available in the environment, but also because people with depression do not engage in forms of behaviour that lead to pleasant consequences. In other words, depression can also be the result of a *lack of the social skills* necessary to obtain rewards. The whole situation may be made worse by the fact that once depressed, depressed subjects are less likely to have contact with other people, and so they become even less likely to experience positive social reinforcement.

Cognitive–behavioural models and depression in young people

Attributions and control

Many of the important ideas behind helplessness theory in adults can be meaningfully applied to explain depression in children. For example, Dweck and Reppucci (1973) found that following failure, some 8-year-old children did not perform the responses required to succeed. They seemed to become "learned helpless". Moreover, as noted in the previous chapter, there seem to be sex differences in reactions to failure. Boys show a greater resilience to failure and are less pessimistic than girls about their future performance (Dweck et al, 1978). In addition, it seems likely that there are strong developmental trends in childrens' abilities to display learned helplessness. Rholes et al (1980) found that, although older children display situation-specific learned helplessness, younger children do not. At about the age of 7 years children begin to shift from the view that task performance and skills are specific, to a conception of general abilities that are both global and stable (Dweck & Elliot, 1983). Clearly, then, learned helplessness theory provides a coherent way of explaining several features of juvenile depressive conditions, such as the increase in rates during early adolescence and the sex differences that appear at around the same time.

To examine the relationship between depressive symptoms and attributional style, Seligman and Peterson (1986) assessed 96 children from two elementary schools with questionnaire measures of these two constructs. Both measures were repeated six months later. Attributional style was measured using the Children's Attributional Style Questionnaire (CASQ), which operationalizes each of the attributional dimensions (internal–external, global–specific, stable–unstable). Attributional style correlated strongly with depressive symptoms. However, among those aged 9–13, girls reported significantly more depressive symptoms, but only slightly more internal attributions for bad events than boys. The implication is that the sex difference in depression may not be due to the kind of sex difference in attributional style described by Dweck et al (1978).

This study, like other studies of depressed children (e.g. Kaslow, Rehm & Siegel, 1984) relied on hypothetical situations to assess attributional style. The question therefore arises as to whether depressed young people make depressogenic causal attributions in response to *actual events*. This question was examined by Meyer, Dyck and Petrinack (1989) in a sample obtained from schools. Students were asked to solve picture arrangement problems, some of which were unsolvable, and afterwards completed a measure of causal attributions. Depressed children evaluated themselves more negatively than their peers, despite similar performance on the tasks, and displayed more negative expectations for themselves both before and after task performance. However, contrary to predictions based on attribution theory, depressed children did not view the situation as beyond their control and they were no more likely than nondepressed children to externalize their success to factors such as task difficulty and luck.

The results from these studies of school samples may not of course generalize to clinical settings. However, Weisz et al (1987, 1989) have conducted several studies of outpatient and inpatient samples and have found that depressive symptoms in such settings are associated with a perceived lack of self-control. They emphasized the importance of "personal helplessness", in which people perceive themselves as less competent than others to produce the outcome behaviour, rather than "universal helplessness", in which there is the belief that desired outcomes are not contingent on the actions that either the individual or others may take. Kaslow et al (1988) reported that depressed clinic children had a more depressive attributional style than nondepressed children.

Although few investigators would quarrel with the idea that depressed young people see themselves as less competent than others, it will be appreciated that these cognitions could just as well be a consequence of depression as a cause. There have been several attempts to demonstrate causality using longitudinal data. Seligman and Peterson (1986) administered questionnaire measures of depression and attributional style to subjects in a nonclinical sample on two occasions, six months apart. Measures of attributional style at time 1 were stronger predictors of depression at time 2 than depression at time 1 was a predictor of attributional style at time 2. Seligman and Peterson therefore suggested that attributional style leads to depression. However, Hammen, Adrian and Hiroto (1988) were unable to replicate these findings in a follow-up study that included the offspring of women with affective disorders. They found that depression at follow-up was best predicted by initial symptoms and by life events but not by attributions for negative outcomes. Nolen-Hoeksema, Girgus and Seligman (1992) found that helplessness was only a very weak predictor of subsequent depressive symptomatology. Similarly, two studies of children with depressive disorders have found that cases whose depressive disorder has remitted do not show significantly increased rates of negative attributional style (Asarnow & Bates, 1988; Mc-Cauley et al, 1988). Clearly, all these findings suggest that a negative attributional style may be a state-dependent symptom of depressive disorder rather than a trait-like predisposition.

However, let us assume for a moment that certain kinds of attributional styles do lead to depression. How could these styles come about? Seligman and Peterson (1986) suggested that the origins of attributional style may be in part familial. They found a correlation between mother's attributional style for bad events and her child's attributional style. This correlation was as strong as the correlation between depression in the mother and depression in the child, suggesting that attributional style was not simply a result of the depression. Support for the idea that negative attributional styles may be familial also comes from Jaenicke et al's study (1987) of the children of depressed mothers. These researchers found that children's self-critical remarks were strongly related to maternal criticism. The implication seems to be that if children are criticized a great deal they could eventually become excessively critical of themselves.

Cognitive distortions in depressed children

While the models described in the previous section have emphasized the importance of causal attributions in depression, "cognitive" theories have been more concerned with the presence of *cognitive distortions*, such as negative appraisals about the self. Indeed, several studies have now documented an association between negative cognitive biases and depression in young people. Kaslow, Rehm and Siegel (1984) found that children with depressive symptoms were more self-punitive than nondepressed children. Children with depressive symptoms have also been found to have lower self-esteem (Kaslow et al, 1984), to experience hopelessness (Kazdin et al, 1983b; McCauley et al, 1988), and to recall positive experiences less well (Whitman & Leitenberg, 1990). In three studies, using separate samples, Kendall, Stark and Adam (1990) found that the cognitive functioning of depressed children recruited through schools was characterized by more negative self-evaluations than in nondepressed children.

Interestingly, Kendall et al (1990) found no evidence that depressed young people had reduced cognitive tempo or a processing deficit, as judged by their ability to match familiar figures. The implication is that depression in young people is associated with a distortion in thinking not a deficiency in thinking. Cognitive treatments should therefore aim at modifying distorted patterns of thinking rather than training new cognitive styles.

Social–cognitive models

Since depression in young people is frequently associated with social impairment of various kinds (see Chapter 6), it is not surprising to find that there have been a number of attempts to understand depressive conditions among young people in terms of social learning theory and social competence. *Social competence models* (see Cole, 1991) are based on the observations that children frequently seek and use social comparison information in making self-evaluations, and that others (e.g. family, peers) will develop social expectations about the child that some children may eventually come to believe. In other words, children actively seek social competency feedback from others and if they suffer negative feedback too frequently they can develop negative self-schemata that will predispose to depression, especially when they experience stress. Support for this idea has come from a number of studies. Wilson and Cairns (1988), for example, reported that sex differences in rates of depression among adolescents from the general population might be related to sex differences in perceptions of social competence. Cole (1991) reported an association between peer nominations of social competence and self-reported depressive symptoms.

Other socially-based formulations of depression among the young place greater emphasis on the role of *social skills*. For instance, Patterson and Capaldi (1990) pointed to the possibility that lack of social skills would lead to loss of social support and thence to depression. In their model, particular emphasis was placed on the idea That antisocial behaviour would lead to peer rejection and thence to depression. Parental rejection was hypothesized to act through another route that involved low self-esteem. Adams and Adams (1991) found some evidence to support the idea that depressed youngsters lack social skills. They reported that depressed adolescents were more likely to choose a maladaptive response to a stressful event, such as getting drunk or running away from home, than nondepressed adolescents. On the other hand, Joffe et al (1990) found that adolescent inpatients with major depression did not differ significantly from normal controls in regard to social problem-solving abilities, as assessed by responses to questions about hypothetical social situations. This was in stark contrast to adolescents with conduct disorder, who showed a number of social problem-solving deficits, such as the inability to anticipate obstacles in the pursuit of a social end. The implication is that the social skills deficits of adolescents with conduct disorder may have a different origin from those of children with depression.

Some limitations of cognitive theories of depression in young people

In interpreting the results of the studies of depressive cognitions in young people that have been published so far, a number of points need to be borne in mind. First, much of this research has been conducted using continuous measures of depressive symptomatology in nonclinical samples. It remains to be seen whether or not the results will generalize to children with depressive disorders seen in clinical settings. Second, extensive reliance has been placed on questionnaire measures, and it may well be necessary to use more sensitive measures in future research. There is, for instance, evidence that some self-report measures of social cognitive processing in young people have low internal consistency (Robins & Hinkley, 1989). Third, it is not yet clear whether the kinds of cognitive distortions found to be associated with depressive symptomatology are specific to depression, or whether they are also linked to other kinds of symptomatology. Finally, there is the continuing uncertainty as to whether or not these cognitions are secondary to the depression of mood or whether they are primary and causal.

Having said this, cognitive theories certainly deserve greater scrutiny. They provide a plausible mechanism for linking adverse experiences to depression of mood. "Cognitive" explanations also exist for sex differences in depression and for the increase in frequency in depression and depression-related phenomena that occurs in early adolescence. Moreover, we shall see in the next chapter that they have led to several promising forms of therapy. It is likely therefore that cognitive–behavioural perspectives on depression in young people will continue to be valuable.

Psychosocial models of vulnerability and resilience

Models of adult depressive disorder

Studies of depressive disorder in adults have consistently shown that there is an association with adverse experiences of one kind or another (Paykel & Cooper, 1992). However, as we saw in the previous chapter, the association is typically small and it has become clear that the impact of stressful life events depends a great deal on the context in which they occur, the meaning of these events and on the individual's resources to cope with them. In other words, it has become necessary to understand why it is that some people are more *vulnerable* to adversity than others.

Several different kinds of vulnerability model have been put forward to explain depression in adults. Amongst the most influential has been the theory of Brown and his colleagues in London. In its original form (Brown & Harris, 1978) the model postulated that there were three main aetiological factors: provoking agents, vulnerability factors and symptom formation factors. However, recent revisions to the model (Brown, Harris & Bifulco, 1986) have produced a rather more complicated picture, with several possible causal pathways. Thus, Brown and colleagues suggested that early adverse experiences, such as loss of mother, might have an impact on the later mental health of women through one of two chains. First, they postulated links between unsuccessful coping with a premarital pregnancy and current working-class status. Low social class was thought to increase the rate of experiencing both provoking agents and vulnerability factors such as an unsatisfactory marital relationship. These would then lead to depression. The second strand was hypothesized to involve certain enduring personality characteristics comprising cognitive sets and coping styles. Early loss of mother was postulated to lead to lack of care which in turn led to childhood helplessness. Both childhood helplessness and later factors (particularly premarital pregnancy) led to current helplessness, which in turn caused ongoing poor mastery and low self-esteem, and so produced depression.

In other words, according to Brown et al (1986) vulnerability to depression in adulthood may come about either through a pathway that is largely based on psychosocial factors in the individual's environment, or through a mechanism that involves intrinsic affective–cognitive factors. Early adversity can lead to depression through one or both of these paths.

Vulnerability and resilience in children
Vulnerability has been an important issue in research on the effects of life stress in children, where there has also been great interest in the resilience of children to adverse experiences. Garmezy (1985) described three models of the relationship between personal attributes, stress and adjustment. In the *compensatory model,* stressors tend to lower the level of adjustment and positive personal attributes tend to increase it. In other words the effects are simply counteractive. In the *vulnerability–protective model* there is an interaction between stress and personal attributes in predicting adjustment. If the risk is intensified when the attribute is present, then the variable carries a *vulnerability effect.* If the risk is reduced, then the variable carries a *protective effect.* In either case, there is an interaction between the attribute and the stressor. The *challenge* model postulates a curvilinear relationship between stress and disorder, in which stressors could act to enhance competence provided that the levels of stress were not too high. Thus, stressors can have *steeling effects.* For example, there is some evidence that brief, happy separations may help children to cope with longer ones (Wolkind & Rutter, 1985). So, it should be borne in mind that protective factors are not always positive social experiences: they may in fact be aversive to the child when they occur.

Garmezy (1985) identified three broad groups of factors that protect against stress: (1) attributes of the child, (2) family cohesion and warmth, and (3) the availability of external supports for children and/or parents. Amongst the personal attributes of the child, sex seems to be particularly important in determining vulnerability to adversities such as marital discord, with boys being more at risk than girls (Rutter, 1982). Age may also be important. For example, there are developmental changes in children's responses to the stress of separation (Chapter 1). Temperamental features can also be important. Rutter and Quinton (1984) showed that children of mentally ill parents with high-risk temperamental attributes (mostly attributes of the so-called "difficult" temperament) were twice as likely as temperamentally easy children to develop a psychiatric disturbance. Amongst the family factors that seem to protect children from psychiatric disorders, a good relationship with a parent seems important (Rutter, 1971).

Vulnerability and resilience to depression in children

Several investigators have begun to apply these, or similar, models of vulnerability and resilience to the study of depression in children. For example, Seligman and Peterson (1986) proposed that depression in children generally resulted from characteristics of an individual *in conjunction* with characteristics of the environment. Neither individual characteristics (in their model, attributional style) nor the uncontrollable events alone result in widespread helplessness and depression; only their co-occurrence leads to depression. In other words, like Brown's model of depression in adults, vulnerability factors are seen as important mainly because they increase the risk of disorder in the presence of other factors; they carry a negligible risk in the absence of provoking agents. Similarly, Goodyer (1990) reported some evidence for indirect effects of a lack of social achievements (such as in education or physical skills) on anxiety and depression in children. Children who lacked social achievements did not normally develop psychiatric problems. However, in the presence of poor friendships there was an association between poor social achievements and depression/anxiety. The interesting implication from these findings is that vulnerability or resilience need not necessarily reside in past environmental factors or constitutional qualities. Current factors, such as social achievements, may be just as important. It follows that helping children to succeed may decrease the risk of psychiatric disorder.

These early studies of vulnerability and resilience in depressed children offer promising leads for future research. However, one criticism of this kind of approach is that it implies a linear "cause–effect" model of psychopathology that fails to take into account the possibility of reciprocal interactions between the child and his environment. It has therefore been argued that a *transactional model*, in which the environment and the child are seen as exerting a mutual influence on each other in a dynamic fashion, may be a better formulation of depression in young people (Cicchetti & Schneider-Rosen, 1984, 1986). According to this model, in studying the aetiology of depression at any one point in a child's development, the interplay between a number of factors must be considered. Some of these factors will be *enduring* and others *transient*. Enduring factors can be *protective* or *vulnerability* factors, and transient factors can be either *buffers* or *challenging* factors. For each of these factors there is a relationship with development. Thus, for enduring factors developmental changes may be necessary before they become operative. So, for instance, certain cognitive changes may be required for a child to experience depressive cognitions. Similarly, what constitutes a "challenger" or a "buffer" will vary according to developmental level. For example, the "buffering" effect of a close, confiding friendship may become operative only during adolescence. Cicchetti & Schneider-Rosen (1984) suggested that there would be "coordination" between vulnerability and protective factors; that is, that there would be a tendency for development to be "self-righting" or homeostatic. Thus, for example, as the child develops the cognitive capacity to make causal attributions to the self (a vulnerability factor), so the ability to conceptualize multiple emotions (a protective factor) develops. In their model childhood depression would be expressed "only when potentiating factors override compensatory ones".

Family systems models of child and adolescent depression

Another set of models that emphasize the bidirectional nature of the aetiological factors in childhood depression arises from family systems theory. As described in Chapter 6, it seems that depressed young people often come from families in which there are high rates of psychopathology and/or disturbed family functioning of one kind or another. There are, of course, numerous possible mechanisms that could explain these links, such as genetic processes or exposure to family discord or through the modelling of a parent's negative attributional style. However, all these theories tend to explain depression through a linear series of cause and effect chains. In *systems theory* a different approach is taken in which there is a focus on the *relationship* between members in the family. Systems thinking derives from the ideas of mutual causality, of homeostasis, and from the notion that the whole is qualitatively different from its parts (Gorell Barnes, 1985). Depression can therefore be formulated as a consequence of dysfunctional maintenance of the family equilibrium.

Thus, for example, Oster and Caro (1990) emphasized the importance of placing other possible risk factors for depression, such as genetic make-up, within a family systems perspective. The most important of these factors were family history, past traumas (such as bereavement), "boundaries and structures" and "coping with emotions". According to these authors, the organization and structure of the family predisposes the family either to cope effectively or to experience problems. In families with "enmeshed" boundaries (that is, in which there is little differentiation between generations), the adolescent's move towards independence is seen as leaving the parent's more aware of their own difficulties, such as marital problems or depression. The families are also characterized by avoidance of external relationships and an over-intense loyalty to the family. The adolescent's development of depressive symptoms may therefore serve to maintain the myth of family unity. Depressive symptoms may also occur because the adolescent mirrors the symptoms of the parents or because adolescents in such families are often socially isolated and lonely.

There have been only a handful of attempts to investigate the family environments of depressed children using the kinds of instruments that would be familiar to researchers interested in systems theory. However, the research that has been published so far has produced some positive findings. Forehand et al (1988) reported that depressive symptoms were associated with the number of conflicts that the young people reported with their parents. Stark et al (1990) investigated the family environments of 11 depressed children (mostly diagnosed as dysthymic disorder or depressive disorder not elsewhere classified), 15 children with depression and an anxiety disorder, 10 children with an anxiety disorder and 15 normal controls. Compared with the controls, children with a psychiatric diagnosis perceived their family environments to be less supportive and more "enmeshed". Families with a depressed and anxious child differed from families of children with an anxious child in respect of a variety of variables, such as enmeshment and involvement in decision-making. Moreover, based on the child's perceptions of family environment, the diagnostic status of the child could be predicted with considerable accuracy.

One of the problems with this kind of research is that, although its focus is on bidirectionality, its tools are essentially unidirectional to the extent that one subject is asked to report on his/her view of the family. No attempt is made to study sequences of events, as when A leads to B leads to C leads to A. Moreover, depression of mood is by its very nature an individual behaviour, that does not depend for its definition on the presence of external factors. It is an intrapsychic phenomenon that can, as we saw in Chapter 2, exist in a child without any other person being aware of it. Indeed, this feature of "emotional" symptoms distinguishes them from conduct problems, which are for the most part *defined* by the interaction between the individual and his environment (as occurs, for instance, through the breaking of societal norms in stealing). So, although systems thinking may have a part to play in enhancing understanding of certain aspects of childhood depressive disorders, such as their tendency to run in families, it seems unlikely that it can offer a complete model.

BIOLOGICAL THEORIES

Early formulations of the amine theory of depression

Perhaps the most influential of the biological theories of depression have been the so-called amine hypotheses. The original amine hypotheses of affective disorders stemmed from several observations: first, that certain drugs have effects on mood, and, second, that in animals these same drugs alter brain amine concentrations. During the 1950s it was noticed that a proportion of patients with high blood pressure who were taking reserpine developed depression-like reactions. Subsequently, it was shown in animals that reserpine depletes the brain of certain neurotransmitters, such as noradrenaline and dopamine. At around the same time there were reports that iproniazid, which is closely related to the antituberculosis agent isoniazid, sometimes produced mood elevation. Compounds such as iproniazid were known to inhibit the enzyme monoamine oxidase, whose major function is to metabolize amines such as noradrenaline. Subsequently, numerous controlled trials showed that tricyclic drugs such as amitriptyline, which also have an effect on amine pathways, are effective antidepressants (Paykel, 1989).

Accordingly, two early hypotheses regarding the pathophysiology of the affective disorders were formulated. One hypothesis concentrated on the catecholamine noradrenaline and the other on the indoleamine 5-hydroxytryptamine. The original *catecholamine hypothesis* proposed that some depressions were associated with a deficiency of catecholamines at functionally important sites in the brain (Schildkraut, 1965), and that mania was due to an excess of these same catecholamines. The deficiency was thought to occur because of several different reasons, principally decreased production. Different kinds of deficiencies were linked to different kinds of depressions. The original *indoleamine hypothesis* was very similar, except that it postulated that there was a deficiency of 5-hydroxytryptamine (5HT, also known as serotonin) in depression.

How might these changes in neurotransmitters lead to depression? A variety of different theories have been put forward, but one of the most influential has been the idea that these neurotransmitters have a behavioural function in certain reward systems. Traditionally, noradrenaline has been seen as most important in this regard (Stein, 1962). Deakin and Crow (1986) suggested that catecholamine systems were linked to reward and approach behaviours, and that serotonin systems were linked to punishment and avoidance. They suggested that the amine hypothesis could be formulated as follows: "depression results from hypoactivity of catecholaminergic reward systems, and anxiety from hyperactivity of serotonergic punishment systems, the two systems interacting with each other such that anxiety and depression represent separate but correlated dimensions of disturbance". Siever and Davis (1985) suggested that it was not so much the overall level of activity in these systems that was disordered, but rather that there were abnormalities of homeostatic mechanisms or of the normal periodicities of the system. In other words, it is the *dynamics* of the system that are impaired in depression.

Testing and reformulation of the amine hypothesis
At first the tricyclic antidepressants were thought to act through their ability to increase the concentrations of monoamines by blocking their reuptake into presynaptic neurones (see Green & Goodwin, 1986). Accordingly, the

original amine hypothesis postulated an absolute or relative deficiency in noradrenergic transmission. However, there appeared to be little relationship between time of onset of antidepressant action (weeks) and the speed with which the drugs inhibit monoamine uptake (days). Moreover, some drugs such as cocaine and amphetamine, which are potent blockers of noradrenaline reuptake, did not appear to be as effective as antidepressants. In addition, although there is some evidence that depressed bipolar patients do excrete lower levels of catecholamine metabolites, other diagnostic categories of depressed patients had equal amounts of metabolites as normal subjects (Heninger & Charney, 1986).

Accordingly, recent research on the mechanism of action of antidepressant drugs has tried to understand the *multiple* effects of antidepressants on neurotransmitter systems. There has been particular interest in the idea that they may influence receptor sensitivity (Charney et al, 1991). In other words, net noradrenergic function is changed because antidepressants alter *receptor function*, not primarily because they alter levels of catecholamines. Several studies have attempted to study noradrenergic receptor sensitivity using so-called "challenge" tests. For example, a number of investigations of growth hormone response to the drug clonidine (which is thought to involve noradrenergic pathways) have shown abnormalities of this response in patients with endogenous depression (see Checkley et al, 1986; Cowen & Wood, 1991). However, since the ability to change noradrenergic receptor activity is a property shared by only some antidepressants, it is very likely that other mechanisms are involved as well.

It is likely that the amine hypothesis and its variants will continue to attract much attention from researchers who are interested in the biology of adult depressive disorders. However, as all researchers in this field seem to agree, the current hypotheses are almost certainly an oversimplification. There are many other neurotransmitters in the nervous system that might be involved in the aetiology of depressive disorders. The emphasis on the amines is partly a reflection of the widespread availability of techniques to measure them. Nevertheless, the amine hypothesis is supported by a number of replicable observations, most notably the effects of TCAs on depression and on monoamine function.

Tests of the amine hypothesis in depressed children
Several research groups have investigated the functioning of amine systems in depressed children. Before considering these studies, however, it is important to note that there may be developmental differences in the balance of neural amine systems between childhood and adult life. In a review of developmental differences in psychobiological markers of depression, Puig-Antich (1986) pointed out that in rats catecholamine systems do not develop fully until the beginning of adulthood whereas serotonergic systems develop much earlier in life. He suggested that there was evidence of a similar phenomenon in humans.

In particular, he noted that children do not show the euphoric response to dextro-amphetamine (which is thought to be mediated by monoamine pathways) that is found in adults (Rapoport et al, 1980). There is also evidence that the relative activity of the noradrenergic system in relation to the dopaminergic system (a system that is regulated by the neurotransmitter dopamine) changes with age, and that the development of both systems is affected by environmental as well as genetic factors (Rogeness, Javors and Pliszka, 1992).

In spite of these possible developmental differences, techniques very similar to those used in depressed adults have been used to investigate the functioning of central monoamine neurotransmitters in depressed children and adolescents. Thus, several investigators have studied the excretion of amine metabolites in depressed young people. Cytryn et al (1974) studied urinary metabolites of noradrenaline in depressed children, but possible group heterogeneity based on differences in diagnostic criteria makes it difficult to draw firm conclusions from the results (Lowe & Cohen, 1983). Khan (1987) studied 24-hour urinary noradrenaline metabolites in 33 adolescents with major depression, 6 with dysthymic disorder and 51 nondepressed adolescent inpatients. Neither low nor high concentrations of urinary metabolites were specific to depression, but occurred in other diagnostic categories as well. On the other hand, Rogeness et al (1990) found that a measure of increased noradrenaline function was higher in major depression and anxiety disorder than in conduct disorder.

Challenge tests involving the secretion of growth hormone have produced some evidence for the hypothesis of hypersecretion in depressed young people. Puig-Antich et al (1984a) reported that endogenously depressed prepubertal children hyposecrete growth hormone (GH) in response to insulin-induced hypoglycemia compared with nondepressed psychiatric controls and non-endogenous depressed children. Jensen and Garfinkel (1990) found that among six prepubertal children with major depression, the peak growth hormone response to stimulation with oral clonidine was significantly lower than in normal controls. They interpreted this as evidence of dysregulation of noradrenergic receptors. Unfortunately, the interpretation of these findings is made difficult by the possibility that the results of provocation tests may not necessarily apply to physiological (sleep) GH secretion, which may be regulated by other systems (Mendelson, 1982; Puig-Antich, 1986). In other words it is necessary to establish whether children with major depression differ from controls in nocturnal GH secretion. Puig-Antich et al (1984b) found that prepubertal children with major depression hypersecreted GH during sleep when compared with nondepressed child patients. Kutcher et al (1991) reported similar findings when 12 depressed adolescents were compared with 12 normal controls in respect of nocturnal GH secretion. In addition to 12 midnight differences, adolescents with depression hypersecreted more GH at 1 a.m. and 3 a.m.

However, nocturnal GH secretion does not seem to be influenced by adrenergic or dopamine systems, but is thought to be controlled predominantly by cholinergic systems (i.e. systems using acetylcholine as a neurotransmitter) or by serotonergic (5HT) systems (Mendelson, 1982). Accordingly, Puig-Antich (1986) proposed that there were several possible mechanisms that could account for sleep GH hypersecretion in children with major depression. The main ones were: (1) a functional deficit of hypothalamic serotonin systems (as these systems seem to inhibit nocturnal GH secretion), and/or (2) an increase in cholinergic activity (as these systems seem to increase nocturnal GH secretion). Puig-Antich (1986) concluded that serotonin deficit would explain the findings better than cholinergic hyperactivity, although a simple serotonin deficit alone could not entirely account for all the findings. On the other hand, the few biological studies of serotonergic measures can be interpreted as consistent with either increased or decreased activity in this system (Rogeness, Javors & Pliszka, 1992). Clearly, in this area even when positive findings are replicated their interpretation is far from easy!

A variety of other neuroendocrine tests have been used to examine the functioning of amine systems in depressed children and adolescents, some of which will be considered in more detail later. In addition, since receptors to particular amine neurotransmitters exist in peripheral tissues, such as blood platelets, there have been attempts to study the functioning of these receptors *in vitro* (e.g. Carstens et al, 1988). All these techniques offer exciting prospects for future investigations of depressive conditions in young people, but at this point it has to be said that there is a paucity of good evidence to support the role of abnormal amine systems in depressive conditions among the young. Several studies, such as those of GH secretion, have provided some general support for the notion of a biochemical abnormality of amine systems. However, it must be remembered that in adult depressive disorders probably the most important set of observations that has supported the amine hypothesis has been the response of these disorders to antidepressants. We shall see later in this book that so far there is little evidence that antidepressants have a specific effect on depressive conditions in either prepubertal children or adolescents. Now, it may be that this lack of effect is a result of developmental differences in amine systems or of the difficulties in conducting systematic drug trials in this age group. Nevertheless, the absence of a specific and replicable therapeutic effect of antidepressants among young people (see Chapter 9) certainly does undermine the amine hypothesis of the aetiology of depressive conditions in this age group.

ENDOCRINE ABNORMALITIES

Three lines of evidence have suggested that abnormalities of the endocrine system may be important in the aetiology of depression. First, endocrine disorders are sometimes associated with affective reactions. Second, abnormalities of the endocrine system have been found in people with affective disorders. Third, endocrine organs are controlled by the hypothalamic system which in turn is controlled by nerve pathways involving monoamines. Biological theories of depression that involve the endocrine system are also popular because this system is involved in determining bodily responses to stress. So, such theories can readily accommodate the notion of an interaction between biological predispositions and environmental adversity.

Endocrine disorders

Several kinds of endocrine disorder have been linked with affective phenomena. In hypoadrenalism (underactivity of the adrenal gland) symptoms such as apathy, fatigue, withdrawal and mood disturbance are frequent and may appear at an early stage of the disease. Emotional disorder is also common in patients with hyperadrenalism (overactivity of the adrenal gland). Haskett (1985) described a series of 30 patients with Cushing's disease, of whom 25 had had some form of affective disorder. Twenty had depression and eight had had mania or hypomania. Other psychiatric symptoms are also common in adults with Cushing's disease.

Cushing's disease in adults is commonly due to disease of the pituitary gland. Such cases are rare in childhood. Frank and Doerr (1989) found only eight cases among referrals to a department of paediatric endocrinology over an 18-year period. These authors described a case of mania occurring in a pubescent 13-year-old girl with Cushing's disease. She presented with typical features of mania including mood elevation, pressure of speech, decreased need for sleep and grandiose delusions. On physical examination several features of hyperadrenalism were present, such as Cushingoid facies and obesity. Her mental state improved with neuroleptics, and after removal of a pituitary adenoma no further medication was required.

Psychiatric symptoms are also found in subjects with thyroid disease. In hyperthyroidism there are usually some psychological symptoms, some of which resemble those occurring in hypomania or mania, such as distractibility, restlessness and irritability. However, probably the most common psychiatric symptom is anxiety. A lack of thyroid hormones, hypothyroidism, is also associated with mental effects. If undiscovered early in infancy, hypothyroidism may lead to mental retardation. Later in life, thyroid disease may present as a dementia or depressive disorder. Mental symptoms include depression, retardation of speech and movement, and muddled thinking. Serious mental disorders may be associated with prolonged hypothyroidism, such as affective and schizophreniform psychoses.

Endocrine abnormalities in depressed people

Cortisol secretion in depressed adults and children
Cortisol is one of the chief glucocorticoids, so-called because of the blood glucose raising properties of this group of hormones. The glucocorticoids are one of a number of different types of steroidal hormone that are secreted by the cortex of the adrenal glands. They have a wide range of physiological actions. For example, they promote the formation of glucose from protein, they increase the retention of sodium by the kidney and are involved in inflammatory reactions. Glucocorticoids play an important role in modifying the responses of the body to infections, trauma and physical stress. A deficiency may lower the ability to withstand stress and death may occur suddenly from low blood pressure and hypoglycemia. They may also play a role in maintaining catecholamine enzyme activity.

The secretion of glucocorticoids is controlled by the release of adrenocor-ticotrophin hormone (ACTH) from the pituitary gland, which in turn is regu-lated by corticotrophin releasing factor (CRF) secreted by the hypothalamus. Several mechanisms modulate ACTH secretion:

1. There is a circadian rhythm so that ACTH level is highest in the morning and lowest at about midnight, with cortisol following a similar pattern.
2. Plasma cortisol levels influence the secretion of CRF, so that high levels of cortisol suppress ACTH secretion and low levels enhance it.
3. Stress, caused by such factors as surgery or infection, increases CRF and ACTH secretion.

Several abnormalities of the CRF–ACTH–cortisol axis have been reported in adult subjects with depressive disorders. Twenty-four-hour mean cortisol secretion has been shown in several studies to be elevated in a substantial proportion of depressed patients (Gibbons & McHugh, 1963; Sachar, Hell-man & Roffwarg, 1973). Abnormalities of cortisol secretion have also been found using the dexamethasone secretion test (DST). In the DST, cortisol levels are measured at specified intervals (usually 9, 17 and 24 hours) after dexamethasone (a powerful steroid similar to cortisol) has been given. Like cortisol, dexamethasone has a suppressive action on ACTH secretion, so in normal subjects the plasma cortisol level will be suppressed. A proportion of adult patients with major endogenous depression fail to suppress. Early stud-ies suggested that the test was both specific (96%) and sensitive (60%) for endogenous depression (Carroll, 1982). However, subsequent studies have generally found both lower sensitivity and specificity (Berger et al, 1984; Klein et al, 1984). The DST appears to be influenced by nonspecific factors such as weight loss and stress (Mellsop, Hutton & Delahunt, 1985). Nonetheless, among adult psychiatric patients nonsuppression does occur more frequently among depressed cases than among nondepressed cases, and it must be borne in mind that part of the variability in results with the DST may well be the result of methodological factors such as patient selection (Zimmerman, Coryell & Pfohl, 1986). There is, in addition, some evidence of abnormalities of corticotrophin releasing factor mechanisms in depressed patients (Amsterdam et al, 1987).

Similar tests of cortisol secretion have been used with children and adolescents suffering from major depression. Most studies of cortisol levels have failed to find a significant difference between depressed adolescents and controls (Dahl et al, 1989; de Villiers et al, 1989; Kutcher et al, 1991). Dahl et al (1989), for instance, found no significant differences between adolescents with major depression (mean age 15 years) and controls in 24-hour cortisol secretion. Only one of 48 depressed adolescents was a hypersecretor. Similarly, Kutcher et al (1991) found that only 3 out of 12 adolescent inpatients with major depression (mean age 18 years) were hypersecretors. Interestingly, these three patients were the only three who also showed severe, near psychotic, guilty ruminations.

The results of DST studies of depressed children and adolescents have produced conflicting results. Several studies of *prepubertal children* have suggested that children with an endogenous symptom pattern tend to have a positive DST result (e.g. Poznanski et al, 1982; Petty et al, 1985; Weller et al, 1985; Woodside, Brownstone & Fisman, 1987). For instance, Weller et al (1985) studied 50 hospitalized children who met criteria for DSM-III major depression. In 80% of depressed patients there was DST nonsuppression, compared with a nonsuppression rate of 28% in psychiatric control subjects and 11% in normal controls. Poznanski et al (1982) found in a small study of outpatients that the DST showed a specificity of 90% and a sensitivity of 63%.

On the other hand, several other studies have raised questions about the specificity of the DST in children. Livingston and Martin-Canicci (1987) found that a high proportion of children with separation anxiety disorder had a postive DST. Petty et al (1985) found DST nonsuppression in 6/7 children with major depression, 5/6 children with dysthymia and 5/6 nondepressed psychiatric controls, giving a specificity for major depression of 53%. Tyrer et al (1991) reported that the proportion of children (pre- and postpubertal) with nonsuppression on the DST did not differ significantly between children with endogenous depression (48%), children with nonendogenous depression (27%) and children with a nondepressive psychiatric diagnosis (42%).

The specificity of the DST in *adolescents* with major depression seems to be a little higher than in prepubertal depressed children. Thus, Casat and Powell (1988) pooled the data from five early studies of children with depressive disorders and estimated a sensitivity of 70% and a specificity of 70%. Pooled data from six studies of adolescents with major depression showed a sensitivity of 41% and a specificity of 79% (Casat & Powell, 1988). That is, about 40% of adolescents with major depression failed to suppress on the DST.

Similar findings have been reported in recent studies of the DST in adolescents. Appelboom-Fondu, Kerkhofs and Mendlewicz (1988) found that about 50% of adolescents with major depression failed to suppress on the DST, and Khan (1987) found that 70% of depressed adolescents were DST positive (compared with 18% of the nondepressed group). Using salivary cortisol estimates, Foreman and Goodyer (1988) reported that the DST had a sensitivity of 48% and a specificity of 91% for depressive disorder in young people.

Interpretation of reported abnormalities of cortisol secretion in depressed young people

Several issues arise from these generally more positive findings in samples of adolescents with depressive disorders. First, it is still not clear whether they can be accounted for by weight loss, although preliminary findings from two studies suggest that loss of weight was not an important factor (Khan, 1987; Foreman & Goodyer, 1988). Second, there is the question of the meaning of the apparent age differences in DST results. It could be, for instance, that they are a reflection of differences in neurotransmitter control systems across ages, similar to those postulated to occur in the amine systems (see above). Alternatively, it may be that severe "endogenous" kinds of depression (in which cortisol hypersecretion would be expected to be most marked) are less common in younger age groups. Or, perhaps these apparent age trends are artifactual and induced by problems such as lack of equivalence of the dose of dexamethasone across ages or the application of inappropriate criterion levels for cortisol nonsuppression.

Whatever the explanations for these age trends, the uncertainties regarding the interpretation of positive DST results and the generally low positive predictive power of this test even in adolescents (Casat & Powell, 1988) make it unlikely that the DST will become widely used as a diagnostic tool in clinical practice. Few clinicians would take the DST as a "gold standard" above a routine clinical assessment. On the other hand, the DST should certainly continue to be useful in research settings. After all, it has been difficult to establish replicable correlates of depressive disorder in young people. The finding of a correlate that can significantly distinguish depressed cases from controls in a number of studies conducted at different centres certainly warrants further investigation.

What other explanations exist for the abnormalities of cortisol secretion that have been found in depressed young people? The first possibility is that hypersecretion of cortisol in depressed patients is an indication of some kind of central neurochemical abnormality that has also caused the depression. In adults attempts have been made to investigate the roles that different neurotransmitter systems might have in overactivity of the hypothalamic–pituitary axis. One way of doing this is to challenge the system with a pharmacological probe, such as methylamphetamine. The effects of methylamphetamine are thought to be modulated by neurotransmitters like noradrenaline and dopamine, which in turn regulate corticotrophin-releasing factor. When given to normal subjects, amphetamine stimulates cortisol release. However, when given to depressed subjects amphetamine has been reported to produce a lower cortisol response than in the same subjects who have recovered (Checkley, 1980; Delgado et al, 1992). The implication is that the central neural pathways involved in the cortisol response to amphetamine are involved in the hypersecretion of cortisol found in some depressed patients.

It is not certain, however, that these findings will apply to depressed youngsters. Thus, a study of adolescents with major depressive disorder found that their cortisol, growth hormone and prolactin responses to amphetamine did not reliably distinguish them from nondepressed subjects, and nor did they delineate any specific depressive subgroup (Waterman et al, 1991).

Another possible cause of the association between abnormal cortisol secretion and depression is that they are both caused by some third factor. For example, it has been suggested that personality and temperamental factors may play just as important a role in determining cortisol response to stress as the degree of stress itself. Tennes and Kreye (1985) found that among children taking exams, cortisol release was better accounted for by personality variables than by the stresses caused by examination tasks. However, in adults, it seems that the tendency to hypersecrete cortisol is a state marker that normalizes when the depression has remitted (Abou-Saleh, 1988). It is not yet clear whether the same is true of indicators of cortisol hypersecretion in depressed children.

Finally, as described earlier it may be that the association of abnormal cortisol secretion and depression in young people is spurious and due to some factor that is commonly associated with depression—such as weight loss or anxiety. Indeed a recent study of the DST in child and adolescent *outpatients* found that there were no significant differences between depressed and nondepressed subjects (Birmaher et al, 1992a,b). Perhaps, then, some of the positive findings from previous research are due to the stress of hospital admission or other nonspecific factors. Certainly, it seems that the results of studies of the DST vary greatly from sample to sample. Much more needs to be known about the factors that influence this variation.

Thyroid axis abnormalities
The physiological effects of thyroid hormones are widespread and, as described earlier, include effects on mental functioning as well as on metabolic rate, cardiac output and protein metabolism. The synthesis of thyroid hormones is normally regulated by thyroid stimulating hormone (TSH) through a feedback mechanism that depends on the levels of thyroid hormones in the

blood stream. A fall in blood level of thyroid hormone increases the output of thyrotrophin-releasing factor (TRH) from the hypothalamus, which stimulates the release of TSH from the pituitary.

Affective disorders and thyroid disorders may share certain symptoms, such as depression of mood, poor concentration and retardation of speech and movements. Indeed, thyroid axis abnormalities have been explored in numerous studies of depressed adults. Thus, a large number of studies have investigated the response of depressed adults to challenge with TRH. The TRH test involves the administration of TRH and the measurement of TSH response. Blunted responses to TRH have been well described in adult patients with major depression (Loosen & Prange, 1982), though the TRH-induced TSH response is influenced by a number of other factors, such as weight loss, and a blunted response is found in several other conditions (see Checkley, 1992).

Few studies have examined TSH responses to TRH in young people, but the available data suggest that TSH responses are not often abnormal in depressed youngsters (e.g. Khan, 1987; Garcia et al, 1991). For instance, although Khan (1987) found that one third of depressed adolescents had a blunted response to TRH, this proportion was not significantly different from that in a nondepressed group. Kutcher et al (1991) found elevated mean nocturnal levels of TSH in depressed adolescents compared with normal controls, but no TRH challenge test was administered. Overall, it seems that the positive results that have been found in some studies of depressed adults cannot yet be replicated in studies of depressed young people.

SEX HORMONES AND PUBERTY

At puberty, the release of gonadotrophins stimulates the gonads to produce oestrogens and androgens which in turn are responsible for the physical changes of puberty. Production of gonadotrophins by the pituitary is under the control of the hypothalamus. High oestrogen levels will inhibit the pituitary secretion of gonadotrophins. In girls, oestrogen output from the ovaries rises sharply between 8 and 11 years. In boys, testosterone output rises between the ages of 10 and 11 years. Pubescence is the time of accelerated growth that takes place together with the development of secondary sexual characteristics. In girls, it usually begins at about 10–11 years and is complete by 13, whereas in boys it tends to be at least one year later.

In adults, several kinds of mental disorder have been linked to abnormalities of sex hormone secretion. For example, 35% of women report moderate affective symptoms just before menstruation (Andersch et al, 1986). In addition, 50–70% of women experience a mild transient mood disturbance between the third and tenth postpartum day, when there has been a 100-fold decrease in oestradiol and progesterone levels, and about 10% develop a significant degree of depression within the first three months after childbirth (Kendell et al, 1976). Moreover, during the perimenopausal years when oestradiol levels are declining many women experience some depressive symptomatology (Anderson et al, 1987).

Clearly, then, the question arises as to whether the changes in sex hormones at around the time of puberty could account for the increase in rates of depressive disorder that was described in previous chapters. In tackling this question, the first point to be made is that almost all of the research that has been conducted on hormone–mood relationships during adolescence has been concerned with depressive affect rather than depressive disorder. It cannot be assumed that the results from studies of adolescent mood fluctuations will apply to depressive conditions. The second point is that the existing results in regard to mood fluctuations and affect have been complicated and at times contradictory (Buchanan, Eccles & Becker, 1992). Thus, for example, Nottelman et al (1987) investigated the relationship between sex hormone changes, age, puberty and adjustment problems in more than 100 boys and girls from the general population. In boys, *lower* rather than higher levels of sex hormones were associated with increased self-image problems. Indeed, adjustment problems were associated with late maturity. However, for girls, higher androgen levels were associated with problems in self-image. Brooks-Gunn and Warren (1989) found that in girls negative affect increased during times of rapid oestrogen rise, supporting the idea of a link between oestrogen levels and depression. However, there was an interaction with social factors. It seemed that there was some kind of relationship between sex hormone status and social adversity such that, if hormones did influence depression, they did so in individuals who were already vulnerable through psychosocial factors.

The third point is that the literature on hormone–mood relationships in adults suggests that it is a *decrease* in oestrogen and progesterone (such as occurs at childbirth, premenstrually or after the menopause—see back) that is associated with depression, not an increase. Indeed, there is evidence that oestrogen enhances central noradrenaline availability (Paul et al, 1979) and it is prescribed to depressed women whose disorder is refractory to other treatments (Sherwin, 1991). So, it could be argued that puberty (when oestrogen levels increase) should actually protect girls from depression, not be associated with an increase in rates. Of course it may be that it is the *change* in hormone levels rather than the average level that is important in leading to depression. In other words, with the onset of menstruation girls are repeatedly exposed to monthly increases and decreases in sex hormones, and it may be these regular decreases rather than the overall increase in hormone levels that lead to depressive disorder. However, if this was the case then it would be expected that premenstrual syndrome in adolescents would be strongly related to depressive disorder, and this does not seem to be true (Raja et al,

1992). All in all, it cannot be said that existing hormonal explanations for the increase in rates of depressive disorder that occurs in girls during early adolescence are very convincing.

SLEEP ABNORMALITIES IN DEPRESSED CHILDREN

Studies of depressed adults have found that they tend to have polysomnographic (PSG) abnormalities, such as (1) reduced slow (delta) wave sleep time, (2) shortened rapid eye movement (REM) latency (time from the start of sleep to the first period of REM sleep), and (3) sleep continuity disturbances (e.g. time in bed, number of arousals, total sleep time) (see the review by Benca et al, 1992). It has also been suggested that reduced REM latency predicts response to tricyclic medication (Kupfer & Reynolds, 1992).

Early studies of PSG abnormalities in children failed to find differences in sleep electroencephalographic (EEG) measures between depressed children and controls. Puig-Antich et al (1982) found that children with major depression did not differ significantly from nondepressed neurotic children on a variety of sleep EEG measures. Similar negative findings were reported by Young et al (1982). On the other hand, Emslie et al (1990) reported that children with major depression showed reduced REM latencies compared with age-matched controls. As Emslie and colleagues pointed out, it was not clear whether these abnormalities were simply a reflection of a depressive episode or whether they represented a biological trait that might have antedated the depression. It is of interest, then, that Puig-Antich et al (1983b) found that *recovered* prepubertal major depressives had significantly shorter REM latency when compared to themselves when ill and to normal controls and to nondepressed neurotic controls. Although the reasons why the sleep EEG should actually normalize during an episode of depression were not clear, Puig-Antich (1986) suggested that these findings supported the idea that the sleep abnormalities might be a marker of a trait.

Studies of depressed adolescents have also produced mixed findings. Lahmeyer, Poznanski and Bellur (1983) found a shorter REM latency in late adolescent/young adult depressed cases compared with age-matched controls, as did Kutcher et al (1992). On the other hand, although Goetz et al (1987) and Appelboom-Fondu et al (1988) found some sleep continuity disturbances in depressed adolescents, there were no overall differences in REM sleep measurements when comparisons were made with controls.

Puig-Antich (1986) hypothesized that it might be possible to put these findings together using a developmental framework. He pointed to the evidence from studies of adult depressed cases that suggested there was an association between many sleep EEG variables and age. For example, REM latency is shorter in older age groups. He proposed that the largely negative sleep findings in childhood depressed cases were the result of maturational differences in the nature of sleep. Sleep continuity disturbances become evident in adolescence but it is only in late adolescence that REM latency becomes abnormal in depressed cases. The findings of Emslie et al (1990) do not go along with this proposition, but Puig-Antich's hypothesis (1986) reminds us once again of the possibility of developmental changes in the so-called biological measures of depression.

It should also be noted that, as with the DST, the results of sleep EEG studies seem to vary greatly from sample to sample. Thus, for instance, two studies have reported on subgroup analyses suggesting that the sleep EEG is particularly likely to be abnormal in *inpatients* (Dahl et al, 1990; Goetz et al, 1991). Neither of these studies found an overall difference between depressed and control groups on sleep EEG measures. The implication is that the EEG abnormalities reported in some studies (e.g. the study of Emslie et al (1990), which compared depressed inpatients with healthy controls) were simply the result of admission to hospital or other nonspecific factors. On the other hand, it could be that the variability in the results is a reflection of a "true" heterogeneity in juvenile depressive disorders. For instance, Giles et al (1992) found that sleep EEG abnormalities were much more likely to occur when depressed children had both a family history of depression and a parent with sleep abnormalities. In other words, there may be subgroups in which sleep EEG abnormalities reflect a real underlying neurophysiological disturbance.

BIOLOGICAL MEASURES IN CHILDHOOD DEPRESSION: CONCLUSIONS

Psychobiological measures have attracted a great deal of attention from researchers interested in depressive disorders among the young. In part this interest has stemmed from the need to develop a biological test that will distinguish depressed from nondepressed patients. Indeed, there is no doubt that the development of such a test would greatly assist in diagnosis. In part, however, interest in biological markers has also stemmed from the wish to identify the degree of similarity between child and adult depressions. If biological similarities could be demonstrated across the age span, then this would improve the validity of the diagnosis of childhood depression.

So far as the development of a "test" for juvenile depression is concerned, the findings thus far have not been particularly promising. Thus, studies of the DST in depressed children have commonly yielded sensitivities of about 70% and specificities of about the same. In adolescents the sensitivity seems to be lower (about 50%) but the specificity is higher (around 80%) (Casat & Powell, 1988; Yaylayan, Weller & Weller, 1992). Although these percentages may sound impressive, they are in fact no better than can be obtained much more cheaply by using a depression questionnaire (see the sensitivities and specificities of the main depression questionnaires cited by Costello & Angold, 1988). As we saw in Chapter 3, this means that the test is in fact relatively inaccurate. Of course, the low sensitivities and specificities could also be a result of problems with the concept of juvenile depression. The "gold standard" against which the DST is judged, the standardized psychiatric diagnosis, may itself be flawed. It remains to be seen, however, whether the DST or other biological markers will prove to be more useful than this diagnosis.

In regard to the links between child and adult depressive disorders, the results are conflicting but perhaps more encouraging. Indeed, many studies have shown significant differences between the DST results of depressed young people and those of nondepressed controls. Although the DST is plainly not sufficiently specific to work well as a diagnostic test, it may yet prove to be useful as a correlate with which to study the relationship between child and adult disorders.

However, there are a number of caveats that need to be dealt with before we can conclude that these positive findings really do reflect biological similarities across the age span. First, it is clear that the findings from the use of biological tests in depressed adults are often themselves contradictory. For instance, the large World Health Organization collaborative study on the clinical correlates of response to DST has failed to identify a typical symptom profile of a depressive cortisol nonsuppressor (Gastpar et al, 1992). The results of sleep EEGs in depressed adults have also been difficult to interpret (Benca et al, 1992). So, the findings of biological tests in adult depression are a less than entirely reliable standard against which to judge psychobiological research in depressed youngsters.

Second, there is still a big problem in interpreting case-control differences on DST and sleep EEG tests. It seems that many other factors, such as in/ outpatient status and weight loss, alter the results of these measures. Some studies have failed to control for these factors and so the meaning of differences between depressed cases and controls becomes obscured.

Third, there is some evidence that the results of psychobiological measures of depression become progressively more abnormal with age. Thus, the specificity of the DST seems to become higher in older age groups, and something similar may occur for sleep EEG measures. There are several possible explanations for these biological differences between child and adult depressions. It could be that early-onset depressions represent a different kind of condition altogether. However, this seems unlikely because family studies and longitudinal studies (see later) have found strong links between child and adult depressive disorders. Alternatively, it is possible that there are developmental differences in the balance between different neuroregulatory systems. In other words, the variation in psychobiological responses with age may simply be a reflection of maturational differences in biology and not a result of differences in the nature of depression. So, for instance, the failure consistently to demonstrate in prepubertal depression the kinds of sleep abnormalities that have been found in some depressed adults could be due to age differences in the nature of sleep (Puig-Antich, 1986).

The importance of these developmental differences is further underlined by the age and sex trends in the prevalence of depressive disorders that were reviewed earlier in this book. Indeed, it may be that the biological changes of puberty lead to the increase in rates of depressive disorder that occurs during adolescence. However, we have seen in this chapter that the size of the association between depressive affect and indices of these changes (such as hormone levels) appears to be small and may not necessarily apply to depressive disorders. In addition, some studies have failed to find an independent contribution of puberty to the rise in depressive disorder in adolescence once age was controlled for (Angold & Rutter, 1992).

Finally, it will be appreciated that early-onset depressive conditions are likely to be biologically heterogeneous (e.g. Goodyer et al, 1991b). A negative finding in one sample may not necessarily generalize to another. Indeed, it is difficult to know how comparable samples were from study to study as the diagnosis of DSM-III major depression is likely to include a very disparate group of disorders. It may be, therefore, that we need to try defining our groups in terms of biological measures that show particular promise (e.g. the DST) and then study their symptoms and natural history.

Chapter 8

Psychological Treatments

We have seen in the previous two chapters that depression is a disorder with a complex aetiology. Indeed, many overlapping models exist to explain it, including biological, cognitive–behavioural, sociological, and systemic. Probably, there are several different kinds of juvenile depressive disorder, each with a multifactorial aetiology. With the exception of bipolar disorder, where it is possible that single genes may be of overriding importance, no single factor stands out as more important than the others. So, it is unlikely that any one form of therapy will be effective in all cases. Physical, social and psychological therapies are therefore all valid in the treatment of depressed young people.

This chapter starts with a brief overview of the initial management of a young patient with depressive disorder. The remainder of the chapter is concerned with some of the more widely used psychological treatments that are available for the treatment of depressive disorder in children and adolescents.

EARLY MANAGEMENT: ASSESSMENT AND DEFINING THE TREATMENT SETTING

The initial management of depressed young people starts with a thorough evaluation of depressive symptomatology. The assessment and diagnosis of depressive disorders in children and adolescents were described earlier and need not therefore be described again here. Suffice to say that, although the accurate diagnosis of depressive disorder is an important part of clinical management, it should be borne in mind that the assessment of depression in young people only starts with the diagnosis, not stops with it. Depressed children usually have multiple problems, such as educational failure (Forness, 1988) and impaired psychosocial functioning (Puig-Antich et al, 1985a), as well as comorbid psychiatric disorders. Moreover they tend to come from families with high rates of psychopathology and may have experienced recent adverse life events including maltreatment. All these problems need to be identified and the causes of each need to be assessed.

The treatment of depressed children depends greatly on the nature of the problems identified during the assessment procedure. The assessment may indicate that the reaction of the child is appropriate for the situation in which he finds himself. In such a case, and if the depression is mild, a sensible approach can consist of regular meetings, sympathetic discussions with the child and his parents, and encouraging support. These simple interventions, especially if combined with measures designed to alleviate stress, are often followed by an improvement in mood.

In other cases, particularly those with severe depression, a more focused form of treatment is indicated, and it may occasionally be necessary to admit the child to hospital. The decision to admit the child to an inpatient facility is likely to depend on a number of factors, but most especially on the severity of the disorder and on the quality of the patient's supportive network. In judging severity, special attention should be paid to factors that may endanger life, such as reduced eating or drinking, or the risk of suicide. If these risks are absent then even severely depressed youngsters can be treated at home, provided of course that the family are willing and able to care for him outside of hospital.

Wherever treatment is carried out, it should be tailored to the needs of the individual child and his family, rather than prescribed as a standard "package". The multiple problems of the depressed child make it especially important that the goals of treatment are precisely formulated. Depression is a legitimate focus of treatment, but this focus should not distract from the prevention or treatment of associated problems such as impaired peer relationships, which may play a part in the maintenance of depression (Goodyer et al, 1991a). It is clear therefore that multiple treatment approaches are needed.

PSYCHOLOGICAL TREATMENTS

A variety of psychological interventions are available for the treatment of depression in children and adolescents. Unfortunately, there have been very few controlled studies of the efficacy of these interventions and confidence in the findings is often limited by relatively small sample sizes and short durations of follow-up. Moreover, much of the work published so far has been conducted on samples who were recruited through schools and who had not been diagnosed as having major depression. The findings may not therefore generalize to patients suffering from major depression attending mental health services.

Despite these reservations, some psychological interventions show considerable promise. In considering these treatments it must be emphasized that there is a great deal of overlap between them, and so any classification is to some extent arbitrary. For instance, many therapists using cognitive therapy with a child would also involve the family in helping with the child's treatment. Nevertheless, it is possible to identify four broad classes of psychological therapy that are becoming widely used to treat depressed children. The first comprises those forms of treatment that can be classed together under the broad umbrella of "cognitive–behavioural" approaches. As we saw in the previous chapter, there are a number of different cognitive and behavioural formulations of depression and the treatments that stem from each of these formulations all differ in a number of respects. However, all of them are loosely based on cognitive or learning theory, all have a focus on changing depressive symptomatology, and all are based in the "here and now".

The second treatment approach, social skills training, has many similarities with the cognitive–behavioural approaches but there is a greater emphasis on overt activities and the development of specific skills. The third treatment approach, interpersonal psychotherapy, is based on the premise that whatever the cause of depression, it occurs in an interpersonal context (Moreau et al, 1991). The focus of treatment is on issues in current relationships. The fourth approach to treatment, family therapy, can include behavioural interventions aimed at alleviating depression, but there is usually a focus on understanding the child's difficulties within the context of the family. Family interventions are therefore primarily aimed at changing patterns of interaction within the family system.

COGNITIVE–BEHAVIOURAL INTERVENTIONS

As already noted, a variety of different approaches can be included in the category of "cognitive–behavioural" therapy. However, most of these techniques have in common an emphasis on maladaptive cognitions as the most important mechanism in the development of depression and in many there is a focus on changing these cognitions. Most of these therapies also include the following features: goal directedness, the teaching of specific skills, and the practice of these skills through homework exercises.

Cognitive therapy has become a widely used treatment for depressive disorders in adults and has been the subject of a number of controlled trials (Dobson, 1989). Much of the research published so far has been concerned with adult outpatients suffering from mild to moderate rather than severe depressive disorders. In this group, cognitive therapy seems to be effective in reducing depressive symptomatology. Several recent studies have compared cognitive therapies with drug therapy and have found that the two were approximately equally effective (reviewed by Paykel, 1989) although they may have undersampled patients who would have responded to antidepressants (Hollon, Shelton & Loosen, 1991). There is some suggestion that cognitive therapy may be particularly effective at cutting down relapse, which can be quite high after drug therapy has been discontinued.

Treatment components

Recent reviews have identified a number of common treatment components included in cognitive behaviour therapy with depressed young people (Reynolds & Stark, 1987; Matson, 1989; Stark, 1990). These components are designed to be used in an integrated manner and to target problem areas that are specific or related to depression. They include self-monitoring, attribution retraining, self-evaluation training, self-reinforcement, cognitive restructuring and relaxation training.

Self-monitoring
Perhaps the most important component of cognitive therapy with young people is self-monitoring. In its basic form, the concept implies the act of observing one's own behaviour and thoughts and recording one's responses to them. Self-monitoring in one form or another is an essential part of all cognitive therapies since all cognitive methods require that the subject is able to identify maladaptive ways of thinking. Self-control methods (Rehm, 1977), which as we shall see later have been used in several treatment studies with depressed young people (Reynolds & Coats, 1986; Stark, Reynolds & Kaslow, 1987), rely heavily on self-monitoring.

Self-monitoring can be viewed as either an assessment or a therapeutic procedure (Reynolds & Stark, 1987). The information that is gathered through self-monitoring of negative events can often be used at later stages of the therapy to illustrate the relationship between thoughts, feelings and behaviours. However, many younger children have problems in differentiating basic emotions and so before self-monitoring can commence it may be necessary to educate the child about basic emotions. *Affective education* aims to teach the child to make increasingly finer distinctions between emotions. These distinctions are taught through an affective education programme that involves tasks such as teaching the child an "emotional vocabulary" by getting him or her to describe what a particular emotion means (Stark, 1990). Self-monitoring of pleasant events may help the child to direct his or her attention to positive events and hence to break the negative cycle of the child always focusing on gloomy happenings. Young people are instructed to observe and monitor themselves and to record every time they participate in an enjoyable activity. The idea is to get subjects to pay more attention to positive things and less to negative aspects of their lives.

Self-evaluation training
Self-evaluation training is the process of comparing one's own performance with an internal standard. Negative self-evaluation is a common symptom of depression in children (Kendall, Stark & Adam, 1990) and it has been suggested that depression can be the result of setting excessively high, unattain-

able standards of performance (Rehm, 1977). As noted in Chapter 7, the current evidence suggests that depressed children tend to have *distorted* styles of thinking rather than a cognitive *deficit* (Kendall et al, 1990). So, in training depressed children new techniques of self-evaluation the focus should be on changing *how* they evaluate themselves and their behaviour. Self-evaluation training starts with the identification of negative self-evaluations, which can then be modified using a variety of cognitive restructuring techniques.

Cognitive restructuring
The term cognitive restructuring refers to a technique in which an attempt is made to modify the child's maladaptive style of thinking together with the underlying assumptions that are thought to lead to this negative cognitive style. Restructuring techniques have been used in a variety of different approaches to the treatment of depression, including cognitive therapy (Beck, 1967) and rational emotive therapy (Ellis, 1962).

According to Beck's cognitive theory of depression (Beck, 1967), depressed people have a negative view of themselves, the world and the future. Beck identified six basic errors in processing information: (1) arbitrary inferences; (2) selective abstraction; (3) overgeneralization; (4) magnification and minimization; (5) personalization; (6) absolute, dichotomous thinking. Patients are taught to observe and record these maladaptive cognitions and then to question them. Stark (1990) described the use of three techniques derived from Beck's programme that had proved useful in the treatment of depressed children:

1. "What's the evidence?" involves the child working with the therapist to identify or refute automatic thoughts.
2. "Alternative interpretations" involves the child developing alternative constructions for an upsetting event. For instance, a depressed child might feel that someone who had passed them in the corridor without saying hello had done so because they did not like them. The child might be taught that another way of looking at that event was that the other child might have been thinking of something else.
3. "What if" aims to teach the child that an actual outcome of an event may not be as bad as the child predicts.

Each of these exercises can be followed by behavioural assignments that aim to provide the child with immediate evidence that addresses the validity of his or her thinking.

Self-reinforcement training
Self-reinforcement is the process of self-reward, contingent on the occurrence of appropriate behaviour. Training in self-reinforcement is an important part of a self-control programme. Parts of a self-reinforcement programme are often linked with self-control procedures. Rewards can consist either of a

tangible reward (e.g. going out) or a covert reinforcer (e.g. a positive self-statement).

Activity scheduling
Activity scheduling involves the systematic planning of the young person's daily schedule. The aim is to increase the amount of time spent in purposeful activity and to decrease the amount of time spent in depressive ruminations. The therapist and young person draw up a schedule of pleasurable activities. Parental involvement is especially important here as parents will often have to provide assistance so that a child can participate in these activities. In severely depressed children it may be necessary to start with some simple tasks and gradually to increase the level of activity.

Relaxation training
Although not a form of cognitive therapy, relaxation training is often used in conjunction with cognitive techniques as another way of helping depressed youngsters to cope with the stresses that are often associated with depressive conditions. Relaxation training can also be useful in helping young people to deal with the symptoms of anxiety that often accompany depression.

Reynolds and Coats (1986) described a 10-session relaxation training programme for use with depressed children. In an introductory session the rationale for the treatment was described, including an explanation of the relationship between stress-related problems and depression. The next four sessions were spent on helping the subjects to relax using the various major muscle groups, following the procedure developed by Jacobsen (1938). Subjects were expected to undertake homework exercises, which were reviewed in each session. The next four sessions were devoted to helping the subject to generalize these skills to the stressful situations encountered in everyday life. All sessions lasted 50 minutes.

Cognitive–behaviour therapy programmes

Several investigators have developed cognitive or cognitive–behavioural treatment programmes for use with depressed young people. Reynolds and Stark (Reynolds & Coats, 1986; Reynolds & Stark, 1987; Stark, 1990; Reynolds, 1991) have described the general structure of a cognitive–behavioural treatment programme that has components derived from a variety of models of depression, including self-control models (Rehm, 1977) and cognitive therapy (Beck, 1967). Stark (1990) provides a detailed account of a form of this therapy that takes 21 sessions, but a briefer version lasting just 10 sessions is also available (Reynolds, 1991). Both forms were group-administered.

In the first session of the 10-session form (Reynolds, 1991) there is a general discussion of the rationale and goals of therapy. In the second session there is a focus on teaching group members the relationship between mood and activity. They are asked to graph the relationship between positive activities and mood each day. In the third session there is a focus on the tendency of depressed persons to attend to the immediate rather than the long-term outcomes of their behaviour. Cognitive distortions and the tendency to view the world in a negative manner are discussed. Patients are given an immediate versus delayed effects worksheet. In the fourth session the focus of therapy is on the development of self-evaluation skills and attribution retraining. The group are encouraged to make accurate self-evaluations and to set realistic, obtainable goals. An "Attribution of Responsibility" exercise is set to illustrate the way in which depressed individuals often make faulty assumptions about responsibility for positive and negative events. In the fifth session there is a focus on procedures for developing a self-change plan. Members of the group are encouraged to think that they can change and that self-control is a skill that can be learned. In session six there is continued training in self-change skills, with an emphasis on setting realistic, obtainable goals. Session seven introduces the idea of self-reinforcement, and youngsters are encouraged to develop positive self-reinforcement schedules. In session eight the idea of self-reinforcement is extended to cover both overt and covert techniques of reward. The last two sessions serve as check, review and practice sessions. The basic principles of the therapy are outlined again and each individual is praised for his or her performance during the sessions.

Lewinsohn et al (1990) described a cognitive–behavioural group intervention with depressed adolescents, the Coping with Depression Course, which was originally developed for use with adults. The course was designed to address a number of areas that were hypothesized to be a problem for depressed people: "discomfort and anxiety, irrational and negative thoughts, poor social skills, and a low rate of pleasant activities". Treatment sessions were skills-training orientated and focused on teaching methods of relaxation, increasing pleasant events, controlling negative thoughts and increasing social skills. A conflict-resolution component was also included. An important modification in the course for adolescents was the inclusion of parents in the treatment. Parents met in a group on the same night as the adolescents and were provided with an overview of the skills and techniques being taught to the adolescents. Ways of dealing with family difficulties were also addressed in these groups.

Several other forms of cognitive therapy are available for the treatment of depressed young people. For example, *rational–emotive therapy* is based on the notion that people have faulty beliefs about themselves that lead them to a poor self-view and so to depression. The treatment aims to get the depressed individual to develop more positive attitudes and behaviour. Components of this treatment appear as part of several other cognitive behavioural programmes, though some therapists consider that rational emotive therapy is unlikely to become widely used with children (Stark, 1990).

Evaluation of cognitive–behavioural treatments in depressed young people

In one of the first systematic studies to evaluate the efficacy of a cognitive intervention in depressed young people, Butler et al (1980) randomly assigned children identified as depressed (on a questionnaire measure) through a school screening programme to one of four conditions: role-play treatment, cognitive restructuring, attention placebo control, and a waiting-list control condition. The treatments were group-administered. The role-play treatment consisted of training in a number of cognitive and behavioural skills, such as generating problem-solving alternatives and social skills training. The cognitive restructuring group was trained in the kinds of restructuring techniques described above. Children in the attention placebo group were taught to solve academic problems as a group. Children in all four groups reported improvement in depression at the post-treatment assessment.

Reynolds and Coats (1986) examined the efficacy of cognitive–behaviour therapy and relaxation training in adolescents (average age 16 years) who were selected by screening for depression through schools. Depression was defined on the basis of a high score on questionnaire measures. Both treatments (described above) resulted in a substantially and statistically significant reduction in depressive symptomatology when compared with a waiting-list control condition. For instance, in the cognitive–behavioural group scores on the Beck Depression Inventory decreased from an average of 21.1 pre-treatment to an average of 6.4 post-treatment. These gains were maintained at follow-up after 5 weeks. Cognitive–behavioural therapy and relaxation training were equally effective in reducing depression. Kahn et al (1990) reported similar findings in a sample of depressed youngsters from middle school. Cognitive–behavioural, relaxation and self-modelling treatments were all associated with a reduction in depressive symptomatology.

Stark, Reynolds and Kaslow (1987) evaluated self-control therapy and a behavioural intervention in a sample of school children (9 to 12 years) who showed mild to moderate depressive symptomatology across self-report and interview measures of depression. The self-control treatment was designed to teach the children more adaptive skills for self-monitoring and evaluating their own performances and abilities. The behavioural problem-solving therapy consisted of education about feelings and interpersonal behaviour together with a combination of training exercises, including problem-solving and social skills training (Stark, 1990). Children in both treatment conditions reported a significant reduction in depression after treatment, and reported greater improvement in depressive symptomatology than children in the waiting-list condition. These results were maintained at 8-weeks follow-up.

Since children in all these studies improved not only with "cognitive" interventions but also with other psychological treatments, the question arises as to the specificity of the therapeutic mechanisms. Indeed, at first sight it is tempting to conclude that the benefits found in these studies in reality came from general features of the intervention, such as a supportive relationship, rather than from a specific therapeutic effect on depression. On the other hand, Stark (1990) reported a second study that was specially designed to address this question of therapeutic specificity. A multi-component cognitive–behavioural treatment was compared with a traditional nondirective counselling approach in depressed children recruited through schools. Subjects in both treatment conditions reported significantly less depression at the end of treatment compared with baseline. However, subjects who had had the cognitive–behavioural intervention reported significantly lower levels of depression immediately after treatment than subjects in the counselling group. This finding argues for the operation of a specific therapeutic mechanism.

None of these studies was concerned with young people who had been diagnosed as having a depressive disorder, so the question also arises as to whether these favourable results would generalize to the severe depressive disorders that are seen in clinical settings. No such study has yet been published. However, Lewinsohn et al (1990) studied the efficacy of the Coping with Depression Course for Adolescents in a sample aged 14–18 years who met criteria for DSM-III or RDC depressive disorder (major or minor or intermittent depression). Adolescents were selected *via* letters and announcements to health professionals, school counsellors and the media. Only 30% had been in some form of psychological or psychiatric treatment before the study. Adolescents were randomly allocated to the Coping with Depression Course, the Coping with Depression Course plus a parental group, or a waiting-list control. Both treatment groups significantly improved at post-treatment, with substantial reductions in depression scores. There were no differences in depression scores between treatment groups.

All in all, these initial comparative studies provide some support for the idea that focused and planned cognitive–behavioural therapies may be of benefit in mild depressive conditions. However, there is still a grave paucity of systematic controlled comparisons of different forms of treatment. In particular, we need to know which therapy is appropriate for which patient with which problem. And, of course, much more data are needed on the efficacy of psychological treatments with young people who have the kinds of moderate or severe depressive disorders that lead to referral for treatment. Finally, it is worth noting that most of the studies carried out so far have been concerned with *group* treatments for depressive disorders. It is clearly feasible to set up therapeutic groups in projects based on large samples who were recruited from schools or through the media. However, it may be more difficult to set up groups in clinical settings where the number of eligible cases of depression at any one time is likely to be quite small. Individual approaches to therapy need to be investigated further.

SOCIAL SKILLS TRAINING

As previously described, many depressed young people have social skills deficits. Indeed, several investigators have emphasized the importance of social skills problems in the aetiology of depression. Lewinsohn (1974), for example, emphasized the importance of the social environment and the mechanisms by which the child is provided with social reinforcement.

Many of the treatment programmes described in the previous section have included a social skills component (Lewinsohn et al, 1990; Stark, 1990). Several procedures are commonly used to teach social skills to depressed youngsters, including modelling, role-play, positive reinforcement and performance feedback. These procedures can be used with individuals, or in groups if the children are of similar level in terms of social skills. Matson (1989) outlined a model for the training of social skills in depressed children that was based on a system of case vignettes. Each vignette described a real-life situation of the patient and a prompt to which the patient had to make an appropriate social response. Based on the child's response to the role-play situation, he or she was rewarded and given feedback in areas where improvement was needed. Skills were frequently demonstrated so that the child could copy them. After each session a set of homework tasks was given that included, for instance, the task of initiating a conversation. Typically, sessions were held two to four times per week.

Fine et al (1991) used a group setting to teach social skills to depressed adolescents. Skills were learned in a series of progressive steps that were spelled out in a manual. Target skills that were taught and then rehearsed included conversational skills, social problem solving and negotiation to resolve social conflict. A session was devoted to each skill and real-life situations were used for role-playing. Therapists acted as role models. There was then discussion of the ways in which the skills learned in the sessions could be generalized.

Evaluation of social skills training in depressed young people

Matson (1989) described the treatment of two cases using the social skills vignettes outlined above. In the first case, it appeared that the child was unhappy because he had moved to a new school only a few months earlier and had had considerable difficulty making friends. Social skills training was followed by the development of several new friendships and a marked improvement in depressive affect. In the second case, depression seemed to have been precipitated by the parents' strained relationship. Social skills training was undertaken as part of a treatment programme that included several other components. Once again, there was a marked improvement in depressed mood.

Fine et al (1991) conducted a comparison of social skills and therapeutic support groups in a sample of adolescents (ages 13 to 17 years) attending outpatients who met DSM-III-R (American Psychiatric Association, 1987) criteria for either major depression or dysthymia. Subjects in the therapeutic support group did rather better immediately post-treatment than subjects in the social skills group. At 9 months follow-up the two treatments were equivalent, with about two-thirds of adolescents in each group falling into the "nonclinical" range on standardized ratings of depressive symptomatology.

INTERPERSONAL PSYCHOTHERAPY

Interpersonal psychotherapy (IPT) is a standardized treatment approach to relationships and life problems that has been extensively evaluated in the treatment of depressed adults. It was designed as a weekly, brief treatment for outpatients with unipolar depression. Its main aims are to treat the patient's symptoms and to identify and treat the problem areas that are commonly associated with depression, such as interpersonal difficulties.

Weissman et al (1979) reported that the effects of interpersonal psychotherapy on the symptoms of moderately severe depressive disorder in adults were equal to those of amitriptyline and greater than those of contact only. In the large NIMH treatment trial that compared several different types of treatment for depressive disorder, interpersonal psychotherapy was more effective than placebo (Elkin et al, 1989). IPT also shows promise as a maintenance treatment to prevent further episodes of depression (Frank et al, 1991a).

Interpersonal psychotherapy with depressed young people

Moreau et al (1991) provided a clear and interesting description of the development of a treatment manual for a version of IPT that will be used in a controlled clinical trial of interpersonal psychotherapy with depressed adolescents. These authors felt that IPT would be particularly suitable for the treatment of depressed adolescents because IPT's brief nature made it "particularly responsive to the adolescent's reluctance to seek or stay in treatment". IPT was also seen as especially appropriate for adolescents because of its focus on the present and future, and because of its focus on issues that are likely to be relevant to adolescents, such as the resolution of interpersonal disputes with parents or school and the negotiation of key life transitions. In their research, IPT was developed for nonpsychotic, nonsuicidal depressed adolescent outpatients who were not engaging in regular drug use or antisocial activities of a violent nature. It was not designed to handle "adolescents in crisis".

The goals of IPT with depressed adolescents are to identify and treat both the patient's depressive symptoms and the problem areas associated with the onset of depression. In adults, these problem areas include grief, interpersonal role disputes, role transitions and interpersonal deficits. For IPT with adolescents, Moreau et al added the problem area of a single-parent family because of the difficulties that may arise for adolescents living in such families. The treatment was adapted to address developmental issues that are commonly encountered in adolescence. These included separation from parents, issues of authority, development of relationships with members of the opposite sex, and peer pressures.

In the *initial phase* of treatment, time is spent establishing a treatment contract, dealing with depressive symptoms and identifying problem areas. Moreau and colleagues outlined six tasks that needed to be accomplished:

1. A detailed assessment of depressive symptomatology, an explanation to the patient and an assessment of the need for medication (given when depressive symptoms are unresponsive to a four-week course of psychotherapy).
2. Assessing the type and nature of the patient's social and familial relationships.
3. Identifying the problem areas.
4. Explaining the rationale and intent of the treatment.
5. Setting a treatment contract with the patient.
6. Explaining the patient's expected role in treatment.

In the *middle phase* of IPT there is a focus on the problem areas identified in the assessment. The task of the middle phase is to associate the depressive symptoms with the problems identified in the initial phase. For instance, in adolescence role disputes commonly occur with parents over issues such as authority, sexuality or money. Adolescents may act out these disputes with self-punishing or disruptive behaviours. The task of the therapist is to associate these behaviours with feelings and to encourage the development of these feelings directly.

Another important problem area concerns the role transitions that occur during adolescence. Difficulties in coping with some of the so-called "developmental tasks" of adolescence form an important part of psychodynamic theories of depression in young people (e.g. Bemporad, 1988). Moreau and colleagues described how difficulties in making the transition from childhood to mid-adolescence were treated in a 15-year-old using a combination of IPT and family work. The girl had presented with symptoms of depression that occurred in the context of a deteriorating relationship with her parents and entry into a new school. Her attempts to gain independence from her parents were met with resistance. Treatment consisted of individual sessions that were focused on the adolescent's expectations of her parents, and sessions with the parents that aimed to educate them about social maturation and normal adolescent behaviour. Depressive symptoms improved rapidly and by the end of treatment her relationship with her parents was also better.

Termination of treatment is addressed at the beginning of treatment and periodically during treatment. Patients are usually advised that there may be a slight recurrence of symptoms towards the end of therapy.

Evaluation of IPT in depressed adolescents

There have been no published controlled trials of IPT in young people diagnosed as having a depressive disorder. Nevertheless, preliminary findings from open studies and from case reports have been encouraging. Robbins, Allessi and Colfer (1989) used a form of psychotherapy that was similar to IPT in adolescents hospitalized with major depression. About one-half of patients responded with psychotherapy alone. Nonsuppression on the DST and melancholic subtype predicted failure to respond to psychotherapy. Moreau et al (1991) described several cases who responded well to IPT. It is to be hoped that these promising findings will be replicated in controlled trials.

FAMILY WORK AND FAMILY THERAPY

As described earlier, depressed children often come from families in which there are difficulties of one kind or another. For example, there may be mental illness or personality problems in one or both parents, chronic marital difficulties, and/or parenting problems. So, it is important that the treatment of the depressed young person includes a thorough assessment of the family, and it is sometimes necessary to undertake some kind of direct work with family members. Three types of family work can be distinguished, though as was the case with the individual treatments, there is much overlap between them:

1. Advice and counselling about depression and its associated symptoms.
2. Using the family as a treatment agent.
3. Family therapy, in which the family is the main focus for intervention.

Advice and counselling about depression and its symptoms

Families of depressed young people will often benefit from simple advice about the symptoms of depression. They may, for example, interpret the social withdrawal that usually accompanies depression as a rebuff and may be reassured by the explanation that many of the symptoms of depression, especially if it is severe, are beyond the young person's control. Parents are often very guilty that they may have "caused" the depression and a careful discussion of the clinical formulation may help them to understand better their child's problems. Parents of young people who are potentially suicidal need advice about ways of reducing the risk of a successful attempt. It may, for instance, be necessary to remove firearms from the house, and if medication is prescribed then the parents must be warned about the dangers of overdose and of the need to ensure that the young person does not have easy access to it. Indeed, as we have seen in earlier chapters, many parents are unaware of marked suicidal ideation in their children. Finally, it is often helpful to explain to the parents what is known about the rate of recovery in early-onset depressive disorders. We shall see later that the great majority of depressed young people will recover eventually. This knowledge may be very helpful to the parents of severely depressed young people who have failed to respond to the initial treatment.

Family work as an adjunct to individual therapy

Parents and/or siblings can have an important role in helping the child with some of the individual therapies described earlier. For example, they may help the child with the homework exercises that are part of relaxation or social skills. Some cognitive–behavioural therapists have found that the family component of their work has been of growing importance over the years. Stark (1990), for example, described how parents could be used to identify maladaptive thoughts in their children and how they could be taught to help the child directly in his therapy. For instance, they may be used as part of a programme that involves the countering of negative beliefs expressed by the child. Parents may also be encouraged to help their child to become more socially active. The active cooperation of the parents will of course be important in behavioural treatments such as activity scheduling, in which the whole family may be involved in outings.

The family as a focus of treatment

In cases where one of the family members has an overt psychiatric disorder, it may be necessary to encourage that person to seek treatment from a mental health professional. Appropriate consultation with other professionals involved with the family is important, especially if a parent is to be admitted to hospital.

A full discussion of the many family therapy techniques that can be used to help families where there are abnormalities of parenting, boundaries or structure is beyond the scope of this book. Suffice to say that it may be necessary to involve the whole family in therapy if the initial formulation suggests that the child's depression seems to be associated with abnormalities of family functioning. Oster and Caro (1990) provide some case examples of the kinds of family interactions that may be associated with depression, and of some of the strategies that may be used to help. For instance, some family therapists "reframe" the meaning of an adolescent's depression as in one way or another protective to the family.

Evaluation of family interventions with depressed young people

To date, there has been only one systematic published study of the efficacy of family interventions for depression in young people. Lewinsohn et al (1990) randomly allocated depressed adolescents to a group-administered cognitive–behavioural treatment with or without a parent group. The parent group had seven 2-hour sessions and aimed to promote "parental acceptance and reinforcement of the expected positive changes in their teenagers". Parents were also helped with coping skills to address family problems or fights. Contrary to the authors' expectation, there were no differences on the depression measures between the groups. In a thoughtful discussion of this negative result, the authors suggest that the parental treatment module could have been improved by, for example, getting both parent and adolescent together. Much more research is needed on the efficacy of family interventions in the treatment of depressed young people.

SCHOOL-BASED INTERVENTIONS

Depression in children and adolescents has become of increasing concern to those interested in the provision of mental health services to schools. In particular, there has been concern that withdrawn and "quiet" children may get less attention and may be less likely to be referred to special education than children who externalize their problems (Forness, 1988). Teachers, like parents, are often unaware of depression in young people.

Attempts to increase awareness of depressive conditions among teachers and other professionals have been furthered by the publication of articles on depression in school psychology books and journals (e.g. Reynolds & Stark, 1987). In addition, it has been suggested that there should be school-based procedures for identifying depressive conditions among children. Reynolds (1991) has proposed that multi-stage assessment procedures could be used to screen for depressive disorders among young people. The multi-stage assessment aims to reduce the number of false positives. In the first stage a depression questionnaire is administered to the whole classroom. The second stage consists of the administration of the same questionnaire to those identified as positive at the first stage. Those who score positive at both stages are then interviewed using a standardized diagnostic interview. Children who are identified as depressed can then be referred for treatment; children who screen positive but are found not to be depressed at interview can be reassessed at some later point.

As Reynolds (1991) pointed out, the treatment of depression in young people is not an activity that can be entered into without proper training and knowledge of the appropriate treatment modalities. Depressed children have a potentially life-threatening disorder whose management is quite different from that of academic problems or behavioural difficulties. So, it is important that the screening procedures are matched by adequate back-up from professionals experienced in the treatment of depressed young people. Fortunately, there have been several school-based intervention studies with depressed young people that have demonstrated the effectiveness of cognitive–behavioural interventions in depressed young people (Butler et al, 1980; Reynolds and Coats, 1986; Stark, Reynolds & Kaslow, 1987; Stark, 1990: see earlier).

Schools, of course, also have an important role in enhancing treatments carried out by other professionals, such as psychologists and psychiatrists. Proper liaison and consultation between mental health professionals and schools is vital, especially where treatment programmes are closely linked to educational facilities. Stark (1990) describes the kinds of problems that can occur when communication between professionals involved with the child breaks down. For instance, in one case a child was failed a grade by her teacher because she had been missing too much time because of her participation in treatment! He advocates discussing the treatment programme at all levels of the administration and educating other professionals about the humanitarian and fiscal value of treatment.

PREVENTION

Educational settings can be used not only to screen for depressive disorders but perhaps also for studies whose main aim is the primary prevention of depression. It will be appreciated that we are still a very long way from understanding the aetiology of depressive conditions among the young, and the large number of possible aetiological factors makes it unlikely that any one factor could be targeted for a simple intervention. However, it should be possible to increase awareness of depressive conditions among teachers and pupils by simple educational programmes, similar to those mounted for bullying. Indeed, there are a large number of suicide prevention programmes currently being conducted in the United States in which awareness of children at risk is emphasized (Shaffer et al, 1991). Alternatively, it may be possible to set up intervention programmes in schools (e.g. Kellam, 1990).

Another strategy would be to target "high risk" groups such as the children of depressed parents, or children who have just experienced an adverse event (such as a disaster), or children who are just about to experience an adverse event (such as a bereavement). Siegel, Mesagno and Christ (1990), for example, described a prevention programme for children who had a parent with terminal cancer. The programme included a number of elements:

1. Support for the well parent.
2. Provision of knowledge about the bereavement reactions that may be expected in children.
3. A focus on certain key features thought to be crucial in determining the child's reactions to a parent's death, such as maintaining consistency and stability in the child's environment.
4. An emphasis on parent–child communication.
5. An emphasis on a parental guidance model, with only indirect targeting of children.
6. An emphasis on the importance of timing, with the intervention occurring not too soon after diagnosis, yet not after the death had actually occurred.

Interestingly, in a follow-up article the same group described some of the problems of such a prevention programme (Christ et al, 1991). For example, it was difficult to get the timing right. However, perhaps more importantly so far as the generality of the results is concerned, they noted the difficulties of persuading the surviving parent to participate in the programme. Clearly, it may be difficult to persuade parents to take part in a prevention programme for depression when their child is relatively asymptomatic. Nevertheless, the majority of families did participate and were felt to have benefited.

PSYCHOLOGICAL TREATMENTS: CONCLUSIONS

Perhaps the most striking feature of this brief review of psychological treatments in juvenile depressive disorders is the lack of systematic studies on which to base the conclusions. There have been only a handful of controlled studies, and most of these have been concerned with young people selected from nonclinical settings who had not been diagnosed as having major depression. Nevertheless, the published findings certainly suggest that focused and planned psychological interventions may be of benefit in depressive conditions among the young. Moreover, there are a number of treatments that have proved useful in the management of depression among adults, such as IPT, that show promise in the treatment of juvenile depression.

Chapter 9

Drugs and other Physical Treatments

The previous chapter was concerned with the psychological treatment of depressive disorders in young people. This chapter is concerned with physical treatments, particularly antidepressants. The description of physical treatments in a separate chapter does not mean that they are an alternative to psychological treatments. Often the two go hand in hand, and as we shall see they may have different goals. So, it will often be necessary to use physical and psychological treatments in combination.

TRICYCLIC ANTIDEPRESSANTS

There are a variety of different tricyclic antidepressants (TCAs), but all of them have a basic molecular structure consisting of three linked rings to which a side chain is attached. Their therapeutic effect is thought to be due to their ability to increase the availability of catecholamines at central receptor sites (see Chapter 7). In adults, the antidepressant effect of tricyclics is not usually evident until two or more weeks after first administration.

Studies of depressed adults

Tricyclic antidepressants are amongst the most extensively studied of treatments for depressive conditions in adults. Elkins and Rapoport (1983) estimated that there had been over 200 blind placebo-controlled trials, with around three-quarters showing significant benefits of an active drug. Paykel (1989) considered that some of the negative findings could be attributed to poor trial technique, such as short treatment periods, low doses and unsatisfactory outcome measures. Some, however, reflected the lack of efficacy of tricyclics.

There may be selective effects of tricyclic antidepressants on certain types of depression. In general, neurovegetative symptoms (anorexia, weight loss, late insomnia, psychomotor retardation) and lack of mood reactivity have been associated with the most favourable response to TCAs (Kocsis, 1990). However, tricyclics also seem to be effective in the less severe depressions

(Paykel & Priest, 1992). It may be that there is a curvilinear relationship between response to antidepressants and type of depression. Abou-Saleh and Coppen (1983), for instance, found that patients with moderate depression scores did better than patients with either mild or severe depression. Severe psychotic depressions do not seem to respond well to TCAs (Abou-Saleh & Coppen, 1983) but seem to do better with electroconvulsive therapy (Scott, 1989).

Comparisons of tricyclics with psychotherapy have generally found that the two are about equally effective in mild or moderate depressions, although there is some suggestion that drugs seem to help vegetative symptoms, and psychological treatments are more effective for interpersonal problems (Paykel, 1989). Comparisons of cognitive therapy with tricyclics have also found that the two are about equal in mild/moderate depression (Hollon, Shelton & Loosen, 1991). However, the most systematic of the large recent studies (the National Institute of Mental Health collaborative study) found that cognitive therapy was a little less effective than drug, especially in moderately severe depression (Elkin et al, 1989).

Early studies of tricyclics in depressed children

Early studies of the efficacy of tricyclics in depressed children produced promising results (reviewed by Petti, 1983), with the suggestion that about three-quarters of depressed children responded to antidepressants (Cantwell, 1983). For instance, Weinberg et al (1973) reported data on 35 depressed children who were felt to need antidepressant treatment. Nineteen were treated with either imipramine or amitriptyline for at least one month by their paediatricians in an "open" design. Fifteen did not receive tricyclics. Twelve of the 19 showed marked improvement, compared with 3 of the 15 who did not receive antidepressants. Only one of the treated children showed no change at all. Puig-Antich et al (1978) gave up to 4.5 mg/kg of imipramine per day for a period of 6–8 weeks to children with major depression. Six out of eight cases were felt to have improved substantially. Petti (1983) described findings from several small studies of imipramine in depressed children that supported the idea that tricyclics were an effective form of treatment.

However, many of these early studies of the use of tricyclics in childhood depression had methodological drawbacks (Elkins & Rapoport, 1983; Petti, 1983). The period of time that the drug was prescribed varied greatly, from a few weeks to several months. The dosage of tricyclic was also very variable. Some studies used very heterogeneous samples (e.g. Lucas, Locket & Grimm, 1965) and the criteria used to define depressive disorder were often different from one study to the next. In addition, very few studies used the double-blind placebo controlled procedures that are now seen as the best way of assessing drug efficacy.

Recent studies of tricyclics in young people with depressive disorders

Children

One of the first systematic studies of tricyclics in childhood depression was conducted by Puig-Antich and his colleagues (1987). This group investigated the efficacy of imipramine in 53 prepubertal children suffering from major depressive disorder. There were no significant differences between placebo and imipramine groups in clinical response rate, which in both groups was quite high (68% versus 56% respectively). There was, however, a linear relationship between the size of response and imipramine and desipramine plasma levels. Puig-Antich et al (1987) therefore suggested that the inability to demonstrate an effect of imipramine might have been the result of the high placebo response rates and/or inadequate drug dosage.

In a study designed to address these methodological issues, Geller et al (1989) compared nortriptyline with placebo in children (aged 5–12 years) with major depression. The design included a 2-week single-blind, placebo washout phase before the main trial so that subjects who responded rapidly to placebo could be excluded. Patients were then begun at a dose based on their 24-hour plasma level that would ensure steady-state nortriptyline plasma levels of 60–100 ng/ml. This plasma level was selected on the basis of a previous study of the relationship between nortriptyline level and response (Geller et al, 1986). Eight out of the 26 patients (31%) on active drug responded during the double-blind phase of the trial, compared with 4 out of the 24 patients (17%) on placebo, the difference falling short of statistical significance.

As Geller et al (1989) pointed out, it could be that this lack of response to TCAs was the result of biological heterogeneity. Indeed, Preskorn et al (1987) reported that superiority of imipramine over placebo was particularly marked in dexamethasone-nonsuppressing children. Hughes et al (1990) reported that comorbidity also had an effect on treatment response. Prepubertal children with depression only or a coexisting anxiety disorder had higher response rates to imipramine and lower placebo response rates than children with depression and conduct disorder. The latter group of children were at increased risk of recurrence of depression and psychosocial problems than depressed children without conduct disorder or oppositional disorder (Hughes et al, 1990). Clearly more work is needed to identify the characteristics of children who are likely to respond to antidepressants. It may be that there is a subgroup of depressed children with relatively "pure" adult-like depressions that will be found to respond to TCAs.

Adolescents

To turn to the treatment of adolescent major depression, studies of the efficacy of TCAs that have been conducted up to now have been unable to show either superiority over placebo or a relationship between plasma level and response. Thus, one small study of amitriptyline versus placebo failed to find any significant differences between the groups (Kramer & Feiguine, 1983). Similarly, Geller et al (1990) stopped their study when 31 depressed adolescents (12–17 years) had completed the 8-week double-blind, placebo-controlled phase because only one patient out of 12 on nortriptyline had responded. Ryan et al (1986) gave a fixed, weight-adjusted dose of imipramine in adolescent depression, but failed to find a relationship between plasma level and response. Only 44% were rated as significantly improved.

Strober, Freeman and Rigali (1990a) found an even lower response rate (one-third) in adolescent inpatients with nondelusional major depression treated with imipramine in an "open" design. The majority of the sample reached the full target dosage of imipramine (mean 222 mg of imipramine daily). Among 10 delusional patients the response rate was even lower (10%). Total imipramine plus desipramine (imipramine is metabolized in the liver to desipramine, an active metabolite) plasma levels did not differ between responders and nonresponders.

In the first published study of the efficacy of desipramine in adolescent major depression, Boulos et al (1991) allocated 30 adolescents to treatment with a fixed dose of 200 mg of desipramine per day for 6 weeks, or to placebo. All subjects who entered the trial had had a pre-treatment score on the Hamilton rating scale of at least 17 for one week and had completed a single-blind placebo washout week. Thirty-three per cent of the placebo treatment group and 50% of the desipramine group met criteria for a positive response, the difference falling short of statistical significance.

Possible reasons for low response rates in clinical trials
Why is it that the TCAs seem to be less efficacious in the treatment of major depression in young people than in the apparently identical condition when it occurs in adults? A variety of different types of explanations have been put forward (reviewed by Ryan, 1990; Strober, 1992b). First, it could be that the low response rate is accounted for by some methodological feature of the studies carried out so far. For example, Ambrosini et al (1992) suggested that the therapeutic response to tricyclics in adolescents with major depression may take longer to develop than the 3–6 weeks that is necessary in adults. In their open trial of nortriptyline in adolescents with major depression the response rate was increased by maintaining the treatment for 10 weeks. Perhaps, then, the duration of the trials carried out so far has been too short.

Alternatively, there may have been difficulties in establishing the correct drug dosage. There is great variation in the rate at which young people metabolize antidepressants (Geller, 1991). The failure consistently to find a relationship between plasma level of antidepressant and clinical response may mean that the relationship between response and level is more complex than was first thought. For instance, perhaps there is a curvilinear relationship between clinical response and TCA level, such that subjects on too high or too low a dose fail to respond. Such a relationship has been suggested to occur in depressed adults (e.g. Asberg et al, 1971), the so-called therapeutic window. However, so far such a "window" has not been found among depressed adolescents (Ryan et al, 1986; Ambrosini et al, 1992), though there is some suggestion of a dose–response relationship in children (Preskorn, Weller & Weller, 1982).

Another methodological problem concerns the high placebo response rates that have been found in some placebo-control studies of depressed young people. High rates of response in the placebo group will reduce effect size. However, although these rates may indeed be higher than in adult studies it is unlikely that they constitute the complete explanation for the failure of placebo-control studies to find a therapeutic effect of TCAs. Response rates of groups of depressed adolescents on TCAs have rarely exceeded 50%, whereas in depressed adults there is often a response rate of around 70% (Goodwin, 1992).

The second type of explanation stems from the possibility that depression in adolescence, though phenotypically similar to adult depression, differs in some important respect that might alter drug responsiveness. For instance, perhaps as several authors have suggested on the basis of the findings from family studies (Weissman et al, 1988; Puig-Antich et al, 1989) early-onset depressive disorders are more severe than late-onset forms. Indeed, one-half of the depressed adolescents in the study of Geller et al (1990) had a duration of problem of more than 5 years (that is, their problems had persisted for more than a third of their average lifetimes!). In addition, as Strober (1992b) pointed out, it may be that some adolescents with major depression have latent bipolar disorders, which could mean that the depression is more resistant to treatment with TCAs. There is surprisingly little information on the treatment of depression arising in subjects who also have mania (Prien & Potter, 1990).

Alternatively, it is possible that the use of the rather broad criteria of DSM-III has led to the inclusion of a very heterogeneous group of depressive conditions, only some of which will respond to TCAs. For instance, as we saw in Chapter 5, it is possible that the juvenile depressive disorders are more often comorbid with other psychiatric conditions than their adult counterparts. Depressions that are comorbid with other problems might respond less well to TCAs. Or, it may be that the use of DSM-III in adolescent populations leads in one way or another to the over-inclusion of very mild cases of depression.

So, perhaps the failure to find a therapeutic effect of TCAs in adolescent major depression has been a result of the inclusion of subjects who had either too severe or too mild a form of disorder. The depressions of moderate severity with endogenous features that seem to do best with TCAs in studies of depressed adults may have been under-represented in the studies of adolescents that have been carried out so far.

A third possible explanation derives from the idea that the neurochemical systems on which the TCAs are thought to act may show developmental differences. Thus, it has been suggested that adolescents differ from adults both in the relative balance of the cerebral neurotransmitters noradrenaline and serotonin (Strober, Freeman & Rigali, 1990a) and in the hormonal milieu of the brain (Ryan et al, 1986). For example, the TCA that has been used most in the published studies of the drug treatment of adolescent depression is nortriptyline, which is a relatively pure noradrenergic agent. As described in Chapter 7, it may be that the noradrenergic system does not develop fully until adulthood, so that noradrenergic agents are relatively ineffective until then.

At the moment, it is not clear which one of these factors best explains the negative results with the TCAs. Probably a combination of factors is responsible. It is, however, important to remember that research on the clinical utility of antidepressants in juvenile depressive conditions is necessarily at an early stage, if only because of the relatively recent identification of depressive disorders among the young using standardized methods of assessment. It could be that the next wave of controlled studies will provide more pointers on which depressed young people are likely to respond to TCAs. In the meantime, it would seem best to restrict the use of these drugs to patients with severe depression, and to those who fail to respond to other forms of treatment. There is little justification for giving small amounts of antidepressant for minor degrees of depression. We shall see in the next two sections that giving TCAs to children is a difficult and potentially hazardous form of treatment.

Administration of TCAs to children and adolescents

The dose of TCAs given to children varies widely. Early workers, the English and Europeans in particular, advocated starting with relatively small doses of imipramine, such as 10 mg per day, going up to a maximum of 30–60 mg per day. On the other hand, in almost all the treatment studies described above, much larger doses of TCA have been used. For example, in the study of prepubertal children with major depression reported by Puig-Antich et al (1987) subjects were given imipramine 1.5 mg/kg/day divided into three daily, roughly equal doses. The dose was raised steadily over a 9-day period to 5 mg/kg/day. The average dose of imipramine for subjects in the controlled trial was 137 mg per day. Petti (1983) describes a similar dosage regimen. For example, in a child weighing 40 kg, the initial dose would be 50 mg, increasing to 200 mg by day 7. Similar dosage levels have been used in trials involving depressed adolescents. Boulos et al (1991) used 200 mg of nortriptyline per day and Strober et al (1990a) an average of 222 mg daily.

In recent clinical trials TCAs have usually been administered for between 5 and 8 weeks. As described earlier, it has been suggested that this period of administration may be too short. However, in the absence of systematic data to the contrary, it would not seem worth continuing with TCAs if there has been no response within 8 weeks. There are no adequate data on how long to continue with TCAs in those young people who show a clinical response to these drugs. However, we shall see in the next chapter that major depressive disorders in young people tend to be recurrent conditions. Moreover, studies of adult depressed patients who have responded to TCAs have indicated that there may be benefits of continuing medication for many months, or even years (Kupfer, 1992). So, there may be something to be said for maintaining young people who have shown a response to TCAs on medication for at least 6 months. Much will depend on the patient's previous history. For example, it is the author's practice to maintain adolescents who have had two or more severe episodes of major depression, and who seem to have responded to TCAs, on full dosage for at least a year.

The TCAs have some important side-effects, particularly their effects on the myocardium and the cardiac conduction system. Therefore, during treatment with tricyclics there needs to be careful monitoring of the ECG, pulse and blood pressure. In the clinical trials, protocols have often included regular cardiac monitoring. For instance, in the study of Puig-Antich et al (1987) ECGs were done at baseline, every three days until the dose had been stabilized, and weekly thereafter. Parents should be counselled about the dangers of overdose with TCAs, which should be kept in a safe place where neither the patient nor siblings have easy access to them. Plasma levels may be helpful if there is concern about toxicity, but as we saw earlier they are probably not a useful guide to clinical response.

Side-effects of the TCAs

The side-effects of the TCAs may be divided into "minor" and "major", although it is important to note that even so-called minor side-effects may be important to patients and/or to the parents, and may lead to withdrawal from treatment.

Minor side-effects of TCAs in children are quite common. For example, in the study of Puig-Antich et al (1987) the following symptoms occurred in more than 30% of the sample: excitement, irritability, nightmares, insomnia, headache, muscle pains, increased appetite, abdominal cramps, constipation, vomiting, hiccups, dry mouth, bad taste, sweating, flushed face, drowsiness, dizziness, tiredness and listlessness. Probably, some of these symptoms were due to the pharmacological properties of the TCAs, such as their effects on the autonomic nervous system. However, many of them also occurred in the placebo group and only one symptom (flushed face on exercise) was significantly more common among patients on active drug. In a survey of the use of antidepressants by British child psychiatrists, Bramble and Dunkley (1992) reported that among children and adolescents who had been pre-scribed TCAs (usually amitriptyline or imipramine) the most common side-effects were dry mouth, drowsiness and constipation.

Among adolescents treated with TCAs, reported side-effects have included tiredness, sleep problems, dizziness and excessive perspiration (Geller et al, 1990). Geller et al (1990) found no anticholinergic side-effects, such as dry mouth or constipation. Neither Geller et al (1990) nor Boulos et al (1991) found significant differences between the group on active drug and the group on placebo. As Boulos et al (1991) pointed out, the presence of somatic complaints during therapy with the TCAs does not therefore necessarily mean that these complaints are due to the medication. As we saw earlier in this book, somatic complaints are quite common in depressed young people.

The major side-effects of the tricyclics are their effects on the cardiovascu-lar and neurological systems.

The TCAs have effects on heart muscle (myocardium) and other parts of the cardiovascular system, even in therapeutic doses (Puig-Antich et al, 1987; Biederman et al, 1989; Bartels et al, 1991). Indeed, Puig-Antich et al (1987) found that almost all children receiving imipramine showed at least minor electrocardiograph (ECG) changes compared with baseline. Most commonly, these involved resting heart rate increases in the interval between the atrium and the ventricle activating (the "PR interval"). The duration of ventricular activation (the "QRS width") and the interval between ventricular activation and ventricular recovery (the "QT interval") also showed an increase. In 17 out of 30 children receiving imipramine the dosage could not be raised to the pre-established dose (5 mg/kg) because the PR interval had lengthened to the safety limit (0.18 seconds), and in one case the heart rate had increased to 130 beats per minute. Orthostatic hypotension (low blood pressure on standing up) led to one child briefly losing consciousness when he got up from bed in the morning.

In a 6-week study of children and adolescents with attention deficit disor-der, Biederman et al (1989) reported that desipramine administration, especially at doses over 3.5 mg/kg, was associated with asymptomatic elec-trocardiographic changes (increase in the PR interval and the QRS duration) as well as minor increases in diastolic blood pressure. Interestingly, 6 out of 61 cases met criteria for incomplete intraventricular conduction deficit in the baseline, untreated, state. Biederman et al (1989) observed no cases of orthostatic hypotension, but two patients in the study of Boulos et al (1991) had to be withdrawn from the study because of this side-effect.

The clinical significance of the ECG changes is unclear (Biederman et al, 1989; Tingelstad, 1991), but a recent report of sudden death in three children taking desipramine (Riddle et al, 1991) has led to increased concern about the cardiovascular effects of tricyclics in children. All were boys, ages 8, 8 and 9 years. There was a family history of cardiac death in two cases, and in one of these there was a history of cardiac conduction problems. The patients' medical histories and autopsy data were incomplete, but it was postulated that the precipitating event was a disturbance of the heart's rhythm (cardiac arrhythmia).

In a thoughtful review of this issue, Tingelstad (1991) suggested that before initiating treatment with a tricyclic a careful medical history should be taken, including information on cardiac arrhythmia, heart disease, syncope, hearing loss, or a family history of heart disease or sudden cardiac death. A 12-lead electrocardiograph should be obtained and, if there is an abnormality, a 2-minute rhythm strip is appropriate. The rate, PR interval, QRS duration and the QT interval should be measured. Calculation of the corrected QT (QT_c) (calculated by dividing the measured QT by the square-root of the RR interval) is important because when this exceeds normal limits (0.45 seconds) there is a risk of ventricular tachyarrhythmias. Tingelstad (1991) pointed out that prolonged QT_c occurs in syncope associated with a family history of sudden death (Romano-Ward syndrome) and may be associated with congenital deafness, syncope and sudden death (Jervell and Lange-Nielsen syndrome). Such a disorder may have been present in one of the boys whose sudden death was associated with desipramine.

Petti (1983) reviewed some of the neurological effects of the TCAs in young people. The main one appears to be exacerbation of the risk of fits. There are reports scattered throughout the literature of fits in children on TCAs, especially those with brain damage. However, an abnormal EEG is not a contraindication to TCA treatment. Petti also described what appeared to be withdrawal symptoms in children who had high doses of TCAs stopped suddenly. Symptoms included "bizarre, psychotic-like behaviour" and gastrointestinal symptoms. He suggested that the dose of TCA should therefore be reduced gradually. Other neurological side-effects that have been reported in adults include movement disorders and sedation (Lejoyeux et al, 1992).

Finally, it should be borne in mind that the TCAs are very toxic in overdose. Indeed, in adults the death toll from TCAs in therapeutic quantities is likely to be dwarfed by the death toll from overdosage (Henry, 1992). Typically, there is a serious clinical picture that includes coma, hypertension, seizures and a variety of cardiac arrhythmias. Sadly, many patients who take overdoses of TCAs do not reach hospital alive.

LITHIUM AUGMENTATION OF THE TCAs

In depressed adults, there is evidence that the antidepressant action of TCAs can be potentiated by lithium (e.g. Heninger, Charney & Sternberg, 1983;

Katona, 1988) and several studies have reported preliminary data on the use of lithium augmentation in young people. Ryan ct al (1988) described 14 adolescents with nonbipolar major depressive disorder who had been treated with TCAs alone for 6 weeks and who had failed to respond. They were given lithium carbonate, titrated to achieve plasma levels of around 0.6–0.7 mEq/L in addition to the TCA. About 40% were felt to have responded to the addition of lithium, a third did not improve, and two-fifths showed some improvement.

Strober et al (1992a) assessed the value of lithium augmentation in a 3-week open trial involving 24 adolescents who remained very depressed following a 6-week course of imipramine. Two patients responded dramatically within a week and an additional 8 patients showed partial improvement during the trial. The size of improvement was greater than in a "historical" control group of nonresponders who had continued on imipramine. However, the proportion who improved with lithium augmentation was considerably less than has been reported in studies of lithium augmentation in tricyclic-resistant depression occurring in adults. The addition of lithium was associated with only a few side-effects (most commonly polyuria and tremor) and in no case did side-effects force early discontinuation of the trial.

As Ryan (1990) and Strober et al (1992a) pointed out, it is necessary to be cautious in interpreting the data from these open trials. Nevertheless, the results suggest that lithium augmentation should be evaluated further in the treatment of depression in adolescence. Indeed, it may be that lithium on its own has an antidepressant effect, but to date there have been no published studies of the efficacy of lithium alone in adolescent major depression. Such studies are needed, especially as there is some evidence that lithium may be an effective maintenance treatment for unipolar depression in adults (Prien, 1992).

MONOAMINE OXIDASE INHIBITORS (MAOIs)

Irreversible MAOIs

The first monoamine oxidase inhibitor (MAOI), iproniazid, was originally developed as an antituberculous agent and it was only by accident that its antidepressant effect was noticed. MAOIs inhibit the group of enzymes known as the monoamine oxidases. These enzymes are widely distributed throughout the body and their main action is to inactivate (by deamination) the amines 5HT, dopamine and noradrenaline. Inhibition of monamine oxidase therefore leads to the build-up in most tissues, including the brain, of these amines. The "old" MAOIs, such as iproniazid, phenelzine and tranylcypromine, are all *irreversible* inhibitors of both types of monoamine oxidase (MAO-A, MAO-B). The activity of monoamine oxidase returns only when new enzyme has been synthesized in sufficient quantity. Their pharmacological effects therefore last for up to 3 weeks beyond their elimination from the tissues.

The antidepressant effects of the MAOIs have been linked to changes in the concentration of amines in central neurochemical pathways (the amine hypothesis—see back). However, as is the case with the TCAs, their biochemical actions are not well understood and are less than perfectly related to their clinical effects. For example, their antidepressant effects are usually delayed for several weeks, but inhibition of monoamine oxidase (at least in blood) occurs very rapidly.

Early reports on the use of the monoamine oxidase inhibitors suggested that there was a syndrome of atypical depression that responded particularly well to MAOIs. The term "atypical depression" has been used in a number of different ways, but the features that have been suggested to predict preferential response to MAOIs include somatic anxiety features, phobias, panics and initial insomnia (Davidson, 1992). However, recent studies suggest that the MAOIs are effective antidepressants across a broad range of types of depressions. For example, among 17 controlled trials of the MAOI phenelzine against placebo in depression, 10 have shown the drug to be clearly superior (Paykel, 1989). There is some evidence that the MAOIs are weakly specific for anxiety and reversed functional shift (i.e. depression with a diurnal pattern of evening worsening: see, for example, Quitkin et al, 1991) although the differences from tricyclics are not especially strong (Paykel, 1989).

Since MAOIs have developed a reputation in the treatment of atypical depressions in adults, which in the past have been called "masked" or "smiling" depressions, it is not surprising to find that they have been used to treat depressions in children, which have also been regarded historically as presenting atypically or in a "masked form" (Chapter 1). One of the first controlled studies of antidepressant medication in depressed children compared a combination of phenelzine and chlordiazepoxide versus phenobarbital in depressed children (Frommer, 1967). Seventy-eight per cent of the children showed improvement within 2 weeks while on the MAOI compared with 50% of those on the barbiturate. Unfortunately, it is difficult to interpret the results of this study because of its design. It is not clear, for instance, whether the active ingredient was the phenelzine, or the chlordiazepoxide, or both.

In an open clinical trial, Ryan and his colleagues (Ryan, 1990) treated adolescents either with MAOIs alone or in combination with the TCAs. All but two of the subjects had received a course of TCAs before the MAOIs were initiated. Fourteen subjects were considered to have made a good response, which is encouraging since the history of previous treatment suggests that this group may have been especially resistant to medication.

On the other hand, this study also illustrates some of the problems of using irreversible MAOIs in young people. One of the best-known side-effects of the MAOIs are their dietary interactions. When monoamine oxidase inhibition is induced, tyramine (a compound that is found in many foods such as mature cheeses and meat) is no longer detoxified by the gut wall and liver but enters the circulation. It is then taken up into nerve endings and a large amount of noradrenaline is released. The result is severe hypertension, with symptoms like headache, vomiting and chest pain. These symptoms usually subside within a few hours, but very occasionally there may be cerebral haemorrhage or death. Accordingly, it is necessary that patients taking MAOIs adhere to a strict diet.

Ryan (1990) reported that dietary noncompliance was an important issue in the prescription of MAOIs to depressed adolescents. Two subjects had significant hypertension after the ingestion of food containing tyramine. One was given the food accidentally as part of the hospital diet, the other ate two cheese sandwiches as part of a suicide attempt. Good clinical response alone did not guarantee good dietary compliance. Three out of the five adolescents whose poor compliance had led to the discontinuation of the MAOI had made a good clinical response to the drug.

The irreversible MAOIs also interact with other drugs. For example, a hypertensive reaction can occur if they are prescribed in conjunction with cough medicines or nasal decongestants. In addition, there are interactions with the TCAs, and some clinicians will not prescribe the two together, although in some studies the MAOIs have been added to the TCAs without serious effects (Ryan 1990).

Other side-effects of the MAOIs include orthostatic hypotension, dry mouth and reduced sweating. Orthostatic hypotension can be a problem and blood pressure needs to be monitored throughout treatment. Hydrazine MAOIs have been associated with hepatocellular jaundice. Acute hypomanic episodes and toxic psychoses have been described in adults and there have been reports of such problems in children treated with MAOIs (Pfefferbaum, Pack & van Eys, 1989). Interactions with other drugs can also be a problem.

Clearly, then, the decision to prescribe irreversible MAOIs to depressed young people should not be taken lightly. They may have a place in the treatment of depressions that are resistant to other forms of medication, but they should not be prescribed to adolescents whom it is felt may be unreliable in sticking to the diet.

Reversible MAOIs

In recent years several compounds have been developed that can inhibit MAO reversibly. As yet, none of them has been systematically tested in child and adolescent patients with major depression. Nevertheless, they have a number of advantages over the older MAOIs that may make them more suitable for the treatment of depressions in young people.

Moclobemide is probably the best known of the "new" MAOIs. Its inhibition of MAO lasts for only a few hours and MAO activity is usually reinstated within 24 hours of the last dose. In addition, it is thought to be a much more specific inhibitor of MAO than the old MAOIs, and less potentially toxic, especially to the liver (Burkard et al, 1989). Moclobemide has been shown to be as effective as TCAs in several studies of depressed adults (e.g. Guelfi et al, 1992). Several investigations (reviewed by Burkard et al, 1989) have found that moclobemide only weakly potentiates the effects of tyramine on blood pressure, so substantially reducing the risk of hypertensive crises (the cheese effect). It remains to be seen whether it will be safe and effective in depressed children.

OTHER NEWER ANTIDEPRESSANTS

A number of other new antidepressants have been introduced, such as lofepramine, mianserin and fluoxetine. Very little has been written about the use of these drugs in depressed young people, but some of them show promise. Fluoxetine, for example, is a selective inhibitor of serotonin uptake, which may make it particularly suitable for depression in young people (see page 139). Several placebo-control trials have demonstrated its efficacy in adult depression, including melancholic and severe depressive disorders (Hale & Stokes, 1991). It seems that the onset of action is comparable to the "standard" antidepressants, though preliminary trials of the combination of fluoxetine and desipramine have suggested that in adults this combination may have a very rapid onset of antidepressant effect (Nelson et al, 1991). However, the efficacy of fluoxetine either alone or in combination with other antidepressants remains to be demonstrated in double-blind placebo-control trials with depressed children and/or adolescents. There has been only one published controlled study among depressed young people. This produced a negative result among a sample of adolescents with major depression, though the high response rate in the placebo group made any other finding difficult (Simeon et al, 1990). More trials are required, as fluoxetine seems to have fewer cardiac effects than the TCAs (Riddle et al, 1990) and it appears to be less toxic in overdose (Riddle et al, 1989).

ELECTROCONVULSIVE THERAPY

Electroconvulsive therapy (ECT) has been used as a treatment in adult psychiatry for many years. The most common indication for ECT in adults is major depression. It is usually prescribed in severe cases of depression where the patient has failed to respond to medication and/or where a rapid response is necessary. It is sometimes given as the primary form of treatment when other treatments are contraindicated or where it is known that previous depressions have responded well to ECT. Typically, ECT is administered two or three times a week, with the total number of treatments between 6 and 12. Electrode placement can be bilateral or unilateral, and some clinicians will change from one form to another depending on response. There have been a number of recent developments in the practice of ECT (Weiner & Coffey, 1991). A growing number of clinicians base the size of the shock on an estimate of the seizure threshold determined after the first session, and EEG monitoring of the induced seizure is becoming increasingly common.

Electroconvulsive therapy is occasionally used in the treatment of severe depressions in children younger than 16 years (Pippard & Ellam, 1981). The literature on the use of ECT in children and adolescents consists almost entirely of case reports, which were reviewed by Bertagnoli and Borchardt (1990). Their review identified a total of 32 cases of affective disorder arising in children and adolescents that were treated with ECT. These cases included 10 unipolar depressions (age range 5–17 years) and 22 cases of bipolar disorder, 9 of whom were manic at the time of ECT. Eighty per cent of the depressed cases and nearly 90% of the manic cases were thought to have improved. It is of course necessary to be very cautious in interpreting the results of these case reports. One cannot be certain about the accuracy of diagnosis or of the measures used to assess improvement. Indeed, that one of these case reports found that 97% of patients with schizophrenia improved (a disorder that is usually thought to do less well with ECT than depression) does raise doubts about their validity. A systematic review of prescribing practices among child and adolescent psychiatrists would be most helpful, and indeed is currently being conducted in Britain by the Royal College of Psychiatrists. Nevertheless, at the moment these reports are all that we have to go on and they do suggest that ECT may be indicated in the kinds of situations in which it is used in adult psychiatry.

Recent research on the adverse effects of ECT has been concerned both with memory function and with structural brain imaging using techniques such as computed axial tomography (CAT) and magnetic resonance imaging (MRI). It seems that bilateral electrode placement is associated with subtle memory deficits detectable at 6-months post-ECT, although unilateral nondominant electrode placement diminishes the severity and persistence of memory impairment (Weiner & Coffey, 1991). A recent magnetic resonance imaging study found that ECT was not associated with evidence of gross brain damage. In a prospective study, 35 inpatients with depression underwent MRI scans before and twice after ECT (Coffey et al, 1991). There was no relationship between ECT and brain damage.

There have been reports of neuropsychological impairment in young people who have had ECT. For example, Carr et al (1983) described the case of a 12-year-old girl with a severe manic disorder who had developed side-effects on neuroleptics but who was successfully treated with unilateral ECT. Neuropsychological testing at follow-up revealed some persisting impairment of auditory information memory. On the other hand, Bertagnoli and Borchardt (1990) identified a number of case reports in which the authors reported that there were no long-term effects. They concluded that, although there was some cognitive impairment within a few days of ECT, this usually clears quickly. There may be some mild impairment for a few months.

It is likely that there will be increasing interest in the use of ECT among adolescents with severe affective disorders because of the side-effects of psychotropics in this age group and because of the poor response to medication that such patients commonly show. The available data suggest that effects on cognitive functioning are not major, and these effects need to be balanced against the severe impairments that can be associated with acute affective disorders among the young. However, there is a great need for systematic, prospective neuropsychological studies with adequate periods of follow-up.

TREATMENT OF BIPOLAR DISORDERS

The physical treatment of bipolar disorders among young people can be divided into three main areas:

1. The treatment of acute mania.
2. The treatment of the depressed phase.
3. Maintenance treament.

It should be noted that in this section we are concerned with the treatment of bipolar conditions resembling adult bipolar disorders. The treatment of "atypical" bipolar disorders will be discussed in the next section.

Treatment of mania

Neuroleptics
Neuroleptics such as chlorpromazine and haloperidol seem to suppress manic symptoms more rapidly than lithium (Prien, Caffey & Klett, 1972). Accordingly, for many psychiatrists they are the drug of first choice in the treatment of acute mania, either alone or in combination with lithium. However, neuroleptics have a number of troublesome side-effects, most notably acute extrapyramidal reactions such as dystonia, and prolonged administration is associated with the development of tardive dyskinesia. Children may be

especially susceptible to these effects (Taylor, 1985). There may also be effects on learning.

Lithium

There have been few double-blind controlled studies of lithium in juvenile manic disorders and interpretation of the published research is complicated by uncertainties over diagnosis (Strober, Hanna & McCracken, 1989). Nonetheless, a variety of studies and case reports have described the beneficial effects of lithium for mania both in children and adolescents. Carlson and Strober (1978), for example, found that three of six adolescents with mania showed a good response to lithium. Delong and Nieman (1983) found greater improvement in manic children whilst on lithium than during a placebo period.

It has, however, been suggested that mania in young people may be more resistant to treatment with lithium than its adult counterpart. Strober et al (1988) found that prepubertal onset of psychopathology (mostly nonaffective symptoms such as conduct problems) was associated with a worse antimanic response to lithium. Thus, by the sixth week of treatment only 40% of prepubertal-onset probands were responders, whereas in the postpubertal-onset group 80% had responded. These findings are consistent with studies of adults that suggest that a longer history of problems preceding treatment predicts a worse response to lithium (Prien, Caffey & Klett, 1974).

Children and adolescents who are prescribed lithium need a careful physical work-up, including a full medical history and examination, ECG, thyroid function, haemoglobin and red cell indices, serum creatinine and blood biochemistry. Lithium is contraindicated in renal failure and severe cardiac disorders. It is cleared from the body by the kidney, and since renal clearance varies from person to person it is necessary to adjust the dose to maintain a steady plasma level. In general, plasma levels in adolescents should be in the same range as that recommended for adults (Prendergast, 1992)—between 0.6 and 1.0 mmol/l. Blood for plasma levels should be taken each week until a steady plasma level has been achieved and thereafter once every 6 weeks. The blood should be drawn in the morning, about 12 hours after the last dose of lithium.

Early side-effects of lithium include a mild diuresis, fine tremor and mild fatigue. Thyroid enlargement occurs in about 5% of adults taking lithium but is readily reversible with thyroxine. Some patients, mostly older women, will develop hypothyroidism, so thyroid function needs to be tested periodically during the administration of lithium. Reversible ECG changes occur. Lithium may induce lowering of the renal concentrating ability, and some patients develop mild polyuria and polydipsia. Morphological changes have been found in the kidneys of patients during long-term lithium treatment, but mortality from renal disorders does not appear to be increased (Abou-Saleh,

1992). Symptoms of acute intoxication with lithium include ataxia, muscle twitching, slurred speech and confusion. There can be progression to coma and fits. Lithium intoxication is especially likely to occur when the patient is dehydrated, such as during illness or after surgery.

Lithium has interactions with a number of drugs. Any drug that reduces the elimination of lithium may lead to toxicity. Thiazide diuretics are an important example, but reduced clearance of lithium may also occur with nonsteroidal anti-inflammatory drugs such as indomethacin. There have been reports of serious toxic reactions when lithium is given with large doses of neuroleptic, especially haloperidol, but low doses (less than 20 mg haloperidol per day) are usually not a problem (Abou-Saleh, 1992).

Anticonvulsants
Lithium has a number of other drawbacks. It takes one to two weeks to work, it is less effective in severe mania, and in adults about 25% fail to respond (Prien & Potter, 1990). As a result, a variety of other treatments have been investigated, especially anticonvulsants. Of these, carbamazepine has been the most thoroughly examined, with several controlled trials showing superiority over placebo in adult samples (Small et al, 1991). Carbamazepine seems to be as effective as lithium in the treatment of acute mania, though neither drug alone is sufficient for the management of adult manic patients referred for tertiary care. Another anticonvulsant, sodium valproate, has now been evaluated in several placebo-control studies of adults with mania, and also appears to have an antimanic effect (Pope et al, 1991). It remains to be seen whether anticonvulsants will prove effective in juvenile manic disorders.

Other treatments of mania
As described above, there is some evidence that ECT may be effective in mania, but it is usually reserved for cases that are resistant to other forms of treatment.

Treatment of the depressed phase

It might be thought that treatment of the depressed phase of bipolar disorder would not differ from the treatment of depressions arising in subjects who have never had an episode of mania, especially as the symptoms of depression are very similar (Brockington et al, 1982). In fact, however, there is some evidence that depressions occurring as part of a bipolar disorder are more resistant to antidepressant treatment than other depressions. Strober and Carlson (1982) studied prospectively a group of adolescent subjects who had been diagnosed as major depressive disorder. Some went on to have manic episodes. Twenty-four of 45 patients with nonbipolar outcomes (53%) were thought to have responded well to antidepressants compared with only 2 out of 11 with bipolar outcomes. Interestingly, the two cases of pharmacologically precipitated mania both occurred in the bipolar outcome group.

The possibility that antidepressants might precipitate mania in subjects with bipolar disorder has been seen as one of the main reasons for the lack of placebo-controlled trials of antidepressants in the depressed phase of bipolar disorder (Prien & Potter, 1990). The evidence, such as it is, suggests that lithium can be effective in bipolar depression (Prien & Potter, 1990) and some psychiatrists combine lithium with an antidepressant, especially if the depression is severe.

Maintenance treatment

In adults there is convincing evidence that prolonged administration of lithium prevents both manic and depressive episodes (Prien, 1992). However, in recent years there has been a search for new ways of preventing relapse in bipolar disorders. This search has been prompted by three problems associated with the long-term use of lithium. First, it seems that a growing number of people have to stop lithium because of medical risks (such as possible cardiovascular teratogenicity in the fetus or the risks associated with certain medical illnesses), or because of side-effects. Second, there has been increasing recognition that, although lithium does reduce the rate of relapse, it does not eliminate the risk altogether. Indeed, recent research has suggested that only about one-third of patients on lithium remain completely episode-free for two years (reviewed by Prien & Potter, 1990). Third, lithium seems to be relatively ineffective in the treatment of patients whose mood state cycles rapidly or who have "dysphoric mania" (Bauer & Whybrow, 1991).

Various alternative treatments now exist for the maintenance treatment of bipolar disorders. The most thoroughly studied has been carbamazepine, which has been compared with lithium in several trials. Some have shown that carbamazepine is a little more effective than lithium, others that it is a little less effective (Prien, 1992). Interpretation of the results has been made difficult by various methodological issues (Prien & Gelenberg, 1989), such as that in many of these trials other medication was prescribed in addition to carbamazepine. This has also occurred in studies where carbamazepine has been evaluated in patients who fail to respond to lithium, so the efficacy of carbamazepine therapy alone remains to be conclusively demonstrated. Nevertheless, it will probably continue to be a useful second-line treatment for bipolar disorders that have failed to respond to lithium or where lithium is contraindicated.

The other main maintenance treatment for bipolar disorders has been the augmentation of lithium with either an antidepressant, so as to prevent "breakthrough" depression, or a neuroleptic, so as to prevent "breakthrough" mania. As described earlier, the prescription of TCAs to patients with bipolar disorder has caused concern because of the possibility of inducing mania in these subjects. Nevertheless, in practice TCAs are very commonly prescribed as a maintenance treatment in such circumstances, although the benefits have not been conclusively demonstrated (Quitkin et al, 1981). At present, it is not clear whether the addition of a neuroleptic to lithium maintenance therapy is effective in the prevention of breakthrough mania (Prien & Potter, 1990).

In young people, there have been no systematic long-interval placebo-control studies of lithium maintenance therapy. Nevertheless, many clinicians prescribe lithium prophylactically to adolescents with bipolar disorder on the grounds that it has proved to be effective in adults and because open trials suggest that it may be effective in some adolescents. Carlson and Strober (1978), for example, found that in adolescents with mania diagnosed according to RDC criteria, lithium did in some cases seem to be effective in the prevention of recurrence. Similarly, Strober et al (1990b) reported a naturalistic study in which adolescent bipolar patients who complied with lithium had a lower risk of relapse than those who were noncompliant.

TREATMENT OF CYCLIC BEHAVIOURAL DISORDERS RESEMBLING BIPOLAR ILLNESS

Many clinicians will be familiar with the adolescent patient who has a cyclical illness that resembles in one way or another manic disorder and in whom there are reasons for believing that the disorder may in fact be "atypical" mania, such as that there is a family history of bipolar disorder. Indeed, as Carlson (1990) pointed out, although unambiguous bipolar disorders certainly do occur in adolescence it is far from clear where the boundaries of the disorder lie. In such cases a trial of lithium may be justified, especially as there have been case reports of young people presenting atypically who have seemed to respond to lithium (Carlson et al, 1992).

CONCLUSIONS

Drug treatments have been established as useful interventions in a variety of types of adult affective disorder. Early studies suggested that they might be effective in the treatment of depressive conditions arising in young people. However, recent controlled studies have been unable to show any benefits beyond those that can be ascribed to their placebo effects. It must be remembered, however, that systematic studies of the use of antidepressants in the major depressive conditions of young people are at an early stage. It may be that one or more of the methodological problems that have been encountered in these early studies accounts for the negative findings. In view of the similarities between child and adult depressions, and the large amount of research showing that antidepressants are effective in adult-onset affective disorders, more research on the use of antidepressants in young people is certainly warranted. In the meantime, antidepressants are probably best re-served for those severe cases of depression that have failed to respond to other forms of intervention.

Chapter 10

Course and Outcome

This chapter deals with the outcomes of depressive disorders in young people. The chapter begins with a brief review of some of the conceptual issues surrounding the definition of outcome. Next, the risk of further episodes of affective disorder is reviewed. Finally, other aspects of outcome are considered, such as the impact of early depression on later social functioning and the risk of suicide.

CONCEPTUAL ISSUES SURROUNDING THE DEFINITION OF OUTCOME

Recent reviews (e.g. Frank et al, 1991b) have highlighted the problems involved in defining change points in the course of depressive disorder in adults. For example, when does partial remission become recovery? How should an episode of depression be defined?

In considering studies of the natural history of depression in young people, it is immediately apparent that the same problems arise. Thus, many authors use different concepts and definitions of "recovery" and "relapse". For example, in the study of Kovacs et al (1984a) the definition of "recovery" included mental states in which there was persistence of some subclinical symptoms, whereas in the study of Goodyer et al (1991a) recovery was defined as "no mental state abnormalities" whatsoever. Moreover, it seems that there is only moderate agreement between different informants on the classification of recovery. Thus, Goodyer et al (1991a) reported that the level of agreement between the child and the mother on whether or not the child had recovered was only moderate ($\kappa = 0.49$, calculated by the author from the data in Goodyer et al's table 1).

The problems of defining and measuring recovery and relapse are formidable enough, but a further problem in the interpretation of follow-ups of depressed children arises from the fact that these children often have other psychiatric problems such as conduct disorder. The problem is that few follow-ups of depressed young people have used a comparison group who were closely matched according to the *presence* of nondepressive symptomatology. Rather, comparison groups have been defined primarily by the mere *absence* of depression. Clearly, the question arises as to how much the outcome of childhood depression is the result of the earlier depression and how much it relates to the comorbid psychiatric problems.

RISK OF FURTHER EPISODES OF DEPRESSION IN DEPRESSED YOUNG PEOPLE

It is necessary therefore to be cautious in interpreting the follow-ups of depressed children published so far, especially as most studies have hitherto been carried out on samples of patients, thus limiting the range of severity. Nevertheless, one conclusion seems reasonably secure: *young people diagnosed as depressed are at increased risk of subsequent episodes of depression.*

Thus, many early uncontrolled studies reported that children who had had one episode of depression were at risk of another. Poznanski, Kraheneuhl and Zrull (1976), for example, found that 5 out of 10 depressed children who were re-evaluated on average 6½ years later were depressed. Eastgate and Gilmour (1984) followed up 19 depressed subjects 7–8 years after first presentation: 8 still had moderate or severe disability, and of these 4 had depression, 1 was schizophrenic and 3 had marked personality disorders.

Controlled studies have by and large confirmed that the risk of subsequent depression among depressed young people is more than would be expected by chance. Studies of preadolescent children meeting DSM-III criteria for depressive disorder have shown that depression in childhood often recurs (Kovacs et al, 1984b; McGee & Williams, 1988). For example, Kovacs et al (1984b) undertook a systematic follow-up of child patients with a major depressive disorder, a dysthymic disorder, an adjustment disorder with depressed mood, and some other psychiatric disorder. The development of subsequent episodes of depression was virtually confined to children with major depressive disorders and dysthymic disorders. Asarnow et al (1988) found that children who had been hospitalized with major depression were at high risk of rehospitalization because of suicidal behaviour or increasing depression. Within a little less than two years 45% were rehospitalized, a rate that was not significantly different from that found for children with schizophrenia spectrum disorders.

Studies of the short-term stability of depressive symptoms in community samples of adolescents have also found significant correlations over time. Larsson et al (1991) found that the correlation over a period of 4–6 weeks on the BDI was 0.66. Garrison et al (1990) reported that the stability of adolescents' scores on the CES-D was 0.53 at one year and 0.36 at two years after the initial assessment.

None of these studies has yet extended beyond late-adolescence. However, a similarly high rate of subsequent psychiatric morbidity has been reported in follow-up studies of depressed adolescents that have extended into late adolescence or early adult life (Garber et al, 1988; Kandel & Davies, 1986; King & Pittman, 1970; Strober & Carlson, 1982). These studies have suggested both that self-ratings of depression in adolescent community samples predict similar problems in early adulthood (Kandel & Davies, 1986), and that adolescent patients with depressive disorders are at high risk of subsequent major affective disturbance (Garber et al, 1988; Strober & Carlson, 1982). Although the findings of these studies are limited by issues such as the uncertainty regarding the connection between depression questionnaire scores and clinical depressive disorder (Kandel & Davies, 1986) and high rates of sample attrition (Garber et al, 1988), they clearly suggest that adolescents with depression are at increased risk of depression in early adulthood.

Moving still further into adult life, Harrington et al (1990) followed up 63 depressed children and adolescents on average 18 years after their initial contact. The depressed group had a significantly greater risk of depression in adulthood than a control group who had been matched on a large number of variables, including nondepressive symptoms. Depressed children were no more likely than control children to suffer nondepressive disorders in adulthood, suggesting that the risk for adult major depression was specific and unrelated to comorbidity with other psychiatric problems. Zeitlin (1986), in a study of child psychiatric patients who attended the same hospital as adults, has also found strong child to adult continuities for depression.

Predictors of outcome

Depressed young people, then, seem to be at increased risk of subsequent depression, sometimes for many years after the initial episode. What mechanisms might be responsible for this poor outcome? Unfortunately, as yet little is known about this issue and the only risk factor that has consistently been associated with an adverse outcome is the type of depression that the child showed during the index episode. Two studies have shown that children with DSM-III "double depression" (major depression and dysthymic disorder) have a worse short-term outcome than children with major depression alone (Asarnow et al, 1988; Kovacs et al, 1984b), and it appears that the adult prognosis of childhood depression is also influenced by the characteristics of the index depression (Harrington et al, 1990).

There is some suggestion that comorbidity with other child psychiatric disorders may also influence the outcome, but the findings have varied between different studies. Thus, in the study of Kovacs and her colleagues (Kovacs et al, 1988, 1989) neither comorbid anxiety disorder nor comorbid conduct disorder was significantly associated with an increased risk of subsequent major depression. By contrast, in our child to adult follow-up, conduct disorder during the index episode was associated with a tendency towards a *lower* risk of subsequent major depression (Harrington et al, 1991). Interestingly, two studies have found that older depressed children have a worse prognosis than younger depressed children (Harrington et al, 1990; Kovacs et al, 1989).

There is evidence that certain kinds of stressors, particularly those occurring within the family, may be important in predicting the outcome of depressed young people (Garrison et al, 1990; Hammen, Burge & Adrian, 1991). Hammen et al (1991) examined the influence of initial depression in the child, stressful events, maternal depressive symptoms and the interaction between events and symptoms in predicting depression at 6-month follow-up. The level of initial depression in the child was the strongest predictor of subsequent depression, but maternal symptoms were also a strong independent predictor of subsequent depression. Of course, it could be that this association is simply a reflection of the fact that both maternal depression and depression in the child are the result of some third factor, such as a genetic predisposition. However, Hammen and colleagues also found a close *temporal* relationship between maternal and child depression, suggesting that the links may have been a reflection of some kind of environmental mechanism. Perhaps, for example, depressed mothers are less able to comfort their children or offer support, or perhaps they are more critical. Support for the latter suggestion came from the follow-up study of Asarnow et al (1992) in which relapse of major depression was strongly linked with maternal expressed emotion.

Alternatively, it may be that both the child and the mother were reacting to some external adverse event. Thus, Burge and Hammen (1991) described a relationship between two aspects of mother–child interaction, ability to focus on a task and affective quality, and children's subsequent depression and school behaviour. Chronic environmental stress was predictive of more negative, critical maternal behaviour, whereas maternal depressed mood was associated with less task involvement. In other words, there seemed to be a complex relationship between mother–child interactions, environmental adversity and depression in children. Some aspects of the mother's parenting were directly influenced by the social environment, whereas others were affected by her mental state.

These findings regarding the role of environmental stressors, such as negative maternal interactions, in the persistence of depression in young people require replication. However, they are important because they suggest that the strong continuities that have been found for early-onset depressive disorder may be a reflection not only of processes that are intrinsic to the child, but also of continuities of adverse environments.

RISK OF OTHER FORMS OF ADVERSE OUTCOME

Social and cognitive functioning

There are a number of reasons for thinking that depression in young people may not only predict further episodes of depression but also might be associated with effects on social and cognitive functioning. Depression in young people is frequently associated with social withdrawal and irritability, and so depressed young people may find it more difficult to establish and maintain social relationships. Similarly, symptoms such as loss of concentration and psychomotor retardation may interfere with the process of learning. This in turn might lead to low self-esteem and so lead to further academic failure. Kovacs and Goldston (1991) pointed out that young people suffering from major depression are impaired for a significant proportion of the lifespan. Moreover, they are impaired at a time when learning takes place rapidly. Perhaps, then, they will eventually become delayed both socially and cognitively.

Several studies have examined the social outcomes of depressed young people. Puig-Antich and his colleagues (1985b) found that some impairment of peer relationships persisted several months after recovery from depression. In the longer term, Kandel and Davies (1986) reported that self-ratings of dysphoria in adolescence were associated with heavy cigarette smoking, greater involvement in delinquent activities, and impairments of intimate relationships as young adults. Garber et al (1988) found that depressed adolescent inpatients reported more marital and relationship problems when they were followed 8 years after discharge than non-depressed psychiatric control subjects.

These findings have important theoretical as well as clinical implications since they suggest that the social isolation and lack of a supporting relationship that have been found in cross-sectional studies of adult depression (Brown & Harris, 1978) may reflect social selection as much as social causation (Kandel & Davies, 1986). However, none of these studies excluded the effects that childhood conduct problems, which are commonly associated with adolescent depression, could have on these outcomes. Harrington et al (1991) found that juvenile depression seemed to have little direct impact on social functioning in adulthood, whereas comorbid conduct disorder was a strong predictor of subsequent antisocial personality development. The implication is that it is important to differentiate the course of depressive disorder from the course of other disorders.

Association with suicidal behaviour and suicide

Depressed young people very commonly have suicidal thoughts and some of them make suicide attempts. For instance, Ryan et al (1987) found that about

60% of children and adolescents with major depression had suicidal ideation. Mitchell et al (1988) reported that 67% of depressed children and adolescents had suicidal ideation and 39% had made a suicide attempt. Myers et al (1991) examined the cross-sectional correlates of suicidality in the sample described by Mitchell et al (1988). Conduct problems and depressive thinking were the strongest correlates. The best predictors of subsequent suicidality at 3 year follow-up were level of initial suicidality, anger and age.

Conversely, it seems that suicidal children are at increased risk of depression (Pfeffer, 1992). For example, Pfeffer et al (1991) found that young people who had attempted suicide were ten times more likely to have a mood disorder during the follow-up period of 6–8 years than young people who had not made an attempt.

Little is known about the risk of completed suicide in depressed children and adolescents. However, in our child to adult follow-up of 80 depressed probands and 80 controls, all of the deaths in adult life were "unnatural". Of the three deaths in the depressed group, two were definite suicides and the third died of pneumonia following a prolonged period of self-neglect. The only death in the control group was also by suicide. Interestingly, the "control" who committed suicide was probably misdiagnosed in childhood; shortly after her index attendance she developed a definite bipolar illness. Although no statistical weight should be attached to these figures because of the small numbers, the rate of suicide is clearly far in excess of that expected in the general population of young adults.

Another way of looking at the relationship of depression and suicide is through psychological autopsy studies of young people who have killed themselves. Such studies involve the interviewing of relatives and the collection of data from a variety of other sources in order to make a diagnostic assessment on the young person before the suicide. It will be appreciated that such studies are necessarily limited by their reliance on indirect sources of data. This may have led to an underestimation of the prevalence of depressive phenomena in young people who have committed suicide. Nonetheless, most recent psychological autopsy studies of suicide in young people have found high rates of affective disorders (Shaffer, 1988; Brent et al, 1988; Marttunen et al, 1991). The type of affective disorder that has been found has, however, differed between studies. Brent et al (1988) found that bipolar symptoms were quite common, whereas Shaffer (1988) and Marttunen et al (1991) found that such symptoms were uncommon.

It is important to note that other mental disorders may also be important in suicide. Several studies have found that antisocial behaviours are quite common among young people who have killed themselves (Brent et al, 1988; Shaffer, 1988). In a prospective study of the predictors of completed suicide in young men from the general population, Allebeck, Allgulander and Fisher (1988) found that several early indicators predicted suicide. These included poor emotional control, contact with a child welfare authority or the police and lack of friends. Marttunen et al (1991) found nearly one-fifth of suicides aged between 13 and 19 years had a conduct disorder or antisocial personality and that a quarter abused alcohol or drugs. Perhaps, then, it is the combination of depression and certain personality characteristics, such as aggression or the propensity to take risks, that is especially likely to lead to suicide in young people.

In adults, one of the characteristics of depression that has been closely linked to suicide is the symptom of hopelessness. Scales now exist to measure hopelessness in young people (Kazdin, Rodgers & Colbus, 1986). However, so far the relationship between suicidal behaviour and hopelessness in young people has not been confirmed (Cole, 1989). In studies of two separate populations, Cole (1989) found that suicidal ideation and/or behaviour was much more strongly related to depression scores than to hopelessness scores. He postulated that extreme hopelessness in adolescents might be attenuated by the adolescent's belief that future life changes (e.g. leaving school or home) might be beneficial.

The risk factors for completed suicide among depressed young people have not yet been systematically investigated. However, if it is assumed that they are similar to the risk factors for suicide that have been identified in psychological autopsy studies of young people, then they would include the following: male sex, increased age, a diagnosis of severe depression, conduct disorder or alcohol/drug use, easy access to the means of committing suicide, comorbidity, presence of a precipitant, and a previous attempt (especially if of high suicidal intent).

RECOVERY FROM THE INDEX EPISODE

Although the recurrence rate for depression in young people seems to be quite high, the available data suggest that many children with major depression will recover from that depression within two years. For example, Kovacs et al (1984a) reported that the cumulative probability of recovery from major depression by one year after onset was 74% and by two years was 92%. This study included many subjects who had previous emotional–behavioural problems and some form of treatment. However, very similar results were reported by Keller et al (1988) in a retrospective study of time to recovery from first episode of major depression in young people who had mostly not received treatment (Keller et al, 1991). Goodyer et al (1991a) found that 50 per cent of depressed children were completely free of symptoms within on average one year of their first assessment. Adolescents with major depression usually recover within a year (Strober et al, 1992b).

CHRONIC DEPRESSION

Unfortunately, in some cases depression among young people can become chronic and unremitting. Different definitions of chronicity have been used. Ryan et al (1987), for example, defined chronicity as a duration of depression for more than two years, whereas Shain et al (1991) defined it as a duration of just one year. In the study of Ryan et al (1987) nearly one-half of subjects had either chronic major depression or fluctuating dysthymia and major depression, and roughly the same proportion were found to be chronic cases in the study of Shain et al. Chronicity seems to be associated with increased suicidality (Ryan et al, 1987) but not, surprisingly, with an increased length of stay in hospital.

OUTCOMES OF EARLY-ONSET BIPOLAR DISORDERS

It is unclear whether there is a difference in the course of bipolar illness when it arises early in life (Strober, Hanna & McCracken, 1989). Carlson, Davenport and Jamison (1977) compared bipolar patients with an onset at around the age of 16 years with later-onset bipolars and found no significant difference in episode frequency. Werry, McClellan and Chard (1991) reported that the outcome of bipolar disorder arising in adolescence seemed to be better than early-onset schizophrenia. However, compliance with treatment was poor in one-third of cases, so active follow-up is required. Premorbid functioning was the best predictor of outcome (Werry & McClellan, 1992).

CONCLUSIONS AND IMPLICATIONS

Longitudinal studies of early-onset affective disorders are at an early stage, and numerous methodological issues remain to be tackled. It is scarcely likely, therefore, that the studies would give rise to the same conclusions. Nevertheless, there has been general agreement between investigators on the finding that juvenile affective disorders tend to be recurrent. This finding is important because it has been taught for many years that, while behavioural difficulties such as conduct disorders show strong continuity over time, "emotional" problems among the young tend to be short-lived. The studies described here suggest that this view is mistaken, at least so far as clinical cases of depressive disorders are concerned. They are associated with considerable impairment of psychosocial functioning and in severe cases vulnerability extends into adult life.

What, then, are the clinical implications that arise from these findings? The clearest conclusions apply to the long-term management of juvenile depressive disorders. It is sometimes assumed that the rapid recovery of depressed children means that treatment endeavours need only focus on the short-term. The evidence reviewed here firmly contradicts this sanguine view. It is apparent that both assessment and treatment need to be viewed as extending over a prolonged period of time. Young people with depressive disorders are likely to have another episode, and so it is important that we develop effective maintenance and/or prophylactic treatments. Thus, for example, it may be necessary in severe cases of adolescence-onset depressive disorder to consider long-term medication and/or psychological treatment. In milder cases who are relatively well between episodes it is important that we teach the child and his or her parents early recognition of the signs of a relapse, and encourage them to return for help when the first symptoms appear.

Since severe forms of early-onset depressive disorder seem to have a significant self-perpetuating quality, there is clearly a need to help individuals to develop coping strategies that will enable them to deal with the illness in the long-term. However, there is also evidence that relapses are linked to changes in environmental circumstances, especially family disturbances such as parenting difficulties and mental illness. Accordingly, clinicians treating young people with depressive disorders need to assess the extent to which these factors are relevant. It may be possible to intervene therapeutically to improve patterns of family relationships. Parents who are depressed or suffering from some other form of mental disorder also need to be helped. In other words, there needs to be a concern with the family as a whole and not just with the patient as an individual.

The evidence on the course of early-onset depressive disorders also has implications for preventive policies. For example, it may be that intensive work with at-risk groups such as the children of depressed parents will reduce the risk of depression in the children. Unfortunately, so far data are lacking on the extent to which primary preventive interventions are in fact protective, so it may be better to concentrate on the early recognition and intensive treatment of the first episode of depression. There is some evidence that in adults the earlier the intervention the shorter the episode (Kupfer, Frank & Perel, 1989) and it could be that the same will be found to occur in juvenile depressions.

Finally, the multiple problems of the depressed young person make it especially important that multimodal approaches to treatment are used. Reduction of depression is a legitimate focus of treatment but should not distract from the treatment of comorbid difficulties. Some of these difficulties, such as problems in peer relationships, may play a part in prolonging depression. Others, such as conduct disorder, appear to exert an independent influence on the prognosis (Harrington et al, 1991). Depressed young people therefore require a range of therapeutic interventions. It remains to be seen whether these will alter the long-term outcome.

Chapter 11

Future Lines of Research

Future directions for research into depression among young people have been touched on at various points in this book. Too many questions remain for it to be helpful to review them all comprehensively. In conclusion, therefore, this chapter will highlight just a few of the key unresolved issues and outline some of the research avenues that seem to be a priority.

LONGITUDINAL RESEARCH STRATEGIES

Longitudinal research into child and adolescent affective disorders is still at an early stage. Therefore, perhaps the most immediately pressing need is for more longitudinal research designed to replicate the findings of the studies reviewed in the previous chapter. For example, it should be possible within the next few years to mount *prospective* long-interval follow-ups of children diagnosed as depressed using standardized interviews and present-day diagnostic criteria. Indeed, several of the research programmes cited in this book have systematic data on depressed children who were first seen during the late 1970s and early 1980s. New generations of child to adult longitudinal studies could be based on these children.

Such studies will be relatively expensive, but they need to be undertaken. Their starting point should be a reconsideration of some of the main findings of existing research. For example, it will be important that these studies use strategies that allow the investigators to control for childhood symptomatology other than depression. One of the most striking findings in all studies of depressed children undertaken up to now has been that these children frequently have other, nondepressive, psychiatric symptoms. The extent to which these nondepressive symptoms determine the poor prognosis of early-onset depressive conditions still requires investigation. Future longitudinal research will also benefit from larger numbers. Two groups stand out as particularly in need of further investigation: (1) children with depression and conduct disorder; and (2) prepubertal depressed children. Children with depression and conduct disorder need to be studied further because of the uncertainty surrounding the nosological status of children diagnosed as having both conditions. Prepubertal depressed children are of interest not only in their own right, but also because of the provocative finding from our research that they seem to differ from postpubertal depressed children in regard to prognosis (Harrington et al, 1990). It would be advantageous if further longitudinal studies were able to stratify subjects according to both age and pubertal status, and had systematic measures of puberty.

Future long-term follow-up studies also need to extend the questions from those of simple continuities and discontinuities over time to the nature of the mechanisms involved. To intervene effectively it is crucial that we know more about the factors that *mediate* the strong continuities found in previous research, rather than just the factors that *predict* continuity. One of the most promising postulated mechanisms that could account for continuity concerns genetic mediation. The notion here would be that the persistence of depression over time is a function of the intrinsic qualities of a genetically determined condition. Indeed, there is well replicated evidence from twin studies showing a major genetic component for bipolar affective disorder with an onset in adulthood. So far, however, there is a paucity of direct evidence on the extent to which genetic factors operate in juvenile depression. The indirect evidence from family studies suggests that juvenile probands with major affective conditions have a high familial loading for affective disorders. It will be appreciated, however, that even if it is assumed that early-onset bipolar and major affective disorders have a strong genetic component, no extrapolation to the broader range of juvenile depressive conditions is warranted. Childhood depressive disorders differ in a number of key respects from the severe depressive conditions of adulthood in which genetic factors seem to predominate. For instance, there is a strong degree of overlap with other psychiatric conditions. Genetic studies of childhood depression will therefore need to take into account patterns of comorbidity.

Moreover, that a family history of psychiatric disorder predicts continuity does not necessarily mean that the continuities are mediated genetically. A number of other mechanisms could be involved. For example, it could be that there is constancy of environmental forces. After all, there is no doubt that some family features, such as marital discord, can be highly persistent. Alternatively, it is possible that even when the environment changes, there may be links between different adverse environments. Or, continuities might be mediated by the establishment of certain cognitive sets.

In short, the goal of future longitudinal studies of juvenile depressive disorders should be not only to describe the frequency of further episodes but also to observe under what conditions the predicted links occur. In this regard, it should be emphasized that there is also a need for short-interval follow-ups of no more than a year or two. Such studies are relatively inexpensive and could provide important clues about mediating mechanisms. Indeed, for some purposes short-interval longitudinal studies are preferable to longer-interval studies. This is particularly the case when it is crucial that the dating of events is accurate, as it is for instance in the study of acute adversity and the onset of psychiatric disorder.

FAMILY STUDIES

Family studies will continue to be an important tool in the study of juvenile affective disorders. There are, however, a number of methodological issues that need to be considered in designing future family studies of depressed children. One of the most important concerns the choice of cases and controls. Clearly, many family studies will have to be based on clinical groups because of the need to obtain an adequate sample of major depressive disorders and because of the uncertainties about the links between the severe depressive disorders seen in clinics and the less severe conditions identified in community populations. However, it is possible that family studies of samples referred to child psychiatrists will be biased because the relatives' problems play a part in the decision to seek referral. It will therefore be necessary to use child controls who have been treated for another psychiatric disorder. By this means, it should be possible to examine the *degree of specificity* of familial loading.

A second important methodological issue concerns the need to combine family studies with a longitudinal element. Almost all of the family studies of depressed children that have been conducted up to now have been cross-sectional. There are three main reasons for thinking that a longitudinal component would be a valuable addition to family studies. First, the longitudinal element can be used to "strengthen" the diagnosis of depressive disorder in the proband. As we saw in Chapters 2 and 3, there are still substantial problems in the measurement of depressive disorders in young people. Repeated measurements could be used to ensure that the proband's disorder was stable. This strategy proved very useful in our family study of depressed probands (Harrington et al, 1992), in which familial aggregation was found to be considerably higher when "cases" and "controls" were redefined using longitudinal data. Second, continuity of family environmental effects can only be studied in a longitudinal design. Hammen's (1991) research showed how depressed children often had multiple episodes and how these were often linked to illness in the parent. The implication is that it is necessary to focus on the experience of family adversity *over time*. Third, the temporal sequencing of a longitudinal design makes it easier to tackle causal questions concerning the relationship between mental illness in parents and psychopathology in children.

What, then, are the uses that a new generation of family studies could be put to? One important use for such studies would be as a method of examining links between disorders. Thus, in the absence of a biological test, familial aggregation of depression could be used as a "marker" to examine the degree of similarity between conditions. For instance, family studies could be employed to study the relationship between comorbid conditions such as depression and anxiety. The strategy would be to stratify groups of relatives according to the presence or absence of anxiety disorder in the proband and then to assess the rates of depressive and anxiety disorders in the relatives. By this means the degree of similarity between "mixed" cases, and cases with either "pure" anxiety or "pure" depression, could be examined.

Another important use for family studies will be to investigate the mechanisms that might be involved in linking parental and child disorders. For example, Hammen's (1991) study has shown that there are several ways in which depression in parents can impact on children. Thus, in her research it seemed that depressed mothers were not only more negative towards their children but also that they acted in ways that increased the likelihood that the child was exposed to other kinds of adversity. So, future family studies will need to consider the multiple pathways that may link parental difficulties to psychopathology in children. Hammen's research (1991) also reminds us of the importance of looking for *bidirectional* effects. Difficulties in children can trigger depression in parents. Moreover, depressed children may be more likely to perceive their environments in a negative fashion and even to *cause* their own stressors.

SOME GENETIC RESEARCH STRATEGIES

It will be appreciated, however, that there are reasons for thinking that environments may follow the same distribution as that expected on the basis of genetic predictions, so it will also be necessary to use research strategies that can more accurately differentiate between genetic and environmental mediation. One such method is the twin study, by which concordance in monozygotic (MZ) pairs is compared with that in dizygotic (DZ) pairs. This strategy relies upon the fact that MZ twins are genetically identical whereas DZ twins share on average 50% of their genes. The difference between the correlation for MZ and DZ pairs can be used to estimate heritability.

A number of conditions have to be met for the results of twin studies to be valid, and there are numerous biases that can affect the results. For example, we have seen in previous chapters that there are likely to be strong biases in referrals to child psychiatrists. Nevertheless, this method has deservedly become one of the most popular ways of separating genetic and environmental effects, and of calculating "heritability". Twin studies also have a number of other uses that make them especially valuable in the study of juvenile depression. First, they can be helpful in defining the range of the phenotype. The basic design here is to estimate the level of concordance between MZ pairs for a range of different "phenotypes". This technique has obvious applications in the study of comorbidity between childhood depressive disorders and other psychiatric conditions. If, for example, MZ pairs that were discordant for depression were usually concordant for a broader range of emotional problems (such as anxiety), then this would suggest that we should broaden our view of the "phenotype" of juvenile depression to include other emotional problems. Second, discordant MZ pairs can be used to examine the role of environmental factors. This strategy relies on the fact that discordance in MZ pairs, which is not due to variable expression of the phenotype, must be due to nongenetic factors. Hypotheses about the role of environmental factors can be tested by examining the rates of these factors in discordant MZ pairs.

Sadly, there have been no published twin studies of child- or adolescence-onset depressive disorders. Such investigations are much needed, though they are going to be difficult to accomplish because of the rarity of twins who have severe depressive conditions with an onset in childhood. In the first place, it might therefore be necessary to conduct these studies retrospectively in one or two centres where systematic case records and accurate registers of twin attendances have been kept over many years. The idea would be to ascertain all twins who attended child psychiatrists for depression at these centres, and then to contact and interview the twins and their co-twins regarding their "lifetime" psychiatric histories. One of the great advantages of this strategy is that it would necessarily involve a longitudinal element. Thus, concordance within MZ and within DZ pairs could be analysed according to psychiatric status in childhood and in adult life, as well as according to persistence across those two age periods. It could be, for instance, that heritability changes with age. It should also be possible to assess possible genetic shaping of the environment by examining concordance for putative environmental variables in adulthood.

Of course, the problem with this approach is that to obtain data on the co-twin's childhood, it would be necessary to rely on retrospective recall. An alternative approach would be to mount a prospective study based on a large number of child psychiatric clinics. The strategy here would be for each clinic to keep a register of twin subjects who could then be interviewed in a second, more intensive, phase of the study. However, ultimately it is likely that the most informative of strategies will be large-scale twin studies based on community samples, as these will for the most part avoid the numerous biases that can occur when twin studies are conducted on referrals to clinical centres.

The effects of genes and environment may also be teased apart by studying individuals who have been fostered or adopted early in life, and their adopted and biological families. Several different designs are available (Rutter et al, 1990b). Unfortunately, in many countries there are formidable difficulties in obtaining the data required to use most of these designs. It is particularly difficult to collect information on the biological father. However, such studies are possible in some countries where systematic registers of adoptions are kept.

EPIDEMIOLOGICAL STUDIES

As discussed earlier, clinical samples are still required for research in juvenile depressive conditions, if only because of the need to study adolescents with uncommon but potentially highly informative disorders, such as bipolar conditions. Thus, for instance, the important findings of Strober et al (1988) regarding the substantially increased familial loading for affective disorder in adolescents with manic-depression need to be replicated in a study that includes a systematic comparison with adult-onset bipolar disorders.

There are, however, several outstanding general issues that are best tackled using an epidemiological approach. For example, general population studies will be required to compare categorical and dimensional approaches to diagnosis, since clinical samples will necessarily be biased towards the most severe cases. Moreover, community-based samples will be needed to tackle in more detail the problem of comorbidity. For instance, the links between "depressive conduct disorder" and "pure" conduct disorder need to be studied further. We also need to know much more about the relationship between depression and anxiety in nonreferred samples.

More importantly, general population studies are needed to explore further the age changes in the rate of depressive disorders that have now been documented by several research groups. Much of the epidemiological research that has been conducted on juvenile depression has been concerned with the question of establishing the rate of disorder. However, few studies have attempted to explore systematically the various features that might explain these age trends. The time seems particularly ripe for a multiple-cohort study that is combined with a longitudinal follow-up. Hence, age changes in the same individuals could be examined. Ideally, such a study would cover several of the transitions that may be relevant to the increment in depression, such as puberty and leaving school. It would be particularly important that the study starts at a time when the sex ratio for depressive disorders is equal, so that the reasons for the apparently rapid increase in girls can be mapped out. The delineation of the processes involved in these age trends should throw important light on the factors responsible for depression at all ages, child, adolescent and adult. Such information would have clear implications for prevention and treatment.

It will, however, be necessary that this proposed epidemiological study takes into account several methodological considerations. First, it seems that developmental trends for affective disorders vary according to the type of phenomenon that is being studied. For example, during childhood negative mood is common at all ages, but some affective phenomena decline in frequency with age (e.g. tearfulness) while some increase at adolescence (e.g. mood swings) (Shepherd, Oppenheim & Mitchell, 1971). Clearly, then, any study looking at age trends for depression would have to differentiate between different types of affect, and there would be a particular need to distinguish feelings of misery from depressive disorders. Second, it may well be that patterns of comorbidity vary with age (Chapter 5) and it will be necessary therefore to relate these patterns to factors such as age, puberty and life events. Third, there is the basic question of the type of epidemiological strategy that should be used to study age trends in depressive conditions. We saw in Chapter 4 that in recent years there has been an increasing tendency in psychiatric epidemiology to use one-stage studies in which a large number of subjects are assessed using highly structured interviews. However, such a strategy is likely to be very inefficient when studying age trends for affective conditions, as depression will be so uncommon in the younger (especially prepubertal) age groups. Accordingly, it would seem better to use a two-stage design with questionnaires completed by parents, teachers and children, which will be used to screen for general disturbance as well as for depression. However, it will be important that data are available on the efficiency of the screening questionnaires across ages and that age-related variations in sensitivity and specificity are taken into account.

TREATMENT

Chapters 8 and 9 reviewed psychological and pharmacological methods of treatment. In both areas there has been substantial progress, but important questions still remain about both therepeutic modalities.

With regard to psychological treatments, the main current issue is whether or not the therapies that have been developed for use with nonclinical samples of children and adolescents will be effective in young people attending mental health clinics with major depressive conditions. If therapies such as cognitive–behavioural treatment or interpersonal psychotherapy prove to be successful then we might envisage further studies in which types of treatment could be comparatively evaluated. For example, it would be very informative to compare individual versus family therapy. In addition, there will be a need to examine differential outcome associated with various clinical features, particularly developmental stage and the association with other psychiatric problems.

In regard to pharmacological treatments, there are a number of lines of research that seem to be a priority. First, there need to be further studies of the effectiveness of the TCAs, especially among adolescent samples. The evidence for their efficacy in adults is so strong that we must continue to search for subgroups of children or adolescents who may respond. Thus, for example, it may be that further studies will benefit from the exclusion of patients with depressions that are accompanied by conduct disorder. Alternatively, it may be better to focus on young people suffering from depressions characterized by endogenous or melancholic features, or who have abnormal results on the kinds of biological measures described in Chapter 7.

A second promising line of drug research will be the study of the "new" antidepressants. Chapters 7 and 9 documented some evidence to support the idea that drugs that have a greater activity on serotinergic systems might for theoretical reasons be expected to be more effective in early-onset depressive conditions. It has to be said that the evidence to support this suggestion is very weak at the moment, but the apparently low toxicity of these drugs in overdose certainly does make them an attractive proposition in the treatment of adolescent depressive disorders, where there is often concern about suicidality.

However, perhaps the most important issue in the treatment of juvenile depressive conditions relates not to the treatment of the acute episode, but to long-term management. Enough is known about the later outcome of diagnosed depressive disorder to be clear that it does indeed constitute a significant vulnerability to later psychiatric problems, and to social impairment. These disorders need to be taken seriously, and long-term approaches to treatment need to be devised. Of course, 2-year or 3-year randomized trials will be very difficult to mount and maintain. Nevertheless, the need for them is clear. Many of the therapies that were described in Chapters 8 and 9 are of unknown long-term value.

MEASUREMENT

All the studies outlined in this chapter will make it necessary to advance systems of diagnosis and classification. Thus, for instance, there need to be systematic comparisons of different sets of diagnostic criteria. What, for example, are the consequences of the proposal within DSM-IV to include impairment as part of the definition of depressive disorder? How would this alter the rates of depressive disorders in children? Is it possible to partial out the impairment that results from depression and the impairment that results from, say, anxiety?

Research is also needed on the extent to which children at various ages are able to give information on their problems. Several standardized instruments have been devised over the past few years. However, Chapters 2 and 3 showed that there are still many unresolved questions concerning the measurement of depression among the young. For instance, we need to know much more about the assessment of depression in the younger age groups. It is difficult to justify the expense of developing new instruments until the old ones have been thoroughly tested across the age span.

CONCLUSIONS

This brief overview of some of the research tasks that remain has not attempted to provide a complete agenda for the next decade, but rather just to highlight a few of the issues that need to be tackled together with the types of studies that seem to be immediately feasible. The findings of existing research are encouraging to the extent that they show that the concept of depressive disorder in young people is useful. However, the data also suggest that, as in their adult counterparts, depressive disorders in young people tend to be recurrent and they are associated with a great deal of morbidity. It is nevertheless reasonable to hope that the knowledge gained from the kinds of research projects outlined here will eventually be of great benefit to depressed children and their families.

References

Abou-Saleh, M.T. (1988). How useful is a dexamethasone suppression test? *Current Opinion in Psychiatry*, **1**, 60–65.

Abou-Saleh, M.T. (1992). Lithium. In E.S. Paykel (ed.), *Handbook of Affective Disorders*, 2nd edn. Edinburgh: Churchill Livingstone, pp. 369–385.

Abou-Saleh, M.T. & Coppen, A. (1983). Classification of depression and response to antidepressive therapies. *British Journal of Psychiatry*, **143**, 601–603.

Abramson, L.Y., Seligman, M.E.P. & Teasdale, J.D. (1978). Learned helplessness in humans: critique and reformulation. *Journal of Abnormal Psychology*, **87**, 49–74.

Abramson, L.Y., Metalsky, G.I. & Alloy, L.B. (1989). Hopelessness depression: a theory-based subtype of depression. *Psychological Review*, **96**, 358–372.

Achenbach, T.M. & Edelbrock, C.S. (1983). *Manual for the Child Behavior Checklist and the Revised Child Behavior Profile.* Burlington, VT: University Associates in Psychiatry.

Achenbach, T.M., Conners, C.K., Quay, H.C., Verhulst, F.C. & Howell, C.T. (1989). Replication of empirically derived syndromes as a basis for taxonomy of child/adolescent psychopathology. *Journal of Abnormal Child Psychology*, **17**, 299–323.

Adams, M. & Adams, J. (1991) Life events, depression, and perceived problem solving alternatives in adolescents. *Journal of Child Psychology and Psychiatry*, **32**, 811–820.

Adams-Tucker, C. (1982). Proximate effects of sexual abuse in childhood. *American Journal of Psychiatry*, **139**, 1252–1256.

Albert, N. & Beck, A.T. (1975). Incidence of depression in early adolescence. *Journal of Youth and Adolescence*, **4**, 301–306.

Allebeck, P., Allgulander, C. & Fisher, L.D. (1988). Predictors of completed suicide in a cohort of 50,465 young men: role of personality and deviant behaviour. *British Medical Journal*, **297**, 176–178.

Allen, D.M. & Tarnowski, K.J. (1989). Depressive characteristics of physically abused children. *Journal of Abnormal Child Psychology*, **17**, 1–11.

Altmann, E.O. & Gotlib, I.H. (1988). The social behaviour of depressed children: an observational study. *Journal of Abnormal Child Psychology*, **16**, 29–44.

Ambelas, A. (1979). Psychologically stressful events in the precipitation of manic episodes. *British Journal of Psychiatry*, **135**, 15–21.

Ambrosini, P.J., Metz, C., Prabucki, K. & Lee, J. (1989). Videotape reliability of the Third Revised Edition of the K-SADS. *Journal of the American Academy of Child and Adolescent Psychiatry*, **28**, 723–728.

Ambrosini, P.J., Metz, C., Bianchi, M.D., Rabinovich, H. & Undie, A. (1991). Concurrent validity and psychometric properties of the Beck depression inventory in outpatient adolescents. *Journal of the American Academy of Child Psychiatry*, **30**, 51–57.

Ambrosini, P.J., Bianchi, M.D., Metz, C. & Rabinovich, H. (1992). Response patterns of open nortriptyline pharmacotherapy in adolescent major depression. Submitted for publication.

American Psychiatric Association (1980). *Diagnostic and Statistical Manual of Mental Disorders.* Washington: American Psychiatric Association.

American Psychiatric Association (1987). *Diagnostic and Statistical Manual of Mental Disorders—DSM-III-R*, 3rd edn: revised. Washington: American Psychiatric Association.

American Psychiatric Association (1991). *DSM-IV Options Book: Work in Progress (9/1/91).* Washington: American Psychiatric Association.

Amsterdam, J.D., Maislin, G., Winokur, A., Kling, M. & Gold, P. (1987). Pituitary and adrenocortical responses to the ovine corticotropin releasing hormone in depressed patients and healthy volunteers. *Archives of General Psychiatry*, **44**, 775–781.

Andersch, B., Wendelstam, C., Hahn, L. & Ohman, R. (1986). Premenstrual complaints. I: Prevalence of premenstrual symptoms in a Swedish urban population. *Journal of Psychosomatic Obstetrics and Gynaecology*, **5**, 39–49.,

Anderson, E., Hamburger, S., Liu, J.H. & Rebar, R.W. (1987). Characteristics of menopausal women seeking assistance. *American Journal of Obstetrics and Gynecology*, **156**, 428–433.

Anderson, J.C., Williams, S., McGee, R. & Silva, P.A. (1987). DSM-III disorders in preadolescent children: prevalence in a large sample from the general population. *Archives of General Psychiatry*, **44**, 69–76.

Andreasen, N.C. (1982). Concepts, diagnosis and classification. In E.S. Paykel (ed.), *Handbook of Affective Disorders.* Edinburgh: Churchill Livingstone, pp. 24–44.

Andreasen, N.C., Scheftner, W., Reich, T., Hirschfeld, R.M.A., Endicott, J. & Keller, M.B. (1986). The validation of the concept of endogenous depression: a family study approach. *Archives of General Psychiatry*, **43**, 246–251.

Andreasen, N.C., Rice, J., Endicott, J., Coryell, W., Grove, W.M. & Reich, T. (1987). Familial rates of affective disorder: a report from the National Institute of Mental Health collaborative study. *Archives of General Psychiatry*, **44**, 461–469.

Angold, A. (1988a). Childhood and adolescent depression. I: Epidemiological and aetiological aspects. *British Journal of Psychiatry*, **152**, 601–617.

Angold, A. (1988b). Childhood and adolescent depression. II: Research in clinical populations. *British Journal of Psychiatry*, **153**, 476–492.

Angold, A. (1988c). Child and adolescent psychiatric assessment (CAPA). Unpublished paper presented at the Annual Meeting of the Child Psychiatry Section of the Royal College of Psychiatrists, Durham, England.

Angold, A. (1989). Structured assessments of psychopathology in children and adolescents. In C. Thompson (ed.), *The Instruments of Psychiatric Research.* Chichester: John Wiley, pp. 271–304.

Angold, A., Weissman, M.M., John, K., Merikangas, K.R., Prusoff, P., Wickramaratne, G., Gammon, G.D. & Warner, V. (1987a). Parent and child reports of depressive symptoms in children at low and high risk of depression. *Journal of Child Psychology and Psychiatry*, **28**, 901–915.

Angold, A., Costello, E.J., Pickles, A. & Winder, F. (1987b). The development of a questionnaire for use in epidemiological studies of depression in children and adolescents. Unpublished manuscript, London University.

Angold, A. & Rutter, M. (1992). The effects of age and pubertal status on depression in a large clinical sample. *Developmental Psychopathology.* In press.

Appelboom-Fondu, J., Kerkhofs, M. & Mendlewicz, J. (1988). Depression in adolescents and young adults—polysomnographic and neuroendocrine aspects. *Journal of Affective Disorders*, **14**, 35–40.

Apter, A., Orvaschel, H., Laseg, M., Moses, T. & Tyano, S. (1989). Psychometric properties of the K-SADS-P in an Israeli adolescent inpatient population. *Journal of the American Academy of Child and Adolescent Psychiatry*, **28**, 61–65.

Armsden, G.C., McCauley, E., Greenberg, M.T., Burke, P.M. & Mitchell, J.R. (1990). Parent and peer attachment in early adolescent depression. *Journal of Abnormal Child Psychology*, **18**, 683–697.,

Asarnow, J.R. & Carlson, G.A. (1985). Depression self-rating scale. *Journal of Consulting and Clinical Psychology*, **53**, 491–499.

Asarnow, J.R. & Bates, S. (1988). Depression in child psychiatric inpatients: cognitive and attributional patterns. *Journal of Abnormal Child Psychology*, **16**, 601–615.

Asarnow, J.R., Goldstein, M.J., Carlson, G.A., Perdue, S., Bates, S. & Keller, J. (1988). Childhood-onset depressive disorders: a follow-up study of rates of rehospitalization and out-of-home placement among child psychiatric inpatients. *Journal of Affective Disorders*, **15**, 245–253.

Asarnow, J.R., Goldstein, M.J., Tompson, M. & Guthrie, D. (1992). One-year outcomes of depressive disorders in child psychiatric inpatients: evaluation of the prognostic power of a brief measure of expressed emotion. *Journal of Child Psychology and Psychiatry*. In press.

Asberg, M., Cronholm, B., Sjoqvist, F. & Tuck, D. (1971). Relationship between plasma level and therapeutic effect of nortriptyine. *British Medical Journal*, **3**, 331–334.

Barkley, A. (1988). Child behaviour rating scales and checklists. In M. Rutter, A.H. Tuma & I.S. Lann (eds), *Assessment and Diagnosis in Child Psychopathology*. New York: Guilford, pp. 113–155.

Barlow, D.H., Dinardo, P.A., Vermilyea, B.B., Vermilyea, J. & Blanchard, E.B. (1986). Comorbidity and depression among the anxiety disorders: issues in diagnosis and classification. *The Journal of Nervous and Mental Disease*, **174**, 63–72.

Baron, M., Endicott, J. & Ott, J. (1990). Genetic linkage in mental illness: limitations and prospects. *British Journal of Psychiatry*, **157**, 645–655.

Barraclough, B.M., Bunch, J., Nelson, B. & Sainsbury, P. (1974). A hundred cases of suicide. *British Journal of Psychiatry*, **125**, 355–373.,

Barrera, M. & Garrison-Jones, C.V. (1988). Properties of the Beck Depression Inventory as a screening instrument for adolescent depression. *Journal of Abnormal Child Psychology*, **16**, 263–273.

Barrett, M.L., Berney, T.P., Bhate, S., Famuyiwa, O., Fundudis, T., Kolvin, I. & Tyrer, S. (1991). Diagnosing childhood depression: who should be interviewed—parent or child? The Newcastle Child Depression Project. *British Journal of Psychiatry*, **159**, (suppl. 11), 22–27.

Bartels, M.B., Varley, C.K., Mitchell, J. & Stamm, S.J. (1991). Pediatric cardiovascular effects of imipramine and desipramine. *Journal of the American Academy of Child Psychiatry*, **30**, 100–103.

Bauer, M.S. & Whybrow, P.C. (1991). Rapid cycling bipolar disorder: clinical features, treatment, and etiology. In J.D. Amsterdam (ed.), *Advances in Neuropsychiatry and Psychopharmacology. Vol. 2: Refractory Depression*. New York: Raven Press, pp. 191–208.

Beardslee, W.R., Bemporad, J., Keller, M.B. & Klerman, G.L. (1983). Children of parents with major affective disorder: a review. *American Journal of Psychiatry*, **140**, 825–832.

Beardslee, W.R., Schultz, L.H. & Selman, R.L. (1987). Level of social-cognitive development, adaptive functioning, and DSM-III diagnoses in adolescent offspring of parents with affective disorders: implications of the development of the capacity for mutuality. *Developmental Psychology*, **23**, 807–815.

Bebbington, P.E., Brugha, T., MacCarthy, B. et al. (1988). The Camberwell Collaborative Depression Study. I: Depressed probands: adversity and the form of depression. *British Journal of Psychiatry*, **152**, 754–765.

Beck, A.T. (1967). *Depression: Clinical, Experimental, and Theoretical Aspects*. New York: Harper & Row.

Beck, A.T. (1976). *Cognitive Therapy and the Emotional Disorders*. New York: International Universities Press.

Beck, A.T., Ward, C.H., Mendelsohn, M., Mock, J. & Erbaugh, J. (1961). An inventory for measuring depression. *Archives of General Psychiatry*, **4**, 53–63.

Bemporad, J.R. (1988). Psychodynamic treatment of depressed adolescents. *Journal of Clinical Psychiatry*, **49** (suppl. 9), 26–31.

Benca, R.M., Obermeyer, W.H., Thisted, R.A. & Gillin, J.C. (1992). Sleep and psychiatric disorders: a meta-analysis. *Archives of General Psychiatry*, **49**, 651–668.,

Benfield, C.Y., Palmer, D.J., Pfefferbaum, B. & Stowe, M.L. (1988). A comparison of depressed and nondepressed disturbed children on measures of attributional style, hopelessness, life stress, and temperament. *Journal of Abnormal Child Psychology*, **16**, 397–410.

Berger, M., Pirke, K., Doerr, P., Krieg, J. & von Zerssen, D. (1984). The limited utility of the dexamethasone suppression test for the diagnostic process in psychiatry. *British Journal of Psychiatry*, **145**, 372–382.

Berkson, J. (1946). Limitations of the application of fourfold table analysis to hospital data. *Biometrics*, **2**, 47–53.

Berndt, T.J. (1983). Social cognition, social behaviour and children's friendships. In D. Higgins, D. Ruble & W. Hartup (ed.), *Social Cognition and Social Development*. Cambridge: Cambridge University Press.

Berney, T.P., Bhate, S.R., Kolvin, I., Famuyiwa, O., Barrett, M.L., Fundudis, T. & Tyrer, S.P. (1991). The context of childhood depression: the Newcastle Childhood Depression Project. *British Journal of Psychiatry*, **159** (suppl. 11), 28–35.,

Bernstein, G.A. (1991). Comorbidity and severity of anxiety and depressive disorders in a clinic population. *Journal of the American Academy of Child Psychiatry*, **30**, 43–50.

Bernstein, G.A. & Garfinkel, B.D. (1986). School phobia: the overlap of affective and anxiety disorders. *Journal of the American Academy of Child Psychiatry*, **25**, 235–241.

Bernstein, G.A. & Garfinkel, B.D. (1988). Pedigrees, functioning, and psychopathology in families of school phobic children. *American Journal of Psychiatry*, **145**, 70–74.,

Bernstein, G.A. & Borchardt, C.M. (1991). Anxiety disorders of childhood and adolescence: a critical review. *Journal of the American Academy of Child Psychiatry*, **30**, 519–532.

Bertagnoli, M.W. & Borchardt, C.M. (1990). A review of ECT for children and adolescents. *Journal of the American Academy of Child Psychiatry*, **29**, 302–307.

Biederman, J., Baldessarini, R.J., Wright, V., Knee, D., Harmatz, J.S. & Goldblatt, A. (1989). Double-blind placebo controlled study of desipramine in the treatment of ADD. II: Serum drug levels and cardiovascular findings. *Journal of the American Academy of Child Psychiatry*, **28**, 903–911.

Biederman, J., Newcorn, J. & Sprich, S. (1991). Comorbidity of attention deficit hyperactivity disorder with conduct, depressive, anxiety, and other disorders. *American Journal of Psychiatry*, **148**, 564–577.

Bifulco, A., Brown, G.W. & Harris, T.O. (1987). Childhood loss of parent, lack of adequate parental care and adult depression: a replication. *Journal of Affective Disorders*, **12**, 115–118.

Bifulco, A., Brown, G.W. & Adler, Z. (1991). Early sexual abuse and clinical depression in adult life. *British Journal of Psychiatry*, **159**, 115–122.

Bird, H.R., Canino, G., Rubio-Stipec, M. & Gould, M.S. (1988). Estimates of prevalence of childhood maladjustment in a community survey in Puerto Rico. *Archives of General Psychiatry*, **45**, 1120–1126.

Bird, H.R., Gould, M.S., Yager, T., Staghezza, B. & Canino, G. (1989). Risk factors for maladjustment in Puerto Rican children. *Journal of the American Academy of Child Psychiatry*, **28**, 847–850.

Bird, H.R., Yager, T.J., Staghezza, B., Gould, M.S., Canino, G. & Rubio-Stipec, M. (1990). Impairment in the epidemiological measurement of childhood psychopathology in the community. *Journal of the American Academy of Child Psychiatry*, **29**, 796–803.

Bird, H.R., Gould, M.S. & Staghezza, B. (1992). Aggregating data from multiple informants in child psychiatry epidemiological research. *Journal of the American Academy of Child Psychiatry*, **31**, 78–85.

Birleson, P. (1981). The validity of depressive disorder in childhood and the development of a self-rating scale: a research project. *Journal of Child Psychology and Psychiatry*, **22**, 73–88.

Birleson, P., Hudson, I., Buchanan, D.G. & Wolff, S. (1987). Clinical evaluation of a self-rating scale for depressive disorder in childhood (Depression Self-Rating Scale). *Journal of Child Psychology and Psychiatry*, **28**, 43–60.

Birmaher, B., Ryan, N.D., Dahl, R., Rabinovich, H., Ambrosini, P., Williamson, D.E., Novacenko, H., Nelson, B., Sing Lo, E. & Puig-Antich, J. (1992a). Dexamethasone Suppression Test in children with major depressive disorder. *Journal of the American Academy of Child Psychiatry*, **31**, 291–297.

Birmaher, B., Dahl, R.E., Ryan, N.D., Rabinovich, H., Ambrosini, P., Al-Shabbout, M., Novacenko, H., Nelson, B. & Puig-Antich, J. (1992b). The dexamethasone suppression test in adolescent outpatients with major depressive disorder. *American Journal of Psychiatry*, **149**, 1040–1045.

Block, J., Block, J.H. & Gjerde, P.F. (1988). Parental functioning and home environment in families of divorce: prospective and concurrent analyses. *Journal of the American Academy of Child Psychiatry*, **27**, 207–213.

Boulos, C., Kutcher, S., Marton, P., Simeon, J., Ferguson, B. & Roberts, N. (1991). Response to desipramine treatment in adolescent major depression. *Psychopharmacology Bulletin*, **27**, 59–65.

Bowlby, J. (1969). *Attachment and Loss: Vol. I: Attachment.* London: Hogarth Press.

Bowlby, J. (1973). *Attachment and Loss. Vol. II: Separation, Anxiety and Anger.* London: Hogarth Press.

Bowlby, J. (1980). *Attachment and Loss. Vol. III: Sadness and Depression.* New York: Basic Books.

Bowring, M.A. & Kovacs, M. (1992). Difficulties in diagnosing manic disorders among children and adolescents. *Journal of the American Academy of Child Psychiatry*, **31**, 611–614.

Boyle, M.H., Offord, D.R., Hofmann, H.G., Catlin, G.P., Byles, J.A., Cadman, D.T., Crawford, J.W., Links, P.S., Rae-Grant, N.I. & Szatmari, P. (1987). Ontario Child Health Study. I: Methodology. *Archives of General Psychiatry*, **44**, 826–831.

Brady, E.U. & Kendall, P.C. (1992). Comorbidity of anxiety and depression in children and adolescents. *Psychological Bulletin*, **111**, 244–255.

Bramble, D.J. & Dunkley, S.D. (1992). The use of antidepressants by British child psychiatrists. *Psychiatric Bulletin*, **16**, 396–398.

Brandenburg, N.A., Friedman, R.M. & Silver, S.E. (1990). The epidemiology of childhood psychiatric disorders: prevalence findings from recent studies. *Journal of the American Academy of Child Psychiatry*, **29**, 76–83.

Brent, D.A., Perper, J.A., Goldstein, C.E., Kolko, D.J., Allan, M.J., Allman, C.J. & Zelenak, J.P. (1988). Risk factors for adolescent suicide: a comparison of adolescent suicide victims with suicidal inpatients. *Archives of General Psychiatry*, **45**, 581–588.

Breslau, N. (1987). Inquiring about the bizarre: false positives in Diagnostic Interview Schedule for Children (DISC) ascertainment of obsessions, compulsions and psychotic symptoms. *Journal of the American Academy of Child Psychiatry*, **26**, 639–644.

Breslau, N., Davis, G.C. & Prabizki, K. (1988). Depressed mothers as informants in family history research—are they accurate? *Psychiatry Research*, **24**, 345–359.

British Medical Journal (1981). Editorial: The new psychiatry. *British Medical Journal*, **283**, 513–514.

Brockington, I.F., Altman, E., Hillier, V., Meltzer, H.Y. & Nand, S. (1982). The clinical picture of bipolar affective disorder in its depressed phase: a report from London and Chicago. *British Journal of Psychiatry*, **141**, 558–562.

Bronisch, T. & Hecht, H. (1990). Major depression with and without a coexisting anxiety disorder: social dysfunction, social integration, and personality features. *Journal of Affective Disorders*, **20**, 151–157.

Brooks-Gunn, J. & Warren, M.P. (1989). Biological and social contributions to negative affect in young adolescent girls. *Child Development*, **60**, 40–55.

Brown, G.W., Sklair, F., Harris, T.O. & Birley, J.L.T. (1973). Life events and psychiatric disorders. 1: Some methodological issues. *Psychological Medicine*, **3**, 74–87.

Brown, G.W. & Harris, T. (1978). *Social Origins of Depression*. London: Tavistock.

Brown, G.W., Harris, T.O. & Bifulco, A. (1986). Long-term effects of early loss of parent. In M. Rutter, C.E. Izard & P.B. Read (eds), *Depression in Young People: Clinical and Developmental Perspectives*. New York: Guilford, pp. 251–296.

Brugha, T.S. & Conroy, R. (1985). Categories of depression: reported life events in a controlled design. *British Journal of Psychiatry*, **147**, 641–646.

Buchanan, C.M., Eccles, J.S. & Becker, J.B. (1992). Are adolescents the victims of raging hormones: evidence for activational effects of hormones on moods and behavior at adolescence. *Psychological Bulletin*, **111**, 62–107.

Burge, D. & Hammen, C. (1991). Maternal communication: predictors of outcome at follow-up in a sample of children at high and low risk for depression. *Journal of Abnormal Psychology*, **100**, 174–180.

Burkard, W.P., Prada, M.D., Keller, H.H., Kettler, R. & Haefely, W. (1989). Preclinical pharmacology of moclobemide: a review of published studies. *British Journal of Psychiatry*, **155** (suppl. 6), 84–88.

Burke, P., Kocoshis, S.A., Chandra, R., Whiteway, M. & Sauer, J. (1990). Determinants of depression in recent onset pediatric inflammatory bowel disease. *Journal of the American Academy of Child Psychiatry*, **29**, 608–610.

Butler, L., Miezitis, S., Friedman, R. & Cole, E. (1980). The effect of two school-based intervention programs on depressive symptoms in preadolescents. *American Educational Research Journal*, **17**, 111–119.

Cairns, E., McWhirter, L., Barry, R. & Duffy, U. (1991). The development of psychological well-being in late adolescence. *Journal of Child Psychology and Psychiatry*, **32**, 635–643.

Cantwell, D.P. (1983). Depression in childhood: clinical picture and diagnostic criteria. In D.P. Cantwell & G.A. Carlson (eds), *Affective Disorders in Childhood and Adolescence: An Update*. Lancaster: MTP Press, pp. 3–18.

Cantwell, D.P. & Baker, L. (1987). Assessment of childhood affective disorders. In R.J. Prinz (ed.), *Advances in Behavioural Assessment of Children and Families*. Connecticut: JAI Press, pp. 267–287.

Carlson, G.A. (1983). Bipolar affective disorders in childhood and adolescence. In D.P. Cantwell, & G.A. Carlson (eds), *Affective Disorders in Childhood and Adolescence*. Lancaster: MTP Press, pp. 61–83.

Carlson, G.A. (1990). Child and adolescent mania—diagnostic considerations. *Journal of Child Psychology and Psychiatry*, **31**, 331–341.

Carlson, G.A., Davenport, Y.B. & Jamison, K. (1977). A comparison of outcome in adolescent and late onset bipolar manic depressive illness. *American Journal of Psychiatry*, **134**, 919–922.

Carlson, G.A. & Strober, M. (1978). Manic-depressive illness in early adolescence: a study of clinical and diagnostic characteristics in six cases. *Journal of the American Academy of Child Psychiatry*, **17**, 138–153.

Carlson, G.A. & Cantwell, D.P. (1980a). Unmasking masked depression in children and adolescents. *American Journal of Psychiatry*, **137**, 445–449.

Carlson, G.A. & Cantwell, D.P. (1980b). A survey of depressive symptoms, syndrome and disorder in a child psychiatric population. *Journal of Child Psychology and Psychiatry*, **21**, 19–25.

Carlson, G.A. & Strober, M. (1983). Affective disorders in adolescence. In D.P. Cantwell, & G.A. Carlson (eds), *Affective Disorders in Childhood and Adolescence*. Lancaster: MTP Press, pp. 85–96.,

Carlson, G.A. & Garber, J. (1986). Developmental issues in the classification of depression in children. In M. Rutter, C.E. Izard & P.B. Read (eds), *Depression in Young People: Developmental and Clinical Perspectives*. New York: Guilford, pp. 399–434.

Carlson, G.A., Kashani, J.H., Thomas, M.D.F., Vaidya, A. & Daniel, A.E. (1987). Comparison of two structured interviews on a psychiatrically hospitalized population of children. *Journal of the American Academy of Child Psychiatry*, **26**, 645–648.

Carlson, G.A. & Kashani, J.H. (1988). Phenomenology of major depression from childhood through adulthood: analysis of three studies. *American Journal of Psychiatry*, **145**, 1222–1225.

Carlson, G.A., Rich, C.L., Grayson, P. & Fowler, R.C. (1991). Secular trends in psychiatric diagnoses of suicide victims. *Journal of Affective Disorders*, **21**, 127–132.

Carlson, G.A., Rapport, M.D., Pataki, C.S. & Kelly, K.L. (1992). Lithium in hospitalized children at 4 and 8 weeks: mood, behaviour and cognitive effects. *Journal of Child Psychology and Psychiatry*, **33**, 411–425.

Caron, C. & Rutter, M. (1991). Comorbidity in child psychopathology: concepts, issues and research strategies. *Journal of Child Psychology and Psychiatry*, **32**, 1063–1080.

Caron, C., Wickramaratne, P., Warner, V., Weissman, M. & Merette, C. (1992). A search for pathways to comorbidity of major depression and conduct disorder. Unpublished manuscript.

Carr, V., Dorrington, C., Schader, G. & Wale, J. (1983). The use of ECT in childhood bipolar disorder. *British Journal of Psychiatry*, **143**, 411–415.

Carroll, B.J. (1982). The dexamethasone suppression test for melancholia. *British Journal of Psychiatry*, **140**, 292–304.

Carstens, M.E., Engelbrecht, A.H., Russell, V.A., van Zyl, A.M. & Taljaard, J.J.F. (1988). Biological markers in juvenile depression. *Psychiatry Research*, **23**, 77–88.

Casat, C.D. & Powell, K. (1988). The dexamethasone suppression test in children and adolescents with major depressive disorder: a review. *Journal of Clinical Psychiatry*, **49**, 390–393.

Chambers, W., Puig-Antich, J., Hirsch, M., Paez, P., Ambrosini, P.J., Tabrizi, M.A. & Davies, M. (1985). The assessment of affective disorders in children and adolescents by semi-structured interview: test–retest reliability of the K-SADS-P. *Archives of General Psychiatry*, **42**, 696–702.

Charney, D.S., Delgado, P.L., Southwick, S.M., Krystal, J.H., Price, L.H. & Heninger, G.R. (1991). Current hypotheses of the mechanism of antidepressant treatments: implications for the treatment of refractory depression. In J.D. Amsterdam (ed.), *Advances in Neuropsychiatry and Psychopharmacology. Vol. 2: Refractory Depression*. New York: Raven Press, pp. 23–52.

Checkley, S. (1980). Neuroendocrine tests of monoamine function in man: a review of basic theory and its application to the study of depressive illness. *Psychological Medicine*, **10**, 35–53.

Checkley, S. (1992). Neuroendocrinology. In E.S. Paykel (ed.), *Handbook of Affective Disorders*, 2nd edn. Edinburgh: Churchill Livingstone, pp. 255–266.

Checkley, S.A., Corn, T.H., Glass, I.B., Burton, S.W. & Burke, C.A. (1986). The responsiveness of central alpha2 adrenoreceptors in depression. In J.F.W. Deakin (ed.), *The Biology of Depression*. London: Royal College of Psychiatrists, pp. 100–120.

Chess, S., Thomas, A. & Hassibi, M. (1983). Depression in childhood and adolescence: prospective study of six cases. *Journal of Nervous and Mental Disease*, **171**, 411–420.

Chiles, J.A., Miller, M.L. & Cox, G.B. (1980). Depression in an adolescent delinquent population. *Archives of General Psychiatry*, **37**, 1179–1184.

Christ, G.H., Siegel, K., Mesagno, F.P. & Langosch, D. (1991). A preventive intervention program for bereaved children: problems of implementation. *American Journal of Orthopsychiatry*, **61**, 168–178.

Cicchetti, D. & Schneider-Rosen, K. (1984). Toward a transactional model of childhood depression. In D. Cicchetti & K. Schneider-Rosen (eds), *Childhood Depression (New Directions for Child Development*, No. 26). San Francisco: Jossey-Bass, pp. 5–27.

Cicchetti, D. & Schneider-Rosen, K. (1986). An organizational approach to childhood depression. In M. Rutter, C.E. Izard & P.B. Read (eds), *Depression in Young People: Developmental and Clinical Perspectives*. New York: Guilford, pp. 71–134.

Clayton, P. (1982). Bereavement. In E.S. Paykel (ed.), *Handbook of Affective Disorders*. Edinburgh: Churchill Livingstone, pp. 403–415.

Coffey, C.E., Weiner, R.D., Djang, W.T. Figiel, G.S., Soady, S.A.R., Patterson, L.J., Holt, P.D., Spritzer, C.E. & Wilkinson, W.E. (1991). Brain anatomic effects of electroconvulsive therapy: a prospective magnetic resonance imaging study. *Archives of General Psychiatry*, **48**, 1013–1021.

Cohen, P., O'Connor, P., Lewis, S., Velez, C.N. & Malachowski, B. (1987). Comparison of DISC and K-SADS-P interviews of an epidemiological sample of children. *Journal of the American Academy of Child Psychiatry*, **26**, 662–667.

Cole, D.A. (1989). Psychopathology of adolescent suicide: hopelessness, coping beliefs, and depression. *Journal of Abnormal Psychology*, **98**, 248–255.

Cole, D.A. (1990). Relation of social and academic competence to depressive symptoms in childhood. *Journal of Abnormal Psychology*, **99**, 422–429.

Cole, D.A. (1991). Preliminary support for a competency-based model of depression in children. *Journal of Abnormal Psychology*, **100**, 181–190.

Coopersmith, S. (1967). *The Antecedents of Self-esteem*. San-Francisco: W.H. Freeman.

Copeland, J.R.M. (1983). Psychotic and neurotic depression: discriminant function analysis and five-year outcome. *Psychological Medicine*, **13**, 373–383.

Costello, A.J. (1986). Assessment and diagnosis of affective disorders in children. *Journal of Child Psychology and Psychiatry*, **27**, 565–574.,

Costello, E.J., Edelbrock, C., Dulcan, M.K., Kalas, R. & Klaric, S. (1984). *Report on the NIMH Diagnostic Interview Schedule for Children (DISC)*. Washington, DC: NIMH.

Costello, E.J. & Angold, A. (1988). Scales to assess child and adolescent depression: checklists, screens, and nets. *Journal of the American Academy of Child Psychiatry*, **27**, 726–737.,

Costello, E.J. (1989). Child psychiatric disorders and their correlates: a primary care pediatric sample. *Journal of the American Academy of Child Psychiatry*, **28**, 851–855.

Costello, E.J., Edelbrock, C. & Costello, A.J. (1985). The validity of the NIMH Diagnostic Interview Schedule for Children: a comparison between pediatric and psychiatric referrals. *Journal of Abnormal Child Psychology*, **13**, 579–595.

Costello, E.J., Benjamin, R., Angold, A. & Silver, D. (1991). Mood variability in adolescents: a study of depressed, nondepressed and comorbid patients. *Journal of Affective Disorders*, **23**, 199–212.

Cowen, P.J. & Wood, A.J. (1991). Biological markers of depression. *Psychological Medicine*, **21**, 831–836.,

Cox, A., Hopkinson, K.F. & Rutter, M. (1981). Psychiatric interview techniques. II: Naturalistic study: eliciting factual information. *British Journal of Psychiatry*, **138**, 283–291.

Cox, A. & Rutter, M. (1985). Diagnostic appraisal and interviewing. In M. Rutter and L. Hersov (eds.), *Child and Adolescent Psychiatry: Modern Approaches*. Oxford: Blackwell Scientific, pp. 233–248.

Cox, A.D., Puckering, C., Pound, A. & Mills, M. (1987). The impact of maternal depression in young children. *Journal of Child Psychology and Psychiatry*, **28**, 917–928.,

Crook, T. & Elliot, J. (1980). Parental death during childhood and adult depression: a critical review of the literature. *Psychology Bulletin*, **87**, 252–259.

Culp, R.E., Little, V., Letts, D. & Lawrence, H. (1991). Maltreated children's self-concept: effects of a comprehensive treatment program. *American Journal of Orthopsychiatry*, **61**, 114–121.

Cytryn, L. & McKnew, D.H. (1972). Proposed classification of childhood depression. *American Journal of Psychiatry*, **129**, 149–155.

Cytryn, L., McKnew, D.H., Logue, M. & Desai, R.B (1974). Biochemical correlates of affective disorders in children. *Archives of General Psychiatry*, **31**, 659–661.

Cytryn, L., McKnew, D.H. & Bunney, W.E. (1980). Diagnosis of depression in children: a reassessment. *American Journal of Psychiatry*, **137**, 22–25.

Dahl, R., Puig-Antich, J., Ryan, N., Nelson, B., Novacenko, H., Twomey, J., Williamson, D., Goetz, R. & Ambrosini, P.J. (1989). Cortisol secretion in adolescents with major depressive disorder. *Acta Psychiatrica Scandinavica*, **80**, 18–26.

Dahl, R.E., Puig-Antich, J., Ryan, N.D., Nelson, B., Dachille, S., Cunningham, S.L., Trubnick, L. & Klepper, T.P. (1990). EEG sleep in adolescents with major depression: the role of suicidality and inpatient status. *Journal of Affective Disorders*, **19**, 63–75.

Damon, W. & Hart, D. (1982). The development of self-understanding from infancy through adolescence. *Child Development*, **53**, 841–864.

Davidson, J.R.T. (1992). Monoamine oxidase inhibitors. In E.S. Paykel (ed.), *Handbook of Affective Disorders*, 2nd edn. Edinburgh: Churchill Livingstone, pp. 345–358.

Deakin, J.F.W. & Crow, T.J. (1986). Monoamines, rewards and punishments—the anatomy and physiology of the affective disorders. In J.F.W. Deakin (ed.), *The Biology of Depression*. London: Royal College of Psychiatrists, pp. 1–25.

Delong, G.R. & Nieman, G.W. (1983). Lithium induced changes in children with symptoms suggesting manic-depressive illness. *Psychopharmacology Bulletin*, **19**, 258–265.

de Villiers, A.S., Russell, V.A., Carstens, M.E., Searson, J.A., van Zyl, A.M., Lombard, C.J. & Taljaard, J.J. (1989). Noradrenergic function and hypothalamic–pituitary–adrenal axis activity in adolescents with major depressive disorder. *Psychiatry Research*, **27**, 101–109.

Delgado, P.L., Price, L.H., Heninger, G.R. & Charney, D.S. (1992). Neurochemistry. In E.S. Paykel (ed.), *Handbook of Affective Disorders,* 2nd edn. Edinburgh: Churchill Livingstone, pp. 219–253.,

Dobson, K.S. (1989). A meta-analysis of the efficacy of cognitive therapy for depression. *Journal of Consulting and Clinical Psychology*, **57**, 414–419.

Dodge, K.A. (1990). Developmental psychopathology in children of depressed mothers. *Developmental Psychology*, **26**, 3–6.

Dunn, J. & Kendrick, C. (1982). Temperamental differences, family relationships and young children's response to change within the family. In R. Porter & G.M. Collins (ed.), *Temperamental Differences in Infants and Young Children*. London: Pitman, pp. 87–100.

Dweck, C.S. & Reppucci, N.D. (1973). Learned helplessness and reinforcement responsibility in children. *Journal of Personality and Social Psychology*, **25**, 109–116.

Dweck, C.S., Davidson, W., Nelson, S. & Enna, B. (1978). Sex differences in learned helplessness. II: The contingencies of evaluative feedback in the classroom; and III: An experimental analysis. *Developmental Psychology*, **14**, 268–276.

Dweck, C.S. & Elliot, E.S. (1983). Achievement motivation. In E.M. Hetherington (ed.), *Socialization, Personality and Social Development*, vol. 4 (*Mussen's Handbook of Child Psychology,* 4th edn). New York: John Wiley, pp. 643–691.

Dwyer, J.T. & Delong, G.R. (1987). A family history study of twenty probands with childhood manic–depressive illness. *Journal of the American Academy of Child Psychiatry*, **26**, 176–180.

Earls, F. (1987). On the familial transmission of child psychiatric disorder. *Journal of Child Psychology and Psychiatry*, **28**, 791–802.

Earls, F., Jacobs, G., Goldfein, D., Silbert, A., Beardslee, W. & Rivinus, T. (1982). Concurrent validation of a behaviour problem scale for use with three-year-olds. *Journal of the American Academy of Child Psychiatry*, **21**, 47–57.

Eastgate, J. & Gilmour, L. (1984). Long-term outcome of depressed children: a follow-up study. *Developmental Medicine and Child Neurology*, **26**, 68–72.

Eddy, B.A. & Lubin, B. (1988). The children's depression adjective checklists (C-DACL) with emotionally disturbed adolescent boys. *Journal of Abnormal Child Psychology*, **16**, 83–88.

Edelbrock, C., Costello, A.J., Dulcan, M.K., Kalas, R. & Conover, N.C. (1985). Age differences in the reliability of the psychiatric interview with the child. *Child Development*, **56**, 265–275.

Edelbrock, C., Costello, A.J., Dulcan, M.K., Conover, M.C. & Kalas, R. (1986). Parent–child agreement on child psychiatric symptoms assessed via structured interview. *Journal of Child Psychology and Psychiatry*, **27**, 181–190.

Edelbrock, C. & Costello, A.J. (1988a). Structured psychiatric interviews for children. In M. Rutter, A.H. Tuma & I.S. Lann (eds), *Assessment and Diagnosis in Child Psychopathology*. New York: Guilford, pp. 87–112.

Edelbrock, C. & Costello, A.J. (1988b). Convergence between statistically derived behavior problem syndromes and child psychiatric diagnoses. *Journal of Abnormal Child Psychology*, **16**, 219–231.

Egeland, J.A., Gerhard, D.S., Pauls, D.L., Sussex, J.N., Kidd, K.K., Allen, C.R., Hostetter, A.N. & Housman, D.E. (1987). Bipolar affective disorders linked to DNA markers on chromosome 11. *Nature*, **325**, 783–787.

Elkin, I., Shea, T., Watkins, J.T., Imber, S.D., Sotsky, S.M., Collins, J.F., Glass, D.R., Pilkonis, P.A., Leber, W.R., Docherty, J.P., Fiester, S.J. & Parloff, M.B. (1989). National Institute of Mental Health treatment of depression collaborative research programme: general effectiveness of treatments. *Archives of General Psychiatry*, **46**, 971–982.

Elkins, R. & Rapoport, J.L. (1983). Psychopharmacology of adult and childhood depression: an overview. In D.P. Cantwell & G.A. Carlson (eds), *Affective Disorders in Childhood and Adolescence*. Lancaster: MTP Press, pp. 363–374.

Ellis, A. (1962). *Reason and Emotion in Psychotherapy*. New York: Lyle Stuart.

Emslie, G.J., Rush, A.J., Weinberg, W.A., Rintelmann, J.W. & Roffward, H.P. (1990). Children with major depression show reduced rapid eye movement latencies. *Archives of General Psychiatry*, **47**, 119–124.

Endicott, J. & Spitzer, R.L. (1978). A diagnostic interview: the SADS. *Archives of General Psychiatry*, **35**, 837–853.

Everitt, B.S. & Dunn, G. (1983). *Advanced Methods of Data Exploration and Modelling*. London: Heinemann.

Ezpeleta, L., Polaino, A., Domenech, E. & Domenech, J.M. (1990). Peer nomination inventory of depression: characteristics in a Spanish sample. *Journal of Abnormal Child Psychology*, **18**, 373–391.

Farmer, A. & McGuffin, P. (1989). The classification of the depressions: contemporary confusion revisited. *British Journal of Psychiatry*, **155**, 437–443.

Feighner, J.P., Robins, E., Guze, S.B., Woodruff, R.A. & Winokur, G. (1972). Diagnostic criteria for use in psychiatric research. *Archives of General Psychiatry*, **26**, 57–63.

Ferguson, H.B. & Bawden, H.N. (1988). Psychobiological measures. In M. Rutter, A.H. Tuma & I.S. Lann (eds), *Assessment and Diagnosis in Child Psychopathology*. New York: Guilford, pp. 232–263.,

Fergusson, D.M. & Horwood, L.J. (1987). The trait and methods components of ratings of conduct disorder. I: Maternal and teacher evaluations of conduct disorder in young children. *Journal of Child Psychology and Psychiatry*, **28**, 249–260.

Fergusson, D.M., Horwood, L.J. & Lloyd, M. (1991). Confirmatory factor models of attention deficit and conduct disorder. *Journal of Child Psychology and Psychiatry*, **32**, 257–274.

Field, T., Healy, B., Goldstein, S. & Guthertz, M. (1990). Behavior state matching and synchrony in mother–infant interactions of nondepressed versus "depressed" dyads. *Developmental Psychology*, **26**, 7–14.

Finch, A.J., Saylor, C.F. & Edwards, G.L. (1985). Children's Depression Inventory: sex and grade norms for normal children. *Journal of Consulting and Clinical Psychology*, **53**, 424–425.

Fine, S., Forth, A., Gilbert, M. & Haley, G. (1991). Group therapy for adolescent depressive disorder: a comparison of social skills and therapeutic support. *Journal of the American Academy of Child Psychiatry*, **30**, 79–85.

Finlay-Jones, R.A., Brown, G.W., Duncan-Jones, P., Murphy, E. & Prudo, R. (1980). Depression and anxiety in the community: replicating the diagnosis of a case. *Psychological Medicine*, **10**, 445–454.

Finlay-Jones, R.A. & Brown, G.W. (1981). Types of stressful life event and the onset of anxiety and depressive disorders. *Psychological Medicine*, **11**, 803–815.

Firth, M.A. & Chaplin, L. (1987). Research note: the use of the Birleson depression scale with a non-clinical sample of boys. *Journal of Child Psychology and Psychiatry*, **28**, 79–85.

Fleming, J.E., Offord, D.R. & Boyle, M.H. (1989). Prevalence of childhood and adolescent depression in the community: Ontario child health study. *British Journal of Psychiatry*, **155**, 647–654.

Fleming, J.E. & Offord, D.R. (1990). Epidemiology of childhood depressive disorders: a critical review. *Journal of the American Academy of Child Psychiatry*, **29**, 571–580.,

Forehand, R., Brody, G., Slotkin, J., Fauber, R., McCombs, A. & Long, N. (1988). Young adolescent and maternal depression: assessment, inter-relations and predictors. *Journal of Consulting and Clinical Psychology*, **56**, 422–426.

Forehand, R., Neighbors, B. & Wierson, M. (1991). The transition to adolescence: the role of gender and stress in problem behavior and competence. *Journal of Child Psychology and Psychiatry*, **32**, 929–937.

Foreman, D.M. & Goodyer, I.M. (1988). Salivary cortisol hypersecretion in juvenile depression. *Journal of Child Psychology and Psychiatry*, **29**, 311–320.

Forness, S.R. (1988). School characteristics of children and adolescents with depression. In R.B. Rutherford, C.M. Nelson & S.R. Forness (eds), *Bases of Severe Behavioural Disorders in Children and Youth*. Boston, Mass: Little, Brown, pp. 177–203.

Fox, S.J., Barrnett, R.J., Davies, M. & Bird, H.R. (1990). Psychopathology and developmental delay in homeless children: a pilot study. *Journal of the American Academy of Child Psychiatry*, **29**, 732–735.

Frank, E., Kupfer, D.J., Wagner, E.F., McEachran, A.B. & Cornes, C. (1991a). Efficacy of interpersonal psychotherapy as a maintenance treatment of recurrent depression. *Archives of General Psychiatry*, **48**, 1053–1059.

Frank, E., Prien, R.F., Jarrett, R.B., Keller, M.B., Kupfer, D.J., Lavori, P.W., Rush, A.J. & Weissman, M.M. (1991b). Conceptualization and rationale for consensus definitions of terms in major depressive disorder: remission, recovery, relapse, and recurrence. *Archives of General Psychiatry*, **48**, 851–855.

Frank, R. & Doerr, H.G. (1989). Mania in a girl with Cushing's disease. *Journal of the American Academy of Child Psychiatry*, **28**, 610–611.,

Friedrich, W.N. & Einbender, A.J. (1983). The abused child: a psychological review. *Journal of Clinical Child Psychology*, **12**, 244–256.

Frommer, E.A. (1967). Treatment of childhood depression with antidepressant drugs. *British Medical Journal*, **1**, 729–732.

Frommer, E.A. (1968). Depressive illness in childhood. In A. Coppen & A. Walk (eds), *Recent Developments in Affective Disorders*. Ashford, Kent: Headley Brothers, pp. 117–136.

Fundudis, T., Berney, T.P., Kolvin, I., Famuyiwa, O., Barrett, L., Bhate, S. & Tyrer, S.P. (1991). Reliability and validity of two self-rating scales in the assessment of childhood depression. *British Journal of Psychiatry*, **159** (suppl. 11), 36–40.

Garber, J. (1984). The developmental progression of depression in female children. In D. Cicchetti & K. Schneider-Rosen (eds), *Childhood Depression (New Directions for Child Development*, No. 26). San Francisco: Jossey Bass, pp. 29–58.

Garber, J., Kriss, M.R., Koch, M. & Lindholm, L. (1988). Recurrent depression in adolescents: a follow-up study. *Journal of the American Academy of Child Psychiatry*, **27**, 49–54.

Garber, J., Zeman, J. & Walker, L.S. (1990). Recurrernt abdominal pain in children: psychiatric diagnoses and parental psychopathology. *Journal of the American Academy of Child Psychiatry*, **29**, 648–656.

Garcia, M.R., Ryan, N.D., Rabinovitch, H., Ambrosini, P., Twomey, J., Iyengar, S., Novacenko, H., Nelson, B. & Puig-Antich, J. (1991). Thyroid stimulating hormone response to thyrotropin in prepubertal depression. *Journal of the American Academy of Child Psychiatry*, **30**, 398–406.

Garmezy, N. (1985). Stress-resistant children—the search for protective factors. In: J. Stevenson (ed.), *Recent Advances in Developmental Psychopathology*. Oxford: Pergamon.

Garmezy, N. (1986). Developmental aspects of children's responses to the stress of separation and loss. In M. Rutter, C.E. Izard, P.B. Read (eds), *Depression in Young People: Clinical Developmental Perspectives*. New York: Guilford, pp. 297–324.

Garrison, C.Z., Schluchter, M.D., Schoenbach, V.J. & Kaplan, B.K. (1989). Epidemiology of depressive symptoms in young adolescents. *Journal of the American Academy of Child Psychiatry*, **28**, 343–351.

Garrison, C.Z., Jackson, K.L., Martseller, F., McKeown, R. & Addy, C. (1990). A longitudinal study of depressive symptomatology in young adolescents. *Journal of the American Academy of Child Psychiatry*, **29**, 581–585.

Garrison, C.Z., Addy, C.L., Jackson, K.L., McKeown, R.E. & Waller, J.L. (1991). The CES-D as a screen for depression and other psychiatric disorders in adolescents. *Journal of the American Academy of Child Psychiatry*, **30**, 636–641.

Gastpar, M., Gilsdorf, U., Abou-Saleh, M.T. & Ngo-Khac, T. (1992). Clinical correlates of response to DST. The Dexamethasone Suppression Test in Depression: a World Health Organization collaborative study. *Journal of Affective Disorders*, **26**, 17–24.

Geller, B. (1991). Psychopharmacology of children and adolescents: pharmacokinetics and relationships of plasma/serum levels to response. *Psychopharmacology Bulletin*, **27**, 401–409.

Geller, B., Chestnut, E.C., Miller, M.D., Price, D.T. & Yates, E. (1985). Preliminary data on DSM-III associated features of major depressive disorder in children and adolescents. *American Journal of Psychiatry*, **142**, 643–644.

Geller, B., Cooper, T.B., Chestnut, E.C., Anker, J.A. & Schluchter, M.D. (1986). Preliminary data on the relationship between nortriptyline plasma level and response in depressed children. *American Journal of Psychiatry*, **143**, 1283–1286.

Geller, B., Cooper, T.B., McCombs, H.G., Graham, D.L. & Wells, J. (1989). Double-blind placebo-controlled study of nortriptyline in depressed children using a "fixed plasma level" design. *Psychopharmacology Bulletin*, **25**, 101–108.

Geller, B., Cooper, T.B., Graham, D.L., Marsteller, F.A. & Bryant, D.M. (1990). Double-blind placebo-controlled study of nortriptyline in depressed adolescents using a "fixed plasma level" design. *Psychopharmacology Bulletin*, **26**, 85–90.

George, C. & Main, M. (1979). Social interaction of young abused children: approach, avoidance, and aggression. *Child Development*, **50**, 306–318.

Gershon, E.S., Mark, A., Cohen, N., Belizon, N., Baron, M. & Knobe, K.E. (1975). Transmitted factors in the morbid risk of affective disorders: a controlled study. *Journal of Psychiatric Research*, **12**, 283–299.

Gershon, E.S., Hamovit, J., Guroff, J.J., Dibble, E., Leckman, J.F., Sceery, W., Targum, S.D., Nurnberger, J.I., Goldin, L.R. & Bunney, W.E. (1982). A family study of schizoaffective, bipolar I, bipolar II, unipolar, and normal control probands. *Archives of General Psychiatry*, **39**, 1157–1167.

Gibbons, J. & McHugh, P. (1963). Plasma cortisol in depressive illness. *Journal of Psychiatry Research*, **1**, 162–171.

Gibbs, J.T. (1985). Psychosocial factors associated with depression in urban adolescent females. *Journal of Youth and Adolescence*, **14**, 57–60.

Giles, D.E., Roffwarg, H.P., Dahl, R.E. & Kupfer, D.J. (1992). Electroencephalographic sleep abnormalities in depressed children: a hypothesis. *Psychiatry Research*, **42**, 53–63.

Gittelman, R., Mannuzza, S., Shenker, R. & Bonagura, N. (1985). Hyperactive boys almost grown up. I: Psychiatric status. *Archives of General Psychiatry*, **42**, 937–947.

Gittelman-Klein, R. (1977). Definitional and methodological issues concerning depressive illness in children. In: J.G. Schulterbrandt & A. Raskin (eds), *Depression in Childhood*. New York: Raven Press, pp. 69–80.,

Giuffra, L.A. & Risch, N. (1991). Forgetting and the cohort effect: a simulation study. *Abstracts of the Second World Congress on Psychiatric Genetics*, p. 41.

Glaser, K. (1967). Masked depression in children and adolescents. *American Journal of Psychotherapy*, **21**, 565–574.

Gleser, G.C., Green, B.L. & Winget, C. (1981). *Prolonged Psychosocial Effects of Disaster: a Study of Buffalo Creek*. New York: Academic Press.

Goetz, R.R., Puig-Antich, J., Ryan, N., Rabinovich, H., Ambrosini, P., Nelson, B. & Krawiec, V. (1987). The EEG sleep of adolescents with major depression and normal controls. *Archives of General Psychiatry*, **44**, 53–61.

Goetz, R.R., Puig-Antich, J., Dahl, R.E., Ryan, N.D., Asnis, G.M., Rabinovich, H. & Nelson, B. (1991). EEG sleep of young adults with major depression: a controlled study. *Journal of Affective Disorders*, **22**, 91–100.

Goldston, D.B., Turnquist, D.C. & Knutson, J.F. (1989). Presenting problems of sexually abused girls receiving psychiatric services. *Journal of Abnormal Psychology*, **98**, 314–317.

Goldfarb, W. (1943). The effects of early institutional care on adolescent personality. *Journal of Education*, **12**, 106–129.

Goodwin, G.M. (1992). Tricyclic and newer antidepressants. In E.S. Paykel (ed.), *Handbook of Affective Disorders*, 2nd edn. Edinburgh: Churchill Livingstone, pp. 327–343.

Goodyer, I.M. (1990). *Life Experiences, Development and Childhood Psychopathology*. Chichester: John Wiley.

Goodyer, I.M., Kolvin, I. & Gatzanis, S. (1985). Recent undesirable life events and psychiatric disorder in childhood and adolescence. *British Journal of Psychiatry*, **147**, 517–523.

Goodyer, I.M., Wright, C. & Altham, P.M.E. (1988). Maternal adversity and recent stressful life events in anxious and depressed children. *Journal of Child Psychology and Psychiatry*, **29**, 651–667.

Goodyer, I.M., Wright, C. & Altham, P.M.E. (1989). Recent friendships in anxious and depressed school-age children. *Psychological Medicine*, **19**, 165–174.

Goodyer, I.M. & Altham, P.M.E. (1991a). Lifetime exit events and recent social and family adversities in anxious and depressed school-age children and adolescents—I. *Journal of Affective Disorders*, **21**, 219–228.

Goodyer, I.M. & Altham, P.M.E. (1991b). Lifetime exist events and recent social and family adversities in anxious and depressed school-age children and adolescents— II. *Journal of Affective Disorders*, **21**, 229–238.

Goodyer, I.M., Germany, E., Gowrusankur, J. & Altham, P. (1991a). Social influences on the course of anxious and depressive disorders in school-age children. *British Journal of Psychiatry*, **158**, 676–684.

Goodyer, I., Herbert, J., Moor, S. & Altham, P. (1991b). Cortisol hypersection in depressed school-aged children and adolescents. *Psychiatry Research*, **37**, 237–244.

Gorell Barnes, G. (1985). Systems theory and family theory. In: M. Rutter and L. Hersov (eds), *Child and Adolescent Psychaitry: Modern Approaches.* Oxford: Blackwell Scientific, pp. 216–232.

Graham, P.J. (1981). Depressive disorders in children—a re-consideration. *Acta Paedopsychiatrica*, **46**, 285–296.

Graham, P., Rutter, M. & George, S. (1973). Temperamental characteristics as predictors of behavior disorders in children. *American Journal of Orthopsychiatry*, **43**, 328–339.

Granville-Grossman, K.L. (1968). The early environment in affective disorder. In A. Coppen & A. Walk (eds), *Recent Developments in Affective Disorders.* London: Royal Medico-Psychological Association.

Green, A.R. & Goodwin, G.M. (1986). Antidepressants and monoamines: actions and interactions. In J.F.W. Deakin (ed.), *The Biology of Depression.* London: The Royal College of Psychiatrists, pp. 174–189.

Greenbaum, P.E., Prange, M.E., Friedman, R.M. & Silver, S.E. (1991). Substance abuse prevalence and comorbidity with other psychiatric disorders among adolescents with severe emotional disturbances. *Journal of the American Academy of Child Psychiatry*, **30**, 575–583.

Grigoroiu-Serbanescu, M., Christodorescu, D., Magureanu, S., Jipescu, I., Totoescu, A., Marinescu, E., Ardelean, V. & Popa, S. (1991). Adolescent offspring of endogenous unipolar depressive parents and of normal parents. *Journal of Affective Disorders,* **21**, 185–198.

Guelfi, J.D., Payan, C., Fermanian, J., Pedarriosse, A.-M. & Manfredi, R. (1992). Moclobemide versus clomipramine in endogenous depression: a double-blind randomized clinical trial. *British Journal of Psychiatry*, **160**, 519–524.

Gutterman, E.M., O'Brien, J.D. & Young, J.G. (1987). Structured diagnostic interviews for children and adolescents: current status and future directions. *Journal of the American Academy of Child Psychiatry*, **26**, 621–630.

Hagnell, O., Lanke, J., Rorsman, B. & Ojesjo, L. (1982). Are we entering an age of melancholy? Depressive illness in a prospective epidemiological study over 25 years: the Lundby study, Sweden. *Psychological Medicine*, **12**, 279–289.

Hale, A.S. & Stokes, P.E. (1992). The utility of serotonin reuptake inhibitors in endogenous and severe depression. In H.L. Freeman (ed.), *The Use of Fluoxetine in Clinical Practice.* London: Royal Society of Medicine Services Limited, pp. 15–25.

Hamilton, M. (1960). A rating scale for depression. *Journal of Neurology, Neuro-Surgery and Psychiatry*, **23**, 56–62.

Hamilton, M. (1982). Symptoms and assessment of depression. In E. Paykel (ed.), *Handbook of Affective Disorders.* Edinburgh: Churchill Livingstone, pp. 3–11.

Hammen, C. (1991). *Depression Runs in Families. The Social Context of Risk and Resilience in Children of Depressed Mothers.* New York: Springer-Verlag.

Hammen, C., Gordon, D., Burge, D., Adrian, C., Jaenicke, C. & Hiroto, D. (1987). Maternal affective disorders, illness and stress. *American Journal of Psychiatry*, **144**, 736–741.

Hammen, C., Adrian, C. & Hiroto, D. (1988). A longitudinal test of the attributional vulnerability model in children at risk for depression. *British Journal of Clinical Psychology*, **27**, 37–46.

Hammen, C., Burge, D., Burney, E. & Adrian, C. (1990a). Longitudinal study of diagnoses in children of women with unipolar and bipolar affective disorder. *Archives of General Psychiatry*, **47**, 1112–1117.

Hammen, C., Burge, D. & Stansbury, K. (1990b). Relationship of mother and child variables to child outcomes in a high risk sample: a causal modelling analysis. *Developmental Psychology*, **26**, 24–30.

Hammen, C., Burge, D. & Adrian, C. (1991). Timing of mother and child depression in a longitudinal study of children at risk. *Journal of Consulting and Clinical Psychology*, **59**, 341–345.

Harmon, R.J., Wagonfeld, S. & Emde, R.N. (1982). Anaclitic depression: a follow-up from infancy to puberty with observations and psychotherapy. *Psychoanalytic Study of the Child*, **37**, 67–94.

Harrington, R.C. (1990). Depressive disorder in children and adolescents. *British Journal of Hospital Medicine*, **43**, 108–112.

Harrington, R.C. (1991). Do we need different criteria to diagnose depression in children? Paper presented at the Ninth Meeting of the European Society for Child and Adolescent Psychiatry.

Harrington, R.C. (1992). Affective disorders. In M. Rutter, L. Hersov & E. Taylor (eds), *Child and Adolescent Psychiatry: Modern Approaches,* 3rd edn. Oxford: Blackwell. In press.

Harrington, R.C., Hill, J., Rutter, M., John, K., Fudge, H., Zoccolillo, M. & Weissman, M.M. (1988). The assessment of lifetime psychopathology: a comparison of two interviewing styles. *Psychological Medicine*, **18**, 487–493.

Harrington, R.D., Fudge, H., Rutter, M., Pickles, A. & Hill, J. (1990). Adult outcomes of childhood and adolescent depression. I: Psychiatric status. *Archives of General Psychiatry*, **47**, 465–473.

Harrington, R.C., Fudge, H., Rutter, M., Pickles, A. & Hill, J. (1991). Adult outcomes of childhood and adolescent depression. II: Links with antisocial disorders. *Journal of the American Academy of Child Psychiatry*, **30**, 434–439.

Harrington, R.C., Fudge, H., Rutter, M., Bredenkamp, D., Groothues, C. & Pridham, J. (1992). Child and adult depression: a test of continuities with family-study data. *British Journal of Psychiatry*. In press.

Harris, P.L., Donnelly, K., Guz, G.R. & Pitt-Watson, R. (1986). Children's understanding of the distinction between real and apparent emotion. *Child Development*, **57**, 895–909.

Harter, S. (1983). Developmental perspectives on the self-system. In: E.M. Hetherington (ed.), *Socialization, Personality and Social Development*, vol. 4, (*Musson's Handbook of Child Psychology*, 4th edn) New York: John Wiley, pp 275–385.

Hartup, W. (1983). Peer relations. In: E.M. Hetherington (ed.), *Socialization, Personality and Social Development*, vol. 4, (*Mussen's Handbook of Child Psychology*, 4th edn). New York: John Wiley, pp 103–196.

Haskett, R.F. (1985). Diagnostic categorization of psychiatric disturbance in Cushing's syndrome. *American Journal of Psychiatry*, **142**, 911–916.

Hawton, K. & Goldacre, M. (1982). Hospital admissions for adverse effects of medical agents (mainly self-poisoning) among adolescents in the Oxford region. *British Journal of Psychiatry*, **141**, 166–170.

Helsel, W.J. & Matson, J.L. (1984). The assessment of depression in children: the internal structure of the Children's Depression Inventory (CDI) and its relationship to the Matson Evaluation of Social Skills with Youngsters (MESSY). *Behaviour Research and Therapy*, **23**, 289–298.

Henderson, S. (1982). The significance of social relationships in the aetiology of neurosis. In C.M. Parkes & J. Stevenson-Hinde (ed.), *The Place of Attachment in Human Behaviour*. London: Tavistock.

Henderson, S., Byrne, D.G., Duncan-Jones, P., Scott, R. & Adcock, S. (1980). Social relationships, adversity and neurosis: a study of associations in a general population sample. *British Journal of Psychiatry*, **136**, 574–583.

Henderson, S., Byrne, D.G. & Duncan-Jones, P. (1981). *Neurosis and the Social Environment*. Sydney: Academic Press.

Hendren, R.L. (1983). Depression in anorexia nervosa. *Journal of the American Academy of Child Psychiatry*, **22**, 59–62.

Heninger, G.R., Charney, D.S. & Sternberg, D.E. (1983). Lithium carbonate augmentation of antidepressant treatment. *Archives of General Psychiatry*, **40**, 1336–1342.

Heninger, G.R. & Charney, D.S. (1986). Mechanisms of action of antidepressant treatments: implications for the etiology and treatment of depressive disorders. In H.Y. Meltzer (ed.), *Psychopharmacology: The Third Generation of Progress*. New York: Raven Press, pp. 535–544.

Henry, J.A. (1992). The safety of antidepressants. *British Journal of Psychiatry*, **160**, 439–441.

Herjanic, B., Herjanic, M., Brown, F. & Wheatt, J. (1975). Are children reliable reporters. *Journal of Abnormal Child Psychology*, **3**, 41–48.

Herjanic, B. & Reich, W. (1982). Development of a structured psychiatric interview for children: agreement between child and parent on individual symptoms. *Journal of Abnormal Child Psychology*, **10**, 307–324.,

Hetherington, E.M., Cox, M. & Cox, R. (1982). Effects of divorce on parents and children. In: M.E. Lamb (ed.), *Non-Traditional families: Parenting and Child Development*. New York: Erlbaum.

Hinde, R.A. (1982). Attachment: some conceptual and biological issues. In C.M. Parkes & J. Stevenson-Hinde (ed.), *The Place of Attachment in Human Behaviour*. New York: Basic Books, pp. 60–76.

Hodges, K. (1993). Structured interviews for assessing children. *Journal of Child Psychology and Psychiatry*, **34**, 49–67.

Hodges, K., Kline, J., Stern, L., Cytryn, L. & McKnew, D. (1982). The development of a child assessment interview for research and clinical use. *Journal of Abnormal Child Psychology*, **10**, 173–189.

Hodges, K., McKnew, D., Burbach, D.J. & Roebuck, L. (1987). Diagnostic concordance between the Child Assessment Schedule (CAS) and the Schedule for Affective Disorders and Schizophrenia for school-age children (K-SADS) in an outpatient sample using lay interviewers. *Journal of the American Academy of Child Psychiatry*, **26**, 654–661.

Hodges, K., Cools, J. & McKnew, D. (1989). Test–retest reliability of a clinical research interview for children: the Child Assessment Schedule (CAS). *Psychological Assessment: Journal of Consulting and Clinical Psychology*, **1**, 317–322.

Hodges, K., Saunders, W.B., Kashani, J., Hamlett, K. & Thompson, R.J. (1990). Internal consistency of DSM-III diagnoses using the symptom scales of the Child Assessment Schedule. *Journal of the American Academy of Child Psychiatry*, **29**, 635–641.

Hoier, T.S. & Kerr, M.M. (1988). Extrafamilial information sources in the study of childhood depression. *Journal of the American Academy of Child Psychiatry*, **27**, 21–33.

Hollon, S.D., Shelton, R.C. & Loosen, P.T. (1991). Cognitive therapy and pharmacotherapy for depression. *Journal of Consulting Clinical Psychology*, **59**, 88–99.

Hops, H., Lewinsohn, P.M., Andrews, J.A. & Roberts, R.E. (1990). Psychosocial corre-lates of depressive symptomatology among high school students. *Journal of Clinical Child Psychology*, **19**, 211–220.

Hughes, C.W., Preskorn, S.H., Weller, E., Weller, R., Hassanein, R. & Tucker, S. (1990). The effect of concomitant disorders in childhood depression on predicting clinical response. *Psychopharmacology Bulletin*, **26**, 235–238.

Jacobsen, E. (1938). *Progressive Relaxation*. Chicago: University of Chicago Press.

Jaenicke, C., Hammen, C., Zupan, B., Hiroto, D., Gordon, D., Adrian, C. & Burge, D. (1987). Cognitive vulnerability in children at risk for depression. *Journal of Abnor-mal Child Psychology*, **15**, 559–572.

Jensen, J.B. & Garfinkel, B.D. (1990). Growth hormone dysregulation in children with major depressive disorder. *Journal of the American Academy of Child Psychiatry*, **29**, 295–301.

Jensen, P.S., Traylor, J., Xenakis, S.N. & Davis, H. (1988). Child psychopathology rating scales and interrater agreement. I: Parents' gender and psychiatric symptoms. *Journal of the American Academy of Child and Adolescent Psychiatry*, **27**, 442–450.

Joffe, R.D., Dobson, K.S., Fine, S., Marriage, K. & Haley, G. (1990). Social problem-solving in depressed, conduct-disordered, and normal adolescents. *Journal of Abnormal Child Psychology*, **18**, 565–575.

John, K., Gammon, G., Prusoff, B. & Warner, V. (1987). The Social Adjustment Interview Schedule for Children and Adolescents (SAICA). Testing of a new semi-structured interview. *Journal of the American Academy of Child Psychiatry*, **26**, 898–911.

Joshi, P.T., Capozzoli, J.A. & Coyle, J.T. (1990). The Johns Hopkins Depression Scale: normative data and validation in child psychiatry patients. *Journal of the American Academy of Child Psychiatry*, **29**, 283–288.

Kagan, J., Reznick, J.S. & Snidman, N. (1987). The physiology and psychology of behavioural inhibition in children. *Child Development*, **58**, 1459–1473.

Kahn, J.S., Kehle, T.J., Jenson, W.R. & Clarke, E. (1990). Comparison of cognitive–behavioural, relaxation, and self-modeling interventions for depression among middle-school students. *School Psychology Review*, **19**, 196–211.

Kandel, D.B. & Davies, M. (1982). Epidemiology of depressive mood in adolescents. *Archives of General Psychiatry*, **39**, 1205–1212.

Kandel, D.B. & Davies, M. (1986). Adult sequelae of adolescent depressive symptoms. *Archives of General Psychiatry*, **43**, 255–262.

Kaplan, S.L., Hong, G.K. & Weinhold, C. (1984). Epidemiology of depressive symp-tomatology in adolescents. *Journal of the American Academy of Child Psychiatry*, **23**, 91–98.

Kashani, J.H. & Simonds, J.F. (1979). The incidence of depression in children. *Ameri-can Journal of Psychiatry*, **136**, 1203–1205.

Kashani, J.H., McGee, R., Clarkson, S., Anderson, J., Walton, L., Williams, S., Silva, P., Robins, A., Cytryn, M. & McKnew, D. (1983). Depression in a sample of 9-year-old children: prevalence and associated characteristics. *Archives of General Psychi-atry*, **40**, 1217–1223.

Kashani, J., Holcomb, W.R. & Orvaschel, H. (1986). Depression and depressive symp-toms in preschool children from the general population. *American Journal of Psy-chiatry*, **143**, 1138–1143.

Kashani, J.H., Beck, N.C., Hoeper, E.W., Fallahi, C., Corcoran, C.M., McAllister, J.A., Rosenberg, T.K. & Reid, J.C. (1987). Psychiatric disorders in a community sample of adolescents. *American Journal of Psychiatry*, **144**, 584–589.

Kashani, J.H., Burbach, D.J. & Rosenberg, T.K. (1988). Perception of family conflict resolution and depressive symptomatology in adolescents. *Journal of the American Academy of Child Psychiatry*, **27**, 42–48.

Kashani, J.H., Orvaschel, H., Rosenberg, T.K. & Reid, J.C. (1989). Psychopathology in a community sample of children and adolescents: a developmental perspective. *Journal of the American Academy of Child Psychiatry*, **28**, 701–706.

Kashani, J.H., Sherman, D.D., Parker, D.R. & Reid, J.C. (1990). Utility of the Beck Depression Inventory with clinic-referred adolescents. *Journal of the American Academy of Child Psychiatry*, **29**, 278–282.

Kaslow, N.J., Rehm, L.P. & Siegel, A.W. (1984). Social-cognitive and cognitive correlates of depression in children. *Journal of Abnormal Child Psychology*, **12**, 605–620.

Kaslow, N.J., Rehm, L.P., Pollack, S.L. & Siegel, A.W. (1988). Attributional style and self-control behavior in depressed and nondepressed children and their parents. *Journal of Abnormal Child Psychology*, **16**, 163–175.

Katona, C.L.E. (1988). Lithium augmentation in refractory depression. *Psychiatry Developments*, **6**, 153–172.

Kaufman, J. (1991). Depressive disorders in maltreated children. *Journal of the American Academy of Child Psychiatry*, **30**, 257–265.

Kazdin, A.E. (1987). Children's Depression Scale: validation with child psychiatric inpatients. *Journal of Child Psychology and Psychiatry*, **28**, 29–41.

Kazdin, A.E. (1989a). Identifying depression in children: a comparison of alternative selection criteria. *Journal of Abnormal Child Psychology*, **17**, 437–454.

Kazdin, A.E. (1989b). Evaluation of the Pleasure Scale in the assessment of anhedonia in children. *Journal of the American Academy of Child Psychiatry*, **28**, 364–372.

Kazdin, A.E. (1990). Childhood depression. *Journal of Child Psychology and Psychiatry*, **31**, 121–160.

Kazdin, A.E., French, N.H., Unis, A.S. & Esveldt-Dawson, K. (1983a). Assessment of childhood depression: correspondence of child and parent ratings. *Journal of the American Academy of Child Psychiatry*, **22**, 157–164.

Kazdin, A.E., French, N.H., Unis, A.S., Esveldt-Dawson, K. & Sherick, R.B. (1983b). Hopelessness, depression and suicidal intent among psychiatrically disturbed inpatient children. *Journal of Consulting and Clinical Psychology*, **51**, 504–510.

Kazdin, A.E., Esveldt-Dawson, K., Sherick, R.B. & Colbus, D. (1985a). Assessment of overt behaviour and childhood depression among psychiatrically disturbed children. *Journal of Consulting and Clinical Psychology*, **53**, 201–210.

Kazdin, A.E., Sherick, R.B., Esveldt-Dawson, K. & Rancurello, M.D. (1985b). Nonverbal behavior and childhood depression. *Journal of the American Academy of Child Psychiatry*, **24**, 303–309.

Kazdin, A.E., Moser, J., Colbus, D. & Bell, R. (1985c). Depressive symptoms among physically abused and psychiatrically disturbed children. *Journal of Abnormal Psychology*, **94**, 298–307.

Kazdin, A.E., Rodgers, A. & Colbus, D. (1986). The Hopelessness Scale for Children: psychometric characteristics and concurrent validity. *Journal of Consulting and Clinical Psychology*, **54**, 241–245.

Kellam, S.G. (1990). Developmental epidemiological framework for family research on depression and aggression. In G.R. Patterson (ed.), *Depression and Aggression in Family Interaction*. New Jersey: Erlbaum, pp. 11–24.

Keller, M.B., Beardslee, W.R., Dorer, D.J., Lavori, P.W., Samuelson, H. & Klerman, G.R. (1986). Impact of severity and chronicity of parental affective illness on adaptive functioning and psychopathology in children. *Archives of General Psychiatry*, **43**, 930–937.

Keller, M.B., Beardslee, W., Lavori, P.W., Wunder, J., Drs D.L. & Samuelson, H. (1988). Course of major depression in non-referred adolescents: a retrospective study. *Journal of Affective Disorders*, **15**, 235–243.

Keller, M.B., Lavori, P.W., Beardslee, W.R., Wunder, J. & Ryan, N. (1991). Depression in children and adolescents: new data on "undertreatment" and a literature review on the efficacy of available treatments. *Journal of Affective Disorders*, **21**, 163–171.

Kendall, P.C., Stark, K.D. & Adam, T. (1990). Cognitive deficit or cognitive distortion in childhood depression. *Journal of Abnormal Child Psychology*, **18**, 255–270.

Kendell, R.E. (1976). The classification of depressions: a review of contemporary confusion. *British Journal of Psychiatry*, **129**, 15–28.

Kendell, R.E., Wainwright, S., Hailey, A. & Shannon, B. (1976). The influence of childbirth on psychiatric morbidity. *Psychological Medicine*, **6**, 297–302.

Kendler, K.S. (1988). The impact of diagnostic hierarchies on prevalence estimates for psychiatric disorders. *Comprehensive Psychiatry*, **29**, 218–227.

Kendler, K.S., Neale, M.C., Kessler, R.C., Heath, A.C. & Eaves, L.J. (1992). A population-based twin study of major depression in women: the impact of varying definitions of illness. *Archives of General Psychiatry*, **49**, 257–266.

Khan, A.U. (1987). Biochemical profile of depressed adolescents. *Journal of the American Academy of Child Psychiatry*, **26**, 873–878.

Kiloh, L.G., Andrews, G. & Neilson, M. (1988). The long-term outcome of depressive illness. *British Journal of Psychiatry*, **153**, 752–757.

Kinard, E.M. (1982). Experiencing child abuse: effects of emotional adjustment. *American Journal of Orthopsychiatry*, **52**, 82–91.

King, L.J. & Pittman, G.D. (1970). A six-year follow-up study of 65 adolescent patients: natural history of affective disorders in adolescence. *Archives of General Psychiatry*, **22**, 230–236.

Kinzie, J.D., Sack, W., Angell, R., Clarke, G. & Ben, R. (1989). A three-year follow-up of Cambodian young people traumatized as children. *Journal of the American Academy of Child Psychiatry*, **28**, 501–504.

Klein, H.E., Bender, W., Mayr, H., Niederschweiberer, A. & Schmauss, J. (1984). The DST and its relationship to psychiatric diagnosis, symptoms and treatment outcome. *British Journal of Psychiatry*, **145**, 591–599.

Klerman, G.L., Lavori, P.W., Rice, J., Reich, T., Endicott, J., Andreasen, N.C., Keller, M.B. & Hirschfeld, R.M.A. (1985). Birth cohort trends in rates of major depressive disorder among relatives of patients with affective disorder. *Archives of General Psychiatry*, **42**, 689–695.

Klerman, G.L. (1988). The current age of youthful melancholia: evidence for increase in depression among adolescents and young adults. *British Journal of Psychiatry*, **152**, 4–14.

Kocsis, J.H. (1990). Predicting treatment response in clinical psychopharmacology. *Psychopharmacology Bulletin*, **26**, 49–59.

Kolvin, I., Berney, T.P. & Bhate, S. (1984). Classification and diagnosis of depression in school phobia. *British Journal of Psychiatry*, **145**, 347–357.

Kolvin, I., Barrett, M.L., Bhate, S.R., Berney, T.P., Famuyiwa, O., Fundudis, T. & Tyrer, S. (1991). The Newcastle Child Depression Project: diagnosis and classification of depression. *British Journal of Psychiatry*, **159** (suppl. 11), 9–21.

Kolvin, I., Berney, T.P., Barrett, L.M. & Bhate, S. (1992). Development and evaluation of a diagnostic algorithm for depression in childhood. *European Child and Adolescent Psychiatry*, **1**, 119–129.

Kovacs, M. (1982a). The Interview Schedule for Children (ISC). Unpublished interview schedule, Department of Psychiatry, University of Pittsburgh.

Kovacs, M. (1982b). The Children's Depression Inventory. Unpublished manuscript, University of Pittsburgh.

Kovacs, M. (1983) The Interview Schedule for Children (ISC): inter-rater and parent–child agreement. Unpublished manuscript.

Kovacs, M. (1986). A developmental perspective on methods and measures in the assessment of depressive disorders: the clinical interview. In M. Rutter, C.E. Izard & R.B. Read (eds), *Depression in Young People: Developmental and Clinical Perspectives*. New York: Guilford, pp. 435–465.

Kovacs, M. & Beck, A.T. (1977). An empirical clinical approach toward a definition of childhood depression. In J.G. Schulterbrandt (ed.), *Depression in Childhood: Diagnosis, Treatment and Conceptual Models*. New York: Raven Press, pp. 1–25.

Kovacs, M. & Paulauskas, S.L. (1984). Developmental state and the expression of depressive disorders in children: an empirical analysis. In D. Cicchetti & K. Schneider-Rosen (eds), *Childhood Depression (New Direction for Child Development*, no. 26). San Francisco: Jossey-Bass, pp. 59–80.

Kovacs, M., Feinberg, T.L., Crouse-Novak, M.A., Paulauskas, S.L. & Finkelstein, R. (1984a). Depressive disorders in childhood. I: A longitudinal prospective study of characteristics and recovery. *Archives of General Psychiatry*, **41**, 229–237.

Kovacs, M., Feinberg, T.L., Crouse-Novak, M., Paulauskas, S.L., Pollock, M. & Finkelstein, R. (1984b). Depressive disorders in childhood. II: A longitudinal study of the risk for a subsequent major depression. *Archives of General Psychiatry*, **41**, 643–649.

Kovacs, M., Paulauskas, S., Gatsonis, C. & Richards, C. (1988). Depressive disorders in childhood. III: A longitudinal study of comorbidity with and risk of conduct disorders. *Journal of Affective Disorders,* **15**, 205–217.

Kovacs, M., Gatsonis, C., Paulauskas, S. & Richards, C. (1989). Depressive disorders in childhood. IV: A longitudinal study of comorbidity with and risk for anxiety disorders. *Archives of General Psychiatry*, **46**, 776–782.

Kovacs, M. & Goldston, D. (1991). Cognitive and social cognitive development of depressed children and adolescents. *Journal of the American Academy of Child Psychiatry*, **30**, 388–392.

Kramer, A.D. & Feiguine, R.J. (1983). Clinical effects of amitriptyline in adolescent depression: a pilot study. *Journal of the American Academy of Child Psychiatry*, **20**, 636–644.

Kranzler, E.M., Shaffer, D., Wasserman, G. & Davies, M. (1990). Early childhood bereavement. *Journal of the American Academy of Child Psychiatry*, **29**, 513–520.

Krener, P. (1985). After incest: secondary prevention? *Journal of the American Academy of Child Psychiatry*, **24**, 231–234.

Kupersmidt, J.B., & Patterson, C.J. (1991). Childhood peer rejection, aggression, withdrawal, and perceived competence as predictors of self-reported behavior problems in preadolescence. *Journal of Abnormal Child Psychology*, **19**, 427–449.

Kupfer, D. (1992). Maintenance treatment in recurrent depression: current and future directions. *British Journal of Psychiatry*, **161**, 309–316.

Kupfer, D.J., Frank, E. & Perel, J.M. (1989). The advantage of early treatment intervention in recurrent depression. *Archives of General Psychiatry*, **46**, 771–775.

Kupfer, D.J. & Reynolds, C.F. (1992). Sleep and affective disorders. In E.S. Paykel (ed.), *Handbook of Affective Disorders,* 2nd edn. Edinburgh: Churchill Livingstone, pp. 311–323.

Kutcher, S. & Marton, P. (1991). Affective disorders in first degree relatives of adolescent onset bipolars, unipolars, and normal controls. *Journal of the American Academy of Child Psychiatry*, **30**, 75–78.

Kutcher, S., Malkin, D., Silverberg, J., Marton, P., Williamson, P., Malkin, A., Szalai, J. & Katic, M. (1991). Nocturnal cortisol, thyroid stimulating hormone, and growth hormone secretory profiles in depressed adolescents. *Journal of the American Academy of Child Psychiatry*, **30**, 407–414.

Kutcher, S., Williamson, P., Marton, P. & Szalai, J. (1992). REM latency in endogenously depressed adolescents. *British Journal of Psychiatry*, **161**, 399–402.

Lahmeyer, H.W., Poznanski, E.O. & Bellur, S.N. (1983). EEG sleep in depressed adolescents. *American Journal of Psychiatry*, **140**, 1150–1153.

Lancet (1989). Editorial: Outcome of depression. *Lancet*, **i**, 650–651.

Lang, M. & Tisher, M. (1978). *Children's Depression Scale*. Melbourne: Australian Council for Educational Research.

Lapouse, R. & Monk, M.A. (1964). Behavior deviations in a representative sample of children: variation by sex, age, race, social class and family size. *American Journal of Orthopsychiatry*, **34**, 436–446.

Larson, R. & Lampman-Petraitis, C. (1989). Daily emotional states as reported by children and adolescents. *Child Development*, **60**, 1250–1260.

Larson, R.W. Raffaelli, M., Richards, M.H., Ham, M. & Jewell, L. (1990). Ecology of depression in late childhood and early adolescence: a profile of daily states and activities. *Journal of Abnormal Psychology*, **99**, 92–102.

Larson, R. & Richards, M.H. (1991). Daily companionship in late childhood and early adolescence: changing developmental contexts. *Child Development*, **62**, 284–300.

Larsson, B.S. (1991). Somatic complaints and their relationship to depressive symptoms in Swedish adolescents. *Journal of Child Psychology and Psychiatry*, **32**, 821–832.

Larsson, B. & Melin, L. (1990). Depressive symptoms in Swedish adolescents. *Journal of Abnormal Child Psychology*, **18**, 91–103.

Larsson, B., Melin, L., Breitholtz, E., & Andersson, G. (1991). Short-term stability of depressive symptoms and suicide attempts in Swedish adolescents. *Acta Psychiatrica Scandinavica*, **83**, 385–390.

Leckman, J.F., Sholomskas, D., Thompson, W.D., Belanger, A. & Weissman, M.M. (1982). Best estimate of lifetime psychiatric diagnosis: a methodological study. *Archives of General Psychiatry*, **39**, 879–883.

Leckman, J.F., Weissman, M.M., Prusoff, B.A., Caruso, K.A., Merikangas, K.R., Pauls, D.L. & Kidd, K.K. (1984). Subtypes of depression: family study perspective. *Archives of General Psychiatry*, **41**, 833–838.

Lee, A.S. & Murray, R.M. (1988). The long-term outcome of Maudsley depressives. *British Journal of Psychiatry*, **153**, 741–751.

Leff, M.J., Roatch, J.F. & Bunney, W.E. (1970). Environmental factors preceding the onset of severe depressions. *Psychiatry*, **33**, 293–311.

Lefkowitz, M.M. & Burton, N. (1978). Childhood depression: a critique of the concept. *Psychological Bulletin*, **85**, 716–726.

Lefkowitz, M.M. & Tesiny, E.P. (1980). Assessment of childhood depression. *Journal of Consulting and Clinical Psychology*, **48**, 43–50.

Lefkowitz, M.M., Tesiny, E.P. & Gordon, N.H. (1980). Childhood depression, family income, and locus of control. *Journal of Nervous and Mental Disease*, **168**, 732–735.

Lefkowitz, M.M. & Tesiny, E.P. (1985). Depression in children: prevalence and correlates. *Journal of Consulting and Clinical Psychology*, **53**, 647–656.

Lefkowitz, M.M., Tesiny, E.P. & Solodow, W. (1989). A rating scale for assessing dysphoria in youth. *Journal of Abnormal Child Psychology*, **17**, 337–347.

Leon, G., Kendall, P. & Garber, J. (1980). Depression in children: parent, teacher and child perspectives. *Journal of Abnormal Child Psychology*, **8**, 221–235.

Lewinsohn, P.M. (1974). A behavioural approach to depression. In R.J. Friedman & M.M. Katz (eds), *Th Psychology of Depression: Contemporary Theory and Research*. Washington, DC: Winston.

Lewinsohn, P.M., Clarke, G.N., Hops, H. & Andrews, J. (1990). Cognitive–behavioural treatment for depressed adolescents. *Behaviour Therapy*, **21**, 385–401.

Lewinsohn, P.M., Rohde, P., Seeley, J.R. & Hops, H. (1991). Comorbidity of unipolar depression. I: Major depression with dysthymia. *Journal of Abnormal Psychology*, **100**, 205–213.

Lewis, M., Feiring, C., McGuffog, C. & Jaskir, J. (1984). Predicting psychopathology in six-year-olds from early social relations. *Child Development*, **55**, 123–136.

Lejoyeux, M., Rouillon, F., Ades, J. & Gorwood, P. (1992). Neural symptoms induced by tricyclic antidepressants: phenomenology and pathophysiology. *Acta Psychiatrica Scandinavica*, **85**, 249–256.

Ling, W., Oftedal, G. & Weinberg, W. (1970). Depressive illness in childhood presenting as severe headache. *American Journal of Diseases of Childhood*, **120**, 122–124.

Livingston, R. (1987). Sexually and physically abused children. *Journal of the American Academy of Child Psychiatry*, **26**, 413–415.

Livingston, R., Nugent, H., Rader, L. & Smith, G.R. (1985). Family histories of depressed and severely anxious children. *American Journal of Psychiatry*, **142**, 1497–1499.

Livingston, R. & Martin-Cannici (1987). Depression, anxiety and the dexamethasone suppression test in hospitalised prepubertal children. *Journal of Clinical Psychiatry*, **9**, 55–63.

Lobovits, D.A. & Handal, P.J. (1985). Childhood depression: prevalence using DSM-III criteria and validity of parent and child depression scales. *Journal of Pediatric Psychology*, **10**, 45–54.

Loosen, P.T. & Prange, A.J. (1982). Serum thyrotropin response to thyrotropin-releasing hormone in psychiatric patients: a review. *American Journal of Psychiatry*, **139**, 405–416.

Lowe, T.L. & Cohen, D.J. (1983). Biological research on depression in childhood. In D.P. Cantwell & G.A. Carlson (eds), *Affective Disorders in Childhood and Adolescence*. Lancaster: MTP Press, pp. 229–248.

Lucas, A.R., Locket, H.J. & Grimm, F. (1965). Amitriptyline in childhood depressions. *Diseases of the Nervous System*, **26**, 105–110.

McCauley, E., Mitchell, J.R., Burke, P. & Moss, S. (1988). Cognitive attributes of depression in children and adolescents *Journal of Consulting Clinical Psychology*, **56**, 903–908.

McCauley, E., Carlson, G.A. & Calderon, R. (1991). The role of somatic complaints in the diagnosis of depression in children and adolescents. *Journal of the American Academy of Child Psychiatry*, **30**, 631–635.

McClellan, J.M., Rubert, M.P., Reichler, R.J. & Sylvester, C.E. (1990). Attention deficit disorder in children at risk for anxiety and depression. *Journal of the American Academy of Child Psychiatry*, **29**, 534–539.

McClure, G.M.G. (1984). Trends in suicide rate for England and Wales 1975–1980. *British Journal of Psychiatry*, **144**, 119–126.

McClure, G.M.G. (1986). Recent changes in suicide among adolescents in England and Wales. *Journal of Adolescence*, **9**, 135–143.

McClure, G.M.G. (1988). Suicide in children in England and Wales. *Journal of Child Psychology and Psychiatry*, **29**, 345–349.

McConville, B.J., Boag, L.C. & Purohit, A.P. (1973). Three types of childhood depression. *Canadian Psychiatric Association Journal*, **18**, 133–138.

McFarlane, A.C. (1987). Life events and psychiatric disorder: the role of natural disaster. *British Journal of Psychiatry*, **151**, 362–367.

McFarlane, A.C. (1988). Recent life events and psychiatric disorder in children: the interaction with preceding extreme adversity. *Journal of Child Psychology and Psychiatry*, **29**, 677–691.

McGee, R., Williams, S., Kashani, J.H. & Silva, P.A. (1983). Prevalence of self-reported depressive symptoms and associated social factors in mothers in Dunedin. *British Journal of Psychiatry*, **143**, 473–479.

McGee, R. & Williams, S. (1988). A longitudinal study of depression in nine-year-old children. *Journal of the American Academy of Child Psychiatry*, **27**, 342–348.

McGee, R., Feehan, M., Williams, S., Partridge, F., Silva, P.A. & Kelly, J. (1990). DSM-III disorders in a large sample of adolescents. *Journal of the American Academy of Child Psychiatry*, **29**, 611–619.

McGee, R., Feehan, M., Williams, S. & Anderson, J. (1992). DSM-III disorders from age 11 to age 15 years. *Journal of the American Academy of Child Psychiatry*, **31**, 50–59.

McGuffin, P. (1991). Genetic models of mental illness. In P. McGuffin & R. Murray (ed.), *The New Genetics of Mental Illness*. Oxford: Butterworth–Heinemann, pp. 27–43.

McGuffin, P. & Katz, R. (1986). Nature, nurture and affective disorder. In J.F.W. Deakin (ed.), *The Biology of Depression*. London: Royal College of Psychiatrists, pp. 26–52.

McGuffin, P., Katz, R., Aldrich, J. & Bebbington, P. (1988). The Camberwell Collaborative Depression Study. II: Investigation of family members. *British Journal of Psychiatry*, **152**, 766–774.

McGuffin, P. & Sargeant, M.P. (1991). Genetic markers and affective disorder. In P. McGuffin & R. Murray (eds), *The New Genetics of Mental Illness*. Oxford: Butterworth–Heinemann, pp. 165–181.

Malmquist, C.P. (1971). Depressions in childhood and adolescence. *New England Journal of Medicine*, **284**, 887–893.

Marks, I. (1987). The development of normal fear: a review. *Journal of Child Psychology and Psychiatry*, **28**, 667–698.

Marriage, K., Fine, S., Moretti, M. & Haley, G. (1986). Relationship between depression and conduct disorder in children and adolescents. *Journal of the American Academy of Child Psychiatry*, **25**, 687–691.

Martini, D.R., Strayhorn, J.M. & Puig-Antich, J. (1990). A symptom self-report measure for preschool children. *Journal of the American Academy of Child Psychiatry*, **29**, 594–600.

Marttunen, M.J., Aro, H.M., Henrikson, M.M. & Lonnqvist, J.K. (1991). Mental disorders in adolescent suicide. DSM-III-R axes I and II diagnoses in suicides among 13- to 19-year-olds in Finland. *Archives of General Psychiatry*, **48**, 834–839.

Matson, J.L. (1989). *Treating Depression in Children and Adolescents*. New York: Pergamon.

Mellsop, G.W., Hutton, J.D. & Delahunt, J.W. (1985). Dexamethasone suppression test as a simple measure of stress? *British Medical Journal*, **290**, 1804–1806.

Mendelson, W.B. (1982). The clock and the blue guitar: studies of human growth hormone secretion in sleep and waking. *International Review of Neurobiology*, **23**, 367–389.

Mendlewicz, J. & Baron, M. (1981). Morbidity risks in subtypes of unipolar depressive illness: differences between early and late onset forms. *British Journal of Psychiatry*, **139**, 463–466.

Merikangas, K.R., Leckman, J.F., Prusoff, B.A., Pauls, D.L. & Weissman, M.M. (1985). Familial transmission of depression and alcoholism. *Archives of General Psychiatry*, **42**, 367–372.

Meyer, N.E., Dyck, D.G. & Petrinack, R.J. (1989). Cognitive appraisal and attributional correlates of depressive symptoms in children. *Journal of Abnormal Child Psychology*, **17**, 325–336.

Milin, R., Halikas, J.A., Meller, J.E. & Morse, C. (1991). Psychopathology among substance abusing juvenile offenders. *Journal of the American Academy of Child Psychiatry*, **30**, 569–574.

Mitchell, J., McCauley, E., Burke, P. & Moss, S.J. (1988). Phenomenology of depression in children and adolescents. *Journal of the American Academy of Child Psychiatry*, **27**, 12–20.

Mitchell, J., McCauley, E., Burke, P., Calderon, R. & Schloredt, K. (1989). Psychopathology in parents of depressed children and adolescents. *Journal of the American Academy of Child Psychiatry*, **28**, 352–357.

Mokros, H.B., Poznanski, E., Grossman, J.A. & Freeman, L.N. (1987). A comparison of child and parent ratings of depression for normal and clinically referred children. *Journal of Child Psychology and Psychiatry*, **28**, 613–624.

Moreau, D., Mufson, L., Weissman, M.M. & Klerman, G.L. (1991). Interpersonal psychotherapy for adolescent depression: description of modification and preliminary application. *Journal of the American Academy of Child Psychiatry*, **30**, 642–651.

Moretti, M.M., Fine, S., Haley, G. & Marriage, K. (1985). Childhood and adolescent depression: child-report versus parent-report information. *Journal of the American Academy of Child Psychiatry*, **24**, 298–302.

Mullen, P.E., Romans-Clarkson, S.E., Walton, V.A. & Herbison, G.P. (1988). Impact of sexual and physical abuse on women's mental health. *Lancet*, **i**, 841–845.

Myers, K., McCauley, E., Calderon, R. & Treder, R. (1991). The 3-year longitudinal course of suicidality and predictive factors for subsequent suicidality in youths with major depressive disorder. *Journal of the American Academy of Child Psychiatry*, **30**, 804–810.

Nelson, J.C. & Charney, D.S. (1981). The symptoms of major depressive illness. *American Journal of Psychiatry*, **138**, 1–13.

Nelson, J.C., Mazure, C.M., Bowers, M.B. & Jatlow, P.I. (1991). A preliminary, open study of the combination of fluoxetine and desipramine for rapid treatment of major depression. *Archives of General Psychiatry*, **48**, 303–307.

Nelson, W.M., Politano, P.M., Finch, A.J., et al (1987). Children's Depression Inventory. *Journal of the American Academy of Child Psychiatry*, **26**, 43–48.

Nolen-Hoeksema, S., Girgus, J.S. & Seligman, M.E.P. (1992). Predictors and consequences of childhood depressive symptoms: a 5-year longitudinal study. *Journal of Abnormal Psychology*, **101**, 405–422.

Nottelman, E.D., Susman, E.J., Inoff-Germain, G., Cutler, G., Loriaux, D.L. & Chrousos, G.P. (1987). Developmental processes in early adolescence: relations between adolescent adjustment problems and chronological age, pubertal stage, and puberty-related serum hormone levels. *Journal of Pediatrics*, **110**, 473–480.

Nurcombe, B., Seifer, R., Scioli, A., Tramontana, M.G., Grapentine, W.L. & Beauchesne, H.C. (1989). Is major depressive disorder in adolescence a distinct diagnostic entity? *Journal of the American Academy of Child Psychiatry*, **28**, 333–342.

Oates, R.K., Forrest, D. & Peacock, A. (1985). Self-esteem of abused children. *Child Abuse and Neglect*, **9**, 159–163.

Office of Population Census and Surveys (1990). *1990 Mortality Statistics—Cause, England and Wales*, series DH2, no. 17, London: HMSO.

Orvaschel, H. (1989). Diagnostic interviews for children and adolescents. In C.G. Last & M. Hersen (eds), *Handbook of Child Psychiatric Diagnosis*. New York: John Wiley, pp. 483–495.

Orvaschel, H., Weissman. M.M., Padian, N. & Lowe, T. (1981). Assessing psychopathology in children of psychiatrically disturbed parents: a pilot study. *Journal of the American Academy of Child Psychiatry*, **20**, 112–122.

Orvaschel, H., Puig-Antich, J., Chambers, W., Tabrizi, M.A. & Johnson, R. (1982). Retrospective assessment of child psychopathology with the Kiddie-SADS-E. *Journal of the American Academy of Child Psychiatry*, **21**, 392–397.

Oster, G.D. & Caro, J.E. (1990). *Understanding and Treating Depressed Adolescents and their Families*. New York: John Wiley.

Overall, J.E., Hollister, L.E., Johnson, M. & Pennington, V. (1966). Nosology of depression and differential response to drugs. *Journal of the American Medical Association*, **195**, 946–950.

Parker, G. (1992). Early environment. In E.S. Paykel (ed.), *Handbook of Affective Disorders*, 2nd edn. Edinburgh: Churchill Livingstone, pp. 171–183.

Patterson, G.R. & Capaldi, D.M. (1990). A mediational model for boys' depressed mood. In J. Rolf, A.S. Masten, D. Cicchetti, K.H. Nuechterlein & S. Weintraub (ed.), *Risk and Protective Factors in the Development of Psychopathology*. Cambridge: Cambridge University Press, pp. 141–163.

Paul, S.M., Axelrod, J., Saaveda, J.M. & Skolnick, P. (1979). Estrogen-induced afflux of endogenous catecholamines from the hypothalamus in vitro. *Brain Research*, **178**, 479–505.

Paykel, E.S. (1971). Classification of depressed patients: a cluster analysis derived grouping. *British Journal of Psychiatry*, **118**, 275–288.

Paykel, E.S. (1974). Recent life events and clinical depression. In E.K. Gunderson & R.H. Rahe (eds), *Life Stress and Psychiatric Illness*. Springfield, Ill.: Charles Thomas, pp. 134–163.

Paykel, E.S. (1978). Contribution of life events to causation of psychiatric illness. *Psychological Medicine*, **8**, 245–253.

Paykel, E.S. (1982). Life events and early environment. In E.S. Paykel (ed.), *Handbook of Affective Disorders*. Edinburgh: Churchill Livingstone, pp. 146–161.

Paykel, E.S. (1986). Recent advances in the treatment of depression. In J.F.W. Deakin (ed.), *The Biology of Depression*. London: Royal College of Psychiatrists, pp. 153–173.

Paykel, E.S. (1989). Treatment of depression: the relevance of research for clinical practice. *British Journal of Psychiatry*, **155**, 754–763.

Paykel, E.S., Myers, J.K., Dienelt, M.N., Klerman, G.L., Lindenthal, J.J. & Pepper, M.P. (1969). Life events and depression: a controlled study. *Archives of General Psychiatry*, **21**, 753–760.

Paykel, E.S. & Cooper, Z. (1992). Life events and social stress. In E.S. Paykel (ed.), *Handbook of Affective Disorders*, 2nd edn. Edinburgh: Churchill Livingstone, pp. 149–170.

Paykel, E.S., Priest, R.G., on behalf of conference participants (1992). Recognition and management of depression in general practice: consensus statement. *British Medical Journal*, **305**, 1198–1202.

Pearce, J.B. (1974). *Childhood Depression*, MPhil thesis: University of London.

Pearce, J.B. (1978). The recognition of depressive disorder in children. *Journal of the Royal Society of Medicine*, **71**, 494–500.

Perris, C. (1982). The distinction between bipolar and unipolar affective disorders. In E.S. Paykel (ed.), *Handbook of Affective Disorders.* Edinburgh: Churchill Livingstone, pp. 45–58.

Petti, T.A. (1978). Depression in hospitalized child psychiatry patients: approaches to measuring depression. *Journal of the American Academy of Child Psychiatry*, **22**, 11–21.

Petti, T.A. (1983). Imipramine in the treatment of depressed children. In D.P. Cantwell & G.A. Carlson (eds.), *Affective Disorders in Childhood and Adolescence: an Update.* Lancaster: MTP Press, pp. 375–415.

Petty, L.K., Asarnow, J.R., Carlson, G.A., et al (1985). The dexamethasone suppression test in depressed, dysthymic and nondepressed children. *American Journal of Psychiatry*, **142**, 631–633.

Pfeffer, C., Klerman, G.L., Hunt, S.W., Lesser, M., Peskin, J.R. & Siefker, C.A. (1991). Suicidal children grown up: demographic and clinical risk factors for adolescent suicidal attempts. *Journal of the American Academy of Child Psychiatry*, **30**, 609–616.

Pfeffer, C.R. (1992). Relationship between depression and suicidal behaviour. In M. Shafii & S.L. Shafii (eds), *Clinical Guide to Depression in Children and Adolescents.* Washington: American Psychiatric Press, pp. 115–126.

Pfefferbaum, B., Pack, R. & van Eys, J. (1989). Monoamine oxidase inhibitor toxicity. *Journal of the American Academy of Child Psychiatry*, **28**, 954–955.

Pinneau, S.R. (1955). The infantile disorders of hospitalism and anaclitic depression. *Psychological Bulletin*, **52**, 429–452.

Pippard, J. & Ellam, L. (1981). *Electroconvulsive Therapy in Great Britain.* London: Gaskell.

Pope, H.G., McElroy, S.L., Keck, P.E. & Hudson, J.I. (1991). Valproate in the treatment of acute mania: a placebo-controlled study. *Archives of General Psychiatry*, **48**, 62–68.

Poznanski, E.O., Kraheneuhl, V. & Zrull, J.P. (1976). Childhood depression—a longitudinal perspective. *Journal of the American Academy of Child Psychiatry*, **15**, 491–501.

Poznanski, E.O., Cook, S.C. & Carroll, B.J. (1979). A depression rating scale for children. *Pediatrics*, **64**, 442–450.

Poznanski, E.O., Carroll, B.J., Banegas, M.C., Cook, S.C. & Grossman, G.A. (1982). The dexamethasone suppression test in prepubertal depressed children. *American Journal of Psychiatry,* **193**, 321–324.

Poznanski, E.O., Grossman, J.A., Buchsbaum, Y., Banegas, M., Freeman, L. & Gibbons, R. (1984). Preliminary studies of the reliability and validity of the Children's Depression Rating Scale. *Journal of the American Academy of Child Psychiatry*, **23**, 191–197.

Prendergast, M. (1992). Drug treatment. *Archives of Disease in Childhood*, **67**, 1488–1494.

Preskorn, S.H., Weller, E.B. & Weller, R.A. (1982). Depression in children: relationship between plasma imipramine levels and response. *Journal of Clinical Psychiatry*, **43**, 450–453.

Preskorn, S.H., Weller, E.B., Hughes, C.W., Weller, R.A. & Bolte, K. (1987). Depression in prepubertal children: dexamethasone nonsuppression predicts differential response to imipramine vs. placebo. *Psychopharmacology Bulletin*, **23**, 128–133.

Prien, R.F. (1992). Maintenance treatment. In E.S. Paykel (ed.), *Handbook of Affective Disorders,* 2nd edn. Edinburgh: Churchill Livingstone, pp. 419–435.

Prien, R.F., Caffey, F.M. & Klctt, C.J. (1972). A comparison of lithium carbonate and chlorpromazine in the treatment of acute mania. *Archives of General Psychiatry*, **26**, 146–153.

Prien, R.F., Caffey, F.M. & Klett, C.J. (1974). Factors associated with treatment success in lithium prophylaxis. *Archives of General Psychiatry*, **31**, 189–192.

Prien, R.F. & Gelenberg, A.J. (1989). Alternatives to lithium for preventive treatment of bipolar disorder. *American Journal of Psychiatry*, **146**, 840–848.

Prien, R.F. & Potter, W.Z. (1990). NIMH workshop report on treatment of bipolar disorder. *Psychopharmacology Bulletin*, **26**, 409–427.

Prior, M. (1992). Childhood temperament. *Journal of Child Psychology and Psychiatry*, **33**, 249–279.

Puckering, C. (1989). Maternal depression. *Journal of Child Psychology and Psychiatry*, **30**, 807–817.

Puig-Antich, J. (1982). Major depression and conduct disorder in prepuberty. *Journal of the American Academy of Child Psychiatry*, **21**, 118–128.

Puig-Antich, J. (1986). Psychobiological markers: effects of age and puberty. In M. Rutter, C.E. Izard & P.B. Reads (eds), *Depression in Young People: Developmental and Clinical Perspectives*. New York: Guilford Press, pp. 341–382.

Puig-Antich, J. & Chambers, W. (1978). The Schedule for Affective Disorders and Schizophrenia for school-aged children. Unpublished interview schedule, New York State Psychiatric Institute.

Puig-Antich, J., Blau, S., Marx, N., Greenhill, L.L. & Chambers, W. (1978). Prepubertal major depressive disorder: a pilot study. *Journal of the American Academy of Child Psychiatry*, **17**, 695–707.

Puig-Antich, J., Tabrizi, M.A., Davies, M., Chambers, W., Halpern, F. & Sachar, E.J. (1981). Prepubertal endogenous major depressives hyposecrete growth hormone in response to insulin-induced hypoglycaemia. *Journal of Biological Psychiatry*, **16**, 801–818.

Puig-Antich, J. & Gittelman, R. (1982). Depression in childhood and adolescence. In E.S. Paykel (ed.), *Handbook of Affective Disorders*. Edinburgh: Churchill Livingstone, pp. 379–392.

Puig-Antich, J., Goetz, R., Hanlon, C., Tabrizi, M.A. & Weitzman, E. (1982). Sleep architecture and REM sleep measures in prepubertal major depressives during an episode. *Archives of General Psychiatry*, **39**, 932–939.

Puig-Antich, J., Chambers, W.J. & Tabrizi, M.A. (1983a). The clinical assessment of current depressive episodes in children and adolescents: interviews with parents and children. In D.P. Cantwell & G.A. Carlson (eds), *Affective Disorders in Childhood and Adolescence*. Lancaster: MTP Press, pp. 157–180.

Puig-Antich, J., Goetz, R., Hanlon, C., Tabrizi, M.A., Davies, M. & Weitzman, E. (1983b). Sleep architecture and REM sleep measures in prepubertal major depressives: studies during recovery from a major depressive episode in a drug free state. *Archives of General Psychiatry*, **40**, 187–192.

Puig-Antich, J., Novacenko, H., Tabrizi, M.A., Ambrosini, P., Goetz, R., Bianca, J. & Sachar, E.J. (1984a). Growth hormone secretion in prepubertal major depressive children. III: Response to insulin induced hypoglycemia in a drug-free, fully recovered clinical state. *Archives of General Psychiatry*, **41**, 471–475.

Puig-Antich, J., Goetz, R., Davies, M., Fein, M., Hanlon, C., Chambers, W.J., Tabrizi, M.A., Sachar, E.J. & Weitzman, E.D. (1984b). Growth hormone secretion in prepubertal major depressive children. II: Sleep related plasma concentration during a depressive episode. *Archives of General Psychiatry*, **41**, 463–466.

Puig-Antich, J., Lukens, E., Davies, M., Goetz, D., Brennan-Quattrock, J. & Todak, G. (1985a). Psychosocial functioning in prepubertal major depressive disorders. I: Interpersonal relationships during the depressive episode. *Archives of General Psychiatry*, **42**, 500–507.

Puig-Antich, J., Lukens, E., Davies, M., Goetz, D., Brennan-Quattrock, J. & Todak, G. (1985b). Psychosocial functioning in prepubertal major depressive disorders. II: Interpersonal relationships after sustained recovery from affective episode. *Archives of General Psychiatry*, **42**, 511–517.

Puig-Antich, J. & Rabinovich, H. (1986). Relationship between affective and anxiety disorders in childhood. In R. Gittelman (ed.), *Anxiety Disorders of Childhood*. New York: Guilford Press, pp. 136–156.

Puig-Antich, J., Perel, J.M., Lupatkin, W., Chambers, W.J., Tabrizi, M.A., King, J., Goetz, R., Davies, M. & Stiller, R.L. (1987). Imipramine in prepubertal major depressive disorders. *Archives of General Psychiatry*, **44**, 81–89.

Puig-Antich, J., Goetz, D., Davies, M., Kaplan, T., Davies, S., Ostrow, L., Asnis, L., Twomey, J., Iyengar, S. & Ryan, N.D. (1989). A controlled family history study of prepubertal major depressive disorder. *Archives of General Psychiatry*, **46**, 406–418.

Quay, H.C. (1979). Classification. In H.C. Quay & J.S. Werry (eds), *Psychopathological Disorders of Childhood*, 2nd edn. New York: John Wiley, pp. 1–42.

Quay, H.C. & Peterson, D.R. (1987). *Manual for the Revised Behaviour Problem Checklist.* Miami: Authors.

Quinton, D., Rutter, M. & Liddle, C. (1984). Institutional rearing, parenting difficulties and marital support. *Psychological Medicine*, **14**, 107–124.

Quinton, D. & Rutter, M. (1985). Family pathology and child psychiatric disorder: a four year prospective study. In A.R. Nicol (ed.), *Longitudinal Studies in Child Psychology and Psychiatry.* Chichester: John Wiley.

Quinton, D., Rutter, M. & Gulliver, L. (1990). Continuities in psychiatric disorders from childhood to adulthood in the children of psychiatric patients. In L.N. Robins & M. Rutter (ed.), *Straight and Devious Pathways from Childhood to Adulthood.* Cambridge: Cambridge University Press, pp. 259–278.

Quitkin, F.M., Kane, J., Rifkin, A., Ramos-Lorenzi, J.R., Saraf, K., Howard, A. & Klein, D.F. (1981). Prophylactic lithium with and without imipramine for bipolar I patients. *Archives of General Psychiatry*, **38**, 902–907.

Quitkin, F.M., Harrison, W., Stewart, J.W., McGrath, P.J., Tricamo, E., Ocepek-Welikson, K., Rabkin, J.G., Wager, S.G. Nunes, E. & Klein, D.F. (1991). Response to phenelzine and imipramine in placebo nonresponders with atypical depression: a new application of the crossover design. *Archives of General Psychiatry*, **48**, 319–323.

Radloff, L.S. (1977). A CES-D scale: a self-report depression scale for research in the general population. *Applied Psychological Measurement*, **1**, 385–401.

Radke-Yarrow, M., Cummings, E.S., Kuczynski, L. & Chapman, M. (1985). Patterns of attachmemt in two- and three-year olds in normal families and families with parental depression. *Child Development*, **56**, 884–893.

Radke-Yarrow, M. & Sherman, T. (1990). Hard growing: children who survive. In J. Rolf, A. Masten, D. Cicchetti, K. Nuechterlein & S. Weintraub (eds), *Relationships Within Families: Mutual Influences.* Cambridge: Cambridge University Press.

Radke-Yarrow, M., Nottelmann, E., Martinez, P., Fox, M.B. & Belmont, B. (1992). Young children of affectively ill parents: a longitudinal study of psychosocial development. *Journal of the American Academy of Child Psychiatry*, **31**, 68–77.

Raja, S.N., Feehan, M., Stanton, W.R. & McGee, R. (1992). Prevalence and correlates of the premenstrual syndrome in adolescence. *Journal of the American Academy of Child Psychiatry*, **31**, 783–789.

Rapoport, J.L., Buchsbaum, M.S., Weingartner, H., Zahn, T., Ludlow, C. & Mikkelsen, E. (1980). Dextro-amphetamine: its cognitive and behavioral effects in hyperactive boys and normal men. *Archives of General Psychiatry*, **37**, 933–943.

Registrar General for England and Wales (1961). *Statistical Reviews: Part III*. London: HMSO, pp. 240–266.

Rehm, L.P. (1977). A self-control model of depression. *Behaviour Therapy*, **8**, 787–804.

Reich, W., Herjanic, B., Welner, Z. & Gandhy, P.R. (1982). Development of a structured psychiatric interview for children: agreement on diagnosis comparing child and parent interviews. *Journal of Abnormal Child Psychology*, **20**, 325–336.

Reich, W. & Earls, F. (1987). Rules for making psychiatric diagnoses in children on the basis of multiple sources of information: preliminary strategies. *Journal of Abnormal Child Psychology*, **15**, 601–616.

Reid, J.B., Baldwin, D.V., Patterson, G.R. & Dishion, T.J. (1988). Observations in the assessment of childhood disorders. In M. Rutter, A.H. Tuma & I.S. Lann (eds), *Assessment and Diagnosis in Child Psychopathology*. New York: Guilford, pp. 156–195.

Reinherz, H.Z., Stewart-Berghauer, G., Pakiz, B., Frost, A.K., Moeykens, B.A. & Holmes, W.M. (1989). The relationship of early risk and current mediators to depressive symptomatology in adolescence. *Journal of the American Academy of Child Psychiatry*, **28**, 942–947.

Rey, J.M. & Morris-Yates, A. (1991). Adolescent depression and the Child Behaviour Checklist. *Journal of the American Academy of Child Psychiatry*, **30**, 423–427.

Reynolds, W.M. (1987). *Reynolds Adolescent Depression Scale*. Odessa, FI: Psychological Assessment Resource Inc.

Reynolds, W.M. (1989). Suicidal ideation and depression in adolescents: assessment and research. In P. Lovibond and P. Wilson (eds), *Clinical and Abnormal Psychology*. Amsterdam: Elsevier Science Publishers, pp. 125–135.

Reynolds, W.M. (1990). Development of a semistructural clinical interview for suicidal behaviors in adolescents. *Psychological Assessment: A Journal of Consulting and Clinical Psychology*, **2**, 382–390.

Reynolds, W.M. (1991). Psychological interventions for depression in children and adolescents. In G. Stoner, M.R. Shinn & H.M. Walker (eds), *Interventions for Achievement and Behaviour Problems*. Washington, DC: National Association of School Psychologists, pp. 649–683.

Reynolds, W.M., Anderson, G. & Bartell, N. (1985). Measuring depression in children: a multimethod assessment investigation. *Journal of Abnormal Child Psychology*, **13**, 513–526.

Reynolds, W.M. & Coats, K.I. (1986). A comparison of cognitive–behavioural therapy and relaxation training for the treatment of depression in adolescents. *Journal of Consulting and Clinical Psychology*, **54**, 653–660.

Reynolds, W.M & Stark, K.D. (1987). School-based intervention strategies for the treatment of depression in children and adolescents. In S.G. Forman (ed.), *School-Based Affective and Social Intervention*. New York: Haworth Press, pp. 69–88.

Rholes, W.S., Blackwell, J., Jordan, C. & Walters, C. (1980). A developmental study of learned helplessness. *Developmental Psychology*, **16**, 616–624.

Richman, N. & Graham, P. (1971). A behavioural screening questionnaire for use with three-year-old children: preliminary findings. *Journal of Child Psychology and Psychiatry*, **12**, 5–33.

Richman, N., Stevenson, J. & Graham, P. (1975). Prevalence of behaviour problems in three-year-old children: an epidemiologic study in a London borough. *Journal of Child Psychology and Psychiatry*, **16**, 277–287.

Riddle, M.A., Brown, N., Dzubinski, D., Jetmalani, A.N., Law, Y. & Woolston, J.L. (1989). Fluoxetine overdose in an adolescent. *Journal of the American Academy of Child Psychiatry*, **28**, 587–588.

Riddle, M.A., Hardin, M.T., King, R., Scahill, L., Woolston, J.L. (1990). Fluoxetine treatment of children and adolescents with Tourette's and obsessive–compulsive disorders: preliminary clinical experience. *Journal of the American Academy of Child Psychiatry*, **29**, 45–48.

Riddle, M.A., Nelson, J.C., Kleinman, C.S., Rasmusson, A., Leckman, J.F., King, R.A. & Cohen, D.J. (1991). Sudden death in children receiving norpramin: a review of three reported cases and commentary. *Journal of the American Academy of Child Psychiatry*, **29**, 45–48.

Rie, H.E. (1966). Depression in childhood: a survey of some pertinent contributions. *Journal of the American Academy of Child Psychiatry*, **5**, 653–685.

Robbins, D.R., Allessi, N.E. & Colfer, M.V. (1989). Treatment of adolescents with major depression: implications of the DST and the melancholic clinical subtype. *Journal of Affective Disorders*, **17**, 99–104.

Roberts, R.E., Lewinsohn, P.M. & Seeley, J.R. (1991). Screening for adolescent depression: a comparison of depression scales. *Journal of the American Academy of Child Psychiatry*, **30**, 58–66.

Robins, C.J. & Hinkley, K. (1989). Social–cognitive processing and depressive symptoms in children: a comparison of measures. *Journal of Abnormal Child Psychology*, **17**, 29–36.

Robins, E., Murphy, G.E., Wilkinson, R.H., Gassner, S. & Kayes, J. (1959). Some clinical considerations in the prevention of suicide based on a study of 134 successful suicides. *American Journal of Public Health*, **49**, 888–889.

Robins, E. & Guze, S.B. (1970). Establishment of diagnostic validity in psychiatric illness: its application to schizophrenia. *American Journal of Psychiatry*, **126**, 107–111.

Robins, L.N. (1966). *Deviant Children Grown Up*. Baltimore: Williams & Williams.

Robins, L.N. (1991). Conduct disorder. *Journal of Child Psychology and Psychiatry*, **32**, 193–212.

Robins, L.N., Helzer, J.E., Crougan, J. & Ratcliff, K.S. (1981). National Institute of Mental Health Diagnostic Interview Schedule. *Archives of General Psychiatry*, **38**, 381–389.

Robins, L.N., Helzer, J.E., Weissman, M.M., Orvaschel, H., Gruenberg, E., Burke, J.D. & Regier, D.A. (1984). Lifetime prevalence of specific psychiatric disorders in three sites. *Archives of General Psychiatry*, **41**, 949–958.

Robins, L.N. & McEvoy, L. (1990). Conduct problems as predictors of substance abuse. In L. Robins & M. Rutter (eds), *Straight and Devious Pathways from Childhood to Adulthood*. Cambridge: Cambridge University Press, pp. 182–204.

Rochlin, G. (1959). The loss complex. *Journal of the American Psychoanalytic Association*, **7**, 299–316.

Rodgers, B. (1990). Influences of early-life and recent factors on affective disorder in women: an exploration of vulnerability models. In L.N. Robins, & M. Rutter (eds), *Straight and Devious Pathways from Childhood to Adulthood*. Cambridge: Cambridge University Press, pp. 314–327.

Rogeness, G.A., Javors, M.A., Maas, J.W. & Macedo, C.A. (1990). Catecholamines and diagnosis in children. *Journal of the American Academy of Child Psychiatry*, **29**, 234–241.

Rogeness, G.H., Javors, M.A. & Pliszka, S.R. (1992). Neurochemistry and child and adolescent psychiatry. *Journal of the American Academy of Child Psychiatry*, **31**, 765–781.

Rohde, P., Lewinsohn, P.M. & Seeley, J.R. (1991). Comorbidity of unipolar depression. II: Comorbidity with other mental disorders in adolescents and adults. *Journal of Abnormal Psychology*, **100**, 214–222.

Rothenberg, A. (1988). Differential diagnosis of anorexia nervosa and depressive illness: a review of 11 studies. *Comprehensive Psychiatry*, **29**, 427–432.

Rotundo, N. & Hensley, V.R. (1985). The Children's Depression Scale. *Journal of Child Psychology and Psychiatry*, **26**, 917–927.

Rubin, R.T. (1990). Mood changes during adolescence. In J. Bancroft & J. Reinisch (eds), *Adolescence and Puberty*. Oxford: Oxford University Press.

Rutter, M. (1966). *Children of Sick Parents: An Environmental and Psychiatric Study*. London: Oxford University Press.

Rutter, M. (1971). Parent–child separation: psychological effects on the children. *Journal of Child Psychology and Psychiatry*, **12**, 233–260.

Rutter, M. (1980). *Changing Youth in a Changing Society: Patterns of Adolescent Development and Disorder*. Cambridge: MA: Harvard University Press.

Rutter, M. (1982). Epidemiological–longitudinal approaches to the study of development. In W.A. Collins (ed.), *The Concept of Development* (Minnesota Symposia on Child Psychology, vol. 15). New Jersey: Erlbaum, pp. 105–144.

Rutter, M. (1986a). The developmental psychopathology of depression: issues and perspectives. In M. Rutter, C.E. Izard & P.B. Read (eds), *Depression in Young People: Developmental and Clinical Perspectives*. New York: Guilford, pp. 3–30.

Rutter, M. (1986b). Depressive feelings, cognitions, and disorders: a research postscript. In M. Rutter, C.E. Izard & P.B. Read (eds), *Depression in Young People: Developmental and Clinical Perspectives*. New York: Guilford, pp. 491–519.

Rutter, M. (1988a). Depressive disorders. In M. Rutter, A.H. Tuma & I.S. Lann (eds), *Assessment and Diagnosis in Child Psychopathology*. New York: Guilford, pp. 347–376.

Rutter, M. (1988b). Epidemiological approaches to developmental psychopathology. *Archives of General Psychiatry*, **45**, 486–495.,

Rutter, M. (1989). Isle of Wight revisited: twenty-five years of child psychiatric epidemiology. *Journal of the American Academy of Child Psychiatry*, **28**, 633–653.

Rutter, M. (1991). Age changes in depressive disorders: some developmental considerations. In J. Garber & K.A. Dodge (eds), *The Development of Emotion Regulation and Dysregulation*. Cambridge: Cambridge University Press, pp. 273–300.

Rutter, M., Tizard, J. & Whitmore, K. (1970). *Education, Health and Behaviour*. London: Longman.

Rutter, M., Graham, P., Chadwick, O.F. & Yule, W. (1976). Adolescent turmoil: fact or fiction? *Journal of Child Psychology and Psychiatry*, **17**, 35–56.

Rutter, M. & Quinton, D. (1984). Parental psychiatric disorder: effects on children. *Psychological Medicine*, **14**, 853–880.

Rutter, M., Macdonald, M., Le Couteur, A., Harrington, R.C., Bolton, P. & Bailey, A. (1990a). Genetic factors in child psychiatric disorders. II: Empirical findings. *Journal of Child Psychology and Psychiatry*, **31**, 39–83.

Rutter, M., Bolton, P. Harrington, R.C., Le Couteur, A., Macdonald, H. & Simonoff, E. (1990b). Genetic factors in psychiatric disorders. I: A review of research strategies. *Journal of Child Psychology and Psychiatry*, **31**, 3–37.

Rutter, M. & Sandberg, S. (1992). Psychosocial stressors: concepts, causes and effects. *European Child and Adolescent Psychiatry*, **1**, 3–13.

Ryan, N.D. (1990). Pharmacotherapy of adolescent major depression: beyond TCAs. *Psychopharmacology Bulletin*, **26**, 75–79.

Ryan, N.D., Puig-Antich, J., Cooper, T., Rabinovich, H., Ambrosini, P., Davies, M., King, J., Torres, D. & Fried, J. (1986). Imipramine in adolescent major depression: plasma level and clinical response. *Acta Psychiatrica Scandinavica*, **73**, 275–288.

Ryan, N.D., Puig-Antich, J., Ambrosini, P., Rabinovich, H., Robinson, D., Nelson, B., Iyengar, S. & Twomey, J. (1987). The clinical picture of major depression in children and adolescents. *Archives of General Psychiatry*, **44**, 854–861.

Ryan, N.D., Meyer, V., Dachille, S., Mazzie, D. & Puig-Antich, J. (1988). Lithium antidepressant augmentation in TCA-refractory depression in adolescents. *Journal of the American Academy of Child Psychiatry*, **27**, 371–376.

Ryan, N.D., Williamson, D.E., Iyengar, S., Orvaschel, H., Reich, T., Dahl, R.E. & Puig-Antich, J. (1992). A secular increase in child and adolescent onset affective disorder. *Journal of the American Academy of Child Psychiatry*, **31**, 600–605.

Sachar, E., Hellman, L. & Roffwarg, H. (1973). Disrupted 24-hour patterns of cortisol secretion in psychotic depression. *Archives of General Psychiatry*, **28**, 19–24.

Sandberg, S., Rutter, M., Champion, L., Drinnan, D., Giles, S., McGuinness, D., Nicholls, J., Owen, A. & Prior, V. (1992). Assessment of psychosocial experiences in childhood: methodological issues and some illustrative findings. Submitted for publication.

Scarr, S. (1992). Developmental theories for the 1990s: development and individual differences. *Child Development*, **63**, 1–19.

Schildkraut, J.J. (1965). The catecholamine hypothesis of affective disorders; a review of supporting evidence. *American Journal of Psychiatry*, **112**, 509–522.

Schoenbach, V.J., Kaplan, B.H., Grimson, R.C. & Wagner, E.H. (1982). Use of a symptom scale to study the prevalence of a depressive syndrome in young adolescents. *American Journal of Epidemiology*, **116**, 791–800.

Schwartz, C.E., Dorer, D.J., Beardslee, W.R., Lavori, P.W. & Keller, M.B. (1990). Maternal expressed emotion and parental affective disorder: risk for childhood depressive disorder, substance abuse, or conduct disorder. *Journal of Psychiatry Research*, **24**, 231–250.

Scott, A.I.F. (1989). Which depressed patients will respond to electroconvulsive therapy? The search for biological predictors of recovery. *British Journal of Psychiatry*, **154**, 8–17.

Seligman, M.E.P. (1975). *Helplessness: On Depression, Development and Death*. San Francisco: Freeman.

Seligman, M.E.P. & Peterson, C. (1986). A learned helplessness perspective on childhood depression: theory and research. In M. Rutter, C.E. Izard & P.B. Read (eds), *Depression in Young People: Developmental and Clinical Perspectives*. New York: Guilford, pp. 223–250.

Shaffer, D. (1974). Suicide in childhood and early adolescence. *Journal of Child Psychology and Psychiatry*, **15**, 275–291.

Shaffer, D. (1985). Depression, mania and suicidal acts. In M. Rutter and L. Hersov (eds), *Child and Adolescent Psychiatry: Modern Approaches*. Oxford: Blackwell Scientific, pp. 698–719.

Shaffer, D. (1986). Developmental factors in child and adolescent suicide. In M. Rutter, C.E. Izard & P.B. Read (eds), *Depression in Young People: Developmental and Clinical Perspectives*. New York: Guilford Press, pp. 383–398.

Shaffer, D. (1988). The epidemiology of teen suicide: an examination of risk factors. *Journal of Clinical Psychiatry*, **9** (suppl.), 36–41.

Shaffer, D., Gould, M.S., Brasic, J., Ambrosini, P., Fisher, P., Bird, H. & Aluwahlia, S. (1983). A children's Global Assessment Scale (C-GAS). *Archives of General Psychiatry*, **40**, 1228–1231.

Shaffer, D., Campbell, M., Cantwell, D., Bradley, S., Carlson, G., Cohen, D., Denckla, M., Frances, A., Garfinkel, B., Klein, R., Pincus, H., Spitzer, R.L., Volkmar, F. & Widiger, T. (1989). Child and adolescent disorders in DSM-IV: issues facing the working party. *Journal of the American Academy of Child Psychiatry*, **28**, 830–835.

Shaffer, D., Garland, A., Vieland, V., Underwood, M. & Busner, C. (1991). The impact of curriculum-based suicide prevention programs for teachers. *Journal of the American Academy of Child Psychiatry*, **30**, 588–596.

Shain, B.N., King, C.A., Naylor, M. & Alessi, N. (1991). Chronic depression and hospital course in adolescents. *Journal of the American Academy of Child Psychiatry*, **30**, 428–433.

Shepherd, M., Oppenheim, B. & Mitchell, S. (1971). *Childhood Behaviour and Mental Health*. London: University of London Press.

Sherwin, B.B. (1991). Estrogen and refractory depression. In J. Amsterdam (ed.), *Advances in Neuropsychiatry and Psychopharmacology. Vol. 2: Refractory Depression*. New York: Raven Press, pp. 209–218.

Shrout, P.E., Skodel, A.E. & Dohrenwend, B.P. (1986). A multi-method approach for case identification: first stage instruments. In J.E. Barrett & R.M. Rose (eds), *Mental Disorders in the Community: Progress and Challenge*. New York: Guilford Press, pp. 286–303.

Siegel, K., Mesagno, F.P. & Christ, G. (1990). A prevention program for bereaved children. *American Journal of Orthopsychiatry*, **60**, 168–175.

Siever, L.J. & Davis, K.L. (1985). Overview: toward a dysregulation hypothesis of depression. *American Journal of Psychiatry*, **142**, 1017–1031.

Simeon, J.G., Dinicola, V.F., Ferguson, H.B. & Copping, W. (1990). Adolescent depression: a placebo-controlled fluoxetine treatment study and follow-up. *Progress in Neuro-Psychopharmacological Biological Psychiatry*, **14**, 791–795.

Sirles, E.A., Smith, J.A. & Kusama, H. (1989). Psychiatric status of intrafamilial child sexual abuse victims. *Journal of the American Academy of Child Psychiatry*, **28**, 225–229.

Small, J.G., Klapper, M.H., Milstein, V., Kellams, J.J., Miller, M.J., Marhenks, J.D. & Small, I.F. (1991). Carbamazepine compared with lithium in the treatment of mania. *Archives of General Psychiatry*, **48**, 915–921.

Smucker, M.R., Craighead, W.E., Craighead, L.W. & Green, B.J. (1986). Normative and reliability data for the Children's Depression Inventory. *Journal of Abnormal Child Psychology*, **14**, 25–40.

Sokoloff, R.M. & Lubin, B. (1983). Depressive mood in adolescent, emotionally disturbed females: reliability and validity of an adjective checklist (C-DACL). *Journal of Abnormal Child Psychology*, **11**, 531–536.

Spitz, R. (1946). Anaclitic depression. *Psychoanalytic Study of the Child*, **2**, 313–342.

Spitz, R. & Wolf, K.M. (1946). Anaclitic depression: an inquiry into the genesis of early psychiatric conditions. *Psychoanalytic Study of the Child*, **2**, 313–342.

Spitzer, R.L., Endicott, J. & Robins, E. (1978). Research Diagnostic Criteria: rationale and reliability. *Archives of General Psychiatry*, **35**, 773–782.

Stark, K.D. (1990). *Childhood Depression: School-Based Intervention*. New York: Guilford.

Stark, K.D., Reynolds, W.M. & Kaslow, N. (1987) A comparison of the relative efficacy of self-control therapy and a behavioural problem-solving therapy for depression in children. *Journal of Abnormal Child Psychology*, **15**, 91–113.

Stark, K.D., Humphrey, L.L., Crook, K. & Lewis, K. (1990). Perceived family environments of depressed and anxious children: child's and maternal figure's perspectives. *Journal of Abnormal Child Psychology*, **18**, 527–547.

Stein, A., Gath, D.H., Bucher, J., Bond, A., Day, A. & Cooper, P.J. (1991). The relationship between post-natal depression and mother–child interaction. *British Journal of Psychiatry*, **158**, 46–52.

Stein, L. (1962). Effects and interactions of imipramine, chlorpromazine, reserpine and amphetamine on self-stimulation: possible neurophysiological basis of depression. In J. Wortis (ed.), *Recent Advances in Biological Psychiatry*. New York: Plenum, pp. 288–308.

Stoddard, F.J., Norman, D.K., Murphy, J.M. & Beardslee, W.R. (1989). Psychiatric outcome of burned children and adolescents. *Journal of the American Academy of Child Psychiatry*, **28**, 589–595.

Strauss, C.C., Last, C.G., Hersen, M. & Kazdin, A.E. (1988). Association between anxiety and depression in children and adolescents with anxiety disorders. *Journal of Abnormal Child Psychology*, **16**, 57–68.

Strober, M. (1992a). Relevance of early age-of-onset in genetic studies of bipolar affective disorder. *Journal of the American Academy of Child Psychiatry*, **31**, 606–610.

Strober, M. (1992b). The pharmacotherapy of depressive illness in adolescence. III: Diagnostic and conceptual issues in studies of tricyclic drugs. *Journal of Child and Adolescent Psychopharmacology*. In press.

Strober, M. & Carlson, G. (1982). Bipolar illness in adolescents with major depression: clinical, genetic and psychopharmacologic predictors in a three- to four-year prospective follow-up investigation. *Archives of General Psychiatry*, **39**, 549–555.

Strober, M. & Katz, J.L. (1987). Depression in the eating disorders: a review and analysis of descriptive, family, and biological findings. In D. Garner & P. Garfinkel (eds), *Diagnostic Issues in Eating Disorders*. New York: Brunner Mazel, pp. 80–111.

Strober, M., Morrell, W., Burroughs, J., Lampert, C., Danforth, H. & Freeman, R. (1988). A family study of bipolar I disorder in adolescence: early onset of symptoms linked to increased familial loading and lithium resistance. *Journal of Affective Disorders*, **15**, 255–268.

Strober, M., Hanna, G. & McCracken, J. (1989). Bipolar disorder. In C.G. Last & M. Hersen (eds), *Handbook of Child Psychiatric Diagnosis*. New York: John Wiley, pp. 299–316.

Strober, M., Freeman, R. & Rigali, J. (1990a). The pharmacotherapy of depressive illness in adolescence. I: An open label trial of imipramine. *Psychopharmacology Bulletin*, **26**, 80–84.

Strober, M., Morrell, W., Lampert, C. & Burroughs, J. (1990b). Relapse following discontinuation of lithium maintenance therapy in adolescents with bipolar I illness: a naturalistic study. *American Journal of Psychiatry*, **147**, 457–461.

Strober, M., Freeman, R., Rigali, J., Schmidt, S. & Diamond, R. (1992a). The pharmacotherapy of depressive illness in adolescence. II: Effects of lithium augmentation in nonresponders to imipramine. *Journal of the American Academy of Child Psychiatry*, **31**, 16–20.

Strober, M., Lampert, C., Schmidt, S. & Morrell, W. (1992b). The course of major depressive disorder in adolescents. I: Recovery and risk of manic switching in a 24-month prospective naturalistic follow-up of psychotic and nonpsychotic subtypes. *Journal of the American Academy of Child Psychiatry*. In press.

Swift, W.J., Andrews, D. & Barklage, N.E. (1986). The relationship between affective disorder and eating disorders: a review of the literature. *American Journal of Psychiatry*, **143**, 290–299.

Taylor, E. (1985). Drug treatment. In M. Rutter & L. Hersov (eds), *Child and Adolescent Psychiatry: Modern Approaches*. Oxford: Blackwell, pp. 780–793.

Tennant, C. & Bebbington, P. (1978). The social causation of depression: a critique of the work of Brown and his colleagues. *Psychological Medicine*, **8**, 565–575.

Tennant, C., Hurry, J. & Bebbington, P. (1982). The relation of childhood separation experiences to adult depression and anxiety states. *British Journal of Psychiatry*, **141**, 475–482.

Tennes, K. & Kreye, M. (1985). Adrenocortical responses to classroom activities and tests in elementary school children. *Psychosomatic Medicine*, **47**, 451–460.

Teri, L. (1982). The use of the Beck Depression Inventory with adolescents. *Journal of Abnormal Child Psychology*, **10**, 277–284.

Thomas, A. & Chess, S. (1982). Temperament and follow-up to adulthood. In R. Porter & G.M. Collins (eds), *Temperamental Differences in Infants and Young Children*. New York: NY University Press, pp. 168–175.

Thorley, G. (1987). Factor study of a psychiatric child rating scale: based on ratings made by clinicians on child and adolescent clinic attenders. *British Journal of Psychiatry*, **150**, 49–59.

Tingelstad, J.B. (1991). The cardiotoxicity of the tricyclics. *Journal of the American Academy of Child Psychiatry*, **30**, 845–846.

Tisher, M. & Lang, M. (1983). The Children's Depression Scale: review and further developments. In D.P. Cantwell & G.A. Carlson (eds), *Affective Disorders in Childhood and Adolescence*. Lancaster: MTP Press, pp. 81–203.

Trad, P.V. (1986). *Infant Depression*. New York: Springer-Verlag.

Treiber, F.A. & Mabe, P.A. (1987). Child and parent perceptions of children's psychopathology in psychiatric outpatient children. *Journal of Abnormal Child Psychology*, **15**, 115–124.

Tsuang, M.T., Winokur, G. & Crowe, R.R. (1980). Morbidity risks of schizophrenia and affective disorders among first degree relatives of patients with schizophrenia, mania, depression and surgical conditions. *British Journal of Psychiatry*, **137**, 497–504.

Tyrer, S.P., Barrett, M.L., Berney, T.P., Bhate, S., Watson, M.J., Fundudis, T. & Kolvin, I. (1991). The dexamethasone suppression test in children: lack of an association with diagnosis. *British Journal of Psychiatry*, **159**, (suppl. 11), 41–48.

Van Eerdewegh, M., Bieri, M., Parilla, R. & Clayton, P. (1982). The bereaved child. *British Journal of Psychiatry*, **140**, 23–29.

Velez, C.N., Johnson, J. & Cohen, P. (1989). A longitudinal analysis of selected risk factors for childhood psychopathology. *Journal of the American Academy of Child Psychiatry*, **28**, 861–864.

Walker, M., Moreau, D. & Weissman, M.M. (1990). Parents' awareness of children's suicidal attempts. *American Journal of Psychiatry*, **147**, 1364–1366.

Wallerstein, J.S. & Kelly, J.B. (1980). *Surviving the Breakup: How Children and Parents Cope with Divorce*. London: Grant McIntyre.

Warshaw, M.G., Klerman, G.L. & Lavori, P.W. (1991). Are secular trends in major depression an artifact of recall? *Journal of Psychiatric Research*, **25**, 141–151.

Waterman, G.S., Ryan, N.D., Puig-Antich, J., Meyer, V., Ambosini, P.J., Rabinovich, H., Stull, S., Novacenko, H., Williamson, D.E. & Nelson, B. (1991). Hormonal responses to dextroamphetamine in depressed and normal adolescents. *Journal of the American Academy of Child Psychiatry*, **30**, 415–422.

Weinberg, W.A., Rutman, J., Sullivan, L., Penick, E.C. & Dietz, S.G. (1973). Depression in children referred to an educational diagnostic center: diagnosis and treatment. *Journal of Pediatrics*, **83**, 1065–1072.

Weinberg, W. & Rehmet, A. (1983). Childhood affective disorder and school problems. In Cantwell, D.P. & Carlson, G.A. (eds), *Affective Disorders in Childhood and Adolescence: an Update*. Lancaster: MTP Press, pp. 109–128.

Weiner, R.D. & Coffey, C.E. (1991). Electroconvulsive therapy in the United States. *Psychopharmacology Bulletin*, **27**, 9–15.

Weinstein, S.R., Stone, K., Noam, G.G., Grimes, K. & Schwab-Stone, M. (1989). Comparison of DISC with clinicians' DSM-III diagnoses in psychiatric inpatients. *Journal of the American Academy of Child Psychiatry*, **28**, 53–60.

Weissman, M.M. & Paykel, E. (1974). *The Depressed Woman: A Study of Social Relations*. Chicago: University of Chicago Press.

Weissman, M.M. & Klerman, G.L. (1977). Sex differences and the epidemiology of depression. *Archives of General Psychiatry*, **34**, 98–111.

Weissman, M.M., Prusoff, B.A., DiMascio, A., et al (1979). The efficacy of drugs and psychotherapy in the treatment of acute depressive episodes. *American Journal of Psychiatry*, **136**, 555–558.

Weissman, M.M., Orvaschel, H. & Padium, N. (1980). Children's symptoms and social functioning self report scales: comparison of mothers' and children's reports. *Journal of Nervous and Mental Disease*, **168**, 736–740.

Weissman, M.M., Gershon, E.S., Kidd, K.K., Prusoff, B.A., Leckman, J.F., Dibble, E., Hamovit, J., Thompson, W.D., Pauls, D.L. & Guroff, J.J. (1984a). Psychiatric disorders in the relatives of probands with affective disorders: the Yale University–National Institute of Mental Health collaborative study. *Archives of General Psychiatry*, **41**, 13–21.

Weissman, M.M., Wickramaratne, P., Merikangas, K.R., Leckman, J.F., Prusoff, B.A., Caruso, K.A., Kidd, K.K. & Gammon, G.D. (1984b). Onset of major depression in early adulthood: increased familial loading and specificity. *Archives of General Psychiatry*, **41**, 1136–1143.

Weissman, M.M., Gammon, D., John, K., Merikangas, K.R., Warner, V., Prusoff, B.A. & Sholomskas, D. (1987). Children of depressed parents: increased psychopathology and early onset of major depression. *Archives of General Psychiatry*, **44**, 847–853.

Weissman, M.M., Warner, V., Wickramaratne, P. & Prusoff, B.A. (1988). Early-onset major depression in parents and their children. *Journal of Affective Disorders*, **15**, 269–277.

Weissman, M.M., Fendrich, M., Warner, V. & Wickramaratne, P. (1992). Incidence of psychiatric disorder in offspring at high and low risk for depression. *Journal of the American Academy of Child Psychiatry*, **31**, 640–648.

Weisz, J.R., Weiss, B., Wasserman, A.A. & Rintoul, B. (1987). Control related beliefs and depression among clinic-referred children and adolescents. *Journal of Abnormal Psychology*, **96**, 58–63.

Weisz, J.R., Stevens, J.S., Curry, J.F., Cohen, R., Craighead, W.E., Burlingame, W.V., Smith, A., Weiss, B. & Parmelee, D.X. (1989). Control-related cognitions and depression among inpatient children and adolescents. *Journal of the American Academy of Child Psychiatry*, **28**, 358–363.

Weller, E.B., Weller, R.A., Fristad, M.A., Preskorn, S.H. & Teare, M. (1985). The dexamethasone suppression test in prepubertal depressed children. *Journal of Clinical Psychiatry*, **46**, 511–513.

Weller, R.A., Weller, E.B., Fristad, M.A. & Bowes, J.M. (1991). Depression in recently bereaved prepubertal children. *American Journal of Psychiatry*, **148**, 1536–1540.

Wells, V.E., Klerman, G.L. & Deykin, E.Y. (1987). The prevalence of depressive symptoms in college students. *Social Psychiatry*, **22**, 20–28.

Welner, Z., Reich, W., Herjanic, B., Jung, K.G. & Amado, H. (1987). Reliability, validity, and parent–child agreement studies of the Diagnostic Interview for Children and adolescents (DICA). *Journal of the American Academy of Child Psychiatry*, **26**, 649–653.

Werry, J.S., McClellan, J.M. & Chard, L. (1991). Childhood and adolescent schizophrenic, bipolar, and schizoaffective disorders: a clinical and outcome study. *Journal of the American Academy of Child Psychiatry*, **30**, 457–465.

Werry, J.S. & McClellan, J.M. (1992). Predicting outcome in child and adolescent (early onset) schizophrenia and bipolar disorder. *Journal of the American Academy of Child Psychiatry*, **31**, 147–150.

Whitaker, A., Johnson, J., Shaffer, D., Rapoport, J.L., Kalikow, K., Walsh, B.T., Davies, M., Braiman, S. & Dolinsky, A. (1990). Uncommon troubles in young people: prevalence estimates of selected psychiatric disorders in a nonreferred adolescent population. *Archives of General Psychiatry*, **47**, 487–496.

Whitman, P.B. & Leitenberg, H. (1990). Negatively biased recall in children with self-reported symptoms of depression. *Journal of Abnormal Child Psychology*, **18**, 15–27.

Wierzbicki, M. (1987). A parent form of the Children's Depression Inventory: reliability and validity in non-clinical populations. *Journal of Clinical Psychology*, **43,** 390–397.

Wilde, E.J., Kienhorst, I.C.W.M., Diekstra, R.F.W. & Wolters, W.H.G. (1992). The relationship between adolescent suicidal behaviour and life events in childhood and adolescence. *American Journal of Psychiatry*, **149**, 45–51.

Williams, J.G., Barlow, D.H. & Agras, W.S. (1972). Behavioural measurement of severe depression. *Archives of General Psychiatry*, **27**, 330–333.

Williams, S., McGee, R., Anderson, J. & Silva, P.A. (1989). The structure and correlates of self-reported symptoms in 11-year-old children. *Journal of Abnormal Child Psychology*, **17**, 55–71.

Wilner, P. (1984). Cognitive functioning in depression: a review of theory and research. *Psychological Medicine*, **14**, 807–823.

Wilson, R. & Cairns, E. (1988). Sex-role attributes, perceived competence and the development of depression in adolescence. *Journal of Child Psychology and Psychiatry*, **29**, 635–650.

Wing, J.K., Cooper, J.E. & Sartorius, N. (1974). *Measurement and Classification of Psychiatric Symptoms.* London: Cambridge University Press.

Wing, J.K., Mann, S.A., Leff, J.P. & Nixon, J.M. (1978). The concept of a "case" in psychiatric population surveys. *Psychological Medicine*, **8**, 203–217.

Winokur, G., Clayton, P.J. & Reich, T. (1969). *Manic Depressive Illness.* St Louis: Mosby.

Winokur, G. (1979). Unipolar depression: is it divisable into autonomous subtypes? *Archives of General Psychiatry*, **36**, 47–51.

Wolkind, S. & Rutter, M. (1985). Separation, loss and family relationships. In M. Rutter & L. Hersov (ed.), *Child and Adolescent Psychiatry: Modern Approaches.* Oxford: Blackwell, pp. 34–57.

Woodside, D.B., Brownstone, D. & Fisman, S. (1987). The dexamethasone suppression test and the Children's Depression Inventory in psychiatric disorders in children. *Canadian Journal of Psychiatry*, **32**, 2–4.

Worchel, F.F., Hughes, J.N., Hall, B.M., Stanton, S.B., Stanton, H. & Little, V.Z. (1990). Evaluation of subclinical depression in children using self-, peer-, and teacher-report measures. *Journal of Abnormal Child Psychology*, **18**, 271–282.

World Health Organization (1992). *The ICD-10 Classification of Mental and Behavioural Disorders: Clinical Descriptions and Diagnostic Guidelines.* Geneva: WHO.

Yaylayan, S., Weller, E.B. & Weller, R.A. (1992). Neurobiology of depression. In M. Shafii & S.L. Shafii (ed.), *Clinical Guide to Depression in Children and Adolescents.* Washington: American Psychiatric Press, pp. 65–88.

Young, W., Knowles, J.B., Maclean, A.W., Boag, L. & McConville, B.J. (1982). The sleep of childhood depressives: a comparison with age matched controls. *Biological Psychiatry*, **17**, 1163–1168.

Yule, W., Udwin, O. & Murdoch, K. (1990). The 'Jupiter' sinking: effects on children's fears, depression and anxiety. *Journal of Child Psychology and Psychiatry*, **31**, 1051–1061.

Zeitlin, H. (1986). *The Natural History of Psychiatric Disorder in Children* (Maudsley monograph no. 29). Oxford: Oxford University Press.

Zimmerman, M., Coryell, W. & Pfohl, B. (1986). The validity of the dexamethasone suppression test as a marker for endogenous depression. *Archives of General Psychiatry*, **43**, 347–355.

Index